GIBBON'S DECLINE AND FALL OF THE ROMAN EMPIRE

GIBBON'S DECLINE AND FALL OF THE ROMAN EMPIRE

ABRIDGED AND ILLUSTRATED

Grange
BOOKS

This edition published in 2000 by
Grange Books, an imprint of
Grange Books PLC,
The Grange,
Kingsnorth Industrial Estate
Hoo, nr. Rochester,
Kent ME3 9ND

Produced by PRC Publishing Ltd,
Kiln House, 210 New Kings Road,
London SW6 4NZ

ISBN 1 84013 413 5

Printed and bound in Hong Kong

Editor: Rosemary Williams
Designer: John Fitzmaurice
Cartographer: Richard Natkiel
Picture Research: Rosemary Williams

Introduction

G IBBON's *Decline and Fall of the Roman Empire* is a monumental work of scholarship and after two hundred years it still retains its position as a standard work of reference on the Roman Empire covering the period from 2 AD to the fall of Constantinople in 1453. Gibbon meticulously documented his history, and his work anticipates the modern scholar's use of the scientific analysis of source material.

Today the use of original source material in historical works is taken for granted, but in Gibbon's day this approach was rare. The wealth of archeological data we are accustomed to have access to today was scarcely available in the eighteenth century. In this respect Gibbon set a new standard. He explored, studied and tabulated every possible piece of information accessible to him from the works of Herodotus, the writings of the early Church fathers, St Augustine and Jerome, to the study of ancient maps, ruins and coins.

On the publication of the first volume in 1776 by Thomas Cadell and William Strahan the *Decline and Fall* was immediately acclaimed as a masterpiece. Gibbon's success was due to a number of different factors including the style and architectonic quality of his composition and in particular to the great breadth of his work which can be seen as the direct result of his total identification with his theme.

But it is his style which singles him out as one of the greatest literary figures of the eighteenth century. His skillful use of epithet and adjective fills each page with phrases that linger in the mind long after the book has been put down. This style enabled him to express his own opinions with an aplomb that would not have been possible had he chosen a more direct form. It owed a lot to the humanist writers such as Jonathan Swift (1667–1745), who provided inspiration for the bitter irony of his attacks on the early Church. Indeed his treatment of the rise and influence of Christianity was strongly criticized and some readers even thought it blasphemous and immoral. He was thus condemned by the clerics of the day. Recently, with the second centenary of its publication in 1976, the *Decline and Fall* has received wide attention once again. It is eminently readable and particularly well-adapted for the use of illustrative material. No abridgement can ever do justice to the whole and for the greatest enjoyment the original work should be read at leisure. This illustrated edition should, however, help to make the *Decline and Fall* more accessible to the general reader. Through careful editing of the many digressions and asides that appear in the original work this edition makes clearer the flow of history over the centuries of the late Roman Empire. It follows the succession of Emperors from the glories of Caesar Octavius Augustus (63 BC–14 AD) through the division of the Empire under Diocletian (Gaius Aurelius Valerius Diocletianus 245–313) and the fall of the Western Empire under Romulus Augustulus (b.461) to the last glimmer of glory during the restoration of the Eastern Empire under Justinian I (c.482–565).

Gibbon originally intended to finish his work with the fall of Rome and the Western Empire at the end of the first volumes, and this is the logical stopping point. His last three volumes, which deal with the vicissitudes of the Byzantine Empire starting from Justinian and following the Comnenian dynasty through to the final fall of Constantinople in 1453, were a considered afterthought. His whole treatment of this history is different. Rather than giving a chronological account he tends to make jumps in sequence of time in order to pursue the discussion of individual themes. In addition Gibbon's sympathies lay totally with Rome itself. The Byzantine Empire was summarily dismissed by him as one which 'subsisted one thousand and forty-eight years in a state of premature and perpetual decay.' However, Justinian and his wife Theodora are perhaps the most colorful figures in his history and are included here to show how Gibbon's history provided a bridge between the Classical period and what came to be known as the Dark Ages and the later medieval period. As Thomas Carlyle (1795–1881) put it, 'It is a kind of bridge that connects the antique and modern ages: And how gorgeously does it swing across the gloomy and tumultuous chasms of those barbarous centuries . . . The perusal of his work forms an epoch in the history of one's mind.'

Inevitably cuts have been necessary, but every attempt has been made to keep Gibbon's style intact. The pictures have been carefully chosen wherever possible from contemporary sources (whether archeological remains, frescoes, mosaics or statues). Both captions and pictures are intended to complement Gibbon's text and to bring the period alive through the use of portraits of the main protagonists and illustrations depicting such aspects of everyday life as religious customs, gladiatorial sports and changes in fashion.

Left: The Forum in Rome.
Below: Edward Gibbon (1737–94), author of *The History of the Decline and Fall of the Roman Empire*. This engraving was copied from a painting by Sir Joshua Reynolds (1729–92).

In order to appreciate Gibbon one must examine his background. He was born and died in the eighteenth century, otherwise known as the Age of Enlightenment and the Age of Reason, and was acquainted with the great encyclopedists Claude-Adrien Helvétius (1715–71), Jean Le Rond d'Alembert (1717–83) and Denis Diderot (1713–84). He was a man of many parts: a scholar, man of letters and active participant in the society of his day. He was familiar with the literary scene and frequented the same clubs as Samuel Johnson (1709–84), James Boswell (1740–95) and David Hume (1711–76). In the political arena he hobnobbed with the giants of statesmanship and for a time was himself a Member of Parliament. Nor was he without military experience, having served four years as a commanding officer in the Hampshire grenadiers. He was as familiar with the Continent as England, and, through his varied religious experiences, acquainted with both Roman Catholicism and Protestant beliefs.

A short résumé of the biographical details of his life will serve to illuminate the temper and outlook of the man and his period. Edward Gibbon (1737–94) was born into a minor aristocratic family from Kent. His first home was at Lime Grove, Putney, where he spent a somewhat sickly childhood. His own mother died in 1747 giving birth to her sixth child. Edward Gibbon was accordingly brought up by his aunt, Catherine Porten. It was she who nursed him through his childhood complaints and instilled in him a passion for reading. Frequent bouts of illness denied him a regular education. In 1751, on a visit to Stourhead House, Wiltshire, he found a copy of Echard's *Roman History* in the library and was soon absorbed in the text:

> For me the reigns of the successors of Constantine were absolutely new, and I was immersed in the passage of the Goths over the Danube when the summons of the dinnerbell reluctantly dragged me from my intellectual feast.

This chance episode was to shape the course of all subsequent reading in his life.

By the age of 16 Gibbon had outgrown his childhood ailments and was ready to begin his studies at Oxford University. In his own words he 'arrived at Oxford with a stock of erudition which might have puzzled a doctor and a degree of learning of which a schoolboy would have been ashamed.'

At Magdalen College, Gibbon was virtually ignored by the authorities and his youthful curiosity and inquiring mind strayed into readings in theology. This resulted in his embracing the Roman Catholic faith; a high-minded and impetuous decision. Eighteenth-century England was anti-Catholic and the established church hierarchy still extremely powerful. Gibbon's decision therefore had serious consequences. A distressed father, fearing that his son would be forever cut off from the envisaged political career, dispatched him to Lausanne, Switzerland. Gibbon stayed there from July 1753 to the spring of 1758.

After the semi-luxury of Oxford, life in Lausanne seemed to Gibbon one of virtual exile. But here, under the wise tutelage of the Calvinist pastor, Dr Pavillard, Gibbon was persuaded to return to the Protestant fold. Here also he passed five of the most fruitful years of his life. Gibbon had been disappointed with the academic life of Magdalen and later was to look back on it as a time of idleness:

> To the University of Oxford I acknowledge no obligation and she will as cheerfully renounce me as son, as I am willing to disdain her as mother. I spent fourteen months at Magdalen College, the most idle and unprofitable of my whole life. . . .

At Lausanne, however, he found the intellectual life he had been seeking. It was here he learned the disciplines of a scholar and acquired much of the vast storehouse of knowledge of Classical Latin and European writers, especially French, which he later used to such profit.

As a result of his stay in Switzerland, he became increasingly more European in his outlook, and learned a great deal about the Continent and the geography of countries which he had hitherto studied only through his reading. He had time to visit, among other places, the

Roman soldiers with barbarian captives from a Roman sarcophagus. (First – second century AD, National Museum Rome)

museums and libraries of Zurich and the Abbey of Saint-Urbain. This enabled him to acquaint himself with original source material such as the Carolingian manuscript Bible and collected texts of Graevius, Gronovius, Montfaucon, Muratori and the Byzantine writers.

While at Lausanne, Gibbon also formed two of the most important attachments of his life: his lifelong friendship with the Swiss scholar, Georges Deyverdun, who provided invaluable help with the writing of the *Decline and Fall* and his romance, the only one of any consequence in his life, with Suzanne Curchod. Witty, erudite and charming, Suzanne Curchod was the daughter of a Swiss pastor and later became the mother of Madame de Stael. Gibbon's love for her has never been questioned. However, he seems to have been one of those natural bachelors whose energies are channelled with single-minded devotion into their work. He himself confessed to a fear of any deep involvement which might lead to matrimony. His father also opposed any marriage. Gibbon therefore broke off the relationship. He sums up the affair in classic phraseology: 'I sighed as a lover, I obeyed as a son.' For two years thereafter he lived the life of a man of letters at his parents' house, fulfilling the busy round expected of him and producing a first sortie into the literary field, *Essay on the Study of Literature*.

The outbreak of the Seven Years' War in 1759 saw him enroll for military service. To all accounts he fulfilled his commission with characteristic diligence and when his military service ended in 1763 he took lodgings in London where he lived comfortably on the allowance provided by his father. A year later he set out for an extensively prepared Grand Tour with Italy as his ultimate destination: 'I might boast few travellers more completely armed and instructed ever followed the footsteps of Hannibal.' During this tour he visited the ruins of the Capitol in Rome, and it was while there that the idea of composing a history of the decline and fall of the Roman Empire first came to him:

> It was at Rome, on the 15 October 1764, as I sat musing amidst the ruins of the Capitol, while the bare-footed friars were singing vespers in the Temple of Jupiter, that the idea of writing the decline and fall of the City first started on my mind.

Twelve years, however, elapsed before Gibbon completed the first volume. In the interim period his father's death in 1770 provided him with the independent income for which he had always longed, and four years later in 1774, he purchased a seat in Parliament, as member for Liskeard, through the auspices of his cousin, Edward Eliot. He soon became a loyal and devoted follower of Lord North. He was appointed to the position of Commissioner of Trade and Plantations, a post he held until 1781.

The first volume of his history eventually appeared in 1776; to Gibbon's astonishment it immediately ran into three editions:

> I am at a loss to describe the success of the work without betraying the vanity of the writer. The impression was exhausted in a few days; a second and third edition were scarcely adequate to the demand and the Bookseller's property was twice invaded by pirates from Dublin. My book was on every table, and on almost every toilette. . . .

His work was unequivocally applauded by David Hume, who wrote:

> Whether I consider the dignity of your style, the extensiveness of your learning, I must regard the work as equally the object of esteem. . . .

But his comments on the early Church and Christianity, particularly chapters 15 and 16, caused a furor among the hierarchy of the Church, who denounced him as a pagan philosopher scornfully deriding the tenets of the Gospel.

Gibbon was piqued not so much by criticism of his attitude towards Christianity, but by the criticisms which threw doubt on his credibility as a historian. These he refuted in his *Vindication* (1779). In this he was also defended by the eminent classical scholar Richard Porson (1759–1808), who affirmed that he could find no inaccuracy in Gibbon's use of quotation or in the deductions he drew from his sources.

Undoubtedly Gibbon's lack of sympathy with Christianity stems from his own agnosticism and from the bitterness over his own religious experiences which he laid at the door of the Church. The sarcasm of Gibbon's attacks on some of the adherents of the Church,

particularly those in reference to the monastic movement, should be understood in this light. But in spite of the fact that he lacked any understanding of a deeply held religious faith, which prejudiced his views, he tried to be honest and fair in his judgments.

The second and third volumes of *Decline and Fall* were published in 1781 and these bring the history through to the end of the Empire in the West. The final three volumes were completed in 1787 and published in 1788.

Gibbon's last days were marred by illness. By 1790, largely as a result of a liver condition brought on by his fondness for madeira, he had become extremely corpulent and was suffering from swollen ankles.

By 1793 the deterioration in his health was such that he was persuaded to seek medical advice and as a result underwent three operations from which he made an apparently successful recovery. So much so that on 15 January, 1794, he thought himself good for another twelve or twenty years. Gibbon celebrated by indulging himself in a wing of chicken and three glasses of his favorite madeira. The next day, however, abdominal pain set in and Gibbon died peacefully attended by his manservant. He was buried at Fletching Church near Sheffield Place.

Gibbon's work brought out very forcibly the internal decay and other underlying causes which brought about the gradual fall of the Empire. These appear as recurring themes throughout the book. In his own words:

> The decline of Rome was the natural and inevitable effect of immoderate greatness. Prosperity ripened the principle of decay, the cause of destruction multiplied with the extent of conquest; and as soon as time or accident had removed the artificial supports, the stupendous fabric yielded to the pressure of its own weight.

That is to say the very prosperity and peace of the Empire undermined and sapped its vital energy, its moral fiber and its patriotic vigor, while the corruption of the despotic rulers such as Commodus and Caracalla and their excessive taxation undermined the economy of the Empire and prompted severe civil disorders. Thus in spite of every effort to stem the fatal tide of events the Roman Empire disintegrated from within. The ignominious defeats inflicted on the Romans by the barbarians were only the last push to an already crumbling edifice. It all happened so quickly. In the year 300 AD Rome was still a powerful empire and yet a hundred years later it had vanished.

The tragedy of Rome's fall impressed Gibbon and yet his humanist belief in the ultimate triumph of human progress and that of civilization over barbarianism led him to the final conclusion that such a tragedy could never happen again, and he reassured his readers 'that Europe is secure from any future irruption of barbarians since before they can conquer they must cease to be barbarian.' Today his conclusion seems over-optimistic reflecting as it does the rationale of an eighteenth-century man.

There was, however, no simple overriding cause for the destruction of so great and complex an empire as Rome. Gibbon himself identified no less than twelve underlying causes of disunity which brought about its eventual downfall, among which were the concentration of power in the hands of one ruler for whom there was no constitutional form of election, a widening gap between rich and poor, a pampered soldiery, defense cuts and a run down of military forces in spite of massive taxation and a failure of this army to meet its commitments, suppression of the middle classes while the rich pursued a life of luxury and avoided shouldering the responsibilities of government, the alienation of a bureaucratic central government from the people and a breakdown of law and order. It was such internal weaknesses which reduced Rome's resistance to external aggression. While we should not delude ourselves into thinking that any society can exist without some form of internal conflict we must recognize that when these become too marked they undermine the whole fabric of society. This is the fate that overtook Rome. Some have drawn parallels with contemporary Western civilization and its potential for decline.

However, Gibbon need not be read for such sombre parallels. The sheer pleasure that his picture of a glorious empire affords is reason enough and the impact of this is further heightened by the use of stunning visual material.

CHAPTER ONE

The extent and military force of the Empire in the Age of the Antonines

IN THE second century of the Christian era, the Empire of Rome comprehended the fairest part of the earth, and the most civilized portion of mankind. The frontiers of that extensive monarchy were guarded by ancient renown and disciplined valor. The gentle but powerful influence of laws and manners had gradually cemented the union of the provinces. Their peaceful inhabitants enjoyed and abused the advantages of wealth and luxury. The image of a free constitution was preserved with decent reverence: the Roman senate appeared to possess the sovereign authority, and devolved on the emperors all the executive powers of government. During a happy period (AD 98–180) of more than fourscore years, the public administration was conducted by the virtue and abilities of Nerva, Trajan, Hadrian, and the two Antonines. It is the design of this, and of the two succeeding chapters, to describe the prosperous condition of their empire; and afterwards, from the death of Marcus Antoninus, to deduce the most important circumstances of its decline and fall; a revolution which will ever be remembered, and is still felt by the nations of the earth.

The principal conquests of the Romans were achieved under the republic; and the emperors, for the most part, were satisfied with preserving those dominions which had been acquired by the policy of the senate, the active emulation of the consuls, and the martial enthusiasm of the people. The seven first centuries were filled with a rapid succession of triumphs; but it was reserved for Augustus to relinquish the ambitious design of subduing the whole earth, and to introduce a spirit of moderation into the public councils.

His generals, in the early part of his reign, attempted the reduction of Æthiopia and Arabia Felix. They marched near a thousand miles to the south of the tropic; but the heat of the climate soon repelled the invaders, and protected the unwarlike natives of those sequestered regions. The northern countries of Europe scarcely deserved the expense and labor of conquest. The forests and morasses of Germany were filled with a hardy race of barbarians, who despised life when it was separated from freedom; and though, on the first attack, they seemed to yield to the weight of the Roman power, they soon, by a signal act of despair, regained their independence, and reminded Augustus of the vicissitude of fortune. On the death of that emperor, his testament was publicly read in the senate. He bequeathed, as a valuable legacy to his successors, the advice of confining the empire within those limits, which Nature seemed to have placed on its permanent bulwarks and boundaries: the Atlantic Ocean on the west; the Rhine and Danube on the north; the Euphrates on the east; and toward the south, the sandy deserts of Arabia and Africa.

Happily for the repose of mankind, the moderate system recommended by the wisdom of Augustus, was adopted by the fears and vices of his immediate successors. Engaged in the pursuit of pleasure, or in the exercise of tyranny, the first Cæsars seldom showed themselves to the armies, or to the provinces; nor were they disposed to suffer, that those triumphs which *their* indolence neglected should be usurped by the conduct and valor of their lieutenants. The military fame of a subject was considered as an insolent invasion of the Imperial prerogative; and it became the duty, as well as interest, of every Roman general, to guard the frontiers intrusted to his care, without aspiring to conquests which might have proved no less fatal to himself than to the vanquished barbarians.

The only accession which the Roman empire received, during the first century of the Christian era, was the province of Britain. In this single instance the successors of Cæsar and Augustus were persuaded to follow the example of the former, rather than the precept of the latter. After a war of about forty years, undertaken by the most stupid, maintained by the most dissolute, and terminated by the most timid of all the emperors, the far greater part of the island submitted to the Roman yoke.

Such was the state of the Roman frontiers, and such the maxims of Imperial policy, from the death of Augustus to the accession of Trajan. That virtuous and active prince had received the education of a soldier, and possessed the talents of a general. The peaceful system of his predecessors was interrupted by scenes of war and conquest; and the legions, after a long interval, beheld a military emperor at their head. The first exploits of Trajan were against the Dacians, the most warlike of men, who dwelt beyond the Danube, and who, during the reign of Domitian, had insulted with impunity the Majesty of Rome. This memorable war, with a very short suspension of hostilities, lasted five years; and as the emperor could exert, without control, the whole force of the state, it was terminated by an absolute submission of the barbarians.

Trajan was ambitious. Yet the success of Trajan, however transient, was rapid and specious. The degenerate Parthians, broken by intestine discord, fled before his arms. He descended the river Tigris in triumph, from the mountains of Armenia to the Persian Gulf. He enjoyed the honor of being the first, as he was the last, of the Roman generals, who ever navigated that remote sea. His fleets ravaged the coasts of Arabia; and Trajan vainly flattered himself that he was approaching toward the confines of India. But the death of Trajan soon clouded the splendid prospect; and it was justly to be dreaded, that so many distant nations would throw off the unaccustomed yoke, when they were no longer restrained by his powerful hand. The new emperor Hadrian recognizing the impossibility of defending the conquests of Trajan, resigned all the eastern conquests of Trajan. He restored to the Parthians the election of an independent sovereign, withdrew the Roman garrisons from the provinces of Armenia, Mesopotamia, and Assyria, and in compliance with the precept of Augustus, once more established the Euphrates as the frontier of the empire.

Hadrian and the two Antonines persisted in the design of maintain-

Left: Bronze bust of Hadrian (Publius Aelius Hadrianus AD 176–138; Roman Emperor AD 117–138) found in the River Thames, London. (British Museum)
Right: Emperor Augustus (Gaius Julius Caesar Octavianus Augustus 63 BC– AD 14; Roman Emperor 27 BC–AD 14). (Sardonyx cameo, British Museum)

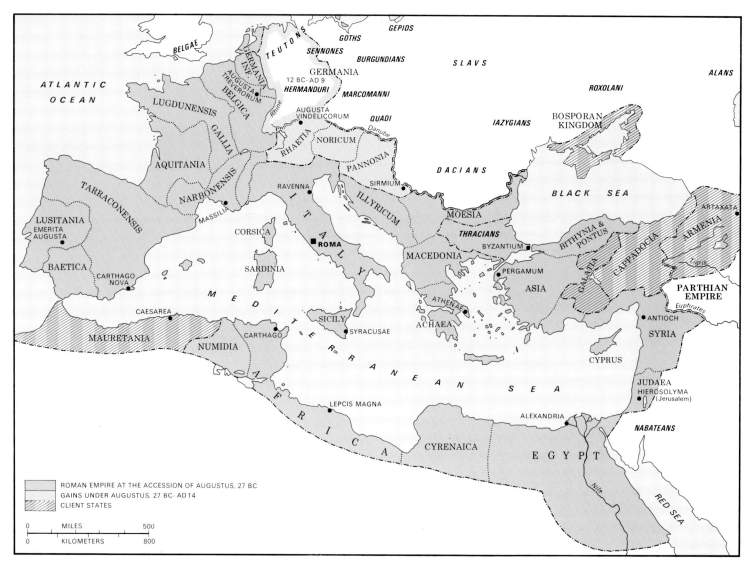

Full extent of the Roman Empire under Augustus.

ing the dignity of the empire, without attempting to enlarge its limits. They invited the friendship of the barbarians and endeavored to convince them that Roman power was actuated only by the love of order and justice. The terror of the Roman arms added weight and dignity to the moderation of emperors. This military strength was merely on display during the time of Hadrian and the elder Antoninus. The emperor Marcus, however, was provoked into using the force as a result of attacks by the Parthians against the Germans. His armies won many signal victories on both the Euphrates and on the Danube.

The military establishment of the Roman empire, which thus assured either its tranquillity or success, will now become the proper and important object of our attention. In the purer ages of the commonwealth, the use of arms was reserved for those ranks of citizens who had a country to love, a property to defend, and some share in enacting those laws which it was their interest, as well as duty, to maintain. But in proportion as the public freedom was lost in extent of conquest, war was gradually improved into an art, and degraded into a trade. The legions themselves, even at the time when they were recruited in the most distant provinces, were supposed to consist of Roman citizens. That distinction was generally considered either as a legal qualification

or as a proper recompense for the soldier; but a more serious regard was paid to the essential merit of age, strength, and military stature. A just preference was given to the climates of the North over those of the South: to men born in the country rather than in the cities; and it was very reasonably presumed, that the hardy occupations of smiths, carpenters, and huntsmen, would supply more vigor and resolution than the sedentary traders which are employed in the service of luxury. After every qualification of property had been laid aside, the armies of the Roman emperors were still commanded, for the most part, by officers of a liberal birth and education; but the common soldiers were drawn from the meanest and the most profligate of mankind.

That public virtue which among the ancients was denominated by patriotism, is derived from a strong sense of our own interests in the preservation and prosperity of the free government of which we are members. Such a sentiment, which had rendered the legions of the

Right: Roman–British pottery. (First century, London Museum)
Left: Coins of Hadrian and Antonius Pius (AD 86–161; Roman Emperor AD 138–161).

republic almost invincible, could make but a very feeble impression on the mercenary servants of a despotic prince; and it became necessary to supply that defect by other motives, of a different, but not less forcible nature; honor and religion. The peasant, or mechanic, imbibed the useful prejudice that he was advanced to the more dignified profession of arms, in which his rank and reputation would depend on his own valor; and that, although the prowess of a private soldier must often escape the notice of fame, his own behavior might sometimes confer glory or disgrace on the company, the legion, or even the army, to whose honors he was associated. On his first entrance into the service, an oath was administered to him, with every circumstance of solemnity. He promised never to desert his standard, to submit his own will to the commands of his leaders, and to sacrifice his life for the safety of the emperor and the empire. The attachment of the Roman troops to their standards was inspired by the united influence of religion and honor. The golden eagle, which glittered in the front of the legion, was the object of their fondest devotion; nor was it esteemed less impious than it was ignominious, to abandon that sacred ensign in the hour of danger. These motives, which derived their strength from the imagination, were enforced by fears and hopes of a more substantial kind.

Above: Funerary stelae of a boatbuilder. (First century, National Museum, Ravenna)
Below left: Roman soldiers preparing to embark: detail from Trajan's Column. (c 144 BC)

Regular pay, occasional donatives, and a stated recompense, after the appointed time of service, alleviated the hardships of the military life, while, on the other hand, it was impossible for cowardice or disobedience to escape the severest punishment. The centurions were authorized to chastise with blows, the generals had a right to punish with death; and it was an inflexible maxim of Roman discipline, that a good soldier should dread his officers far more than the enemy.

All these were included under the general name of auxiliaries; and howsoever they might vary according to the difference of times and circumstances, their numbers were seldom much inferior to those of the legions themselves. Among the auxiliaries, the bravest and most faithful bands were placed under the command of præfects and centurions, and severely trained in the arts of Roman discipline; but the far greater part retained those arms, to which the nature of their country, or their early habits of life, more peculiarly adapted them. By this institution each legion, to whom a certain proportion of auxiliaries were allotted, contained within itself every species of lighter troops, and of missile weapons; and was capable of encountering every nation, with

the advantages of its respective arms and discipline. Nor was the legion destitute of what, in modern language, would be styled a train of artillery. It consisted in ten military engines of the largest, and fifty-five of a smaller size; but all of which, either in an oblique or horizontal manner, discharged stones and darts with irresistible violence.

The camp of a Roman legion presented the appearance of a fortified city. As soon as the space was marked out, the pioneers carefully levelled the ground, and removed every impediment that might interrupt its perfect regularity. Its form was an exact quadrangle; and we may calculate that a square of about seven hundred yards was sufficient for the encampment of twenty thousand Romans; though a similar

Seated figure of Augustus.

Above: Roman soldiers crossing a bridge made of boats during the Dacian wars. (Detail from Trajan's Column)
Left: Roman warship.
Right: Roman standard bearer (*Aquilifero*). The Roman standard or eagle was jealously guarded and the loss of it was considered a grave disgrace. (Relief from the grave stelae of Gneo Musio, early first century AD)

number of our own troops would expose to the enemy a front of more than treble that extent. In the midst of the camp, the prætorium, or general's quarters, rose above the others; the cavalry, the infantry, and the auxiliaries occupied their respective stations; the streets were broad and perfectly straight, and a vacant space of two hundred feet was left on all sides, between the tents and the rampart. The rampart itself was usually twelve feet high, armed with a line of strong and intricate palisades, and defended by a ditch of twelve feet in depth as well as in breadth. This important labor was performed by the hands of the legionaries themselves, to whom the use of the spade and the pick-axe was no less familiar than that of the sword or *pilum*. Active valor may often be the present of nature; but such patient diligence can be the fruit only of habit and discipline.

Whenever the trumpet gave the signal of departure, the camp was almost instantly broke up, and the troops fell into their ranks without delay or confusion. Besides their arms, which the legionaries scarcely

The *Ara Pacis Augustae*: the altar built by Augustus to commemorate the peace established by Augustus, consecrated 4th July 13 BC.

considered as an encumbrance, they were laden with their kitchen furniture, the instruments of fortification, and the provision of many days. Under this weight, which would oppress the delicacy of a modern soldier, they were trained by a regular step to advance, in about six hours, near twenty miles. On the appearance of an enemy, they threw aside their baggage, and by easy and rapid evolutions converted the column of march into an order of battle. The slingers and archers skirmished in the front; the auxiliaries formed the first line, and were seconded or sustained by the strength of the legions: the cavalry covered the flanks, and the military engines were placed in the rear.

Such were the arts of war by which the Roman emperors defended their extensive conquests, and preserved a military spirit, at a time when every other virtue was oppressed by luxury and despotism. If, in the consideration of their armies, we pass from their discipline to their numbers, we shall not find it easy to define them with any tolerable accuracy. We may compute, however, that the legion, which was itself a body of six thousand eight hundred and thirty-one Romans, might, with its attendant auxiliaries, amount to about twelve thousand five hundred men. The peace establishment of Hadrian and his successors was composed of no less than thirty of these formidable brigades; and most probably formed a standing force of three hundred and seventy-five thousand men.

The navy maintained by the emperors might seem inadequate to their greatness; but it was fully sufficient for every useful purpose of government. The ambition of the Romans was confined to the land; nor was that warlike people ever actuated by the enterprising spirit which had prompted the navigators of Tyre, of Carthage, and even of Marseilles, to enlarge the bounds of the world, and to explore the most remote coasts of the ocean. To the Romans the ocean remained an object of terror rather than of curiosity; the whole extent of the Mediterranean, after the destruction of Carthage, and the extirpation of the pirates, was included within their provinces. The policy of the emperors was directed only to preserve the peaceful dominion of that sea, and to protect the commerce of their subjects. If we review this general state of the Imperial forces; of the cavalry as well as infantry; of the legions, the auxiliaries, the guards, and the navy; the most liberal computation will not allow us to fix the entire establishment by sea and by land at more than four hundred and fifty thousand men; a military power, which, however formidable it may seem, was equalled by a monarch of the last century, whose kingdom was confined within a single province of the Roman empire.

We have attempted to explain the spirit which moderated, and the strength which supported, the power of Hadrian and the Antonines.

Above: Vergil (Publius
Vergilius Maro 70–19 BC)
writing the *Aeneid* inspired by
the Muses Clio and Melpone.
(Detail from a Roman mosaic
at Sousse, Tunisia,
second–third century AD)
Right: Roman cavalry officer.
(Detail from a sarcophagus
found in Turkey, Asia Minor)
Below: Roman soldiers
building a fort during the
Dacian campaigns. (Detail
from Trajan's Column)

The Roman Army

The army *(exercitus)* under the early empire was divided into legions *(legiones)* and auxiliaries *(auxiliares)* the former being descendants of the early citizens and farmers who had left the plow to fight – and the auxiliaries who were drawn from subject peoples. Notwithstanding changes in the customary qualifications of land ownership by the time of the Antonines, which had led to the influx of mercenary troops, the officers were still usually men of education.

The legions were distinguished by number in much the same way as the divisions of the modern army and generally comprised 4500–6000 heavy infantry soldiers divided into ten cohorts. Attached to each cohort were 120 dispatch riders and scouts, clerks *(librarii)*, the standard bearer *(aquilifer)*, the master builder *(architectus)*, the surveyor *(mensor)*, the water engineer *(hydraulus)*, the catapult maker *(ballistarius)*, and the various medical orderlies *(medici)*. An army in the field would consist of three or more legions and auxiliary troops. Each legion was commanded by a senator nominated by the emperor as commander-in-chief *(Legatus Augusti Legionis)*, six military tribunes of high social standing, and a senior professional officer *(præfectus castrorum)*. Beneath him were 60 centurions who equalled the rank of major and captain and who were promoted from the ranks, specialists such as the horn blowers *(cornicines)* and other inferior officers. The ordinary soldiers down to the late period of the Empire were designated *Manipulares*.

The legionaries served with their cohort for 20 years and were then pensioned off with a suitable reward and allotted a certain amount of land on discharge where they were usefully employed in the construction of new towns.

The victories of the Roman army were derived from the strength of the legions. The first cohort, which was given the place of honor, consisted of 1105 men armed with helmets, greaves, breastplates and shields of bull's hide strongly reinforced with plates of brass as their main protection. The other nine cohorts were made up of 555 men; and each who were armed with the heavy Roman javelin known as the *pilum*. The *pilum* was a wooden spear roughly six feet in length and fitted with a triangular steel head 18 inches long. The weight of this head stabilized the path of the javelin in flight keeping its course straight. It was able to strike a man down at 30 yards. After throwing his javelin the legionary would then rush in on his enemy to fight in close combat with his sword *(gladius)*.

CAVALRY

The cavalry was divided into ten squadrons: the first cohort comprised 132 men and the other nine of about 66 men and the entire regiment of roughly 725. The cavalry men wore protective helmets, light boots, coats of mail and were armed mainly with javelins, lances, maces and broad swords.

The armor they wore was either formed by plates which were riveted together by internal straps or external laces *(lorica segmentata)* or made up of small scales of bronze or iron *(lorica squamata)*. Lamellar armor was also common and the cuirass was the popular form of breastplate covering for generals.

AUXILIARY TROOPS

The auxiliary troops provided specialist support for the legions. The Sarmatians were skilled archers and horsemen, the Thracians were adept cavalry spearmen and the Moorish troops excelled in desert warfare. The auxiliary troops were usually more lightly equipped wearing merely a simple leather jerkin and armed with an oval shield whether they were mounted or on foot. Their main function was to guard the legionary forces from the first onset of enemy attack. They were usually made up of three types of units composed of the cavalry, infantry and mounted infantry. These troops were organized into units of 500 *(quinguenaria)* or 1000 men *(miliaria)*, the cavalry *(alae)* were made up of sixteen troops *(turmae)* each under an individual commander *(decurio)*; the infantry were divided into nine cohorts some of which were mounted *(cohortes equitatae)*. Slingers, archers, stone throwers and *pioneers*, armed with a type of pick-axe known as the dolabra, made up the rest of the forces.

MEDALS, DECORATIONS AND ENSIGNS

Officers wore a *phalerae* on the breast and a torc from the neck of his enemies might hang from his shoulders. Crowns were awarded for bravery: the triumphant general being assigned the *corona triumphalis* and a wreath of oak leaves being assigned to the hero who had saved the life of a comrade. On the whole the crown took the form of the deed

Below: Helmet with shoulder guard.

mounted on small carts drawn by horses. The arms of the bow were similar to those of the Turkish bow and the ends fitted into the skeins which passed through holes drilled in the frame of the engine and then into large washers. The skeins were then fixed by a pin and could be further tightened by hand spikes which protruded from the edge of the washers. Safety catches secured them from springing back. As the bow string was drawn back the skein would be tightened even further by a winch at the end and as the bowstring was released the javelin would take flight.

The Onager
The onager was also powered by torsion, making use of twisted skin. The skeins were tightened by hand spikes and the vertical arm pulled down by a windlass. The arm was padded to break the force of the impact as it met the cross-piece of the frame. A leather sling was fitted with heavy stone balls or rocks and a small trigger released the arm which then projected the missile through the air with sufficient velocity to plummet onto the roofs of the enemy.

Battering Ram
This was one of the oldest forms of siege instrument known as far back as the Ancient Syrians and frequently adapted by the Romans in various forms.

Left: Bronze figure of a Roman soldier. (First century AD, British Museum, London)
Below: Lerica segmentata: showing the rivets. (Reconstruction of a drawing of a suit of armor found at Corbridge, Northumberland)

commemorated; thus the crown in the shape of a wall signified that the wearer had been first over the wall; the prow of a ship signified the one who had been first to board the enemy ship – a crown of pure gold was awarded for bravery and one in the shape of a rampart for the soldier who had invaded a camp.

ENSIGNS

Ensigns were carried by the soldiers and were made up of lion's or leopard's skins and enabled the commander of each unit to identify his troops. In addition to this each legion had its own standard *(aquila)*, the emblem of an eagle which was they defended proudly. The loss of the 'eagle' was considered the gravest disgrace.

SIEGE EQUIPMENT

In addition to the regular weapons carried by the troops each legion would be equipped with military engines, moveable towers, catapults, onagers, battering rams and other siege instruments.

The Catapult
The catapult was worked by means of torsion obtained by using a bow of horn or sinew, and rope skeins of twisted hair and gut which acted like twisted rubber. The engine was often

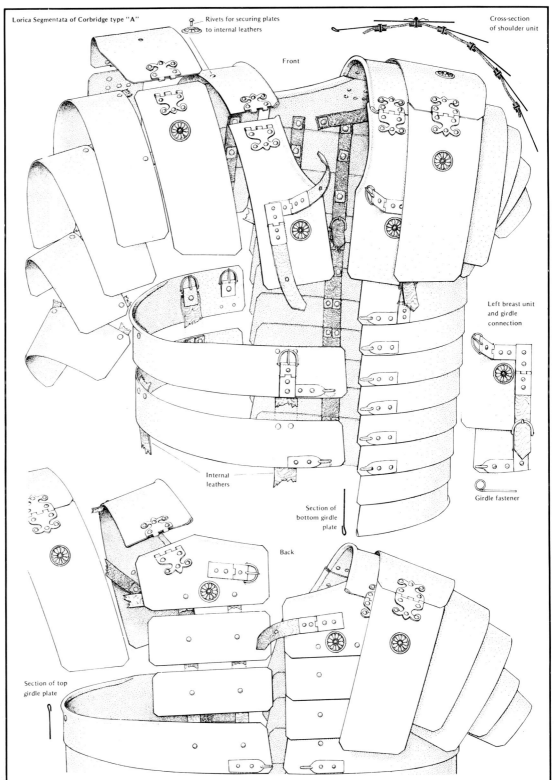

Lorica Segmentata of Corbridge type "A"
Rivets for securing plates to internal leathers
Cross-section of shoulder unit
Front
Left breast unit and girdle connection
Internal leathers
Section of bottom girdle plate
Girdle fastener
Back
Section of top girdle plate

THE PEACEKEEPING FORCES

In time of peace as well as war a standing army was deployed throughout the empire on the barbarian borders and on the banks of rivers. At various points along the frontiers hospitals were situated similar to our modern dressing stations and castellated fortresses were constructed. Fortified walls such as Hadrian's were further reinforced by guard posts known as mile castles, square towers placed at regular intervals of a mile distance along the wall. In addition to these were several turrets believed to have been used as signal posts, where torches, flares, semaphore and other signals were used to give the alert in the case of sudden enemy attack.

As a reinforcement to these walls a defense ditch or *vallum* was dug a little short of the Roman side of the wall. These massive fortified walls were usually constructed when the conquest of the country was still envisaged. A further wall of turf similar to that of Hadrian's Wall is the Antonine Wall built by Lollius Urbicus, Governor of Britain during the reign of Antoninus Pius (Tirius Aelius Hadrianus Antoninus Pius 86–161).

Above: Conically shaped bronze helmet. (British Museum, London)
Left: Bronze mask and parade helmet. (Found at Ribchester, Lancashire, late first century, British Museum, London)
Right: Bronze shield found in the Thames, Battersea, London. (First century AD, British Museum)

Left: Legionary's dagger. (London Museum)
Far left, bottom: Roman cavalry officer: detail from a sarcophagus found in Turkey, Asia Minor.
Right: Bronze helmet found at Hawkedon, Suffolk. (British Museum, London)

THE ROMAN CAMP

The first priority of the Roman army was to construct a camp whether it was for a single night or as in the case of prolonged campaigns for a year or more. Many modern towns in Britain and Europe owe their existence to a prolonged encampment. The camp was always erected in the form of a quadrangle. The tents were placed at regular intervals from each other in straight lines and the two principal roads which divided the various quarters were also straight. The general's quarters were known as the *Prætorium* and were situated in the center of the camp. A defensive rampart was raised on the outer wall of the camp.

Military discipline was enforced and every type of military exercise undertaken. A trumpet blast gave the signal for the camp to break up and the army immediately fell into order for the ensuing march. Slingers and archers to the fore, and the cavalry and auxiliary protecting the main column of the legionaries on the wings. In spite of cumbersome military equipment and kitchen utensils, the men would maintain a speed of 20 miles in six hours.

Military Sports

Wherever they went the milit took their sports with them whether this took the form of chariot racing, gladiatorial fighting, or tournaments. Gladiators first made their appearance at religious ceremonies and funerals but gladiatorial combats soon became a favorite military sport in their own right.

Cavalry tournaments were also popular pastimes. Combatants wore visors crested with yellow plumes, carried gaily decorated shields and wore tunics of scarlet, purple or multi-colors often protected by frontlets and trappings to shield them from the showers of arrows.

Above: Roman warship: relief of a trireme.
Left: Horse armor: leather chamfron decorated with intricate tooled and studded ornamentation. (From the fort at Newstead AD 98–100, Museum of Antiquities, Edinburgh)
Below: Iron and bronze armor scales.

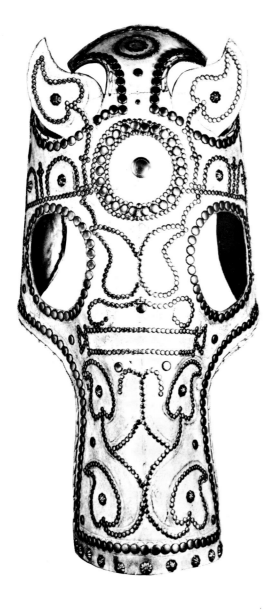

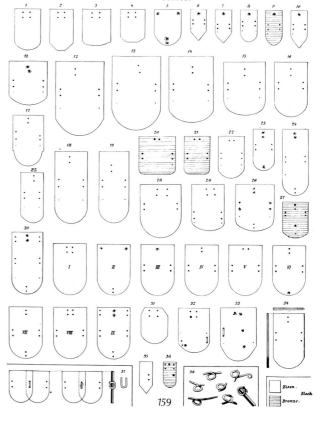

159

Above: Bronze helmet found in London showing a protective nasal piece. (London Museum)

Right: Reconstruction of a suit of armor found at Corbridge, Northumberland.

Below right: Iron helmet of the Imperial Gallic type with embossed cheekpieces and slender bronze rim. (Second half of the first century AD, Mainz Museum)

Below: Cavalry sports greaves. (Mid-third century AD)

CHAPTER TWO

Of the union and internal prosperity of the Roman Empire in the Age of the Antonines

At this time the general principle of government was wise, simple, and beneficient. Each province enjoyed the religion of its ancestors, and in civil honors and advantages its peoples were exalted, by just degrees to an equality with their conquerors. This toleration produced not only mutual indulgence but even religious concord. The visible powers of Nature, the planets, and the elements, were the same throughout the universe. The invisible governors of the moral world were inevitably cast in a similar mold of fiction and allegory. Every virtue, and even vice, acquired its divine representative; every art and profession its patron, whose attributes, in the most distant ages and countries, were uniformly derived from the character of their peculiar votaries. A republic of gods of such opposite tempers and interest required, in every system, the moderating hand of a supreme magistrate, who, by the progress of knowledge and flattery, was gradually invested with the sublime perfections of an Eternal Parent, and an Omnipotent Monarch. Such was the mild spirit of antiquity, that the nations were less attentive to the difference than to the resemblance of their religious worship. The Greek, the Roman, and the Barbarian, as they met before their respective altars, easily persuaded themselves, that under various names, and with various ceremonies, they adorned the same deities. The elegant mythology of Homer gave a beautiful, and almost a regular form, to the polytheism of the ancient world.

The philosophers of Greece deduced their morals from the nature of man, rather than from that of God. They meditated, however, on the Divine Nature, as a very curious and important speculation; and in the profound inquiry, they displayed the strength and weakness of the human understanding. Of the four most celebrated schools, the Stoics and the Platonists endeavored to reconcile the jarring interests of reason and piety. They have left us the most sublime proofs of the existence and perfections of the first cause; but, as it was impossible for them to conceive the creation of matter, the workman in the Stoic philosophy was not sufficiently distinguished from the work; while, on the contrary, the spiritual God of Plato and his disciples resembled an idea rather than a substance. The opinions of the Academics and Epicureans were of a less religious cast; but whilst the modest science of the former induced them to doubt, the positive ignorance of the latter urged them to deny, the providence of a Supreme Ruler. The spirit of inquiry, prompted by emulation, and supported by freedom, had divided the public teachers of philosophy into a variety of contending sects; but the ingenious youth who, from every part, resorted to Athens, and the other seats of learning in the Roman empire, were alike instructed in every school to reject and to despise the religion of the multitude. How, indeed, was it possible, that a philosopher should accept, as divine truths, the idle tales of the poets, and the incoherent traditions of antiquity; or, that he should adore, as gods, those imperfect beings whom he must have despised, as men! Against such unworthy adversaries, Cicero condescended to employ the arms of reason and eloquence; but the satire of Lucian was a much more adequate, as well as more efficacious weapon. We may well be assured, that a writer conversant with the world would never have ventured to expose the gods of his country to public ridicule, had they not already been the objects of secret contempt among the polished and enlightened orders of society.

Rome, the capital of a great monarchy, was incessantly filled with subjects and strangers from every part of the world who all introduced and enjoyed the favorite superstition of their native country. Every city in the Empire was justified in maintaining the purity of its ancient ceremonies and the freedom of the city was bestowed on all the Gods of mankind.

If we study the growth of the Roman republic we may discover that notwithstanding the incessant demands of wars and colonies, the citizens who in the first census of Servius Tullius amounted to no more than eighty-three thousand were multiplied before the commencement of the social war, to the number of four hundred and sixty-three thousand men, able to bear arms in the service of their country. This in contrast with the experience of the Athenian commonwealth which did not admit foreigners to its citizenship during its most flourishing period and actually saw its number of citizens decrease from about thirty to twenty-one thousand. If the Romans had adopted this policy the city would have been deprived of some of its noblest ornaments. Virgil was a native of Mantua; Horace was inclined to doubt whether he should call himself an Apulian or a Lucanian: it was in Padua that an historian was found worthy to record the majestic series of Roman victories. The patriot family of the Catos emerged from Tusculum; and the little town of Arpinum claimed the double honor of producing Marius and Cicero, the former of whom deserved, after Romulus and Camillus, to be styled the Third Founder of Rome; and the latter, after saving his country from the designs of Catiline, enabled her to contend with Athens for the palm of eloquence.

Public authority was everywhere exercised by the ministers of the senate and of the emperors, and that authority was absolute, and without control. But the same salutary maxims of government, which had secured the peace and obedience of Italy, were extended to the most distant conquests. A nation of Romans was gradually formed in the provinces, by the double expedient of introducing colonies, and of admitting the most faithful and deserving of the provincials to the freedom of Rome.

Left: Temple of Apollo with bronze statue of Apollo against a backdrop of Vesuvius, Pompeii (c AD 60).
Below: The household *lares*: each Roman house had its own altar dedicated to the household gods. (Detail from the wall-painting, the House of Vettii, Pompeii, c AD 60)

'Wheresoever the Roman conquers, he inhabits,' is a very just observation of Seneca, confirmed by history and experience. Voluntary exiles were engaged for the most part, in the occupations of commerce and agriculture. Veterans from the legions whether they received the reward of their service in land or in money, usually settled with their families in the country where they had honorably spent their youth. Throughout the empire, but more particularly in the western parts, the most fertile districts, and the most convenient situations, were reserved for the establishment of colonies; some of which were of a civil, and others of a military nature. Such colonies effectually diffused a reverence for the Roman name, and a desire, which was seldom disappointed, of sharing, in due time, its honors and advantages among the natives.

The number of subjects who acknowledged the laws of Rome, of citizens, of provincials, and of slaves, cannot now be fixed with such a degree of accuracy, as the importance of the object would deserve. We are informed that when the emperor Claudius exercised the office of censor, he took an account of six millions nine hundred and forty-five thousand Roman citizens, who, with the proportion of women and children, must have amounted to about twenty millions of souls. The multitude of subjects of an inferior rank was uncertain and fluctuating. But, after weighing with attention every circumstance which could influence the balance, it seems probable that there existed, in the time of Claudius, about twice as many provincials as there were citizens, of either sex, and of every age; and that the slaves were at last equal in number to the free inhabitants of the Roman world. The total amount of this imperfect calculation would rise to about one hundred and twenty millions of persons; a degree of population which possibly exceeds that of modern Europe, and forms the most numerous society that has ever been united under the same system of government.

Domestic peace and union were the natural consequences of the moderate and comprehensive policy embraced by the Romans. In contrast the monarchies of Asia were plagued by despotism in the center, and weakness in the extremities; the collection of the revenue, or the administration of justice, enforced by the presence of an army; hostile barbarians established in the heart of the country, hereditary satraps usurping the dominion of the provinces, and subjects inclined to rebellion, though incapable of freedom. But the obedience of the Roman world was uniform, voluntary and permanent. The vanquished

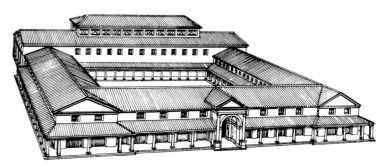

Above: Reconstruction of a Roman basilica and forum.

Above: Bust of the Roman god Oceanus.
Below: Bust of the Roman god Mithras.

Below: Specimens of Roman-British glass. (First century AD, British Museum)

nations, blended into one great people resigned the hope, nay even the wish, of resuming their independence, and scarcely considered their own existence as distinct from the existence of Rome. The established authority of the emperors pervaded without an effort the wide extent of their dominions, and was exercised with the same facility on the banks of the Thames, or of the Nile, as on those of the Tiber. The legions were destined to serve against the public enemy, and the civil magistrate seldom required the aid of a military force. In this state of general security, the leisure as well as opulence both of the prince and people were devoted to improve and to adorn the Roman empire.

Whatever evils either reason or declamation have imputed to extensive empire, the power of Rome was attended with some beneficial consequences to mankind; and the same freedom of intercourse which extended the vices, diffused likewise the improvements of social life. In the more remote ages of antiquity, the world was unequally divided. The east was in the immemorial possession of arts and luxury; while the west was inhabited by rude and warlike barbarians, who either disdained agriculture, or to whom it was totally unknown. Under the protection of an established government, the productions of happier climates, and the industry of more civilized nations, were gradually introduced into the western countries of Europe; and the natives were encouraged, by an open and profitable commerce, to multiply the former, as well as to improve the latter.

The cultivation of flax was transported from Egypt to Gaul, and enriched the whole country, however it might impoverish the particular lands on which it was sown. The use of artificial grasses became familiar to the farmers both of Italy and the provinces, particularly the Lucerne, which derived its name and origin from Media. To all these improvements may be added an assiduous attention to mines and fisheries, which, by employing a multitude of laborious hands, serve to increase the pleasures of the rich, and the subsistence of the poor.

Agriculture is the foundation of manufactures; since the productions of nature are the materials of art. Under the Roman empire, the labor of an industrious and ingenious people was variously, but incessantly employed, in the service of the rich. In their dress, their table, their houses, and their furniture, the favorites of fortune united every refinement of conveniency, of elegance, and of splendor, whatever could soothe their pride or gratify their sensuality. Such refinements, under the odious name of luxury, have been severely arraigned by the moralists of every age; and it might perhaps be more conducive to the virtue, as well as happiness, of mankind, if all possessed the necessaries,

The thriving agriculture of the empire greatly added to its buoyant economy. (Bas-relief, first century AD, Munich Museum)

and none the superfluities, of life. But in the present imperfect condition of society, luxury, though it may proceed from vice or folly, seems to be the only means that can correct the unequal distribution of property.

It was scarcely possible that the eyes of contemporaries should discover in the public felicity the latent causes of decay and corruption. This long peace, and the uniform government of the Romans, introduced a slow and secret poison into the vitals of the empire. The minds of men were gradually reduced to the same level, the fire of genius was extinguished, and even the military spirit evaporated. The natives of Europe were brave and robust, Spain, Gaul, Britain, and Illyricum supplied the legions with excellent soldiers, and constituted the real strength of the monarchy. Their personal valor remained, but they no longer possessed that public courage which is nourished by the love of independence, the sense of national honor, the presence of danger, and the habit of command. They received laws and governors from the will of their sovereign, and trusted for their defense to a mercenary army. The posterity of their boldest leaders was contented with the rank of citizens and subjects. The most aspiring spirits resorted to the court or standard of the emperors; and the deserted provinces, deprived of political strength or union, insensibly sunk into the languid indifference of private life.

The love of letters, almost inseparable from peace and refinement, was fashionable among the subjects of Hadrian and the Antonines, who were themselves men of learning and curiosity. It was diffused over the whole extent of their empire; the most northern tribes of Britons had acquired a taste for rhetoric; Homer as well as Virgil were transcribed and studied on the banks of the Rhine and Danube. But if we accept the inimitable Lucian, this age of indolence passed away without having produced a single writer of original genius, or who excelled in the arts of elegant composition. The beauties of the poets and orators, instead of kindling a fire like their own, inspired only cold and servile imitations: or if any ventured to deviate from those models, they deviated at the same time from good sense and propriety. On the revival of letters, the youthful vigor of the imagination, after a long repose, national emulation, a new religion, new languages, and a new world, called forth the genius of Europe. But the provincials of Rome, trained by a uniform artificial foreign education, were engaged in a very unequal competition with those bold ancients, who, by expressing their genuine feelings in their native tongue, had already occupied every place of honor. The name of Poet was almost forgotten; that of Orator was usurped by the sophists. A cloud of critics, of compilers, of commentators, darkened the face of learning, and the decline of genius was soon followed by the corruption of taste.

Reconstruction of Rome during the first and second centuries AD. Behind the Colosseum is the Palatine Hill, the Circus Maximus and the Tiber.

CHAPTER THREE

Of the Constitution of the Roman Empire in the Age of the Antonines

THE obvious definition of a monarchy seems to be that of a state, in which a single person, by whatsoever name he may be distinguished, is entrusted with the execution of the laws, the management of the revenue, and the command of the army. But, unless public liberty is protected by intrepid and vigilant guardians, the authority of so formidable a magistrate will soon degenerate into despotism. The influence of the clergy, in an age of superstition, might be usefully employed to assert the rights of mankind; but so intimate is the connection between the throne and the altar, that the banner of the church has very seldom been on the side of the people. A martial nobility and stubborn commons, possessed of arms, tenacious of property, and collected into constitutional assemblies, form the only balance capable of preserving a free constitution against enterprises of an aspiring prince.

Every barrier of the Roman constitution has been levelled by the vast ambition of the dictator; every fence had been extirpated by the cruel hand of the Triumvir. After the victory of Actium, the fate of the Roman world depended on the will of Octavianus, surnamed Cæsar, by his uncle's adoption, and afterwards Augustus, by the flattery of the senate.

The reformation of the senate was one of the first steps in which Augustus laid aside the tyrant, and professed himself the father of his country. He was elected censor; and, in concert with his faithful Agrippa, he examined the list of the senators, expelled a few members, whose vices or whose obstinacy required a public example, persuaded near two hundred to prevent the shame of an expulsion by a voluntary retreat, raised the qualification of a senator to about ten thousand pounds, created a sufficient number of Patrician families, and accepted for himself the honorable title of Prince of the Senate, which had always been bestowed, by the censors, on the citizen the most eminent for his honors and services. But while he thus restored the dignity, he destroyed the independence of the senate. The principles of a free constitution are irrecoverably lost, when the legislative power is nominated by the executive.

Before an assembly thus modelled and prepared, Augustus pronounced a studied oration, which displayed his patriotism, and disguised his ambition. 'He lamented, yet excused, his past conduct. Filial piety had required at his hands the revenge of his father's murder; the humanity of his own nature had sometimes given way to the stern laws of necessity, and to a forced connection with two unworthy colleagues: as long as Antony lived, the republic forbade him to abandon her to a degenerate Roman, and a barbarian queen. He was now at liberty to satisfy his duty and his inclination. He solemnly restored the senate and people to all their ancient rights; and wished only to mingle with the crowd of his fellow-citizens, and to share the blessings which he had obtained for his country.'

It would require the pen of Tacitus (if Tacitus had assisted at this assembly) to describe the various emotions of the senate; those that were suppressed, and those that were affected. It was dangerous to trust the sincerity of Augustus; to seem to distrust it was still more dangerous. The respective advantages of monarchy and a republic have often divided speculative inquirers; the present greatness of the Roman state, the corruption of manners, and the license of the soldiers, supplied new arguments to the advocates of monarchy, and these general views of government were again warped by the hopes and fears of each individual. Amidst this confusion of sentiments, the answer of the senate was unanimous and decisive. They refused to accept the resignation of Augustus; they conjured him not to desert the republic, which he had saved. After a decent resistance, the crafty tyrant submitted to the orders of the senate; and consented to receive the government of the provinces, and the general command of the Roman armies, under the well-known names of PROCONSUL and IMPERATOR. But he would receive them only for ten years. Even before the expiration of that period, he hoped that the wounds of civil discord would be completely healed, and that the republic, restored to its pristine health and vigor, would no longer require the dangerous interposition of so extraordinary a magistrate. The memory of this comedy, repeated several times during the life of Augustus, was preserved to the last ages of the empire, by the peculiar pomp with which the perpetual monarchs of Rome always solemnized the tenth years of their reign.

Without any violation of the principles of the constitution, the general of the Roman armies might receive and exercise an authority almost despotic over the soldiers, the enemies, and the subjects of the republic. With regard to the soldiers, the jealousy of freedom had, even from the earliest ages of Rome, given way to the hopes of conquest, and a just sense of military discipline. The dictator, or consul, had a right to command the service of the Roman youth; and to punish an obstinate or cowardly disobedience by the most severe and ignominious penalties, by striking the offender out of the list of citizens, by confiscating his property, and by selling his person into slavery. The most sacred rights of freedom, confirmed by the Porcian and Sempronian laws, were suspended by the military engagement. In his camp the general exercised an absolute power of life and death; his jurisdiction was not confined by any forms of trial or rules of proceeding, and the execution of the sentence was immediate and without appeal. The choice of the enemies of Rome was regularly decided by the legislative authority.

Left: The Emperor Augustus (Emperor 23 BC–AD 14) as Pontifex Maximus or high priest.
Below: The ruins of the Forum as seen from the Capitol. Once the center of Roman activity the Forum today is but a shadow of its former self.

The most important resolutions of peace and war were seriously debated in the senate, and solemnly ratified by the people. But when the arms of the legions were carried to a great distance from Italy, the generals assumed the liberty of directing them against whatever people, and in whatever manner, they judged most advantageous for the public service. It was from the success, not from the justice, of their enterprises, that they expected the honors of a triumph. In the use of victory, especially after they were no longer controlled by the commissioners of the senate, they exercised the most unbounded despotism. When Pompey commanded in the east, he rewarded his soldiers and allies, dethroned princes, divided kingdoms, founded colonies, and distributed the treasures of Mithridates. On his return to Rome, he obtained, by a single act of the senate and people, the universal ratification of all his proceedings. Such was the power over the soldiers, and over the enemies of Rome, which was either granted to, or assumed by, the generals of the republic. They were, at the same time, the governors, or rather monarchs, of the conquered provinces, united the civil with the military character, administered justice as well as the finances, and exercised both the executive and legislative power of the state.

At the time of Augustus the extent of the Empire was so great that it was impossible for the Emperor himself to take command of the legions of so many distant frontiers in person. He was accordingly indulged by the Senate, as Pompey had already been, in the permissions of devolving the execution of his office on a number of lieutenants. In rank and authority these officers seemed not inferior to the ancient proconsuls;

Bas relief of legionaries from the base of the Antonine Column, Rome.

but their station was dependent and precarious. They received and held their commissions at the will of a superior, to whose *auspicious* influence the merit of their action was legally attributed. They were the representatives of the emperor. The emperor alone was the general of the republic, and his jurisdiction, civil as well as military, extended over all the conquests of Rome. It was some satisfaction, however, to the senate, that he always delegated his power to the members of their body. Thus Imperial lieutenants were of consular or prætorian dignity; and the legions were commanded by senators: the præfecture of Egypt was the only important trust committed to a Roman knight.

Within six days after Augustus had been compelled to accept so very liberal a grant, he resolved to gratify the pride of the senate by an easy sacrifice. He represented to them, that they had enlarged his powers, even beyond that degree which might be required by the melancholy condition of the times. They had not permitted him to refuse the laborious command of the armies and the frontiers; but he must insist on being allowed to restore the more peaceful and secure provinces, to the mild administration of the civil magistrate. In the division of the provinces, Augustus provided for his own power, and for the dignity of the republic. The proconsuls of the senate, particularly those of Asia, Greece, and Africa, enjoyed a more honorable character than the lieutenants of the emperor, who commanded in Gaul or Syria. The former were attended by lictors, the latter by soldiers. A law was passed that wherever the emperor was present, his extraordinary commission should supersede the ordinary jurisdiction of the governor; a custom was introduced, that the new conquest belonged to the Imperial portion; and it was soon discovered that the authority of the *Prince*, the favorite epithet of Augustus, was the same in every part of the empire.

The triumph of Marcus Aurelius (Marcus Aurelius Antoninus AD 121–80).

In return for this imaginary concession, Augustus obtained an important privilege, which rendered him master of Rome and Italy. By a dangerous exception to the ancient maxims, he was authorized to preserve his military command, supported by a numerous body of guards, even in time of peace, and in the heart of the capital. His command, indeed, was confined to those citizens who were engaged in the service by the military oath; but such was the propensity of the Romans to servitude, that the oath was voluntarily taken by the magistrates, the senators, and the equestrian order, till the homage of flattery was insensibly converted into an annual and solemn protestation of fidelity.

Although Augustus considered a military force as the firmest foundation, he wisely rejected it, as a very odious instrument of government. It was more agreeable to his temper, as well as to his policy, to reign under the venerable names of ancient magistracy, and artfully to collect, in his own person, all the scattered rays of civil jurisdiction. With this view, he permitted the senate to confer upon him for his life, the powers of the consular and tribunitian offices, which were, in the same manner, continued to all his successors. The consuls had succeeded to the kings of Rome, and represented the dignity of the state. They superintended the ceremonies of religion, levied and commanded the legions, gave audience to foreign ambassadors, and presided in the assemblies both of the senate and people. The general control of the finances was intrusted to their care; and though they seldom had leisure to administer justice in person, they were considered as the supreme guardians of law, equity, and the public peace. Such was their ordinary jurisdiction; but whenever the senate empowered the first magistrate to consult the safety of the commonwealth, he was raised by that degree above the laws, and exercised, in the defense of liberty, a temporary despotism. The character of the tribunes was, in every respect, different from that of the consuls. The appearance of the former was modest and humble; but their persons were sacred and inviolable. Their force was suited rather for opposition than for action. They were instituted to defend the oppressed, to pardon offences, to arraign the enemies of the people, and, when they judged it necessary, to stop, by a single word, the whole machine of government. As long as the republic subsisted, the dangerous influence, which either the consul or the tribune might derive from their respective jurisdiction, was diminished by several important restrictions. Their authority expired with the year in which they were elected; the former office was divided between two, the latter among ten persons; and, as both in their private and public

interest they were averse to each other, their mutual conflicts contributed, for the most part, to strengthen rather than to destroy the balance of the constitution. But when the consular and tribunitian powers were united, when they were vested for life in a single person, when the general of the army was, at the same time, the minister of the senate, and the representative of the Roman people, it was impossible to resist the exercise, nor was it easy to define the limits of his Imperial prerogative.

To these accumulated honors, the policy of Augustus soon added the splendid as well as important dignities of supreme pontiff, and of censor. By the former he acquired the management of the religion, and by the latter a legal inspection over the manners and fortunes, of the Roman people. The emperors, as the first ministers of the republic, were exempted from the obligation and penalty of many inconvenient laws: they were authorized to convoke the senate, to make several motions in the same day, to recommend candidates for the honors of the state, to enlarge the bounds of the city, to employ the revenue at their discretion, to declare peace and war, to ratify treaties; and by a most comprehensive clause, they were empowered to execute whatsoever they should judge advantageous to the empire, and agreeable to the majesty of things private or public, human or divine.

When all the various powers of executive government were committed to the *Imperial magistrate*, the ordinary magistrates of the commonwealth languished in obscurity, without vigor, and almost without business. The names and forms of the ancient administration were preserved by Augustus with the most anxious care. The usual number of consuls, prætors, and tribunes, were annually invested with their respective ensigns of office, and continued to discharge some of their least important functions. Those honors still attracted the vain ambition of the Romans; and the emperors themselves, though invested for life with the powers of the consulship, frequently aspired to the title of that annual dignity, which they condescended to share with the most illustrious of their fellow-citizens. In the election of these magistrates, the people, during the reign of Augustus, were permitted to expose all the inconveniences of a wild democracy. That artful prince, instead of discovering the least symptom of impatience, humbly solicited their suffrages for himself or his friends, and scrupulously practiced all the duties of an ordinary candidate. But we may venture to

Marcus Aurelius sacrificing to the Roman gods. (Museo Capitolino, Rome)

Above: Marble bust of
Marcus Aurelius from
Anatalya, Turkey. (The
Archeological Museum,
Istanbul)
Right: Mounted statue of
Marcus Aurelius, the
Capitoline Hill, Rome.
Far right: Agape: seated
figure of a Roman matron.
(Wall-painting from the Villa
dei Misteri, Pompeii, first
century AD)
Right below: Baths of
Faustina, wife of Marcus
Aurelius and daughter of
Antoninus Pius. View of the
pool in the *frigidarium*
showing statues of a river god
and a lion, formerly two
fountains. (Miletus, Turkey,
AD 161–180)

ascribe to his councils, the first measure of the succeeding reign, by
which the elections were transferred to the senate. The assemblies of
the people were for ever abolished, and the emperors were delivered
from a dangerous multitude, who, without restoring liberty, might
have disturbed, and perhaps endangered, the established government.

The face of the court corresponded with the forms of the administration. The emperors, if we except those tyrants whose capricious folly
violated every law of nature and decency, disdained that pomp and
ceremony which might offend their countrymen, but could add nothing
to their real power. In all the offices of life they affected to confound
themselves with their subjects, and maintained with them an equal
intercourse of visits and entertainments. Their habit, their palace, their
table, were suited only to the rank of an opulent senator. Their family,
however numerous or splendid, was composed entirely of their domestic slaves and freedmen. Augustus or Trajan would have blushed at
employing the meanest of the Romans in those menial offices, which, in
the household and bed-chamber of a limited monarch, are so eagerly
solicited by the proudest nobles of Britain.

The deification of the emperors is the only instance in which they
departed from their accustomed prudence and modesty. The Asiatic
Greeks were the first inventors, the successors of Alexander the first
objects, of this servile and impious mode of adulation. It was easily

transferred from the kings to the governors of Asia; and the Roman
magistrates very frequently were adored as provincial deities, with the
pomp of altars and temples, of festivals and sacrifices. But the conquerors soon imitated the vanquished nations in the arts of flattery and
the imperious spirit of the first Cæsar too easily consented to assume,
during his lifetime, a place among the tutelar deities of Rome. The
milder temper of his successor declined so dangerous an ambition,
which was never afterwards revived, except by the madness of Caligula
and Domitian. Augustus permitted indeed some of the provincial cities
to erect temples to his honor; but he contented himself with being
revered by the senate and people in his human character, and wisely left
to his successor the care of his public deification. A regular custom was
introduced, that on the decease of every emperor who had neither lived
nor died like a tyrant, the senate by a solemn decree should place him in
the number of the gods: and the ceremonies of his Apotheosis were
blended with those of his funeral. As soon as their divinity was established by law, it sunk into oblivion, without contributing either to their
own fame, or to the dignity of succeeding princes.

During a long period of two hundred and twenty years, from the
establishment of this artful system to the death of Commodus, the
dangers inherent to a military government were, in a great measure,
suspended. The soldiers were seldom roused to that fatal sense of their

own strength, and the weakness of the civil authority, which was, before and afterwards, productive of such dreadful calamities. Caligula and Domitian were assassinated in their palace by their own domestics; the convulsions which agitated Rome on the death of the former, were confined to the walls of the city. But Nero involved the whole empire in his ruin. In the space of eighteen months, four princes perished by the sword; and the Roman world was shaken by the fury of the contending armies. Excepting only this short, though violent, eruption of military license, the two centuries from Augustus to Commodus passed away unstained with civil blood, and undisturbed by revolutions. The emperor was elected by *the authority of the senate,* and *the consent of the soldiers.* The legions respected their oath of fidelity; and it requires a minute inspection of the Roman annals to discover three inconsiderable rebellions, which were all suppressed in a few months, and without even the hazard of a battle.

In elective monarchies, the vacancy of the throne is a moment big with danger and mischief. The Roman emperors, desirous to spare the legions that interval of suspense, and the temptation of an irregular choice, invested their designed successor with so large a share of present power, as should enable him, after their decease, to assume the remainder, without suffering the empire to perceive the change of masters. Thus Augustus, after all his fairer prospects had been snatched from him by untimely deaths rested his last hopes on Tiberius, obtained for his adopted son the censorial and tribunitian powers, and dictated a law by which the future prince was invested with an authority equal to his own, over the provinces and the armies. Thus Vespasian subdued the generous mind of his eldest son. Titus was adored by the eastern legions, which, under his command, had recently achieved the conquest of Judæa. His power was dreaded, and, as his virtues were clouded by the intemperance of youth, his designs were suspected. Instead of listening to such unworthy suspicions, the prudent monarch associated Titus to the full powers of the Imperial dignity;

Temple of Antoninus and Faustina in the Roman forum.

the Lower Germany; and immediately, by a degree of the senate, declared him his colleague and successor in the empire. It is sincerely to be lamented, that whilst we are fatigued with the disgustful relation of Nero's crimes and follies, we are reduced to collect the actions of Trajan from the glimmerings of an abridgment, or the doubtful light of a panegyric. There remains, however, one panegyric far removed beyond the suspicion of flattery. Above two hundred and fifty years after the death of Trajan, the senate, in pouring out the customary acclamations on the occasion of a new emperor, wished that he might surpass the felicity of Augustus, and the virtue of Trajan.

We may readily believe, that the father of his country hesitated whether he ought to intrust the various and doubtful character of his kinsman Hadrian with sovereign power. In his last moments, the arts of the empress Plotina either fixed the irresolution of Trajan, or boldly supposed a fictitious adoption; the truth of which could not be safely disputed, and Hadrian was peaceably acknowledged as his lawful successor. Under his reign, as has been already mentioned, the empire

and the grateful son ever approved himself the humble and faithful minister of so indulgent a father.

The good sense of Vespasian engaged him indeed to embrace every measure that might confirm his recent and precarious elevation. The military oath, and the fidelity of the troops, had been consecrated by the habits of an hundred years, to the name and family of the Cæsars; and although that family had been continued only by the fictitious rite of adoption, the Romans still revered, in the person of Nero, the grandson of Germanicus, and the lineal successor of Augustus. It was not without reluctance and remorse that the Prætorian Guards had been persuaded to abandon the cause of the tyrant. The rapid downfall of Galba, Otho, and Vitellius, taught the armies to consider the emperors as the creatures of *their* will, and the instruments of *their* license. The birth of Vespasian was mean; his grandfather had been a private soldier, his father a petty officer of the revenue; his own merit had raised him, in an advanced age, to the empire; but his merit was rather useful, than shining, and his virtues were disgraced by a strict and even sordid parsimony. Such a prince consulted his true interest by the association of a son, whose more splendid and amiable character might turn the public attention from the obscure origin to the future glories of the Flavian house. Under the mild administration of Titus, the Roman world enjoyed a transient felicity, and his beloved memory served to protect, above fifteen years, the vices of his brother Domitian.

Nerva had scarcely accepted the purple from the assassins of Domitian before he discovered that his feeble age was unable to stem the torrent of public disorders, which had multiplied under the long tyranny of his predecessor. His mild disposition was respected by the good; but the degenerate Romans required a more vigorous character, whose justice should strike terror into the guilty. Though he had several relations, he fixed his choice on a stranger. He adopted Trajan, then about forty years of age, and who commanded a powerful army in

Right: Girl with pen and wax writing tablet. (Wall-painting from Pompeii, first century AD, National Museum, Naples)

Below: Portrait of Terentius and his wife. (Wall-painting from Pompeii, first century AD, National Archeological Museum, Naples)

Left: Statue of Marcus Aurelius. (Roman Emperor 161–180 AD)

flourished in peace and prosperity. He encouraged the arts, reformed the laws, asserted military discipline, and visited all his provinces in person. His vast and active genius was equally suited to the most enlarged views, and the minute details of civil policy. But the ruling passions of his soul were curiosity and vanity. As they prevailed, and as they were attracted by different objects, Hadrian was, by turns, an excellent prince, a ridiculous sophist, and a jealous tyrant. The general tenor of his conduct deserved praise for its equity and moderation. Yet in the first days of his reign, he put to death four consular senators, his personal enemies, and men who had been judged worthy of empire; and the tediousness of a painful illness rendered him, at last, peevish and cruel. The senate doubted whether they should pronounce him a god or a tyrant; and the honors decreed to his memory were granted to the prayers of the pious Antoninus.

The caprice of Hadrian influenced his choice of a successor. After revolving in his mind several men of distinguished merit, whom he esteemed and hated, he adopted Ælius Verus, a gay and voluptuous nobleman, recommended by uncommon beauty to the lover of Antoninus. But while Hadrian was delighting himself with his own applause, and the acclamations of the soldiers, whose consent had been secured by an immense donative, the new Cæsar was ravished from his embraces by an untimely death. He left only one son. Hadrian commended the boy to the gratitude of the Antonines. He was adopted by Pius; and, on the accession of Marcus, was invested with an equal share of sovereign power. Among the many vices of this younger Verus he possessed one virtue; a dutiful reverence for his wiser colleagues, to whom he willingly abandoned the ruder cares of empire. The philosophic emperor dissembled his follies, lamented his early death, and cast a decent veil over his memory.

As soon as Hadrian's passion was either gratified or disappointed, he resolved to deserve the thanks of posterity, by placing the most exalted merit on the Roman throne. His discerning eye easily discovered a senator about fifty years of age, blameless in all the offices of life, and a youth of about seventeen, whose riper years opened the fair prospect of every virtue: the elder of these was declared the son and successor of Hadrian, on condition, however, that he himself should immediately adopt the younger. The two Antonines (for it is of them that we are now speaking) governed the Roman world forty-two years, with the same invariable spirit of wisdom and virtue. Although Pius had two sons, he preferred the welfare of Rome to the interest of his family, gave his daughter Faustina in marriage to young Marcus, obtained from the senate the tribunitian and proconsular powers, and with a noble disdain, or rather ignorance of jealousy, associated him to all the labors of government. Marcus, on the other hand, revered the character of his benefactor, loved him as a parent, obeyed him as his sovereign, and,

Left: Detail from the Arch of Marcus Aurelius – a quadrifrontal white marble, Roman triumphal arch. (AD 163)

Above: Nymph Lucurteo.
(Lateran Museum, Rome)
Right: Roman soldiers
fighting a tribe of Germanic
barbarians. (First–second
century AD, sarcophagus,
Museo Nazionale delle
Terme, Rome)
Far right: Roman legionaries,
from the base of the Antonine
Column, Rome.

after he was no more, regulated his own administration by the example and maxims of his predecessor. Their united reigns are possibly the only period of history in which the happiness of a great people was the sole object of government.

Titus Antoninus Pius has been justly denominated a second Numa. The same love of religion, justice, and peace, was the distinguishing characteristic of both princes. But the situation of the former opened a much larger field for the exercise of those virtues. Numa could only prevent a few neighboring villages from plundering each other's harvests. Antoninus diffused order and tranquillity over the greatest part of the earth. His reign is marked by the rare advantage of furnishing very few materials for history; which is, indeed, little more than the register of the crimes, follies, and misfortunes of mankind. In private life, he was an amiable as well as a good man. The native simplicity of his virtue was a stranger to vanity or affectation. He enjoyed with moderation the conveniences of his fortune, and the innocent pleasures of society: and the benevolence of his soul displayed itself in a cheerful serenity of temper.

The virtue of Marcus Aurelius Antoninus was of a severer and more laborious kind. It was the well-earned harvest of many a learned conference, of many a patient lecture, and many a midnight lucub-

ration. At the age of twelve years he embraced the rigid system of the Stoics, which taught him to submit his body to his mind, his passions to his reason; to consider virtue as the only good, vice as the only evil, all things external as things indifferent. His meditations, composed in the tumult of a camp, are still extant; and he even condescended to give lessons of philosophy in a more public manner than was perhaps consistent with the modesty of a sage, or the dignity of an emperor. But his life was the noblest commentary on the precepts of Zeno. He was severe to himself, indulgent to the imperfections of others, just and beneficent to all mankind. He regretted that Avidius Cassius, who excited a rebellion in Syria, had disappointed him, by a voluntary death, of the pleasure of converting an enemy into a friend; and he justified the sincerity of that sentiment, by moderating the zeal of the senate against the adherents of the traitor. War he detested, as the disgrace and calamity of human nature; but when the necessity of a just defense called upon him to take up arms, he readily exposed his person to eight winter campaigns on the frozen banks of the Danube, the severity of which was at last fatal to the weakness of his constitution. His memory was revered by a grateful posterity, and above a century after his death, many persons preserved the image of Marcus Antoninus, among those of their household gods.

If a man were called to fix the period in the history of the world, during which the condition of the human race was most happy and prosperous, he would, without hesitation, name that which elapsed from the death of Domitian to the accession of Commodus. The vast extent of the Roman empire was governed by absolute power, under the guidance of virtue and wisdom. The armies were restrained by the firm but gentle hand of four successive emperors, whose characters and authority commanded involuntary respect. The forms of the civil administration were carefully preserved by Nerva, Trajan, Hadrian, and the Antonines, who delighted in the image of liberty, and were pleased with considering themselves as the accountable ministers of the laws. Such princes deserved the honor of restoring the republic had the Romans of their days been capable of enjoying a rational freedom.

The labors of these monarchs were overpaid by the immense reward that inseparably waited on their success; by the honest pride of virtue, and by the exquisite delight of beholding the general happiness of which they were the authors. A just, but melancholy reflection embittered, however, the noblest of human enjoyments. They must often have recollected the instability of a happiness which depended on the character of a single man. The fatal moment was perhaps approaching, when some licentious youth, or some jealous tyrant, would abuse, to the

destruction, that absolute power which they had exerted for the benefit of their people. The ideal restraints of the senate and the laws might serve to display the virtues, but could never correct the vices, of the emperor. The military force was a blind and irresistible instrument of oppression; and the corruption of Roman manners would always supply flatterers eager to applaud, and ministers prepared to serve the fear or the avarice, the lust or the cruelty, of their masters.

These gloomy apprehensions had been already justified by the experience of the Romans. The annals of the emperors exhibit a strong and various picture of human nature, which we should vainly seek among the mixed and doubtful characters of modern history. In the conduct of those monarchs we may trace the utmost lines of vice and virtue; the most exalted perfection, and the meanest degeneracy of our own species. The golden age of Trajan and the Antonines had been preceded by an age of iron. It is almost superfluous to enumerate the unworthy successors of Augustus. Their unparalleled vices, and the splendid theater on which they were acted, have saved them from oblivion. The dark unrelenting Tiberius, the furious Caligula, the feeble Claudius, the profligate and cruel Nero, the beastly Vitellius, and the timid inhuman Domitian, are condemned to everlasting infamy. During fourscore years (excepting only the short and doubtful respite of Vespasian's reign) Rome groaned beneath an unremitting tyranny, which exterminated the ancient families of the republic, and was fatal to almost every virtue, and every talent, that arose in that unhappy period.

The division of Europe into a number of independent states, connected, however, with each other, by the general resemblance of religion, language, and manners, is productive of the most beneficial consequences to the liberty of mankind. A modern tyrant, who should find no resistance either in his own breast, or in his people, would soon experience a gentle restraint from the example of his equals, the dread of present censure, the advice of his allies, and the apprehension of his enemies. The object of his displeasure, escaping from the narrow limits of his dominions, would easily obtain, in a happier climate, a secure refuge, a new fortune adequate to his merit, the freedom of complaint, and perhaps the means of revenge. But the empire of the Romans filled the world, and when that empire fell into the hands of a single person, the world became a safe and dreary prison for his enemies. The slave of Imperial despotism, whether he was condemned to drag his gilded chain in Rome and the senate, or to wear out a life of exile on the barren rock of Seriphus, or the frozen banks of the Danube, expected his fate in silent despair. To resist was fatal, and it was impossible to fly. On every side he was encompassed with a vast extent of sea and land, which he could never hope to traverse without being discovered, seized, and restored to his irritated master. Beyond the frontiers, his anxious view could discover nothing, except the ocean, inhospitable deserts, hostile tribes of barbarians, of fierce manners and unknown language, or dependent kings, who would gladly purchase the emperor's protection by the sacrifice of an obnoxious fugitive. 'Wherever you are,' said Cicero to the exiled Marcellus, 'remember that you are equally within the power of the conqueror.'

CHAPTER FOUR

The cruelty, follies and murder of Commodus

election of Pertinax – his attempts to reform the state – his assassination by the
Prætorian guards
[AD 180–193]

THE mildness of Marcus, which the rigid discipline of the Stoics was unable to eradicate, formed, at the same time, the most amiable, and the only defective part of his character. His excellent understanding was often deceived by the unsuspecting goodness of his heart. His excessive indulgence to his brother, his wife, and his son, exceeded the bounds of private virtue, and became a public injury, by the example and consequences of their vices.

Faustina, the daughter of Pius and the wife of Marcus, has been as much celebrated for her gallantries as for her beauty. Marcus was the only man in the empire who seemed ignorant or insensible of her irregularities which, according to the prejudices of every age, reflected some disgrace on the injured husband. He promoted several of her lovers to posts of honor and profit, and during a connection of thirty years, invariably gave her proofs of the most tender confidence, and of a respect which ended not with her life. In his Meditations, he thanks the gods, who had bestowed on him a wife, so faithful, so gentle, and of such a wonderful simplicity of manners.

The monstrous vices of the son have cast a shade on the purity of the father's virtues. It has been objected to Marcus, that he sacrificed the happiness of millions to a fond partiality for a worthless boy; and that he chose a successor in his own family, rather than in the republic. Nothing, however, was spared in the education of his son, but Marcus himself blasted the fruits of this labored education, by admitting his son, at the age of fourteen or fifteen, to a full participation of the Imperial power. He lived but four years afterwards; but he lived long enough to repent a rash measure, which raised the impetuous youth above the restraint of reason and authority.

Most of the crimes which disturb the internal peace of society are produced by the restraints which the necessary, but unequal, laws of property have imposed on the appetites of mankind, by confining to a few the possession of those objects that are coveted by many. Of all our passions and appetites, the love of power is of the most imperious and unsociable nature, since the pride of one man requires the submission of the multitude.

Yet Commodus was not, as he has been represented, a tiger born with an insatiate thirst of human blood, and capable, from his infancy, of the most inhuman actions. Nature had formed him of a weak, rather than a wicked, disposition. His simplicity and timidity rendered him the slave of his attendants, who gradually corrupted his mind. His cruelty, which at first obeyed the dictates of others, degenerated into habit, and at length became the ruling passion of his soul.

Upon the death of his father, Commodus found himself embarrassed with the command of a great army, and the conduct of a difficult war against the Quadi and Marcomanni. The servile and profligate youths whom Marcus had banished, soon regained their station and influence about the new emperor. They exaggerated the hardships and dangers of a campaign in the wild countries beyond the Danube; and they assured the indolent prince, that the terror of his name and the arms of his lieutenants would be sufficient to complete the conquest of the dismayed barbarians; or to impose such conditions as were more advantageous than any conquest. By a dexterous application to his sensual appetites, they compared the tranquillity, the splendor, the refined pleasures of Rome, with the tumult of a Pannonian camp, which afforded neither leisure nor materials for luxury. Commodus listened to the pleasing advice; but while he hesitated between his own inclination

and the awe which he still retained for his father's counselors, the summer insensibly elapsed, and his triumphal entry into the capital was deferred till the autumn. His graceful person, popular address, and imagined virtues, attracted the public favor; the honorable peace which he had recently granted to the barbarians diffused an universal joy; his impatience to revisit Rome was fondly ascribed to the love of his country; and his dissolute course of amusements was faintly condemned in a prince of nineteen years of age.

During the three first years of his reign, the forms, and even the spirit, of the old administration were maintained by those faithful counselors, to whom Marcus had recommended his son, and for whose wisdom and integrity Commodus still entertained a reluctant esteem. The young prince and his profligate favorites revelled in all the license of sovereign power; but his hands were yet unstained with blood; and he had even displayed a generosity of sentiment, which might perhaps have ripened into solid virtue. A fatal incident decided his fluctuating character.

One evening (AD 183), as the emperor was returning to the palace through a dark and narrow portico in the amphitheater, an assassin, who waited his passage, rushed upon him with a drawn sword, loudly exclaiming, '*The senate sends you this.*' The menace prevented the deed; the assassin was seized by the guards, and immediately revealed the authors of the conspiracy. It had been formed, not in the state, but within the walls of the palace. Lucilla, the emperor's sister, and widow of Lucius Verus, impatient of the second rank, and jealous of the reigning empress, had armed the murderer against her brother's life. She had not ventured to communicate the black design to her second husband Claudius Pompeianus, a senator of distinguished merit and unshaken loyalty; but among the crowd of her lovers (for she imitated the manners of Faustina), she found men of desperate fortunes and wild ambition, who were prepared to serve her more violent as well as her tender passions. The conspirators experienced the rigor of justice, and the abandoned princess was punished, first with exile, and afterwards with death.

Left: Bust of a young Roman, believed to be the emperor Commodus (Lucius Aurelius Commodus, AD 161–92; Roman emperor AD 337–60), son of Marcus Aurelius Antonius and Faustina.
Below: Roman gladiators, an extreme form of entertainment.

But the words of the assassin sunk deep into the mind of Commodus, and left an indelible impression of fear and hatred against the whole body of the senate. Those whom he had dreaded as importunate ministers, he now suspected as secret enemies. The Delators, a race of men discouraged, and almost extinguished, under the former reigns, again became formidable, as soon as they discovered that the emperor was desirous of finding disaffection and treason in the senate. That assembly, whom Marcus had ever considered as the great council of the nation, was composed of the most distinguished of the Romans; and distinction of every kind soon became criminal. The possession of wealth stimulated the diligence of the informers; rigid virtue implied a tacit censure of the irregularities of Commodus; important services implied a dangerous superiority of merit; and the friendship of the father always insured the aversion of the son. Suspicion was equivalent to proof; trial to condemnation. The execution of a considerable senator was attended with the death of all who might lament or revenge his fate; and when Commodus had once tasted human blood, he became incapable of pity or remorse.

Pestilence and famine contributed to fill up the measure of the calamities of Rome. The first could be only imputed to the just indignation of the gods; but (AD 189) a monopoly of corn, supported by the riches and power of the minister, was considered as the immediate cause of the second. The popular discontent, after it had long circulated in whispers, broke out in the assembled circus. Cleander, who commanded the Prætorian guards, ordered a body of cavalry to sally forth, and disperse the seditious multitude. The tumult became a regular engagement, and threatened a general massacre. The Prætorians, at length, gave way, oppressed with numbers; and the tide of popular fury returned with redoubled violence against the gates of the palace, where Commodus lay, dissolved in luxury, and alone unconscious of the civil war. It was death to approach his person with the unwelcome news. He would have perished in this supine security, had not two women, his elder sister Fadilla, and Marcia, the most favored of his concubines, ventured to break into his presence. Bathed in tears, and with dishevelled hair, they threw themselves at his feet; and with all the pressing eloquence of fear, discovered to the affrighted emperor, the crimes of the minister, the rage of the people, and the impending ruin, which, in a few minutes, would burst over his palace and person. Commodus started from his dream of pleasure, and commanded that the head of Cleander should be thrown out to the people. The desired spectacle instantly appeased the tumult; and the son of Marcus might even yet have regained the affection and confidence of his outraged subjects.

But every sentiment of virtue and humanity was extinct in the mind of Commodus. While he abandoned the reins of empire to unworthy favorites, he valued nothing in sovereign power, except the unbounded license of indulging his sensual appetites. The influence of a polite age, and the labor of an attentive education, had never been able to infuse

Roman gladiators fighting wild beasts.

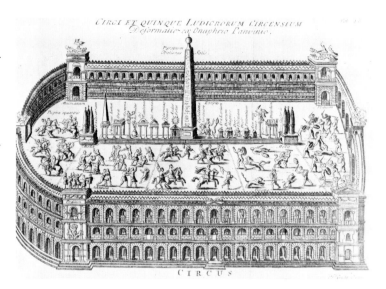

Roman gladiators at the circus. (Seventeenth-century drawing)

into his rude and brutish mind the least tincture of learning; and he was the first of the Roman emperors totally devoid of taste for the pleasures of the understanding. Nero himself excelled, or affected to excel, in the elegant arts of music and poetry; nor should we despise his pursuits had he not converted the pleasing relaxation of a leisure hour into the serious business and ambition of his life. But Commodus, from his earliest infancy, discovered an aversion to whatever was rational or liberal, and a fond attachment to the amusements of the populace; the sports of the circus and amphitheater, the combats of gladiators, and the hunting of wild beasts.

The servile crowd, whose fortune depended on their master's vices, applauded these ignoble pursuits. The perfidious voice of flattery reminded him that by exploits of the same nature, by the defeat of the Nemæan lion, and the slaughter of the wild boar of Erymanthus, the Grecian Hercules had acquired a place among the gods, and an immortal memory among men.

Elated with these praises, which gradually extinguished the innate sense of shame, Commodus resolved to exhibit, before the eyes of the Roman people, those exercises, which till then he had decently confined within the walls of his palace, and to the presence of a few favorites. On the appointed day, the various motives of flattery, fear, and curiosity, attracted to the amphitheater an innumerable multitude of spectators: and some degree of applause was deservedly bestowed on the uncommon skill of the Imperial performer.

But the meanest of the populace were affected with shame and indignation when they beheld their sovereign enter the lists as a gladiator, and glory in a profession which the laws and manners of the Romans had branded with the justest note of infamy.

Commodus had now attained the summit of vice and infamy. Amidst the acclamations of a flattering court, he was unable to disguise, from himself, that he had deserved his contempt and hatred of every man of sense and virtue in his empire. His ferocious spirit was irritated by the consciousness of that hatred, by the envy of every kind of merit, by the just apprehension of danger, and by the habit of slaughter, which he contracted in his daily amusements. His cruelty proved at last fatal to himself. He had shed with impunity the noblest blood of Rome: he perished as soon as he was dreaded by his own domestics. Marcia his favorite concubine, Eclectus his chamberlain, and Lætus his Prætorian præfect, alarmed by the fate of their companions and predecessors, resolved to prevent the destruction which every hour hung over their heads, either from the mad caprice of the tyrant, or the sudden indignation of the people. Marcia seized the occasion of presenting a draught of wine to her lover, after he had fatigued himself with hunting some wild beasts. Commodus retired to sleep; but whilst he was laboring with the effects of poison and drunkenness, a robust youth, by profession a wrestler, entered his chamber, and strangled him without resistance. The body was secretly conveyed out of the palace, before the least suspicion was entertained in the city, or even in the court, of the emperor's death.

The measures of the conspirators were conducted with the deliberate coolness and celerity which the greatness of the occasion required. They resolved instantly to fill the vacant throne with an emperor whose character would justify and maintain the action that had been committed. They fixed on Pertinax, præfect of the city, an ancient senator of consular rank, whose conspicuous merit had broke through the obscurity of his birth, and raised him to the first honors of the state. He now remained almost alone of the friends and ministers of Marcus.

Lætus conducted without delay his new emperor to the camp of the Prætorians, diffusing at the same time through the city a seasonable report that Commodus died suddenly of an apoplexy; and that the virtuous Pertinax had *already* succeeded to the throne.

The memory of Commodus was branded with eternal infamy. The names of tyrant, of gladiator, of public enemy, resounded in every corner.

These effusions of impotent rage against a dead emperor, whom the senate had flattered when alive with the most abject servility, betrayed a just but ungenerous spirit of revenge. The legality of these decrees was however supported by the principles of the Imperial constitution. To censure, to depose, or to punish with death, the first magistrate of the republic, who had abused his delegated trust, was the ancient and undoubted prerogative of the Roman senate; but that feeble assembly was obliged to content itself with inflicting on a fallen tyrant that public justice, from which, during his life and reign, he had been shielded by the strong arm of military despotism.

Pertinax found a nobler way of condemning his predecessor's memory; by the contrast of his own virtues with the vices of Commodus. In public, the behavior of Pertinax was grave and affable. He lived with the virtuous part of the senate (and in a private station, he had been acquainted with the true character of each individual), without either pride or jealousy; considered them as friends and companions, with whom he had shared the dangers of the tyranny, and with whom he wished to enjoy the security of the present time. He very frequently invited them to familiar entertainments, the frugality of which was ridiculed by those who remembered and regretted the luxurious prodigality of Commodus.

To heal, as far as it was possible, the wounds inflicted by the hand of tyranny, was the pleasing, but melancholy, task of Pertinax.

The finances of the state demanded the most vigilant care of the emperor. Though every measure of injustice and extortion had been adopted, which could collect the property of the subject into the coffers of the prince; the rapaciousness of Commodus had been so very inadequate to his extravagance, that, upon his death, no more than

Roman gladiators. (Third-century relief, Museo Nazionale, Rome)

The dying gladiator. (Hellenistic Roman Sculpture, Rome)

eight thousand pounds were found in the exhausted treasury, to defray the current expenses of government, and to discharge the pressing demand of a liberal donative, which the new emperor had been obliged to promise to the Prætorian guards. Yet, Pertinax had the generous firmness to remit all the oppressive taxes invented by Commodus, and to cancel all the unjust claims of the treasury. Economy and industry he considered as the pure and genuine sources of wealth; and from them he soon derived a copious supply for the public necessities. The expense of the household was immediately reduced to one half. At the same time that he obliged the worthless favorites of the tyrant to resign a part of their ill-gotten wealth, he satisfied the just creditors of the state, and unexpectedly discharged the long arrears of honest services. He removed the oppressive restrictions which had been laid upon commerce, and granted all the uncultivated lands in Italy and the provinces to those who would improve them; with an exemption from tribute, during the term of ten years.

A hasty zeal to reform the corrupted state, accompanied with less prudence than might have been expected from the years and experience of Pertinax, proved fatal to himself and to his country. His honest indiscretion united against him the servile crowd, who found their private benefit in the public disorders, and who preferred the favor of a tyrant to the inexorable equality of the laws.

Amidst the general joy, the sullen and angry countenance of the Prætorian guards betrayed their inward dissatisfaction. They had reluctantly submitted to Pertinax; they dreaded the strictness of the ancient discipline, which he was preparing to restore; and they regretted the license of the former reign. Their discontents were secretly fomented by Lætus their præfect, who found, when it was too late, that his new emperor would reward a servant, but would not be ruled by a favorite. On the third day of his reign the soldiers seized on a noble senator, with a design to carry him to the camp, and to invest him with the Imperial purple. Instead of being dazzled by the dangerous honor, the affrighted victim escaped from their violence, and took refuge at the feet of Pertinax. A short time afterwards Sosius Falco, one of the consuls of the year, rash youth, but of an ancient and opulent family, listened to the voice of ambition; and a conspiracy was formed during a short absence of Pertinax, which was crushed by his sudden return to Rome, and his resolute behavior. Falco was on the point of being justly condemned to death as a public enemy, had he not been saved by the earnest and sincere entreaties of the injured emperor; who conjured the senate, that the purity of his reign might not be stained by the blood even of a guilty senator.

These disappointments served only to irritate the rage of the Prætorian guards. On the twenty-eighth day of March, after an eighty-six day rule of temperance and justice, a general sedition broke out in the camp and Pertinax was assassinated. A barbarian of the country of Tongres levelled the first blow against Pertinax, who was instantly dispatched with a multitude of wounds. His head separated from his body, and placed on a lance, was carried in triumph to the Prætorian camp, in the sight of a mournful and indignant people, who lamented the unworthy fate of that excellent prince, and the transient blessings of a reign, the memory of which could serve only to aggravate their approaching misfortunes.

CHAPTER FIVE

Public sale of the Empire to Didius Julianus by the Prætorian guards

Clodius Albinus in Britain, Pescennius Niger in Syria, and Septimius Severus in Pannonia, against the murderers of Pertinax – civil wars and victory of Severus over his three rivals – relaxation of discipline – new maxims of government

[AD 193–193]

THE power of the sword is more sensibly felt in an extensive monarchy than in a small community. It has been calculated by the ablest politicians, that no state, without being soon exhausted, can maintain above the hundredth part of its members in arms and idleness. But although this relative proportion may be uniform, the influence of the army over the rest of the society will vary according to the degree of its positive strength. The advantages of military science and discipline cannot be exerted, unless a proper number of soldiers are united into one body, and actuated by one soul. With a handful of men, such an union would be ineffectual; with an unwieldly host, it would be impracticable; and the powers of the machine would be alike destroyed by the extreme minuteness, or the excessive weight, of its springs. To illustrate this observation we need only reflect, that there is no superiority of natural strength, artificial weapons, or acquired skill, which could enable one man to keep in constant subjection one hundred of his fellow-creatures: the tyrant of a single town, or a small district, would soon discover that an hundred armed followers were a weak defense against ten thousand peasants or citizens; but an hundred thousand well-disciplined soldiers will command, with despotic sway, ten millions of subjects; and a body of ten or fifteen guards will strike terror into the most numerous populace that ever crowded the streets of an immense capital.

The Prætorian bands, whose licentious fury was the first symptom and cause of the decline of the Roman empire, scarcely amounted to the last-mentioned number.

The Prætorians had violated the sanctity of the throne, by the atrocious murder of Pertinax, they dishonored the majesty of it, by their subsequent conduct. The camp was without a leader, for even the Præfect Lætus, who had excited the tempest, prudently declined the public indignation. Amidst the wild disorder Sulpicianus, the emperor's father-in-law, and governor of the city, who had been sent to the camp on the first alarm of mutiny, was endeavoring to calm the fury of the multitude, when he was silenced by the clamorous return of the murderers, bearing on a lance the head of Pertinax. Though history has accustomed us to observe every principle and every passion yielding to the imperious dictates of ambition, it is scarcely credible that, in these moments of horror, Sulpicianus should have aspired to ascend a throne polluted with the recent blood of so near a relation, and so excellent a prince. He had already begun to use the only effectual argument, and to treat for the Imperial dignity; but the more prudent of the Prætorians, apprehensive that, in this private contract, they should not obtain a just price for so valuable a commodity, ran out upon the ramparts; and, with a loud voice, proclaimed that the Roman world was to be disposed of to the best bidder by public auction.

This infamous offer, the most insolent excess of military licence, diffused an universal grief, shame, and indignation throughout the city. It reached at length the ears of Didius Julianus, a wealthy senator, who, regardless of the public calamities, was indulging himself in the luxury of the table. The vain old man (AD 193, 28 March) hastened to the Prætorian camp, where Sulpicianus was still in treaty with the guards; and began to bid against him from the foot of the rampart. Sulpicianus had already promised a donative of five thousand drachms (above one hundred and sixty pounds) to each soldier; when Julian, eager for the prize, rose at once to the sum of six thousand two hundred and fifty drachms, or upwards of six thousand pounds sterling. The gates of the camp were instantly thrown open to the purchaser; he was declared

emperor, and received an oath of allegiance from the soldiers, who retained humanity enough to stipulate that he should pardon and forget the competition of Sulpicianus.

It was now incumbent on the Prætorians to fulfill the conditions of the sale. They placed their new sovereign, whom they served and despised, in the center of their ranks, surrounded him on every side with their shields, and conducted him in close order of battle through the deserted streets of the city. The senate was commanded to assemble; and those who had been the distinguished friends of Pertinax, or the personal enemies of Julian, found it necessary to affect a more than common share of satisfaction at this happy revolution. The obsequious assembly congratulated their own and the public felicity; engaged their allegiance, and conferred on him all the several branches of the Imperial power. From the senate Julian was conducted, by the same military procession, to take possession of the palace. Yet it was observed, that after the crowd of flatterers dispersed, and left him to darkness, solitude, and terrible reflection, he passed a sleepless night; revolving most probably in his mind his own rash folly, the fate of his virtuous predecessor, and the doubtful and dangerous tenure of an empire, which had not been acquired by merit, but purchased by money.

Once he was emperor he had reason to tremble. On the throne of the world he found himself without a friend, and even without an adherent. The guards themselves were ashamed of the prince whom their avarice had persuaded them to accept; nor was there a citizen who did not consider his elevation with horror, as the last insult on the Roman

Left: Street leading to the capitol in the Roman city of Dougga. (Second century AD)
Below: Family scene: Roman matron bathing her baby. (Relief from a sarcophagus, second century AD, Museo Capitolino, Rome)

Left: Coin of Clodius Albinus Augustus, Governor of Britain, who briefly set himself up as emperor after the death of Pertinax (c AD 193). He was subsequently put to death by his successful rival Septimius Severus (Lucius Septimius Severus, 146–211; Roman Emperor, 193–211; London Museum). *Right:* The Arch of Septimius Severus, Rome.

name. The streets and public places of Rome resounded with clamors and imprecations. The enraged multitude affronted the person of Julian, rejected his liberality, and conscious of the impotence of their own resentment, they called aloud on the legions of the frontiers to assert the violated majesty of the Roman empire.

The public discontent was soon diffused from the center to the frontiers of the empire. The armies of Britain, of Syria, and of Illyricum, lamented the death of Pertinax, in whose company, or under whose command, they had so often fought and conquered. They received with surprise, with indignation, and perhaps with envy, the extraordinary intelligence that the Prætorians had disposed of the empire by public auction; and they sternly refused to ratify the ignominious bargain. Their immediate and unanimous revolt was fatal to Julian, but it was fatal at the same time to the public peace; as the generals of the respective armies, Clodius Albinus, Pescennius Niger, and Septimius Severus, were still more anxious to succeed than to revenge the murdered Pertinax. Their forces were exactly balanced. Each of them was at the head of three legions, with a numerous train of auxiliaries; and however different in their characters, they were all soldiers of experience and capacity.

Clodius Albinus, governor of Britain, surpassed both his competitors in the nobility of his extraction, which he derived from some of the most illustrious names of the old republic. A regard to decency induced him to decline the lofty titles of Augustus and Emperor; and he imitated perhaps the example of Galba, who, on a similar occasion, had styled himself the Lieutenant of the senate and people.

Personal merit alone had raised Pescennius Niger from an obscure birth and station to the government of Syria; a lucrative and important command, which in times of civil confusion gave him a near prospect of the throne. Instead of entering into an effectual negotiation with the powerful armies of the west, whose resolution might decide, or at least must balance, the mighty contest; instead of advancing without delay towards Rome and Italy, where his presence was impatiently expected, Niger trifled away in the luxury of Antioch those irretrievable moments which were diligently improved by the decisive activity of Severus.

The country of Pannonia and Dalmatia, which occupied the space between the Danube and the Hadriatic, was one of the last and most difficult conquests of the Romans. In the defense of national freedom, two hundred thousand of these barbarians had once appeared in the field, alarmed the declining age of Augustus, and exercised the vigilant prudence of Tiberius at the head of the collected force of the empire. Pannonians yielded at length to the arms and institutions of Rome. Their recent subjection, however, the neighborhood, and even the mixture, of the unconquered tribes, and perhaps the climate, adapted, as it has been observed, to the production of great bodies and slow minds, all contributed to preserve some remains of their original ferocity, and under the tame and uniform countenance of Roman provincials, the hardy features of the natives were still to be discerned. Their warlike youth afforded an inexhaustible supply of recruits to the legions stationed on the banks of the Danube, and which, from a perpetual warfare against the Germans and Sarmatians, were deservedly esteemed the best troops in the service.

The Pannonian army was at this time commanded by Septimius Severus, a native of Africa, who, in the gradual ascent of private honors, had concealed his daring ambition, which was never diverted from its steady course by the allurements of pleasure, the apprehension of danger, or the feelings of humanity. On the first news of the murder of

Pertinax, he assembled his troops, painted in the most lively colors of the crime, the insolence, and the weakness of the Prætorian guards, and animated the legions to arms and to revenge. He concluded (and the peroration was thought extremely eloquent) with promising every soldier about four hundred pounds; an honorable donative, double in value to the infamous bribe with which Julian had purchased the empire. The acclamations of the army immediately saluted Severus with the names of Augustus, Pertinax, and Emperor; and he (AD 193, 13 April) thus attained the lofty station to which he was invited, by conscious merit and a long train of dreams and omens, the fruitful offspring of his superstition or policy.

The new candidate for empire saw and improved the peculiar advantage of his situation. His province extended to the Julian Alps, which gave an easy access into Italy; and he remembered the saying of Augustus, That a Pannonian army might in ten days appear in sight of Rome.

The wretched Julian had expected, and thought himself prepared, to dispute the empire with the governor of Syria; but in the invincible and rapid approach of the Pannonian legions, he saw his inevitable ruin.

He attempted, however, to prevent, or at least to protract, his ruin. He implored the venal faith of the Prætorians, filled the city with unavailing preparations for war, drew lines round the suburbs, and even strengthened the fortifications of the palace; as if those last entrenchments could be defended without hope or relief against a victorious invader. Fear and shame prevented the guards from desert-

The Prætorian Barracks. (Nineteenth-century engraving)

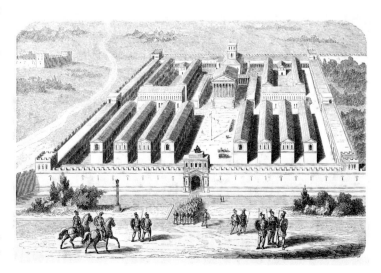

ing his standard; but they trembled at the name of the Pannonian legions, commanded by an experienced general, and accustomed to vanquish the barbarians on the frozen Danube.

Every motion of Julian betrayed his trembling perplexity. He insisted that Severus should be declared a public enemy by the senate. He intreated that the Pannonian general might be associated to the empire. He sent public ambassadors of consular rank to negotiate with his rival; he dispatched private assassins to take away his life. He designed that the Vestal virgins, and all the colleges of priests, in their sacerdotal habits, and bearing before them the sacred pledges of the Roman religion, should advance, in solemn procession, to meet the Pannonian legions; and, at the same time, he vainly tried to interrogate, or to appease, the fates, by magic ceremonies, and unlawful sacrifices.

Severus, who dreaded neither his arms nor his enchantments, guarded himself from the only danger of secret conspiracy, by the faithful attendance of six hundred chosen men, who never quitted his person or their cuirasses, either by night or by day, during the whole march. Advancing with a steady and rapid course, he passed, without difficulty, the defiles of the Apennine, received into his party the troops and ambassadors sent to retard his progress, and made a short halt at Interamnia, about seventy miles from Rome. His victory was already secure; but the despair of the Prætorians might have rendered it bloody; and Severus had the laudable ambition of ascending the throne without drawing the sword. His emissaries, dispersed in the capital, assured the guards, that provided they would abandon their worthless prince, and the perpetrators of the murder of Pertinax, to the justice of the conqueror, he would no longer consider that melancholy event as the act of the whole body. The faithless Prætorians, whose resistance was supported only by sullen obstinacy, gladly complied with the easy conditions, seized the greatest part of the assassins, and signified to the senate that they no longer defended the cause of Julian. That assembly, convoked by the consul, unanimously acknowledged Severus as lawful emperor, decreed divine honors to Pertinax, and pronounced a sentence of deposition and death against his unfortunate successor. Julian was conducted into a private apartment of the baths of the palace, and (AD 193, 2 June) beheaded as a common criminal, after having purchased, with an immense treasure, an anxious and precarious reign of only sixty-six days. The almost incredible expedition of Severus, who, in so short a space of time, conducted a numerous army from the banks of the Danube to those of the Tiber, proves at once the plenty of provisions produced by agriculture and commerce, the goodness of the roads, the discipline of the legions, and the indolent subdued temper of the provinces.

Sensible, however, that arms, not ceremonies, must assert his claim to the empire, he left Rome at the end of thirty days, and, without suffering himself to be elated by this easy victory, prepared to encounter his more formidable rivals.

Both Niger and Albinus were discovered and put to death in their flight from the field of battle. Their fate excited neither surprise nor compassion.

The true interest of an absolute monarch generally coincides with that of his people. Their numbers, their wealth, their order, and their security, are the best and only foundations of his real greatness; and were he totally devoid of virtue, prudence might supply its place, and would dictate the same rule of conduct. Severus considered the Roman empire as his property, and had no sooner secured the possession, than he bestowed his care on the cultivation and improvement of so valuable an acquisition. Salutary laws, executed with inflexible firmness, soon corrected most of the abuses with which, since the death of Marcus, every part of the government had been infected. In the administration of justice, the judgments of the emperor were characterized by attention, discernment, and impartiality; and whenever he deviated from the strict line of equity, it was generally in favor of the poor and oppressed; not so much indeed from any sense of humanity, as from the natural propensity of a despot, to humble the pride of greatness, and to sink all his subjects to the same common level of absolute dependence. His expensive taste for building, magnificent shows, and above all a constant and liberal distribution of corn and provisions, were the surest means of captivating the affection of the Roman people. The misfortunes of civil discord were obliterated. The calm of peace and pros-

The Triumph of Septimius Severus: detail showing the imperial family riding in the triumphal cart, Tripoli.

perity was once more experienced in the provinces; and many cities, restored by the munificence of Severus, assumed the title of his colonies, and attested by public monuments their gratitude and felicity. The fame of Roman arms was revived by that warlike and successful emperor, and he boasted with a just pride, that, having received the empire oppressed with foreign and domestic wars, he left it established in profound, universal, and honorable peace.

Although the wounds of civil war appeared completely healed, its mortal poison still lurked in the vitals of constitution. Severus possessed a considerable share of vigor and ability; but the daring soul of the first Cæsar, or the deep policy of Augustus, were scarcely equal to the task of curbing the insolence of the victorious legions. By gratitude, by misguided policy, by seeming necessity, Severus was induced to relax

The Prætorian guards rose to power under Augustus and they formed a small but powerful group upon which the fate of the empire increasingly depended.

the nerves of discipline. The vanity of his soldiers was flattered with the honor of wearing gold rings; their ease was indulged in the permission of living with their wives in the idleness of quarters. He increased their pay beyond the example of former times, and taught them to expect, and soon to claim, extraordinary donatives on every public occasion of danger or festivity. Elated by success, enervated by luxury, and raised above the level of subjects by their dangerous privileges, they soon became incapable of military fatigue, oppressive to the country, and impatient of a just subordination. Their officers asserted the superiority of rank by a more profuse and elegant luxury. There is still extant a letter of Severus, lamenting the licentious state of the army, and

The Hadrianic Baths, Leptis Magna, Tripolitania, Libya.

Left above: The slim Corinthian columns of the Roman temple, the Capitol, Dougga, Tunisia.
Above: A family outing. (Relief from a sarcophagus, second century, Museo Nazionale, Rome)

exhorting one of his generals to begin the necessary reformation from the tribunes themselves; since, as he justly observes, the officer who has forfeited the esteem, will never command the obedience, of his soldiers. Had the emperor pursued the train of reflection, he would have discovered that the primary cause of this general corruption might be ascribed, not indeed to the example, but to the pernicious indulgence, however, of the commander in chief.

The Prætorians, who murdered their emperor and sold the empire, had received the just punishment of their treason; but the necessary, though dangerous, institution of guards, was soon restored on a new model by Severus, and increased to four times the ancient number. Formerly these troops had been recruited in Italy; and as the adjacent provinces gradually imbibed the softer manners of Rome, the levies were extended to Macedonia, Noricum, and Spain. In the room of these elegant troops, better adapted to the pomp of courts than to the uses of war, it was established by Severus, that from all the legions of the frontiers, the soldiers most distinguished for strength, valor, and fidelity, should be occasionally draughted; and promoted, as an honor and reward, into the more eligible service of the guards. By this new institution, the Italian youth were diverted from the exercise of arms, and the capital was terrified by the strange aspects and manners of a multitude of barbarians. But Severus flattered himself that the legions would consider these chosen Prætorians as the representatives of the whole military order; and that the present aid of fifty thousand men, superior in arms and appointments to any force that could be brought into the field against them, would for ever crush the hopes of rebellion, and secure the empire to himself and his posterity.

The command of these favored and formidable troops soon became the first office of the empire. As the government degenerated into a military despotism, the Prætorian Præfect, who in his origin had been a simple captain of the guards, was placed, not only at the head of the army, but of the finances, and even of the law. In every department of administration he represented the person and exercised the authority of the emperor.

Till the reign of Severus, the virtue and even the good sense of the emperors had been distinguished by their zeal or affected reverence for the senate, and by a tender regard to the nice frame of civil policy instituted by Augustus. But the youth of Severus had been trained in the implicit obedience of camps, and his riper years spent in the despotism of military command. His haughty and inflexible spirit could not discover, or would not acknowledge, the advantage of preserving an intermediate power, however imaginary, between the emperor and the army. He disdained to profess himself the servant of an assembly that detested his person and trembled at his frown; he issued his commands, where his request would have proved as effectual; assumed the conduct and style of a sovereign and a conqueror, and exercised, without disguise, the whole legislative as well as the executive power.

The victory over the senate was easy and inglorious. Every eye and every passion was directed to the supreme magistrate, who possessed

View across the mountains at Djemilah, Algeria with the
ruins of the Septimien family temple in the foreground.
This is one of the many splendid monuments constructed during
the reign of Septimius Severus.

the arms and treasure of the state; whilst the senate, neither elected by
the people, nor guarded by military force, nor animated by public
spirit, rested its declining authority on the frail and crumbling basis of
ancient opinion. The fine theory of a republic insensibly vanished, and
made way for the more natural and substantial feelings of monarchy. As
the freedom and honors of Rome were successively communicated to
the provinces, in which the old government had been either unknown,
or was remembered with abhorrence, the tradition of republican maxims was gradually obliterated. The Greek historians of the age of the
Antonines observe with a malicious pleasure, that although the sovereign of Rome, in compliance with an obsolete prejudice, abstained from
the name of king, he possessed the full measure of regal power. In the
reign of Severus, the senate was filled with polished and eloquent slaves
from the eastern provinces, who justified personal flattery by speculative principles of servitude. These new advocates of prerogative were
heard with pleasure by the court, and with patience by the people,
when they inculcated the duty of passive obedience, and descanted on
the inevitable mischiefs of freedom. The lawyers and the historians
concurred in teaching, that the Imperial authority was held, not by the
delegated commission, but by the irrevocable resignation of the senate;
that the emperor was freed from the restraint of civil laws, could
command by his arbitrary will the lives and fortunes of his subjects, and
might dispose of the empire as of his private patrimony. The most
eminent of the civil lawyers, and particularly Papinian, Paulus, and
Ulpian, flourished under the house of Severus; and the Roman jurisprudence having closely united itself with the system of monarchy, was
supposed to have attained its full maturity and perfection.

The contemporaries of Severus, in the enjoyment of the peace and
glory of his reign, forgave the cruelties by which it had been introduced. Posterity, who experienced the fatal effects of his maxims
and example, justly considered him as the principal author of the
decline of the Roman empire.

CHAPTER SIX

The death of Severus

tyranny of Caracalla – usurpation of Macrinus – follies of Elagabalus – virtues of
Alexander Severus – licentiousness of the army
[AD 208–235]

EVERUS had lost his first wife while he was governor of the
Lyonnese Gaul. In the choice of a second, he sought only to
connect himself with some favorite of fortune; and as soon as
he had discovered that a young lady of Emesa in Syria had *a
royal nativity*, he solicited, and obtained her hand. Julia
Domna possessed, even in an advanced age, the attractions of beauty,
and united to a lively imagination, a firmness of mind, and strength of
judgment, seldom bestowed on her sex.

Two sons, Caracalla and Geta, were the fruit of this marriage, and
the destined heirs of the empire. The fond hopes of the father, and of
the Roman world, were soon disappointed by these vain youths. Without any emulation of virtue or talents, they discovered, almost from
their infancy, a fixed and implacable antipathy for each other. Their
aversion, confirmed by years, and fomented by the arts of their interested favorites, broke out in childish, and gradually in more serious,
competitions; and, at length, divided the theater, the circus, and the
court, into two factions; actuated by the hopes and fears of their
respective leaders. The prudent emperor endeavored, by every expedient of advice and authority, to allay this growing animosity. The
unhappy discord of his sons clouded all his prospects, and threatened to
overturn a throne raised with so much labor, cemented with so much
blood, and guarded with every defense of arms and treasure. With an
impartial hand he maintained between them an exact balance of favor,
confered on both the rank of Augustus, with the revered name of
Antoninus; and for the first time the Roman world beheld three
emperors. Yet even this equal conduct served only to inflame the
contest, whilst the fierce Caracalla asserted the right of primogeniture,
and the milder Geta courted the affections of the people and the
soldiers. In the anguish of a disappointed father, Severus foretold that
the weaker of his sons would fall a sacrifice to the stronger; who, in his
turn, would be ruined by his own vices.

In these circumstances the intelligence of a war in Britain and an
invasion (AD 208) of the province by the barbarians of the North, was
received with pleasure by Severus. Though the vigilance of his lieutenants might have been sufficient to repel the distant enemy, he
resolved to embrace the honorable pretext of withdrawing his sons
from the luxury of Rome, which enervated their minds and irritated
their passions; and of inuring their youth to the toils of war and
government. Notwithstanding his advanced age (for he was above
three-score), and his gout, which obliged him to be carried in a litter, he
transported himself in person into that remote island, attended by his
two sons, his whole court, and a formidable army. He immediately
passed the walls of Hadrian and Antoninus, and entered the enemy's
country, with a design of completing the long-attempted conquest of
Britain. He penetrated to the northern extremity of the island without
meeting an enemy. But the concealed ambuscades of the Caledonians,
who hung unseen on the rear and flanks of his army, the coldness of the
climate, and the severity of a winter march across the hills and morasses
of Scotland, are reported to have cost the Romans above fifty thousand
men. The Caledonians at length yielded to the powerful and obstinate
attack, sued for peace, and surrendered a part of their arms, and a large
tract of territory. But their apparent submission lasted no longer than

the present terror. As soon as the Roman legions had retired, they
resumed their hostile independence. Their restless spirit provoked
Severus to send a new army into Caledonia, with the most bloody
orders, not to subdue but to extirpate the natives. They were saved by
the death of their haughty enemy.

The declining health and last illness of Severus inflamed the wild
ambition and black passions of Caracalla's soul. Impatient of any delay
or division of empire, he attempted, more than once, to shorten the
small remainder of his father's days, and endeavored, but without
success, to excite a mutiny among the troops. The old emperor had
often censured the misguided lenity of Marcus, who, by a single act of
justice, might have saved the Romans from the tyranny of his worthless
son. Placed in the same situation, he experienced how easily the rigor of
a judge dissolves away in the tenderness of a parent. He deliberated, he
threatened, but he could not punish; and this last and only instance of
mercy was more fatal to the empire than a long series of cruelty. The
disorder of his mind irritated the pains of his body; he wished impatiently for death, and hastened the instant of it by his impatience. He

Left: Marble bust of Caracalla. (Museo Nazionale, Naples)
Right: Reconstruction of the Baths of Caracalla, known as the
Thermae Antoninae. (Nineteenth-century engraving)

Julia Domnia (c. AD 158–217), wife of Septimius Severus and mother
of Caracalla and Geta, who was celebrated for her beauty.

expired (AD 211, 4 February) at York in the sixty-fifth year of his life,
and in the eighteenth of a glorious and successful reign. In his last
moments he recommended concord to his sons, and his sons to the
army. The salutary advice never reached the heart, or even the understanding, of the impetuous youths; but the more obedient troops,
mindful of their oath of allegiance, and of the authority of their
deceased master, resisted the solicitations of Caracalla, and proclaimed
both brothers emperors of Rome. The new princes soon left the
Caledonians in peace, returned to the capital, celebrated their father's
funeral with divine honors, and were cheerfully acknowledged as lawful
sovereigns, by the senate, the people, and the provinces. Some pre-
eminence of rank seems to have been allowed to the elder brother; but
they both administered the empire with equal and independent power.

Such a divided form of government would have proved a source of
discord between the most affectionate brothers. It was impossible that
it could long subsist between the two implacable enemies, who neither
desired nor could trust a reconciliation. No communication was allowed between their apartments: the doors and passages were diligently
fortified, and guards posted and relieved with the same strictness as in a
besieged place. The emperors met only in public, in the presence of
their afflicted mother; and each surrounded by a numerous train of
armed followers. Even on these occasions of ceremony, the dissimulation of courts could ill disguise the rancor of their hearts.

This latent civil war already distracted the whole government, when
a scheme was suggested that seemed of mutual benefit to the hostile
brothers. It was proposed, that since it was impossible to reconcile their
minds, they should separate their interest, and divide the empire
between them. The conditions of the treaty were already drawn with
some accuracy. It was agreed that Caracalla, as the elder brother,
should remain in possession of Europe and the western Africa; and that

he should relinquish the sovereignty of Asia and Egypt to Geta. The
tears of the empress Julia interrupted the negotiation, the first idea of
which had filled every Roman breast with surprise and indignation.

Had the treaty been carried into execution, the sovereign of Europe
might soon have been the conqueror of Asia; but Caracalla obtained an
easier though more guilty victory. He artfully listened to his mother's
entreaties, and consented (AD 212, 27 February) to meet his brother in
her apartment, on terms of peace and reconciliation. In the midst of
their conversation, some centurions, who had contrived to conceal
themselves, rushed with drawn swords upon the unfortunate Geta. His
distracted mother strove to protect him in her arms; but, in the
unavailing struggle, she was wounded in the hand, and covered with
the blood of her younger son, while she saw the elder animating and
assisting the fury of the assassins. As soon as the deed was perpetrated,
Caracalla, with hasty steps, and horror in his countenance, ran towards
the Prætorian camp as his only refuge, and threw himself on the ground
before the statues of the tutelar deities. The soldiers attempted to raise
and comfort him. In broken and disordered words he informed them of
his imminent danger and fortunate escape; insinuating that he had
prevented the designs of his enemy, and declared his resolution to live
and die with his faithful troops. Geta had been the favorite of the
soldiers; but complaint was useless, revenge was dangerous, and they
still reverenced the son of Severus. Their discontent died away in idle
murmurs, and Caracalla soon convinced them of the justice of his
cause, by distributing in one lavish donative the accumulated treasures
of his father's reign. The real *sentiments* of the soldiers alone were of
importance to his power or safety. Their declaration in his favor,
commanded the dutiful *professions* of the senate. The obsequious
assembly was always prepared to ratify the decision of fortune; but as
Caracalla wished to assuage the first emotions of public indignation, the
name of Geta was mentioned with decency, and he received the funeral
honors of a Roman emperor. Posterity, in pity to his misfortune, has
cast a veil over his vices. We consider that young prince as the innocent
victim of his brother's ambition, without recollecting that he himself
wanted power, rather than inclination, to consummate the same attempts of revenge and murder.

Caracalla was the common enemy of mankind. He left (AD 213) the
capital (and he never returned to it) about a year after the murder of
Geta. The rest of his reign was spent in the several provinces of the
empire, particularly those of the East, and every province was by turns
the scene of his rapine and cruelty. The senators, compelled by fear to

The vaulted arches and marble columns of the baths at Herculaneum,
AD I.

attend his capricious motions, were obliged to provide daily entertainments at an immense expense, which he abandoned with contempt to his guards; and to erect, in every city, magnificent palaces and theaters, which he either disdained to visit, or ordered to be immediately thrown down. The most wealthy families were ruined by partial fines and confiscations, and the great body of his subjects oppressed by ingenious and aggravated taxes. In the midst of peace, and upon the slightest provocation, he issued his commands, at Alexandria in Egypt, for a general massacre. From a secure post in the temple of Serapis, he viewed and directed the slaughter of many thousand citizens, as well as strangers, without distinguishing either the number or the crime of the sufferers; since, as he coolly informed the senate, *all* the Alexandrians, those who had perished and those who had escaped, were alike guilty.

The wise instructions of Severus never made any lasting impression on the mind of his son, who, although not destitute of imagination and eloquence, was equally devoid of judgment and humanity. One dangerous maxim, worthy of a tyrant, was remembered and abused by Caracalla, 'To secure the affections of the army, and to esteem the rest

The baths of Caracalla were ornately decorated with mosaic inlays such as this panel depicting the figure of a wrestler.

of his subjects as of little moment.' But the liberality of the father had been restrained by prudence, and his indulgence to the troops was tempered by firmness and authority. The careless profusion of the son was the policy of one reign, and the inevitable ruin both of the army and of the empire. The vigor of the soldiers, instead of being confirmed by the severe discipline of camps, melted away in the luxury of cities. The excessive increase of their pay and donatives exhausted the state to enrich the military order, whose modesty in peace, and service in war, is best secured by an honorable poverty. The demeanor of Caracalla was haughty and full of pride; but with the troops he forgot even the proper dignity of his rank, encouraged their insolent familiarity, and, neglecting the essential duties of a general, affected to imitate the dress and manners of a common soldier.

It was impossible that such a character, and such a conduct as that of Caracalla, could inspire either love or esteem; but as long as his vices were beneficial to the armies, he was secure from the danger of rebellion. A secret conspiracy, provoked by his own jealousy, was fatal to the tyrant. The Prætorian præfecture was divided between two ministers. The military department was intrusted to Adventus, an experienced rather than an able soldier; and the civil affairs were transacted by Opilius Macrinus, who, by his dexterity in business, had raised himself, with a fair character, to that high office. But his favor varied with the caprice of the emperor, and his life might depend on the slightest suspicion, or the most casual circumstance. Malice or fanaticism had suggested to an African, deeply skilled in the knowledge of futurity, a very dangerous prediction, that Macrinus and his son were destined to reign over the empire. The report was soon diffused through the province; and when the man was sent in chains to Rome, he still asserted, in the presence of the Præfect of the city, the faith of his prophecy. That magistrate, who had received the most pressing instructions to inform himself of the *successors* of Caracalla, immediately communicated the examination of the African to the Imperial court, which at that time resided in Syria. But, notwithstanding the diligence of the public messengers, a friend of Macrinus found means to appraise him of the approaching danger. The emperor received the letters from Rome; and as he was then engaged in the conduct of a chariot-race, he delivered them unopened to the Prætorian Præfect, directing him to dispatch the ordinary affairs, and to report the more important business that might be contained in them. Macrinus read his fate, and resolved to prevent it. He inflamed the discontents of some inferior officers, and employed the hand of Martialis, a desperate soldier, who had been refused the rank of centurion. The devotion of Caracalla prompted him to make a pilgrimage from Edessa to the celebrated temple of the Moon at Carrhæ. He (AD 217, 8 March) was attended by a body of cavalry; but having stopped on the road for some necessary occasion, his guards preserved a respectful distance, and Martialis approaching his person under a pretence of duty, stabbed him with a dagger. The bold assassin was instantly killed by a Scythian archer of the Imperial guard. Such was the end of a monster whose life disgraced human nature, and whose reign accused the patience of the Romans. The grateful soldiers forgot his vices, remembered only his partial liberality, and obliged the senate to prostitute their own dignity and that of religion by granting him a place among the gods.

After the distinction of the house of Severus, the Roman world remained three days without a master. The choice of the army (for the authority of a distant and feeble senate was little regarded) hung in an anxious suspense; as no candidate presented himself whose distinguished birth and merit could engage their attachment and unite their suffrages. The decisive weight of the Prætorian guards elevated the hopes of their præfects, and these powerful ministers began to assert their *legal* claim to fill the vacancy of the Imperial throne. Adventus, however, the senior præfect, conscious of his age and infirmities, of his small reputation, and his smaller abilities, resigned the dangerous honor to the crafty ambition of his colleague Macrinus, whose well-dissembled grief removed all suspicion of his being accessory to his master's death. A short time after his accession (AD 217, 11 March) he conferred on his son Diadumenianus, at the age of only ten years, the Imperial title and the popular name of Antoninus. The beautiful figure of the youth, assisted by an additional donative, for which the ceremony furnished a pretext, might attract, it was hoped, the favor of the army, and secure the doubtful throne of Macrinus.

But Macrinus was not a senator. The sudden elevation of the Prætorian præfects betrayed the meanness of their origin; and the equestrian order was still in possession of that great office, which commanded with arbitrary sway the lives and fortunes of the senate. A murmur of indignation was heard, that a man whose obscure extraction had never been illustrated by any signal service, should dare to invest himself with the purple, instead of bestowing it on some distinguished senator, equal in birth and dignity to the Imperial station.

As soon as the character of Macrinus was surveyed by the sharp eye of discontent, some vices, and many defects, were easily discovered. The choice of his ministers was in many instances justly censured, and the dissatisfied people, with their usual candor, accused at once his indolent tameness and his excessive severity.

His rash ambition had climbed a height where it was difficult to stand with firmness, and impossible to fall without instant destruction. Trained in the arts of courts, and the forms of civil business, he trembled in the presence of the fierce and undisciplined multitude, over whom he had assumed the command; his military talents were despised, and his personal courage suspected; a whisper that circulated in the camp, disclosed the fatal secret of the conspiracy against the late emperor, aggravated the guilt of murder by the baseness of hypocrisy, and heightened contempt by detestation. To alienate the soldiers, and to provoke inevitable ruin, the character of a reformer was only want-ing: and such was the peculiar hardship of his fate, that Macrinus was compelled to exercise that invidious office. The prodigality of Caracalla had left behind it a long train of ruin and disorder; and if that worthless tyrant had been capable of reflecting on the sure consequences of his own conduct, he would perhaps have enjoyed the dark prospect of the distress and calamities which he bequeathed to his successors.

Above: The Baths of Caracalla: *tepidarium.*

Caracalla spent little time in the Capital and his subjects were subjugated to extortionate taxes in order to support the magnificence of his regime.
Above: The Arch of Caracalla at Volubilis, Morocco.
Right: The road leading to the Arch of Caracalla at Djemilah, Algeria

The empress Julia had experienced all the vicissitudes of fortune. From an humble station she had been raised to greatness, only to taste the superior bitterness of an exalted rank. She was doomed to weep over the death of one of her sons, and over the life of the other. The cruel fate of Caracalla, though her good sense must have long taught her to expect it, awakened the feelings of a mother and of an empress. Notwithstanding the respectful civility expressed by the usurper to-wards the widow of Severus, she descended with a painful struggle into the condition of a subject, and soon withdrew herself by a voluntary death from the anxious and humiliating dependence. Julia Mæsa, her sister, was ordered to leave the court and Antioch. She retired to Emesa with an immense fortune, the fruit of twenty years' favor, accompanied by her two daughters, Soæmias and Mamæa, each of whom was a widow, and each had an only son. Bassianus, for that was the name of the son of Soæmias, was consecrated to the honorable ministry of high priest of the Sun. A numerous body of troops was stationed at Emesa; and, as the severe discipline of Macrinus had constrained them to pass

the winter encamped, they were eager to revenge the cruelty of such unaccustomed hardships. The soldiers, who resorted in crowds to the temple of the Sun, beheld with veneration and delight the elegant dress and figure of a young Pontiff: they recognized, or they thought that they recognized, the features of Caracalla, whose memory they now adored. The artful Mæsa cherished their rising partiality, and insinuated that Bassianus was the natural son of their murdered sovereign. The sums distributed by her emissaries with a lavish hand silenced every objection, and the profusion sufficiently proved the affinity, or at least the resemblance, of Bassianus with the great original. The young Antoninus (for he had assumed and polluted that respectable name) was (AD 218, 16 May) declared emperor by the troops of Emesa, asserted his hereditary right, and called aloud on the armies to follow the standard of a young and liberal prince, who had taken up arms to revenge his father's death and the oppression of the military order. In the ensuing battle of contending forces Macrinus and his son were killed.

The Sun was worshipped at Emesa, under the name of Elagabalus, and under the form of a black conical stone, which, as it was universally believed, had fallen from heaven on that sacred place. To this protecting deity, Antoninus, not without some reason, ascribed his elevation to the throne. The display of superstitious gratitude was the only serious business of his reign. The triumph of the God of Emesa over all the religions of the earth, was the great object of his zeal and vanity: and the appellation of Elagabalus (for he presumed as pontiff and favorite to adopt that sacred name) was dearer to him than all the titles of Imperial greatness.

A rational voluptuary adheres with invariable respect to the temperate dictates of nature, and improves the gratifications of sense by social intercourse, endearing connections, and the soft coloring of taste and the imagination. But Elagabalus corrupted by his youth, his country, and his fortune, abandoned himself to the grossest pleasures with ungoverned fury, and soon found disgust and satiety in the midst of his enjoyments. The inflammatory powers of art were summoned to his aid: the confused multitude of women, of wines, and of dishes, and the studied variety of attitudes and sauces, served to revive his languid appetites. New terms and new inventions in these sciences, the only ones cultivated and patronized by the monarch, signalized his reign, and transmitted his infamy to succeeding times.

The most worthless of mankind are not afraid to condemn in others the same disorders which they allow in themselves; and can readily discover some nice difference of age, character, or station, to justify the partial distinction. The licentious soldiers, who had raised to the throne the dissolute son of Caracalla, blushed at their ignominious choice, and turned with disgust from that monster, to contemplate with pleasure the opening virtues of his cousin Alexander the son of Mamæa. The crafty Mæsa, sensible that her grandson Elagabalus must inevitably destroy himself by his own vices, had provided another and surer support of her family. Embracing a favorable moment of fondness and devotion, she had persuaded the young emperor to adopt Alexander, and to invest him (AD 221) with the title of Cæsar, that his own divine occupations might be no longer interrupted by the care of the earth. In the second rank that amiable prince soon acquired the affections of the public, and excited the tyrant's jealousy, who resolved to terminate the dangerous competition, either by corrupting the manners, or by taking away the life, of his rival. His arts proved unsuccessful; his vain designs were constantly discovered by his own loquacious folly, and disappointed by those virtuous and faithful servants whom the prudence of Mamæa had placed about the person of her son. In a hasty sally of passion, Elagabalus resolved to execute by force what he had been unable to compass by fraud, and by a despotic sentence degraded his cousin from the rank and honors of Cæsar. The message was received in the senate with silence, and in the camp with fury. The Prætorian guards swore to protect Alexander, and to revenge the dishonored majesty of the throne. The tears and promises of the trembling Elagabalus, who only begged them to spare his life, and to leave him in the possession of his beloved Hierocles, diverted their just indignation; and they contented themselves with empowering their præfects to watch over the safety of Alexander, and the conduct of the emperor.

It was impossible that such a reconciliation should last, or that even the mean soul of Elagabalus could hold an empire on such humiliating terms of dependence. He soon attempted by a dangerous experiment, to try the temper of the soldiers. The report of the death of Alexander, and the natural suspicion that he had been murdered, inflamed their passions into fury, and the tempest of the camp could only be appeased by the presence and authority of the popular youth. Provoked at this new instance of their affection for his cousin, and their contempt for his person, the emperor ventured to punish some of the leaders of the mutiny. His unseasonable severity proved instantly fatal to his minions, his mother, and himself. Elagabalus was (AD 222, 10 March) massacred by the indignant Prætorians, his mutilated corpse dragged through the streets of the city, and thrown into the Tiber. His memory was branded with eternal infamy by the senate; the justice of whose decree has been ratified by posterity.

In the room of Elagabalus, his cousin Alexander was raised to the throne by the Prætorian guards. But as Alexander was a modest and dutiful youth, of only seventeen years of age, the reins of government were in the hands of two women, of his mother Mamæa, and of Mæsa, his grandmother. After the death of the latter, who survived but a short time the elevation of Alexander, Mamæa remained the sole regent of her son and of the empire.

The substance, not the pageantry, of power was the object of Mamæa's manly ambition. She maintained an absolute and lasting empire over the mind of her son, and in his affection the mother could not brook a rival. Alexander, with her consent, married the daughter of a Patrician; but his respect for his father-in-law, and love for the empress, were inconsistent with the tenderness or interest of Mamæa. The Patrician was executed on the ready accusation of treason, and the wife of Alexander banished into Africa.

Notwithstanding this act of jealous cruelty, as well as some instances of avarice, with which Mamæa is charged; the general tenor of her administration was equally for the benefit of her son and of the empire. With the approbation of the senate, she chose sixteen of the wisest and most virtuous senators, as a perpetual council of state, before whom every public business of moment was debated and determined. The celebrated Ulpian, equally distinguished by his knowledge of, and his respect for, the laws of Rome, was at their head; and the prudent firmness of this aristocracy restored order and authority to the government. As soon as they had purged the city from foreign superstition and luxury, the remains of the capricious tyranny of Elagabalus, they applied themselves to remove his worthless creatures from every department of public administration, and to supply their places with men of virtue and ability. Learning, and the love of justice, became the only recommendations for civil offices. Valor, and the love of discipline, the only qualifications for military employments.

But the most important care of Mamæa and her wise counselors, was to form the character of the young emperor, on whose personal qualities the happiness or misery of the Roman world must ultimately depend. The fortunate soil assisted, and even encouraged, the hand of cultivation. An excellent understanding soon convinced Alexander of the advantages of virtue, the pleasure of knowledge, and the necessity

The Circus of Caracalla: Caracalla's extravagant building programs filled Rome and the provincial towns with lavish constructions such as this circus, or racing stadium. (Nineteenth-century engraving)

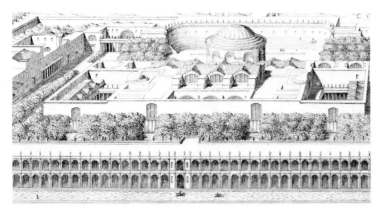

The Baths of Caracalla, some of the most magnificent ever built, were designed to accommodate up to 1500 people. They were enclosed by great walls (350 meters long) and included a stadium and libraries.

of labor. A natural mildness and moderation of temper preserved him from the assaults of passion, and the allurements of vice. His unalterable regard for his mother, and his esteem for the wise Ulpian, guarded his inexperienced youth from the poison of flattery.

In the civil administration of Alexander, wisdom was enforced by power, and the people, sensible of the public felicity, repaid their benefactor with their love and gratitude. There still remained a greater, a more necessary, but a more difficult enterprise; the reformation of the military order, whose interest and temper, confirmed by long impunity, rendered them impatient of the restraints of discipline, and careless of the blessings of public tranquillity. In the execution of his design the emperor affected to display his love, and to conceal his fear, of the army. But his prudence was vain, his courage fatal, and the attempt towards a reformation served only to inflame the ills it was meant to cure.

The Prætorian guards were attached to the youth of Alexander. They loved him as a tender pupil, whom they had saved from a tyrant's fury, and placed on the Imperial throne. That amiable prince was sensible of the obligation; but as his gratitude was restrained within the limits of reason and justice, they soon were more dissatisfied with the virtues of Alexander, than they had ever been with the vices of Elagabalus. Their præfect, the wise Ulpian, was the friend of the laws and of the people; he was considered as the enemy of the soldiers, and to his pernicious counsels every scheme of reformation was imputed. Some trifling accident blew up their discontent into a furious mutiny; and a civil war raged, during three days, in Rome, while the life of that excellent minister was defended by the grateful people. Terrified, at length, by the sight of some houses in flames, and by the threats of a general conflagration, the people yielded with a sigh, and left the virtuous, but unfortunate, Ulpian to his fate. He was pursued into the Imperial palace, and massacred at the feet of his master, who vainly strove to cover him with the purple, and to obtain his pardon from the inexorable soldiers. Such was the deplorable weakness of government, that the emperor was unable to revenge his murdered friend and his insulted dignity, without stooping to the arts of patience and dissimulation. Epagathus, the principal leader of the mutiny, was removed from Rome, by the honorable employment of præfect of Egypt; from that high rank he was gently degraded to the government of Crete; and when, at length, his popularity among the guards was effaced by time and absence, Alexander ventured to inflict the tardy, but deserved punishment of his crimes.

The lenity of the emperor confirmed the insolence of the troops; the legions imitated the example of the guards, and defended their prerogative of licentiousness with the same furious obstinacy. The administration of Alexander was an unavailing struggle against the corruption of his age. In Illyricum, in Mauritania, in Armenia, in Mesopotamia, in Germany, fresh mutinies perpetually broke out; his officers were murdered, his authority was insulted, and his life at last sacrificed to the fierce discontents of the army.

The dissolute tyranny of Commodus, the civil wars occasioned by his death, and the new maxims of policy introduced by the house of Severus, had all contributed to increase the dangerous power of the army, and to obliterate the faint image of laws and liberty that was still impressed on the minds of the Romans. This internal change, which undermined the foundations of the empire, we have endeavored to explain with some degree of order and perspicuity. The personal characters of the emperors, their victories, laws, follies, and fortunes, can interest us no farther than as they are connected with the general history of the Decline and Fall of the monarchy. Our constant attention to the great object will not suffer us to overlook a most important edict of Antoninus Caracalla, which communicated to all the free inhabitants of the empire the name and privileges of Roman citizens. His unbounded liberality flowed not, however, from the sentiments of a generous mind; it was the sordid result of avarice, and will naturally be illustrated by some observations on the finances of that state, from the victorious ages of the commonwealth to the reign of Alexander Severus.

The sentiments, and, indeed, the situation of Caracalla, were very different from those of the Antonines who sought to decrease the public burden of taxation. Inattentive, or rather averse, to the welfare of his people, he found himself under the necessity of gratifying the insatiate avarice, which he had excited in the army. Of the several impositions introduced by Augustus, the twentieth on inheritances and legacies was the most fruitful, as well as the most comprehensive. As its influence was not confined to Rome or Italy, the produce continually increased with the gradual extension of the Roman City. The new citizens, though charged, on equal terms, with the payment of new taxes, which had not affected them as subjects, derived an ample compensation from the rank they obtained, the privileges they acquired, and the fair prospect of honors and fortune that was thrown open to their ambition. But the favor which implied a distinction, was lost in the prodigality of Caracalla, and the reluctant provincials were compelled to assume the vain title, and the real obligations, of Roman citizens. Nor was the rapacious son of Severus contented with such a measure of taxation, as had appeared sufficient to his moderate predecessors. Instead of a twentieth, he exacted a tenth of all legacies and inheritances; and during his reign (for the ancient proportion was restored after his death) he crushed alike every part of the empire under the weight of his iron scepter.

When all the provincials became liable to the peculiar impositions of Roman citizens, they seemed to acquire a legal exemption from the tributes which they had paid in their former condition of subjects. Such were not the maxims of government adopted by Caracalla and his pretended son. The old as well as the new taxes were, at the same time, levied in the provinces. It was reserved for the virtue of Alexander to relieve them in a great measure from this intolerable grievance, by reducing the tributes to a thirtieth part of the sum exacted at the time of his accession. It is impossible to conjecture the motive that engaged him to spare so trifling a remnant of the public evil; but the noxious weed, which had not been totally eradicated, again sprang up with the most luxuriant growth, and in the succeeding age darkened the Roman world with its deadly shade. In the course of this history, we shall be too often summoned to explain the land-tax, the capitation, and the heavy contributions of corn, wine, oil, and meat, which were exacted from the provinces for the use of the court, the army, and the capital.

As long as Rome and Italy were respected as the center of government, a national spirit was preserved by the ancient, and insensibly imbibed by the adopted, citizens. The principal commands of the army were filled by men who had received a liberal education, were well instructed in the advantages of laws and letters, and who had risen, by equal steps, through the regular succession of civil and military honors. To their influence and example we may partly ascribe the modest obedience of the legions during the two first centuries of the Imperial history.

But when the last enclosure of the Roman constitution was trampled down by Caracalla, the separation of professions gradually succeeded to the distinction of ranks. The more polished citizens of the internal provinces were alone qualified to act as lawyers and magistrates. The rougher trade of arms was abandoned to the peasants and barbarians of the frontiers, who knew no country but their camp, no science but that of war, no civil laws, and scarcely those of military discipline. With bloody hands, savage manners, and desperate resolutions, they sometimes guarded, but oftener subverted, the throne of the emperors.

CHAPTER SEVEN

The elevation and tyranny of Maximin

civil wars and the seditions – violent deaths of Maximin and his son, of Maximus and Balbinus, and of the three Gordians – usurpation of secular games of Philip

[AD 235–248]

AFTER the murder of Alexander Severus, and the elevation of Maximin, no emperor could think himself safe upon the throne, and every barbarian peasant of the frontier might aspire to that august, but dangerous station.

Maximin, though born on the territories of the empire, descended from a mixed race of barbarians. His father was a Goth, and his mother of the nation of the Alani. He displayed, on every occasion, a valor equal to his strength; and his native fierceness was soon tempered or disguised by the knowledge of the world. Under the reign of Severus and his son, he obtained the rank of centurion, with the favor and esteem of both those princes, the former of whom was an excellent judge of merit. Gratitude forbade Maximin to serve under the assassin of Caracalla. Honor taught him to decline the effeminate insults of Elagabalus. On the accession of Alexander he returned to court, and was placed by that prince in a station useful to the service and honorable to himself. The fourth legion, to which he was appointed tribune, soon became, under his care, the best disciplined of the whole army. With the general applause of the soldiers, who bestowed on their favorite hero the names of Ajax and Hercules, he was successively promoted to the first military command; and had not he still retained too much of his savage origin, the emperor might perhaps have given his own sister in marriage to the son of Maximin.

Instead of securing his fidelity, these favors served only to inflame the ambition of the Thracian peasant, who deemed his fortune in-adequate to his merit, as long as he was constrained to acknowledge a superior. Though a stranger to real wisdom, he was not devoid of a selfish cunning, which showed him that the emperor had lost the affection of the army, and taught him to improve their discontent to his own advantage. It is easy for faction and calumny to shed their poison on the administration of the best of princes, and to accuse even their virtues, by artfully confounding them with those vices to which they bear the nearest affinity. The troops listened with pleasure to the emissaries of Maximin. They blushed at their own ignominious patience, which, during thirteen years, had supported the vexatious discipline imposed by an effeminate Syrian, the timid slave of his mother and of the senate. It was time, they cried, to cast away that useless phantom of the civil power, and to elect for their prince and general a real soldier, educated in camps, exercised in war, who would assert the glory, and distribute among his companions the treasures, of the empire. A great army was at that time assembled on the banks of the Rhine, under the command of the emperor himself, who, almost immediately after his return from the Persian war, had been obliged to march against the barbarians of Germany. The important care of training and reviewing the new levies was intrusted to Maximin. One day (AD 235, 19 March), as he entered the field of exercise, the troops, either from a sudden impulse or a formed conspiracy, saluted him emperor, silenced by their loud acclamations his obstinate refusal, and hastened to consummate their rebellion by the murder of Alexander Severus.

Left: The only villa left still standing on African soil. (Utica, Tunisia, second century AD)
Below left: A servant carrying food into a banquet. (Mosaic from Carthage, Tunisia, third century, the Louvre, Paris)
Below right: Bikini-clad girl athletes. (Mosaic from the Royal Villa of Piazza Armerina, Sicily, late third century)

The former tyrants, Caligula and Nero, Commodus and Caracalla, were all dissolute and inexperienced youths, educated in the purple, and corrupted by the pride of empire, the luxury of Rome, and the perfidious voice of flattery. The cruelty of Maximin was derived from a different source, the fear of contempt. Though he depended on the attachment of the soldiers, who loved him for virtues like their own, he was conscious that his mean and barbarian origin, his savage appearance, and his total ignorance of the arts and institutions of civil life, formed a very unfavorable contrast with the amiable manners of the unhappy Alexander. He remembered that, in his humbler fortune, he had often waited before the door of the haughty nobles of Rome, and had been denied admittance by the insolence of their slaves. He recollected too the friendship of a few who had relieved his poverty, and assisted his rising hopes. But those who had spurned, and those who had protected the Thracian, were guilty of the same crime, the knowledge of his original obscurity. For this crime many were put to death; and by the execution of several of his benefactors, Maximin published, in characters of blood, the indelible history of his baseness and ingratitude.

The dark and sanguinary soul of the tyrant was open to every suspicion against those among his subjects who were the most distinguished by their birth or merit. Whenever he was alarmed with the sound of treason, his cruelty was unbounded and unrelenting.

As long as the cruelty of Maximin was confined to the illustrious senators, or even to the bold adventurers, who in the court or army expose themselves to the caprice of fortune, the body of the people viewed their sufferings with indifference, or perhaps with pleasure. But the tyrant's avarice, stimulated by the insatiate desires of the soldiers, at length attacked the public property. Every city of the empire was possessed of an independent revenue, destined to purchase corn for the multitude, and to supply the expenses of the games and entertainments. By a single act of authority, the whole mass of wealth was at once confiscated for the use of the Imperial treasury. The temples were stripped of their most valuable offerings of gold and silver, and the statues of gods, heroes, and emperors, were melted down and coined into money. These impious orders could not be executed without tumults and massacres, as in many places the people chose rather to die in their defense of their altars, than to behold in the midst of peace their cities exposed to the rapine and cruelty of war. The soldiers themselves, among whom this sacrilegious plunder was distributed, received it with a blush; and, hardened as they were in acts of violence, they dreaded the just reproaches of their friends and relations. Throughout the Roman world a general cry of indignation was heard, imploring vengeance on the common enemy of human kind; and at length, by an act of private oppression, a peaceful and unarmed province was driven into rebellion.

The procurator of Africa was a servant worthy of such a master, who considered the fines and confiscations of the rich as one of the most fruitful branches of the Imperial revenue. An iniquitous sentence had been (AD 237, April) pronounced against some opulent youths of that country, the execution of which would have stripped them of far the greater part of their patrimony. In this extremity, a resolution that must either complete or prevent their ruin, was dictated by despair. A respite of three days, obtained with difficulty from the rapacious treasurer, was employed in collecting from their estates a great number of slaves and peasants, blindly devoted to the commands of their lords, and armed with the rustic weapons of clubs and axes. The leaders of the conspiracy, as they were admitted to the audience of the procurator, stabbed him with the daggers concealed under their garments, and, by the assistance of their tumultuary train, seized on the little town of Thysdrus, and erected the standard of rebellion against the sovereign

The Roman bridge of Klakta, Syria c AD 200. (Reconstruction, Mostra Augustea, Rome)

The Colosseum of Rome, the site of some of the most extravagant and brutal of Rome's spectacles and martyrdoms, was completed in AD 80 by the Emperor Domitian and seated 50,000 people.

of the Roman empire. They rested their hopes on the hatred of mankind against Maximin, and they judiciously resolved to oppose to that detested tyrant, an emperor whose mild virtues had already acquired the love and esteem of the Romans, and whose authority over the province would give weight and stability to the enterprise. Gordianus, their proconsul, and the object of their choice, refused, with unfeigned reluctance, the dangerous honor, and begged with tears that they would suffer him to terminate in peace a long and innocent life, without staining his feeble age with civil blood. Their menaces compelled him to accept the Imperial purple, his only refuge indeed against the jealous cruelty of Maximin; since, according to the reasoning of tyrants, those who have been esteemed worthy of the throne deserve death, and those who deliberate have already rebelled.

The family of Gordianus was one of the most illustrious of the Roman senate. On the father's side, he was descended from the Gracchi; on his mother's, from the emperor Trajan. A great estate enabled him to support the dignity of this birth, and, in the enjoyment of it, he displayed an elegant taste and beneficent disposition. With the venerable proconsul, his son, who had accompanied him into Africa as his lieutenant, was likewise declared emperor. His manners were less pure, but his character was equally amiable with that of his father. The Roman people acknowledged in the features of the younger Gordian the resemblance of Scipio Africanus, recollected with pleasure that his mother was the grand-daughter of Antoninus Pius, and rested the public hope on those latent virtues which had hitherto, as they fondly imagined, lain concealed in the luxurious indolence of a private life.

As soon as the Gordians had appeased the first tumult of a popular election, they removed their court to Carthage. They were received with the acclamation of the Africans, who honored their virtues, and who, since the visit of Hadrian, had never beheld the majesty of a Roman emperor. But these vain acclamations neither strengthened nor confirmed the title of the Gordians. They were induced by principle, as well as interest, to solicit the approbation of the senate; and a deputation of the noblest provincials was sent, without delay, to Rome, to relate and justify the conduct of their countrymen, who, having long suffered with patience, were at length resolved to act with vigor. The letters of the new princes were modest and respectful, excusing the necessity which had obliged them to accept the Imperial title; but submitting their election and their fate to the supreme judgment of the senate.

The inclinations of the senate were neither doubtful nor divided. By an unanimous decree the election of the Gordians was ratified, Maximin, his son, and his adherents, were pronounced enemies of their country, and liberal rewards were offered to whomsoever had the courage and good fortune to destroy them.

During the emperor's absence, a detachment of the Prætorian guards remained at Rome, to protect, or rather to command, the capital. The Præfect Vitalianus had signalised his fidelity to Maximin, by the alacrity with which he had obeyed, and even prevented, the cruel mandates of the tyrant. His death alone could rescue the authority of the senate, and the lives of the senators, from a state of danger and suspense. Before their resolves had transpired, a quæstor and some tribunes were commissioned to take his devoted life. They executed the order with equal boldness and success; and, with their bloody daggers in their hands, ran through the streets proclaiming to the people and the soldiers the news of the happy revolution. The enthusiasm of liberty was seconded by the promise of a large donative, in lands and money; the statues of Maximin were thrown down; the capital of the empire acknowledged, with transport, the authority of the two Gordians and the senate, and the example of Rome was followed by the rest of Italy.

A new spirit had arisen in that assembly, whose long patience had been insulted by wanton despotism and military license. The senate assumed the reins of government, and, with a calm intrepidity, prepared to vindicate by arms the cause of freedom. Among the consular senators recommended by their merit and services to the favor of the emperor Alexander, it was easy to select twenty, not unequal to the command of an army, and the conduct of a war. To these was the defense of Italy intrusted.

While the cause of the Gordians was embraced with such diffusive ardor, the Gordians themselves (AD 237, 3 July) were no more. The feeble court of Carthage was alarmed with the rapid approach of Capelianus, governor of Mauritania, who, with a small band of veterans, and a fierce host of barbarians, attacked a faithful but unwarlike province. The younger Gordian sallied out to meet the enemy at the head of a few guards, and a numerous undisciplined multitude, educated in the peaceful luxury of Carthage. His useless valor served only to procure him an honorable death, in the field of battle. His aged father, whose reign had not exceeded thirty-six days, put an end to his life on the first news of the defeat. Carthage, destitute of defense, opened her gates to the conqueror, and Africa was exposed to the rapacious cruelty of a slave, obliged to satisfy his unrelenting master with a large account of blood and treasure.

The fate of the Gordians filled Rome with just, but unexpected terror. The senate convoked in the temple of Concord, affected to transact the common business of the day; and seemed to decline, with trembling anxiety, the consideration of their own and the public danger. A silent consternation prevailed on the assembly, till a senator, of the name and family of Trajan, awakened, his brethren from their fatal lethargy. He represented to them, that the choice of cautious dilatory measures had been long since out of their power; that Maximin, implacable by nature, and exasperated by injuries, was advancing towards Italy, at the head of the military force of the empire; and that their only remaining alternative was either to meet him bravely in the field, or tamely to expect the tortures and ignominious death reserved for unsuccessful rebellion. 'We have lost,' continued he, 'two excellent princes; but unless we desert ourselves, the hopes of the republic have not perished with the Gordians. Many are the senators, whose virtues have deserved, and whose abilities would sustain, the Imperial dignity. Let us elect two emperors, one of whom may conduct the war against the public enemy, whilst his colleague remains at Rome to direct the civil administration. I cheerfully expose myself to the danger and envy of the nomination, and give my vote in favor of Maximus and Balbinus. Ratify my choice, conscript fathers, or appoint, in their place, others more worthy of the empire.' The general apprehension silenced the whispers of jealousy; the merit of the candidates was universally acknowledged; and the house resounded with the sincere acclamations, of 'long life and victory to the emperors Maximus and Balbinus. You are happy in the judgment of the senate; may the republic be happy under your administration!'

While in Rome and Africa revolutions succeeded each other with such amazing rapidity, the mind of Maximin was agitated by the most furious passions. He is said to have received the news of the rebellion of the Gordians, and of the decree of the senate against him, not with the temper of a man, but the rage of a wild beast; which, as it could not discharge itself on the distant senate, threatened the life of his son, of his friends, and of all who ventured to approach his person. The grateful intelligence of the death of the Gordians was quickly followed by the assurance that the senate, laying aside all hopes of pardon or accommodation, had substituted in their room two emperors, with whose merit he could not be acquainted. Revenge was the only consolation left to Maximin, and revenge could only be obtained by arms.

When the troops of Maximin, advancing in excellent order, arrived at the foot of the Julian Alps, they were terrified by the silence and desolation that reigned on the frontiers of Italy. The villages and open towns had been abandoned on their approach by the inhabitants, the cattle was driven away, the provisions removed, or destroyed, the bridges broke down, nor was anything left which could afford either shelter or give subsistence to an invader. Such had been the wise orders of the generals of the senate, whose design was to protect the war, to ruin the army of Maximin by the slow operation of famine, and to consume his strength in the sieges of the principal cities of Italy, which they had plentifully stored with men and provisions from the deserted country. Aquileia received and withstood the first shock of the invasion. The streams that issue from the head of the Hadriatic gulf, swelled by the melting of the winter snows, opposed an unexpected obstacle to the arms of Maximin. At length, on a singular bridge, constructed with art and difficulty of large hogsheads, he transported his army to the opposite bank, rooted up the beautiful vineyards in the neighborhood of Aquileia, demolished the suburbs, and employed the timber of the buildings in the engines and towers, with which on every side he attacked the city. The walls, fallen to decay during the security of a long peace, had been hastily repaired on this sudden emergency; but the firmest defense of Aquileia consisted in the constancy of the citizens; all ranks of whom, instead of being dismayed, were animated by the extreme danger, and their knowledge of the tyrant's unrelenting temper. Their courage was supported and directed by Crispinus and Menophilus, two of the twenty lieutenants of the senate, who, with a small body of regular troops had thrown themselves into the besieged place. The army of Maximin was repulsed on repeated attacks, his machines destroyed by showers of artificial fire; and the generous enthusiasm of the Aquileians was exalted into a confidence of success, by the opinion, that Belenus, their tutelar deity, combated in person in the defense of his distressed worshippers.

Statue of a charioteer. (The Vatican, Rome)

Left: Performers fighting leopards at a wild beast show or *venationes.* Somewhat similar to the modern Spanish *corrida,* the *venationes* was the poor man's equivalent to the expensive sport of hunting beloved by the Romans. A lucrative trade was carried on with the African provinces which provided a succession of tigers, ostriches, leopards and lions for the Roman spectacles.
Right: The amphitheater at El Djem, Tunisia believed to have been constructed by Gordian III. The Gordians were members of the Gracchi family, one of the oldest and most distinguished of the patrician families and renowned for their vast estates.

The emperor Maximus, who had advanced as far as Ravenna, to secure that important place, and to hasten the military preparations, beheld the event of the war in the more faithful mirror of reason and policy. He was too sensible, that a single town could not resist the persevering efforts of a great army; and he dreaded lest the enemy, tired with the obstinate resistance of Aquileia, should on a sudden relinquish the fruitless siege, and march directly towards Rome. The fate of the empire and the cause of freedom must then be committed to the chance of a battle; and what arms could he oppose to the veteran legions of the Rhine and the Danube? Some troops newly levied among the generous but enervated youth of Italy; and a body of German auxiliaries, on whose firmness, in the hour of trial, it was dangerous to depend. In the midst of these just alarms, the stroke of domestic conspiracy punished the crimes of Maximin, and delivered Rome and the senate from the calamities that would surely have attended the victory of an enraged barbarian.

A party of Prætorian guards, who trembled for their wives and children in the camp of Alba, near Rome, executed the sentence of the senate. Maximin, abandoned by his guards, was (AD 238, April) slain in his tent, with his son (whom he had associated to the honors of the purple).

It is easier to conceive than to describe the universal joy of the Roman world on the fall of the tyrant. The return of Maximus was a triumphal procession, his colleague and young Gordian went out to meet him, and the three princes made their entry into the capital, attended by the ambassadors of almost all the cities of Italy, saluted with the splendid offerings of gratitude and superstition, and received with the unfeigned acclamations of the senate and people, who persuaded themselves that a golden age would succeed to an age of iron. The conduct of the two emperors correspond with these expectations. They administered justice in person; and the rigor of the one was tempered by the other's clemency. The oppressive taxes with which Maximin had loaded the rights of inheritance and succession were repealed, or at least moderated. Discipline was revived, and with the advice of the senate many wise laws were enacted by their imperial ministers, who endeavored to restore a civil constitution.

When the senate elected two princes, it is probable that, besides the declared reason of providing for the various emergencies of peace and war, they were actuated by the secret desire of weakening by division the despotism of the supreme magistrate. Their policy was effectual, but it proved fatal both to their emperors and to themselves. The jealousy of power was soon exasperated by the difference of character. Maximus despised Balbinus as a luxurious noble, and was in his turn disdained by his colleague as an obscure soldier. Their silent discord was understood rather than seen; but the mutual consciousness prevented them from uniting in any vigorous measures of defense against their common enemies of the Prætorian camp. The whole city was (AD 238, 15 July) employed in the Capitoline games, and the emperors were left almost alone in the palace. On a sudden they were alarmed by the approach of a troop of desperate assassins. Ignorant of each other's situation or designs, for they already occupied very distant apartments, afraid to give or to receive assistance, they wasted the important moments in idle debates and fruitless recriminations. The arrival of the guards put an end to the vain strife. They seized on these emperors of the senate, for such they called them with malicious contempt, stripped them of their garments, and dragged them in insolent triumph through the streets of Rome, with a design of inflicting a slow and cruel death on those unfortunate princes. The fear of a rescue from the faithful Germans of the Imperial guards, shortened their tortures; and their bodies, mangled with a thousand wounds, were left exposed to the insults or to the pity of the populace.

In the space of a few months, six princes had been cut off by the sword. Gordian, who had already received the title of Cæsar, was the only person that occurred to the soldiers as proper to fill the vacant throne. His name was dear to the senate and people; his tender age promised a long impunity of military license; and the submission of Rome and the provinces to the choice of the Prætorian guards, saved the republic, at the expense indeed of its freedom and dignity, from the horrors of a new civil war in the heart of the capital.

As the third Gordian was only nineteen years of age at the time of his death, the history of his life, were it known to us with greater accuracy than it really is, would contain little more than the account of his

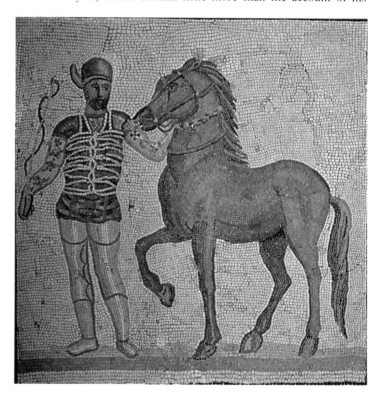

education, and the conduct of the ministers, who by turns abused or guided the simplicity of his inexperienced youth. Immediately after his accession, he fell into the hands of his mother's eunuchs, that pernicious vermin of the East, who, since the days of Elagabalus, had infested the Roman palace. We are ignorant by what fortunate accident the emperor escaped from this ignominious slavery, and devolved his confidence on a minister whose wise counsels had no object except the glory of his sovereign and the happiness of the people. It should seem that (AD 240) love and learning introduced Misitheus to the favor of Gordian. The young prince married the daughter of his master of rhetoric, and promoted his father-in-law to the first offices of the empire. Two admirable letters that passed between them are still extant. The minister, with the conscious dignity of virtue, congratulates Gordian that he is delivered from the tyranny of the eunuchs, and still more that he is sensible of his deliverance. The emperor acknowledges, with an amiable confusion, the errors of his past conduct; and laments, with singular propriety, the misfortune of a monarch, from whom a venal tribe of courtiers perpetually labor to conceal the truth.

The life of Misitheus had been spent in the profession of letters, not of arms; yet such was the versatile genius of that great man, that, when (AD 242) he was appointed Prætorian Præfect, he discharged the military duties of his place with vigor and ability. The Persians had invaded Mesopotamia, and threatened Antioch. By the persuasion of his father-in-law, the young emperor quitted the luxury of Rome, opened, for the last time recorded in history, the temple of Janus, and marched in person into the East. Misitheus watched over the safety and discipline of the army; while he prevented their dangerous murmurs by maintaining a regular plenty in the camp, and by establishing ample magazines of vinegar, bacon, straw, barley, and wheat, in all the cities of the frontier. But the prosperity of Gordian expired with Misitheus,

Left: Charioteer of the Roman Circus wearing the blue racing colors of his master. The cap and leather bands around his chest were for protection. (Mosaic from the Villa dei Settimii, Museo Nazionale, Rome)
Right: Bronze coin of Philip (AD 198–249). Philip was Arab born and he celebrated his accession with a magnificent display of public pomp by inaugurating the secular games.

who died of a flux, not without very strong suspicions of poison. Philip, his successor (AD 243) in the præfecture, was an Arab by birth, and consequently, in the earlier part of his life, a robber by profession. His rise from so obscure a station to the first dignities of the empire, seems to prove that he was a bold and able leader. But his boldness prompted him to aspire to the throne, and his abilities were employed to supplant, not to serve, his indulgent master. The minds of the soldiers were irritated by an artificial scarcity, created by his contrivance in the camp; and the distress of the army was attributed to the youth and incapacity of the prince. It is not in our power to trace the successive steps of the secret conspiracy and open sedition, which were at length fatal to Gordian. A sepulchral monument was erected to his memory on the spot where (AD 244, March) he was killed, near the conflux of the Euphrates with the little river Aboras. The fortunate Philip, raised to the empire by the votes of the soldiers, found a ready obedience from the senate and the provinces.

On his return from the East to Rome, Philip, desirous of obliterating the memory of his crimes, and of captivating the affections of the people, solemnized (AD 248, 21 April) the secular games with infinite pomp and magnificence.

The last three hundred years had been consumed in apparent prosperity and internal decline. The nation of soldiers, magistrates, and legislators, who composed the thirty-five tribes of the Roman people, was dissolved into the common mass of mankind and confounded with the millions of servile provincials, who had received the name without adopting the spirit of Romans. A mercenary army, levied among the subjects and barbarians of the frontier, was the only order of men who preserved and abused their independence. By their tumultuary election, a Syrian, a Goth, or an Arab, was exalted to the throne of Rome, and invested with despotic power over the conquests and over the country of the Scipios.

The limits of the Roman empire still extended from the Western Ocean to the Tigris, and from Mount Atlas to the Rhine and the Danube. To the undiscerning eye of the vulgar, Philip appeared a monarch no less powerful than Hadrian or Augustus had formerly been. The form was still the same, but the animating health and vigor were fled. The industry of the people was discouraged and exhausted by a long series of oppression. The discipline of the legions, which alone, after the extinction of every other virtue, had propped the greatness of the state, was corrupted by the ambition, or relaxed by the weakness, of the emperors. The strength of the frontiers, which had always consisted in arms rather than in fortifications, was insensibly undermined; and the fairest provinces were left exposed to the rapaciousness or ambition of the barbarians, who soon discovered the decline of the Roman empire.

Roman Fashion

MEN'S CLOTHES

Throughout the republican age and well into the Early Empire the national dress for Roman citizens was the cumbersome but dignified toga which the Romans had borrowed from the Etruscans. Its use was prohibited for foreigners and exiles and served to distinguish the Roman citizen from the rank and file, the common dress for freed men and slaves being the tunic, a simple affair made up of two pieces of cloth with neckhole openings which could be gathered in at the waist by a belt *(cingulum)*.

The toga was made of a single piece of cloth of white wool or silk, three times the length of the wearer and eliptical or semicircular in shape. It was worn draped over the shoulders to leave the right arm bare. Youths under the age of sixteen wore a toga bordered with purple *(toga praetexta)*. When they came of age they were able to replace this with the plain white toga known as the *toga pura* or *toga virilis*. The *toga candida* distinguished those in high office and was specially whitened by rubbing the material with white chalk. The *toga palmata*, a more festive affair, was the prerogative of conquering generals and worn on the occasion of their triumph.

During the empire period the toga was customarily worn over tunic. Julius Cæsar (100– 44 BC) had introduced the wearing of a tunic with fringed sleeves and by the time of Commodus (161–92) and the late Empire, the wearing of the sleeved tunic, originally considered effeminate, was an acceptable form of dress. Members of the Equestrian order wore a tunic marked with the *clavis* a broad purple stripe. The wearing of the purple toga was reserved exclusively for the emperor.

For protection against the cold and wet the Roman donned a *lacerna* or *pallium*. The *lacerna* was a dark colored woollen cloak and was the common garment of the militia for whom the toga was considered too impractical. A special white *lacerna* was worn at the circus when the Emperor was present. The *pœnula* a long sleeveless woollen cloak similar to the South American poncho with an opening for the head was worn when travelling.

In the later years of the empire the toga with its complex drapes became over cumbersome. Attempts were made to simplify its form but it eventually grew so ornate that it was relegated to the role of a sumptuous garment worn only for ceremonial occasions. For every day use the people took to the simplified form of the *pallium*: a broad subtle garment that crossed over the body and was gathered on the shoulder with a brooch like a Scottish plaid.

Extreme left: The toga, the normal form of dress for all Roman citizens. (The Vatican Museum, Rome)
Below: Roman matron wearing the *pallia* draped over her head and shoulders. (Museo Nazionale, Rome)

WOMEN'S CLOTHES

Under the Republic Roman women like Roman men wore the toga. But this fashion declined under the Emperors and women tended to adopt a fashion inspired by the Greek *chiton*; they wore a form of simple tunic known as the *tunic interiore* on top of which was worn a *stola* or short supplementary tunic. Over this they would wrap a *palla*, a shawl which fell in graceful folds from the shoulders. In addition a Roman matron or Vestal virgin might wear a veil since it was customary for the head to be covered while sacrificing and during other religious ceremonies. As with the men, the *lacerna* and *pænula* were worn as extra protection while outdoors and when travelling.

Above and right: Roman leather sandals. (London Museum)

HAIR FASHIONS

WOMEN

For the Roman woman one of the most important activities of her morning's beauty routine was the dressing of her hair. The elaborate fashion launched by Messalina had set the tone for the hair arrangements during the Empire period. The simpler style of a single center parting and chignon or the rolled plaits of Livia and Octavia thus gave way to the more elaborate creations of curls and waves that required the help of the hairdresser *(ornatrix)* who features so frequently in the Epigrams of Decimus Junius Juvenalis (c55–c140). These hairdos, which were built up in much the same way as the grandiose eighteenth-century creations, were arranged with the use of suitable died wigs and false hairpieces.

If she did not choose this mode of dressing, she bound her hair simply with a red or purple band *(vitta)* or built it up in a beehive or conical shape *(tutulus)*. On special occasions she would dress her hair as the customs demanded. Weddings for instance required her to dress her hair in a red net the night preceding the ceremony. On the day she would then don an unhemmed tunic made fast by a double knotted woollen girdle; over this was placed a saffron cloak. Sandals of the same color and a metal necklace completed the attire. On her head she wore an orange veil *(flammeum)*, which discreetly hid the upper part of her face. It was supported by six false rolls and crowned by a wreath of marjoram and verbena, later of myrtle and orange blossom. With the advent of Christianity this veil became a traditional feature of every wedding.

MEN

The Roman man too customarily indulged in an elaborate toilet. His face was painted and highlighted here and there with patches, should he deem it necessary – a custom that drew satirical sketches from the pens of contemporary writers; his body was perfumed and his hair arranged according to the fashion set by the reigning emperor. As with the women, this was at first a debonair style that fell simply and naturally into place, but later, after the age of Hadrian, required the art of the *tonsor* who crimped his hair with curling tongs. He took his customary bath in the evening. Beards, too, which had fallen from grace around 2 BC, returned to favor under the Emperor Hadrian.

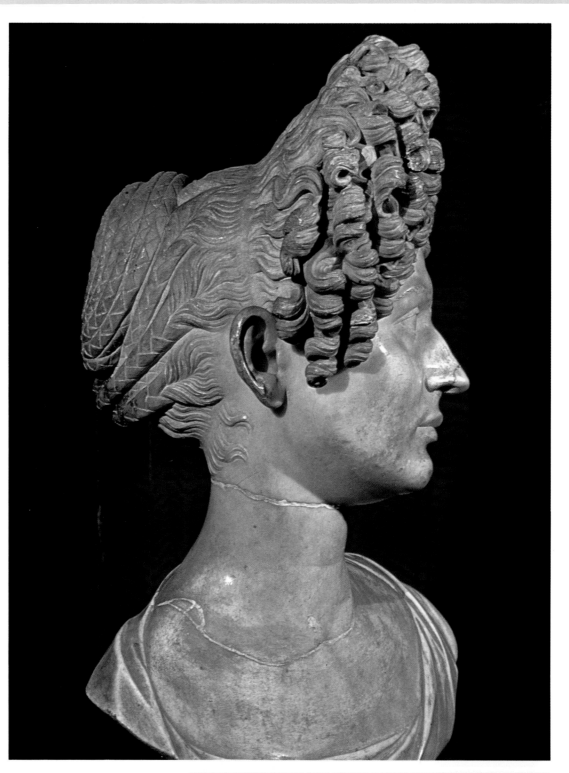

Top: The elaborate curled hairstyles of a Roman lady of the Flavian period. (First century AD, Capitoline Museum, Rome)
Right: The Aldebrandini Wedding. For the wedding the Roman bride would wear an orange veil *(flammeum)* as her headdress. (The Vatican Library, Rome)

Above: Gold earrings wrought with intricate filigree work (Second–third century AD, Granada, Spain, British Museum)
Left: Casually attired in a light tunic a young couple amuse themselves playing the lyre. (Wall-painting from Pompeii, British Museum)
Below: A woman pouring perfume into a small bottle. The most important part of a woman's morning was her toilette. (Wall-painting from the Villa Farnesina formerly Caesar or Augustus, Museo Nazionale, Rome)

FOOTWEAR

The commonest form of footwear was the sandal. This took the form of the *solea* where the sole was fastened on by cords over the instep and was donned for everyday wear in the house. The oldest and simplest form of this sandal was the *carbatinia*. This was made from oxhide and strapped onto the foot over the ankle and instep with thongings.

For outdoor wear the Roman citizen wore a low-slung shoe. This was made out of natural hide, besported a leather sole and thonging over the instep and up the leg. These were reserved for citizens alone and slaves were forbidden to wear them.

For country attire, there was the *pero*, a light-weight boot again laced with thongs and reaching up to the thigh. The *campagnus* was a derivative of this and similar in style except for the openwork over the top of the foot. The most complicated of these sandals was the *calceus senatorum*. The leg covering was open on the inside to reveal a tongue. It laced up with leather thongs decorated with hanging tablets. These were customarily black in color during the period of the early Empire period changing to white in the late Empire. Red thonging was the prerogative of the Emperor and its use was reserved exclusively for him.

Below: Gold snake bracelet, an extremely popular jewelry design throughout the entire Roman period. (The Victoria and Albert Museum, London)

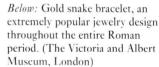

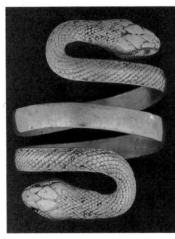

HEADGEAR

Convention portrayed people bareheaded but nonetheless various types of headgear were worn. These included the *galerus*, a type of close-fitting cap; the *petasus*, a wide-brimmed hat often made of straw and of Greek origin that became popular, particularly among women under the reign of Augustus (63 BC– AD 14) – senators were later authorized to wear it at the Circus from the time of Caracalla (176–217) onwards. Also in vogue was the *pileus*, a round, brimless cap made of felt and worn by men. The last piece of headgear was the *cucullus*, a hood that could be worn either on its own or attached to a cape.

Right: The simple coiffure of a young girl. (Graeco-Roman statue, first century AD)

Below: The Rhayader Jewelry – necklet, gold bracelet and ring. The bracelet consists of a broad band in two pieces with applied gold wire ornament and green and blue enamelling. The necklet is wrought of gold plates and bordered with gold filigree which provide a setting for carnelians. (From Rhayader, Radnorshire, Roman, second–third century AD, British Museum)

Above: Formal bandeau style hairdo of the early fourth century, Constantine period.

Above: Seated figure of a Roman matron. (The Uffizzi, Florence)

Above: Tightly set curls of the hairstyle of the Flavian period. (First century AD)
Right: The Desborough Mirror. (From Desborough, Northants, first century AD, British Museum)

JEWELS AND ORNAMENTS

These were worn by men and women alike, although predominantly by women, and included necklaces, pendants, trinkets, armlets, anklets, and rings.

The belt *(cingulum)* was worn both by men and women as a girdle to regulate the length of the tunic or *peplos.* They were often exquisitely wrought and decorated with insets of silver and gold and occasionally crystal and ivory. The lavishness of the jewelry and its rich ornamentation, often Oriental in inspiration, reflected the fortunes of the Empire.

During the periods of conquest the expanding economy transformed Rome into one of the most important manufacturing centers in the whole of the Empire, rivaling the artisans and craftsmen of Antioch and Alexandria in the quality of work and introducing similar techniques of filigree and granulation to produce ornate settings encrusted with precious stones. This tendency towards luxury was particularly noticeable in the neo-classical revival of gracious living. The jewels of this period are noticeable for the opulent and heavy Syrian style settings: earrings hung with huge pendants and snake-ring bracelets.

CHAPTER EIGHT

The Emperors Decius, Gallus, Aemilianus, Valerian and Gallienus

the general irruption of the barbarians
[AD 248–268]

FROM the great secular games celebrated by Philip to the death of the emperor Gallienus there elapsed (AD 248–268) twenty years of shame and misfortune. During that calamitous period every instant of time was marked, every province of the Roman world was afflicted by barbarous invaders and military tyrants, and the ruined empire seemed to approach the last and fatal moment of its dissolution. The confusion of the times, and the scarcity of authentic memorials, oppose equal difficulties to the historian, who attempts to preserve a clear and unbroken thread of narration. Surrounded with imperfect fragments, always concise, often obscure, and sometimes contradictory, he is reduced to collect, to compare, and to conjecture; and though he ought never to place his conjectures in the rank of facts, yet the knowledge of human nature, and of the sure operation of its fierce and unrestrained passions, might, on some occasions supply the want of historical materials.

There is not, for instance, any difficulty in conceiving that since the successive murders of so many emperors had loosened all the ties of allegiance between the prince and people, that all the generals of Philip were disposed to imitate the example of their master; and that the caprice of armies, long since habituated to frequent and violent revolutions, might any day raise to the throne the most obscure of their fellow-soldiers. History can only add that the rebellion against the emperor Philip broke out in the summer of the year two hundred and forty-nine, among the legions of Mæsia; and that a subaltern officer, named Marinus, was the object of their seditious choice. Philip was alarmed. He dreaded lest the treason of the Mæsian army should prove the first spark of a general conflagration. Distracted with the consciousness of his guilt and of his danger, he communicated the intelligence to the senate. A gloomy silence prevailed, the effect of fear, and perhaps of disaffection: till at length Decius, one of the assembly, assuming a spirit worthy of his noble extraction, ventured to discover more intrepidity than the emperor seemed to possess. He treated the whole business with contempt, as a hasty and inconsiderate tumult, and Philip's rival as a phantom of royalty, who in a very few days would be destroyed by the same inconstancy that had created him. The speedy completion of the prophecy inspired Philip with a just esteem for so able a counselor: and Decius appeared to him the only person capable of restoring peace and discipline to an army whose tumultuous spirit did not immediately subside after the murder of Marinus. Decius, who long resisted his own nomination, seems to have insinuated the danger of presenting a leader of merit to the angry and apprehensive minds of the soldiers; and his prediction was again confirmed by the event. The legion of Mæsia forced their judge to become (AD 249) their accomplice. They left him only the alternative of death or the purple. His subsequent conduct, after the decisive measure, was unavoidable. He conducted or followed his army to the confines of Italy, whither Philip, collecting all his force to repel the formidable competitor whom he had raised up, advanced to meet him. The Imperial troops were superior in number; but the rebels formed an army of veterans, commanded by an able and experienced leader. Philip was either killed in the battle or put to death a few days afterwards at Verona. His son and associate in the empire was massacred at Rome by the Prætorian guards; and the victorius Decius, with more favorable circumstances than the ambition of that age can usually plead, was universally acknowledged by the senate and provinces.

The emperor Decius had employed a few months in the works of

peace and the administration of justice, when (AD 250) he was summoned to the banks of the Danube by the invasion of the Goths. This is the first considerable occasion in which history mentions that great people, who afterwards broke the Roman power, sacked the Capitol, and reigned in Gaul, Spain, and Italy. So memorable was the part which they acted in the subversion of the Western empire that the name of Goths is frequently but improperly used as a general appellation of rude and warlike barbarism.

The Goths were now in possession of the Ukraine, a country of considerable extent and uncommon fertility, intersected with navigable rivers, which, from either side, discharge themselves into the Borysthenes; and interspersed with large and lofty forests of oaks. The plenty of game and fish, the innumerable bee-hives, deposited in the hollows of old trees, and in the cavities of rocks, and forming, even in that rude age, a valuable branch of commerce, the size of the cattle, the temperature of the air, the aptness of the soil for every species of grain, and the luxuriancy of the vegetation, all displayed the liberality of Nature, and tempted the industry of man. But the Goths withstood all these temptations, and still adhered to a life of idleness, of poverty, and of rapine.

The Scythian hordes, which, towards the east, bordered on the new settlements of the Goths, presented nothing to their arms except the

Left: Gaius Messius Quintus Trajanus Decius c AD 200–251; Roman Emperor AD 249–251. (British Museum)
Below: Gallienus (Publius Licinius Gallienus c AD 218–268; Roman Emperor from AD 253–268)

doubtful chance of an unprofitable victory. But the prospect of the Roman territories was far more alluring; and the fields of Dacia were covered with rich harvests, sown by the hands of an industrious, and exposed to be gathered by those of a warlike, people. It is probable that the conquests of Trajan maintained by his successors, less for any real advantage than for ideal dignity, had contributed to weaken the empire on that side. The new and unsettled province of Dacia was neither strong enough to resist, nor rich enough to satiate, the rapaciousness of the barbarians. As long as the remote banks of the Dniester were considered as the boundary of the Roman power, the fortifications of the Lower Danube were more carelessly guarded, and the inhabitants of Mæsia lived in supine security, fondly conceiving themselves at an inaccessible distance from any barbarian invaders. The irruptions of the Goths, under the reign of Philip, fatally convinced them of their mistake. The king, or leader, of that fierce nation traversed with contempt the province of Dacia, and passed both the Dniester and the Danube without encountering any opposition capable of retarding his progress. The various multitude of barbarians appeared, at length, under the walls of Marcianopolis, a city built by Trajan in honor of his sister, and at that time the capital of the second Mæsia. The inhabitants consented to ransom their lives and property by the payment of a large sum of money, and the invaders retreated back into their deserts, animated, rather than satisfied, with the first success of their arms against an opulent but feeble country. Intelligence was soon transmitted to the emperor Decius that Cniva, king of the Goths, had passed the Danube a second time, with more considerable forces; that his numerous detachments scattered devastation over the province of Mæsia, whilst the main body of the army, consisting of seventy thousand Germans and Sarmatians, a force equal to the most daring achievements, required the presence of the Roman monarch, and the exertion of his military power.

Decius found (AD 250) the Goths engaged before Nicopolis, on the Jatrus, one of the many monuments of Trajan's victories. On his approach they raised the siege, but with a design only of marching away to a conquest of greater importance, the siege of Philippopolis, a city of Thrace, founded by the father of Alexander, near the foot of mount Hæmus. Decius followed them through a difficult country, and by forced marches; but when he imagined himself at a considerable distance from the rear of the Goths, Cniva turned with rapid fury on his pursuers. The camp of the Romans was surprised and pillaged, and, for the first time, their emperor fled in disorder before a troop of half-armed barbarians. After a long resistance, Philippopolis, destitute of succor, was taken by storm. A hundred thousand persons are reported to have been massacred in the sack of that great city. Many prisoners of

Above: Roman troops and barbarians (detail from the Arch of Constantine, Rome) dating from the time of Hadrian, second century AD. *Left:* Valerian (Publius Licinius Valerian c AD 200–260; Roman Emperor 253–60), proclaimed Emperor by the legions of Rhaetia after the murder of Gallus.

consequence became a valuable accession to the spoil; and Priscus, a brother of the late emperor Philip, blushed not to assume the purple under the protection of the barbarous enemies of Rome. The time, however, consumed in that tedious siege enabled Decius to revive the courage, restore the discipline, and recruit the numbers of his troops. He intercepted several parties of Carpi, and other Germans, who were hastening to share the victory of their countrymen, intrusted the passes

of the mountains to officers of approved valor and fidelity; repaired and strengthened the fortifications of the Danube, and exerted his utmost vigilance to oppose either the progress or the retreat of the Goths. Encouraged by the return of fortune, he anxiously waited for an opportunity to retrieve, by a great and decisive blow, his own glory and that of the Roman arms.

At the same time when Decius was struggling with the violence of the tempest, his mind, calm and deliberate amidst the tumult of war, investigated the more general causes that, since the age of the Antonines, had so impetuously urged the decline of the Roman greatness. He soon discovered that it was impossible to replace that greatness on a permanent basis without restoring public virtue, ancient principles and manners, and the oppressed majesty of the laws. To execute this noble but arduous design, he first resolved to revive the obsolete officer of censor; an office which, as long as it had subsisted in its pristine integrity, had so much contributed to the perpetuity of the state, till it was usurped and gradually neglected by the Cæsars. Conscious that the favor of the sovereign may confer power, but that the esteem of the people can alone bestow authority, he submitted the choice of the censor to the unbiased voice of the senate. By their unanimous votes, or rather acclamations, Valerian, who was afterwards emperor, and who then served with distinction in the army of Decius, was (AD 251, 27 Oct.) declared the most worthy of that exalted honor.

A magistrate, invested with such extensive powers, would have appeared not so much the minister as the colleague of his sovereign. Valerian justly dreaded an elevation so full of envy and suspicion. He modestly urged the alarming greatness of the trust, his own insufficiency, and the incurable corruption of the times. He artfully insinuated that the office of censor was inseparable from the Imperial dignity, and that the feeble hands of a subject were unequal to the support of such an immense weight of cares and of power. The approaching event of war soon put an end to the prosecution of a project so specious but so impracticable; and while it preserved Valerian from the danger, saved the emperor Decius from the disappointment which would most probably have attended it. A censor may maintain, he can never restore, the morals of a state. It is impossible for such a magistrate to exert his authority with benefit, or even with effect, unless he is supported by a quick sense of honor and virtue in the minds of the people, by a decent reverence for the public opinion, and by a train of useful prejudices combating on the side of national manners. In a period when these principles are annihilated, the censorial jurisdiction must either sink into empty pageantry, or be converted into a partial instrument of vexatious oppression. It was easier to vanquish the Goths than to eradicate the public vices; yet even in the first of these enterprises Decius lost his army and his life.

The Goths were now, on every side, surrounded and pursued by the Roman arms but the high-spirited barbarians preferred death to slavery. An obscure town of Mæsia, called Forum Terebronii, was the scene of the battle. The Gothic army was drawn up in three lines, and, either from choice or accident, the front of the third line was covered by a morass. In the beginning of the action, the son of Decius, a youth of the fairest hopes, and already associated to the honors of the purple, was slain by an arrow, in the sight of his afflicted father; who, summoning all his fortitude, admonished the dismayed troops that the loss of a single soldier was of little importance to the republic. The conflict was terrible; it was the combat of despair against grief and rage. The first line of the Goths at length gave way in disorder; the second, advancing to sustain it, shared its fate; and the third only remained entire, prepared to dispute the passage of the morass, which was imprudently attempted by the presumption of the enemy. 'Here the fortune of the day turned, and all things became adverse to the Romans: the place deep with ooze, sinking under those who stood, slippery to such as advanced; their armor heavy, the waters deep; nor could they wield, in that uneasy situation, their weighty javelins. The barbarians, on the contrary, were enured to encounters in the bogs, their persons tall, their spears long, such as could wound at a distance.' In this morass the Roman army, after an ineffectual struggle, was irrecoverably lost; nor could the body of the emperor ever be found. Such was the fate of Decius, in the fiftieth year of his age; an accomplished prince, active in war, and affable in peace; who, together with his son, has deserved to be compared, both in life and death, with the brightest examples of ancient virtue.

This fatal blow humbled, for a very little time, the insolence of the legions. They appear to have patiently expected, and submissively obeyed, the decree of the senate, which regulated the succession to the throne. From a just regard for the memory of Decius, the Imperial title was (AD 251, Dec.) conferred on Hostilianus, his only surviving son; but an equal rank, with more effectual power, was granted to Gallus, whose experience and ability seemed equal to the great trust of guardian to the young prince and the distressed empire. The first care of the new emperor was to deliver the Illyrian provinces from the intolerable weight of the victorious Goths. He (AD 252) consented to leave in their hands the rich fruits of their invasion, an immense booty, and, what was still more disgraceful, a great number of prisoners of the highest merit and quality. He plentifully supplied their camp with every conveniency that could assuage their angry spirits, or facilitate their so much wished-for departure; and he even promised to pay them annually a large sum of gold, on condition they should never afterwards infest the Roman territories by their incursions.

These voluntary marks of bounty were understood to flow not from the fears, but merely from the generosity or the gratitude of the Romans; and whilst presents and subsidies were liberally distributed among friends and suppliants they were sternly refused to such as claimed them as a debt. But this stipulation of an annual payment to a

victorious enemy appeared without disguise in the light of an ignominious tribute; the minds of the Romans were not yet accustomed to accept such equal laws from a tribe of barbarians; and the prince, who by a necessary concession had probably saved his country, became the object of the general contempt and aversion. The death of Hostilianus, though it happened in the midst of a raging pestilence, was interpreted as the personal crime of Gallus; and even the defeat of the late emperor was ascribed by the voice of suspicion to the perfidious counsels of his hated successor. The tranquillity which the empire enjoyed during the first year of his administration served rather to inflame than to appease the public discontent; and, as soon as the apprehensions of war were removed, the infamy of the peace was more deeply and sensibly felt.

But the Romans were irritated to a still higher degree when they discovered that they had not even secured their repose, though at the expense of their honor. The dangerous secret of the wealth and weakness of the empire had been revealed to the world. New swarms of barbarians, encouraged (AD 253) by the success, and not conceiving themselves bound by the obligation, of their brethren, spread devastation through the Illyrian provinces, and terror as far as the gates of Rome. The defense of the monarchy, which seemed abandoned by the pusillanimous emperor, was assumed by Æmilianus, governor of Pannonia and Mæsia; who rallied the scattered forces, and revived the fainting spirits of the troops. The barbarians were unexpectedly attacked, routed, chased, and pursued beyond the Danube. The victorious leader distributed as a donative the money collected for the tribute, and the acclamations of the soldiers proclaimed him emperor on the field of battle. Gallus, who, careless of the general welfare, indulged himself in the pleasures of Italy, was almost in the same instant informed of the success of the revolt and of the rapid approach of his aspiring lieutenant. He advanced to meet him as far as the plains of Spoleto. When the armies came in sight of each other, the soldiers of Gallus compared the ignominious conduct of their sovereign with the glory of his rival. They admired the valor of Æmilianus; they were attracted by his liberality, for he offered a considerable increase of pay to all deserters. The murder of Gallus, and of his son Volusianus, put an end to the civil war; and the senate (AD 253, May) gave a legal sanction to the rights of conquest. The letters of Æmilianus to that assembly displayed a mixture of moderation and vanity. He assured them that he should resign to their wisdom the civil administration; and, contenting himself with the quality of their general, would in a short time assert the glory of Rome, and deliver the empire from all the barbarians both of the North and of the East. His pride was flattered by

Gallus Gaius Cornelius (c 70–c 53). He is memorable for the peace he purchased from the Goths. He was murdered by his own soldiers.

Adamklissi reliefs: guardians of the frontier. (Detail from the monument on the North bank of the Danube commemorating Trajan's victory over the Dacians)

the applause of the senate; and medals are still extant representing him with the name and attributes of Hercules the Victor and of Mars the Avenger.

If the new monarch possessed the abilities, he wanted the time necessary to fulfill these splendid promises. Less than four months intervened between his victory and his fall. He had vanquished Gallus: he sunk under the weight of a competitor more formidable than Gallus. That unfortunate prince had sent Valerian, already distinguished by the honorable title of censor, to bring the legions of Gaul and Germany to his aid. Valerian executed that commission with zeal and fidelity; and as he arrived too late to save his sovereign, he resolved to revenge him. The troops of Æmilianus, who still lay encamped in the plains of Spoleto, were awed by the sanctity of his character, but much more by the superior strength of his army; and as they were now become as incapable of personal attachment as they had always been of constitutional principle, they (AD 253, Aug.) readily imbrued their hands in the blood of a prince who had so lately been the object of their partial choice. The guilt was theirs, but the advantage of it was Valerian's; who obtained the possession of the throne by the means indeed of a civil war, but with a degree of innocence singular in that age of revolutions; since he owned neither gratitude nor allegiance to his predecessor whom he dethroned.

Valerian was about sixty years of age when he was invested with the purple, not by the caprice of the populace, or the clamors of the army, but by the unanimous voice of the Roman world. In his gradual ascent through the honors of the state, he had deserved the favor of virtuous princes, and had declared himself the enemy of tyrants. The consciousness of his decline engaged him to share the throne with a younger and more active associate: the emergency of the times demanded a general no less than a prince; and the experience of the Roman censor might have directed him where to bestow the Imperial purple, as the reward of military merit. But instead of making a judicious choice, which would have confirmed his reign and endeared his memory, Valerian immediately invested with the supreme honors his son Gallienus, a

youth whose effeminate vices had been hitherto concealed by the obscurity of a private station. The joint government of the father and the son subsisted about seven, and the sole administration of Gallienus continued about eight years (AD 253–268). But the whole period was one uninterrupted series of confusion and calamity. As the Roman empire was at the same time, and on every side, attacked by the blind fury of foreign invaders, and the wild ambition of domestic usurpers, we shall consult order and perspicuity by pursuing not so much the doubtful arrangement of dates as the more natural distribution of subjects. The most dangerous enemies of Rome, during the reigns of Valerian and Gallienus, were, 1. The Franks; 2. The Alemanni; 3. The Goths; and 4. The Persians. Under these general appellations we may comprehend the adventures of less considerable tribes, whose obscure and uncouth names would only serve to oppress the memory and perplex the attention of the reader.

The Romans had long experienced the daring valor of the people of Lower Germany. The union of their strength threatened Gaul with a more formidable invasion, and required the presence of Gallienus, the heir and colleague of imperial power. While that prince, and his infant son Salonius, displayed, in the court of Treves, the majesty of the empire, its armies were ably conducted by their general Posthumus, who, though he afterwards betrayed the family of Valerian, was ever faithful for the great interest of the monarchy. The treacherous language of panegyrics and medals darkly announces a long series of victories. Trophies and titles attest (if such evidence can attest) the fame of Posthumus, who is repeatedly styled The conqueror of the Germans, and the savior of Gaul.

But a single fact, the only one indeed of which we have any distinct knowledge, erases, in a great measure, these monuments of vanity and adulation. The Rhine, though dignified with the title of Safeguard of the provinces, was an imperfect barrier against the daring spirit of enterprise with which the Franks were actuated. Their rapid devastations stretched from the river to the foot of the Pyrenees: nor were they stopped by those mountains. Spain, which had never dreaded, was unable to resist, the inroads of the Germans. During twelve years, the greatest part of the reign of Gallienus, that opulent country was the theater of unequal and destructive hostilities. Tarragona, the flourishing capital of a peaceful province, was sacked and almost destroyed, and so late as the days of Orosius, who wrote in the fifth century, wretched cottages, scattered amidst the ruins of magnificent cities, still recorded the rage of the barbarians. When the exhausted country no longer supplied a variety of plunder, the Franks seized on some vessels in the ports of Spain, and transported themselves into Mauritania. The distant province was astonished with the fury of these barbarians, who seemed to fall from a new world, as their name, manners, and complexion were equally unknown on the coast of Africa.

In the reign of the emperor Caracalla, an innumerable swarm of Suevi appeared on the banks of the Mein, and in the neighborhood of

Captives being lead away for slavery. (Nineteenth-Century engraving)

the Roman provinces, in quest either of food, of plunder, or of glory. The hasty army of volunteers gradually coalesced into a great and permanent nation, and as it was composed from so many different tribes, assumed the name of Alemanni, or *All-men*; to denote at once their various lineage and their common bravery. The latter was soon felt by the Romans in many a hostile inroad. The Alemanni fought chiefly on horseback; but their cavalry was rendered still more formidable by a mixture of light infantry, selected from the bravest and most active of the youth, whom frequent exercise had enured to accompany the horsemen in the longest march, the most rapid charge, or the most precipitate retreat.

This warlike people of Germans had been astonished by the immense preparations of Alexander Severus, they were dismayed by the arms of his successor, a barbarian equal in valor and fierceness to themselves. But still hovering on the frontiers of the empire, they increased the general disorder that ensued after the death of Decius. They inflicted severe wounds on the rich provinces of Gaul; they were the first who removed the veil that covered the feeble majesty of Italy. A numerous body of the Alemanni penetrated across the Danube, and through the Rhætian Alps, into the plains of Lombardy, advanced as far as Ravenna, and displayed the victorious banners of barbarians almost in sight of Rome. The insult and the danger rekindled in the senate some sparks of their ancient virtue. Both the emperors were engaged in far distant wars, Valerian in the East and Gallienus on the Rhine. All the hopes and resources of the Romans were in themselves. In this emergency, the senators resumed the defense of the republic, drew out the Prætorian guards, who had been left to garrison the capital, and filled up their numbers by enlisting into the public service the stoutest and most willing of the Plebeians. The Alemanni, astonished with the sudden appearance of an army more numerous than their own, retired into Germany laden with spoil; and their retreat was esteemed as a victory by the unwarlike Romans.

When Gallienus received the intelligence that his capital was delivered from the barbarians, he was much less delighted than alarmed with the courage of the senate, since it might one day prompt them to rescue the public from domestic tyranny as well as from foreign invasion. His timid ingratitude was published to his subjects in an edict which prohibited the senators from exercising any military employment, and even from approaching the camps of the legions. But his fears were groundless. The rich and luxurious nobles, sinking into their natural character, accepted, as a favor, this disgraceful exemption from

Left: The Tower of the Winds, Athens, Greece. Detail showing the sundial and water clock. (Roman, 40 BC)
Right: The submission of Valerian: Valerian was defeated and taken captive by Sapor I at Edessa. (Relief from Nagsha Röstam, third century AD)

military service; and as long as they were indulged in the enjoyment of their baths, their theaters, and their villas, they cheerfully resigned the more dangerous cares of empire to the rough hands of peasants and soldiers.

Under the reigns of Valerian and Gallienus, the frontier of the Danube was perpetually infested by the inroads of Germans and Sarmatians; but it was defended by the Romans with more than usual firmness and success. The provinces that were the seat of war recruited the armies of Rome with an inexhaustible supply of hardy soldiers; and more than one of these Illyrian peasants attained the station and displayed the abilities of a general. Though flying parties of the barbarians, who incessantly hovered on the banks of the Danube, penetrated sometimes to the confines of Italy and Macedonia; their progress was commonly checked, or their return intercepted by the Imperial lieutenants. But the great stream of the Gothic hostilities was diverted into a very different channel. The Goths, in their new settlement of the Ukraine, soon became masters of the northern coast of the Euxine: to the south of that inland sea were situated the soft and wealthy provinces of Asia Minor, which possessed all that could attract, and nothing that could resist, a barbarian conqueror.

The banks of the Borysthenes are only sixty miles distant from the narrow entrance of the peninsula of Crim Tartary, known to the ancients under the name of Chersonesus Taurica. On that inhospitable

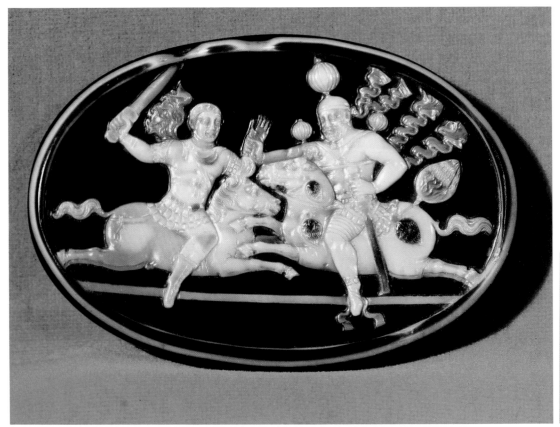

Left: Cameo of Sapor and Valerian. (Cabinet des Médailles, Bibliothèque Nationale, Paris)
Below: Sassanian silver work depicting Dionysos riding in triumph. (Sassanian, second century AD, British Museum)

shore, Euripides, embellishing with exquisite art the tales of antiquity, has placed the scene of one of his most affecting tragedies. The bloody sacrifices of Diana, the arrival of Orestes and Pylades, and the triumph of virtue and religion over savage fierceness, serve to represent an historical truth, that the Tauri, the original inhabitants of the peninsula, were, in some degree, reclaimed from their brutal manners by a gradual intercourse with the Grecian colonies which settled along the maritime coast. The little kingdom of Bosphorus, whose capital was situated on the Straits, through which the Mæotis communicates itself to the Euxine, was composed of degenerate Greeks and half-civilized barbarians. It subsisted, as an independent state, from the time of the Peloponnesian war, was at last swallowed up by the ambition of Mithridates, and, with the rest of his dominions, sunk under the weight of the Roman arms. From the reign of Augustus, the kings of Bosphorus were the humble, but not useless, allies of the empire. By presents, by arms, and by a slight fortification drawn across the Isthmus, they effectually guarded against the roving plunderers of Sarmatia the access of a country which, from its peculiar situation and convenient harbors, commanded the Euxine Sea and Asia Minor. As long as the scepter was possessed by a lineal succession of kings, they acquitted themselves of their important charge with vigilance and success. Domestic factions and the fears, or private interest, of obscure usurpers, who seized on the vacant throne, admitted the Goths into the heart of Bosphorus. With the acquisition of a superfluous waste of fertile soil, the conquerors obtained the command of a naval force, sufficient to transport their armies to the coast of Asia. The ships used in the navigation of the Euxine were of a very singular construction. They were slight flat-bottomed barks framed of timber only, without the least mixture of iron, and occasionally covered with a shelving roof on the appearance of a tempest. In these floating houses, the Goths carelessly trusted themselves to the mercy of an unknown sea, under the conduct of sailors pressed into the service, and whose skill and fidelity were equally suspicious. But the hopes of plunder had banished every idea of danger, and a natural fearlessness of temper supplied in their minds the more rational confidence which is the just result of

knowledge and experience. Warriors of such a daring spirit must have often murmured against the cowardice of their guides, who required the strongest assurances of a settled calm before they would venture to embark; and would scarcely ever be tempted to lose sight of the land. Such, at least, is the practice of the modern Turks, and they are probably not inferior in the art of navigation to the ancient inhabitants of Bosphorus.

The fleet of the Goths, leaving the coast of Circassia on the left hand, first appeared before Pityus, the utmost limits of the Roman provinces; a city provided with a convenient port and fortified with a strong wall. Here they met with a resistance more obstinate than they had reason to expect from the feeble garrison of a distant fortress. They were repulsed; and their disappointment seemed to diminish the terror of the Gothic name. As long as Successianus, an officer of superior rank and merit, defended that frontier, all their efforts were ineffectual; but as soon as he was removed by Valerian to a more honorable but less important station, they resumed the attack of Pityus; and, by the destruction of that city, obliterated the memory of their former disgrace.

Circling round the eastern extremity of the Euxine Sea, the navigation from Pityus to Trebizond is about three hundred miles. The course of the Goths carried them in sight of the country of Colchis, so famous by the expedition of the Argonauts, and they even attempted, though without success, to pillage a rich temple at the mouth of the river Phasis. Trebizond, celebrated in the retreat of the Ten Thousand as an ancient colony of Greeks, derived its wealth and splendor from the munificence of the emperor Hadrian, who had constructed an artificial port on the coast left destitute by nature of secure harbors. The city was large and populous; a double enclosure of walls seemed to defy the fury of the Goths, and the usual garrison had been strengthened by a reinforcement of ten thousand men. But there are not any advantages capable of supplying the absence of discipline and vigilance. The numerous garrison of Trebizond, dissolved in riot and luxury, disdained to guard their impregnable fortifications. The Goths soon discovered the supine negligence of the besieged, erected a lofty pile of fascines, ascended the walls in the silence of the night, and entered the defenseless city sword in hand. A general massacre of the people ensued, while the affrighted soldiers escaped through the opposite gates of the town. The most holy temples, and the most splendid edifices, were involved in a common destruction. The booty that fell into the hands of the Goths was immense: the wealth of the adjacent countries had been deposited in Trebizond, as in a secure place of refuge. The number of captives was incredible, as the victorious barbarians ranged without opposition through the extensive province of Pontus. The rich spoils of Trebizond filled a great fleet of ships that had been found in the port. The robust youth of the sea-coast were chained to the oar; and the Goths, satisfied with the success of their first naval expedition, returned in triumph to their new establishments in the kingdom of Bosphorus.

The second expedition of the Goths was undertaken with greater powers of men and ships; but they steered a different course, and, disdaining the exhausted provinces of Pontus, followed the western coast of the Euxine, passed before the wide mouths of the Borysthenes, the Dniester, and the Danube, and increasing their fleet by the capture of a great number of fishing barks, they approached the narrow outlet through which the Euxine Sea pours its waters into the Mediterranean, and divides the continents of Europe and Asia. The garrison of Chalcedon was encamped near the temple of Jupiter Urius, on a promontory that commanded the entrance of the Strait; and so dreaded were the invasions of the barbarians, that this body of troops surpassed in number the Gothic army. But it was in numbers alone that they surpassed it. They deserted with precipitation their advantageous post, and abandoned the town of Chalcedon, most plentifully stored with arms and money, to the discretion of the conquerors. While they hesitated whether they should prefer the sea or the land, Europe or Asia, for the scene of their hostilities, a perfidious fugitive pointed out Nicomedia, once the capital of the kings of Bithynia, as a rich and easy conquest. He guided the march, which was only sixty miles from the camp of Chalcedon, directed the resistless attack, and partook of the booty; for the Goths had learned sufficient policy to reward the traitor whom they detested. Nice, Prusa, Apamæa, Cius, cities that had sometimes rivalled, or imitated, the splendor of Nicomedia, were involved in the same calamity, which, in a few weeks, raged without control through the whole province of Bithynia. Three hundred years of peace, enjoyed by the soft inhabitants of Asia, had abolished the exercise of arms and removed the apprehension of danger. The ancient walls were suffered to molder away, and all the revenue of the most opulent cities was reserved for the construction of baths, temples, and theaters.

When the city of Cyzicus withstood the utmost effort of Mithridates, it was distinguished by wise laws, a naval power of two hundred galleys, and three arsenals; of arms, of military engines, and of corn. It was still the seat of wealth and luxury; but of its ancient strength nothing remained except the situation, in a little island of the Propontis, connected with the continent of Asia only by two bridges. From the recent sack of Prusa, the Goths advanced within eighteen miles of the city, which they had devoted to destruction; but the ruin of Cyzicus was delayed by a fortunate accident. The season was rainy, and the lake Apolloniates, the reservoir of all the springs of Mount Olympus, rose to an uncommon height. The little river of Rhyndacus, which issues from the lake, swelled into a broad and rapid stream, and stopped the progress of the Goths. Their retreat to the maritime city of Heraclea, where the fleet had probably been stationed, was attended by a long train of wagons, laden with the spoils of Bithynia, and was marked by the flames of Nice and Nicomedia, which they wantonly burned. Some obscure hints are mentioned of a doubtful combat that secured their retreat. But even a complete victory would have been of little moment, as the approach of the autumnal equinox summoned them to hasten their return. To navigate the Euxine before the month of May, or after that of September, is esteemed by the modern Turks the most unquestionable instance of rashness and folly.

When we are informed that the third fleet, equipped by the Goths in the ports of Bosphorus, consisted of five hundred sail of ships, our ready imagination instantly computes and multiplies the formidable armament; but as we are assured, by the judicious Strabo, that the piratical vessels used by the barbarians of Pontus and the Lesser Scythia were not capable of containing more than twenty-five or thirty men, we may safely affirm that fifteen thousand warriors, at the most, embarked in this great expedition. Impatient of the limits of the Euxine, they steered their destructive course from the Cimmerian to the Thracian Bosphorus. When they had almost gained the middle of the Straits, they were suddenly driven back to the entrance of them, till a favorable wind springing up the next day carried them in a few hours into the placid sea, or rather lake, of the Propontis. Their landing on the little island of Cyzicus was attended with the ruin of that ancient and noble city. From thence issuing again through the narrow passage of the Hellespont, they pursued their winding navigation amidst the numerous islands scattered over the Archipelago, or the Ægean Sea. The assistance of captives and deserters must have been very necessary to pilot their vessels and to direct their various incursions, as well on the coast of Greece as on that of Asia. At length the Gothic fleet anchored in the port of Piræus, five miles distant from Athens, which had attempted to make some preparations for a vigorous defense. Cleodamus, one of the engineers employed by the emperor's orders to fortify the maritime cities against the Goths, had already begun to repair the ancient walls fallen to decay since the time of Sylla. The efforts of his skill were ineffectual, and the barbarians became masters of the native seat of the muses and the arts. But while the conquerors abandoned themselves to the license of plunder and intemperance, their fleet, that lay with a slender guard in the harbor of Piræus, was unexpectedly attacked by the brave Dexippus, who, flying with the engineer Cleodamus from the sack of Athens, collected a hasty band of volunteers, peasants as well as soldiers, and in some measure avenged the calamities of his country.

But this exploit, whatever luster it might shed on the declining age of Athens, served rather to irritate than to subdue the undaunted spirit of the northern invaders. A general conflagration blazed out at the same

Left: A carved marble column-drum from the Temple of Artemis (Diana) at Ephesus. It shows Alcestis between Death (left) and Hermes (350–325 BC).
Right: Coins of the Sassanian Dynasty of Persia (AD 224–651): a gold stater of Ardashir (right) and a drachm of Sapor I (far right).

time in every district of Greece. Thebes and Argos, Corinth and Sparta, which had formerly waged such memorable wars against each other, were now unable to bring an army into the field, or even to defend their ruined fortifications. The rage of war, both by land and by sea, spread from the eastern point of Sunium to the western coast of Epirus. The Goths had already advanced within sight of Italy, when the approach of such imminent danger awakened the indolent Gallienus from his dream of pleasure. The emperor appeared in arms; and his presence seems to have checked the ardor and to have divided the strength, of the enemy. Naulobatus, a chief of the Heruli, accepted an honorable capitulation, entered with a large body of his countrymen into the service of Rome, and was invested with the ornaments of the consular dignity, which had never before been profaned by the hands of a barbarian. Great numbers of the Goths, disgusted with the perils and hardships of a tedious voyage, broke into Mæsia, with a design for forcing their way over the Danube to their settlements in the Ukraine. The wild attempt would have proved inevitable destruction if the discord of the Roman generals had not opened to the barbarians the means of an escape. The small remainder of this destroying host returned on board their vessels; and measuring back their way through the Hellespont and the Bosphorus, ravaged in their passage the shores of Troy, whose fame, immortalized by Homer, will probably survive the memory of the Gothic conquests. As soon as they found themselves in safety within the basin of the Euxine, they landed at Anchialus in

Thrace, near the foot of Mount Hæmus; and, after all their toils, indulged themselves in the use of those pleasant and salutary hot baths. What remained of the voyage was a short and easy navigation. Such was the various fate of this third and greatest of their naval enterprises. It may seem difficult to conceive how the original body of fifteen thousand warriors could sustain the losses and divisions of so bold an adventure. But as their numbers were gradually wasted by the sword, by shipwrecks, and by the influence of a warm climate, they were perpetually renewed by troops of banditti and deserters, who flocked to the standard of plunder, and by a crowd of fugitive slaves, often of German or Sarmatian extraction, who eagerly seized the glorious opportunity of freedom and revenge. In these expeditions, the Gothic nation claimed a superior share of honor and danger; but the tribes that fought under the Gothic banners are sometimes distinguished and sometimes confounded in the imperfect histories of that age; and as the barbarian fleets seemed to issue from the mouth of the Tanais, the vague but familiar appellation of Scythians was frequently bestowed on the mixed multitude.

Another circumstance is related of these invasions, which might deserve our notice, were it not justly to be suspected as the fanciful conceit of a recent sophist. We are told that in the sack of Athens the Goths had collected all the libraries, and were on the point of setting fire to this funeral pile of Grecian learning, had not one of their chiefs, of more refined policy than his brethren, dissuaded them from the design; by the profound observation that as long as the Greeks were addicted to the study of books, they would never apply themselves to the exercise of arms. The sagacious counselor (should the truth of the fact be admitted) reasoned like an ignorant barbarian. In the most polite and powerful nations, genius of every kind had displayed itself about the same period; and the age of science has generally been the age of military virtue and success.

The new sovereigns of Persia, Artaxerxes and his son Sapor, had triumphed over the house of Arsaces. Of the many princes of that ancient race, Chosroes, king of Armenia, had alone preserved both his life and his independence. He defended himself by the natural strength of his country; by the perpetual resort of fugitives and malcontents; by the alliance of the Romans, and, above all, by his own courage. Invincible in arms, during a thirty years' war, he was at length assassinated by the emissaries of Sapor, king of Persia. The patriotic satraps of Armenia, who asserted the freedom and dignity of the crown, implored the protection of Rome in favor of Tiridates the lawful heir. But the son of Chosroes was an infant, the allies were at a distance, and the Persian monarch advanced towards the frontier at the head of an irresistible force. Young Tiridates, the future hope of his country, was saved by the fidelity of a servant, and Armenia continued above twenty-seven years a reluctant province of the great monarchy of Persia. Elated with this easy conquest, and presuming on the distresses or the degeneracy of the Romans, Sapor obliged the strong garrisons of Carrhæ and Nisibis to surrender, and spread devastation and terror on either side of the Euphrates.

The loss of an important frontier, the ruin of a faithful and natural ally, and the rapid success of Sapor's ambition, affected Rome with a deep sense of the insult as well as of the danger. Valerian flattered himself that the vigilance of his lieutenants would sufficiently provide for the safety of the Rhine and of the Danube; but he resolved,

notwithstanding his advanced age, to march in person to the defense of the Euphrates. He passed the Euphrates, encountered the Persian monarch near the walls of Edessa, was (AD 260) vanquished and taken prisoner by Sapor.

The voice of history, which is often little more than the organ of hatred or flattery, reproaches Sapor with a proud abuse of the rights of conquest. We are told that Valerian, in chains, but invested with the Imperial purple, was exposed to the multitude, a constant spectacle of fallen greatness; and that whenever the Persian monarch mounted on horseback, he placed his foot on the neck of a Roman emperor. Whatever treatment the unfortunate Valerian might experience in Persia, it is at least certain that the only emperor of Rome who had ever fallen into the hands of the enemy languished away his life in hopeless captivity.

The emperor Gallienus, who had long supported with impatience the censorial severity of his father and colleague, received the intelligence of his misfortunes with secret pleasure and avowed indifference. 'I knew that my father was a mortal,' said he, 'and since he has acted as becomes a brave man, I am satisfied.' It is difficult to paint the light, the various, the inconstant character of Gallienus, which he displayed without constraint, as soon as he became sole possessor of the empire. When the great emergence of the state required his presence and attention, he was engaged in conversation with the philosopher Plotinus, wasting his time in trifling or licentious pleasures, preparing his initiation of the Grecian mysteries, or soliciting a place in the Areopagus of Athens. His profuse magnificence insulted the general poverty; the solemn ridicule of his triumphs impressed a deeper sense of the public disgrace. The repeated intelligence of invasions, defeats, and rebellions, he received with a careless smile; and singling out, with affected contempt, some particular production of the lost province, he carelessly asked whether Rome must be ruined unless it was supplied with linen from Egypt and Arras cloth from Gaul? There were, however, a few short moments in the life of Gallienus when, exasperated by some recent injury, he suddenly appeared the intrepid soldier and the cruel tyrant; till satiated with blood, or fatigued by resistance, he insensibly sunk into the natural mildness and indolence of his character.

At a time when the reins of government were held with so loose a hand, it is not surprising that a crowd of usurpers should start up in every province of the empire against the son of Valerian. The reign of Gallienus, distracted as it was, produced nineteen pretenders to the throne; Cyriades, Macrianus, Balista, Odenathus, and Zenobia in the east; in Gaul, and the western provinces, Posthumus, Lollianus, Victorinus and his mother Victoria, Marius, and Tetricus. In Illyricum and the confines of the Danube, Ignenuus, Regillianus, and Aureolus; in Pontus, Saturninus; in Isauria, Trebellianus; Piso in Thessaly; Valens in Achaia; Æmilianus in Egypt; and Celsus in Africa.

It is sufficiently known that the odious appellation of *Tyrant* was often employed by the ancients to express the illegal seizure of supreme power, without any reference to the abuse of it. Several of the pretenders, who raised the standard of rebellion against the emperor Gallienus, were shining models of virtue, and almost all possessed a considerable share of vigor and ability. Their merit had recommended them to the favor of Valerian.

But of the nineteen tyrants who started up under the reign of Gallienus, there was not one who enjoyed a life of peace or a natural death. As soon as they were invested with the bloody purple, they inspired their adherents with the same fears and ambition which had occasioned their own revolt.

However virtuous was their character, however pure their intentions, they found themselves reduced to the hard necessity of supporting their usurpation by frequent acts of rapine and cruelty. When they fell, they involved armies and provinces in their fall.

While the public forces of the state were dissipated in private quarrels, the defenseless provinces lay exposed to every invader. The bravest usurpers were compelled, by the perplexity of their situation, to conclude ignominious treaties with the common enemy, to purchase with oppressive tributes the neutrality or services of the barbarians, and to introduce hostile and independent nations into the heart of the Roman monarchy.

CHAPTER NINE

Reign of Claudius – defeat of the Goths – victories, triumph and death of Aurelian

[AD 268–275]

NDER the deplorable reigns of Valerian and Gallienus the empire was oppressed and almost destroyed by the soldiers, the tyrants, and the barbarians. It was saved by a series of great princes, who derived their obscure origin from the martial provinces of Illyricum. Within a period of about thirty years, Claudius, Aurelian, Probus, Diocletian and his colleagues, triumphed over the foreign and domestic enemies of the state, re-established, with the military discipline, the strength of the frontiers, and deserved the glorious title of Restorers of the Roman world.

The removal of an effeminate tyrant made way for a succession of heroes. The indignation of the people imputed all their calamities to Gallienus, and the far greater part were, indeed, the consequence of his dissolute manners and careless administration. He was even destitute of a sense of honor, which so frequently supplies the absence of public virtue; and as long as he was permitted to enjoy the possessions of Italy,

must have proved an object of the utmost importance to both armies. The Rhætian usurper, after receiving a total defeat and a dangerous wound, retired into Milan. The siege of that great city was immediately formed; the walls were battered with every engine in use among the ancients; and Aureolus, doubtful of his internal strength and hopeless of foreign succours, already anticipated the fatal consequences of unsuccessful rebellion.

His last resource was an attempt to seduce the loyalty of the besiegers. He scattered libels through their camp, inviting the troops to desert an unworthy master, who sacrificed the public happiness to his luxury, and the lives of his most valuable subjects to the slightest suspicions. The arts of Aureolus diffused fears and discontent among the principal officers of his rival. A conspiracy was formed. The death of Gallienus was resolved, and, notwithstanding their desire of first terminating the siege of Milan, the extreme danger which accompanied every moment's delay obliged them to hasten the execution of their

Left: The ruins of Baalbek, Lebanon.

Left: The ruins of the great Temple of Bacchus, Baalbek. (Second century AD)

a victory of the barbarians, the loss of a province, or the rebellion of a general, seldom disturbed the tranquil course of his pleasures. At length a considerable army, stationed on the Upper Danube, invested with the Imperial purple their leader Aureolus, who, disdaining a confined and barren reign over the mountains of Rhætia, passed the Alps, occupied Milan, threatened Rome, and challenged Gallienus to dispute in the field the sovereignty of Italy. The emperor, provoked by the insult, and alarmed by the instant danger, suddenly exerted that latent vigor which sometimes broke through the indolence of his temper. Forcing himself from the luxury of the palace, he appeared in arms at the head of his legions, and advanced beyond the Po to encounter his competitor. The corrupted name of Pontirolo still preserves the memory of a bridge over the Adda, which, during the action,

daring purpose. Encompassed by his declared or concealed enemies, he soon received a mortal dart from an uncertain hand. Before he expired, a patriotic sentiment rising in the mind of Gallienus induced him to name a deserving successor, and it was his last request that the Imperial ornaments should be delivered to Claudius, who then commanded a detached army in the neighborhood of Pavia. The report at least was diligently propagated, and the order cheerfully obeyed by the conspirators, who had already agreed to place Claudius on the throne. In the first news of the emperor's death the troops expressed some suspicion and resentment, till the one was removed and the other assuaged by a donative of twenty pieces of gold to each soldier. They then ratified the election and acknowledged the merit of their new sovereign.

The obscurity which covered the origin of Claudius, it sufficiently betrays the meanness of his birth. We can only discover that he was a native of one of the provinces bordering on the Danube, that his youth was spent in arms, and that his modest valor attracted the favor and confidence of Decius.

In the arduous task which Claudius had undertaken of restoring the empire to its ancient splendor, it was first necessary to revive among his troops a sense of order and obedience. With the authority of a veteran commander, he represented to them that the relaxation of discipline had introduced a long train of disorders, the effects of which were at length experienced by the soldiers themselves; that a people ruined by oppression, and indolent from despair, could no longer supply a numerous army with the means of luxury, or even of subsistence; that the danger of each individual had increased with the despotism of the military order, since princes who tremble on the throne will guard their safety by the instant sacrifice of every obnoxious subject. The emperor expatiated on the mischiefs of a lawless caprice, which the soldiers could only gratify at the expense of their own blood, as their seditious elections had so frequently been followed by civil wars, which consumed the flower of the legions either in the field of battle or in the cruel abuse of victory. He painted in the most lively colors the exhausted state of the treasury, the desolation of the provinces, the disgrace of the Roman name, and the insolent triumph of rapacious barbarians. It was against those barbarians, he declared, that he intended to point the first effort of their arms. Tetricus might reign for a while over the West, and even Zenobia might preserve the dominion of the East. These usurpers were his personal adversaries, nor could he think of indulging any private resentment till he had saved an empire whose impending ruin would, unless it was timely prevented, crush both the army and the people.

The various nations of Germany and Sarmatia who fought under the Gothic standard had already collected an armament more formidable than any which had yet issued from the Euxine. On the banks of the Dneister, one of the great rivers that discharge themselves into that sea, they constructed a fleet of two thousand, or even six thousand vessels; numbers which, however incredible they may seem, would have been insufficient to transport their pretended army of three hundred and twenty thousand barbarians. Whatever might be the real strength of the Goths, the vigor and success of the expedition were not adequate to the greatness of the preparations. In their passage through the Bosphorus the unskilfull pilots were overpowered by the violence of the current; and while the multitude of their ships were crowded in a narrow channel, many were dashed against each other or against the shore. The barbarians made several descents on the coasts both of Europe and Asia; but the open country was already plundered, and they were repulsed with shame and loss from the fortified cities which they assaulted. A spirit of discouragement and division arose in the fleet, and some of their chiefs sailed away toward the islands of Crete and Cyprus; but the main body, pursuing a more steady course, anchored at length near the foot of Mount Athos, and assaulted the city of Thessalonica, the wealthy capital of all the Macedonian provinces. Their attacks, in which they displayed a fierce but artless bravery, were soon interrupted by the rapid approach of Claudius, hastening to a scene of action that deserved the presence of a warlike prince at the

head of the remaining powers of the empire. Impatient for battle, the Goths immediately broke up their camp, relinquished the siege of Thessalonica, left their navy at the foot of Mount Athos, traversed the hills of Macedonia, and pressed forwards to engage the last defense of Italy.

We still possess an original letter addressed by Claudius to the senate and people on this memorable occasion. 'Conscript fathers,' says the emperor, 'I know that three hundred and twenty thousand Goths have invaded the Roman territory. If I vanquish them, your gratitude will reward my services. Should I fall, remember that I am the successor of Gallienus. The whole republic is fatigued and exhausted. We shall fight after Valerian, after Ingenuus, Regillianus, Lollianus, Posthumus, Celsus, and a thousand others, whom a just contempt for Gallienus provoked into rebellion. We are in want of darts, of spears, and of shields. The strength of the empire, Gaul, and Spain, are usurped by Tetricus; and we blush to acknowledge that the archers of the East serve under the banners of Zenobia. Whatever we shall perform will be sufficiently great.' The melancholy firmness of this epistle announces a hero careless of his fate, conscious of his danger, but still deriving a well-grounded hope from the resources of his own mind.

The event surpassed his own expectations and those of the world. By the most signal victories he delivered the empire from his host of barbarians, and was distinguished by posterity under the glorious appellation of the Gothic Claudius. The imperfect historians of an irregular war do not enable us to describe the order and circumstances of his exploits; but, if we could be indulged in the allusion, we might distribute into three acts this memorable tragedy. The decisive battle was fought near Naissus, a city of Dardania. The legions at first gave way, oppressed by numbers and dismayed by misfortunes. Their ruin was inevitable, had not the abilities of their emperor prepared a seasonable relief. A large detachment, rising out of the secret and difficult passes of the mountains, which by his order they had occupied, suddenly assailed the rear of the victorious Goths. The favorable instant was improved by the activity of Claudius. He revived the courage of his troops, restored their ranks, and pressed the barbarians on every side. Fifty thousand men are reported to have been slain in the battle of Naissus. Several large bodies of barbarians, covering their retreat with a movable fortification of wagons, retired, or rather escaped, from the field of slaughter. We may presume that some insurmountable difficulty – the fatigue, perhaps, or the disobedience, of the conquerors – prevented Claudius from completing in one day the destruction of the Goths. The war was diffused over the provinces of Mæsia, Thrace, and Macedonia, and its operations drawn out into a variety of marches, surprises, and tumultuary engagements, as well as by sea as by land. When the Romans suffered any loss, it was commonly occasioned by their own cowardice or rashness; but the superior talents of the emperor, his perfect knowledge of the country, and his judicious choice of measures as well as officers, assured on most occasions the success of his arms. The immense booty, the fruit of so many victories, consisted for the greater part of cattle and slaves. A select body of the Gothic youth was received among the imperial troops; the remainder was sold into servitude; and so considerable was the number of female

captives that every soldier obtained as his share two or three women. A circumstance from which we may conclude that the invaders entertained some designs of settlement as well as of plunder; since even in a naval expedition they were accompanied by their families. The loss of their fleet, which was either taken or sunk, had intercepted the retreat of the Goths. A vast circle of Roman posts, distributed with skill, supported with firmness, and gradually closing towards a common center, forced the barbarians into the most inaccessible parts of Mount Hæmus, where they found a safe refuge, but a very scanty subsistence. During the course of a rigorous winter, in which they were besieged by the emperor's troops, famine and pestilence, desertion and the sword, continually diminished the imprisoned multitude.

On the return of spring nothing appeared in arms except a hardy and desperate band, the remnant of that mighty host which had embarked at the mouth of the Dniester.

The pestilence which swept away such numbers of the barbarians at length proved fatal to their conqueror. After a short but glorious reign of two years, Claudius expired at Sirmium, amidst the tears and acclamations of his subjects. In his last illness he convened the principal officers of the state and army, and in their presence recommended Aurelian, one of his generals, as the most deserving of the throne, and the best qualified to execute the great design which he himself had been permitted only to undertake. The virtues of Claudius, his valor, affability, justice, and temperance, his love of fame and of his country, place him in that short list of emperors who added luster to the Roman purple. Those virtues, however, were celebrated with peculiar zeal and complacency by the courtly writers of the age of Constantine, who was the great-grandson of Crispus, the elder brother of Claudius. The voice of flattery was soon taught to repeat that the gods, who so hastily had snatched Claudius from the earth, rewarded his merit and piety by the perpetual establishment of the empire in his family.

Notwithstanding these oracles, the greatness of the Flavian family (a name which it had pleased them to assume) was deferred above twenty years, and the elevation of Claudius occasioned the immediate ruin of his brother Quintilius, who possessed not sufficient moderation or courage to descend into the private station to which the patriotism of the late emperor had condemned him. Without delay or reflection he assumed the purple at Aquileia, where he commanded a considerable force; and though his reign lasted only seventeen days, he had time to obtain the sanction of the senate and to experience a mutiny of the troops. As soon as he was informed that the great army of the Danube had invested the well-known valor of Aurelian with Imperial power; he sunk under the fame and merit of his rival; and, ordering his veins to be opened, prudently withdrew himself from the unequal contest.

Above: Reconstruction of the Temple of Bacchus, Baalbek, Lebanon.
Bottom left: Ruins of the once glorious city of Palmyra or Tadmor, Syria, besieged by Aurelian.
Right: Bust of Aqmat, Palmyran princess, daughter of Hagago. (Late second century AD)

The great terrace and the Temple of Bacchus, Baalbek.

The reign of Aurelian lasted only four years and about nine months; but every instant of that short period was filled by some memorable achievement. He put an end to the Gothic war, chastised the Germans who invaded Italy, recovered Gaul, Spain, and Britain out of the hands of Tetricus, and destroyed the proud monarchy which Zenobia had erected in the East on the ruins of the afflicted empire.

The death of Claudius had revived the fainting spirit of the Goths. The troops which guarded the passes of Mount Hæmus and the banks of the Danube had been drawn away by the apprehension of a civil war; and it seems probable that the remaining body of the Gothic and Vandalic tribes embraced the favorable opportunity, abandoned their settlements of the Ukraine, traversed the rivers, and swelled with new multitudes the destroying host of their countrymen. Their united numbers were at length encountered by Aurelian, and the bloody and doubtful conflict ended only with the approach of night. Exhausted by so many calamities, which they had mutually endured and inflicted during a twenty years' war, the Goths and the Romans consented to a lasting and beneficial treaty. It was earnestly solicited by the barbarians, and cheerfully ratified by the legions, to whose suffrage the prudence of Aurelian referred the decision of that important question. The Gothic nation engaged to supply the armies of Rome with a body of two thousand auxiliaries, consisting entirely of cavalry, and stipulated in return an undisturbed retreat, with a regular market as far as the Danube, provided by the emperor's care, but at their own expense.

But the most important condition of peace was understood rather than expressed in the treaty. Aurelian withdrew the Roman forces from Dacia, and tacitly relinquished that great province to the Goths and Vandals. His manly judgment convinced him of the solid advantages, and taught him to despise the seeming disgrace, of thus contracting the frontiers of the monarchy. The Dacian subjects, removed from those distant possessions which they were unable to cultivate or defend, added strength and populousness to the southern side of the Danube.

While the vigorous and moderate conduct of Aurelian restored the Illyrian frontier, the nation of the Alemanni violated the conditions of peace which either Gallienus had purchased, or Claudius had imposed, and, inflamed by their impatient youth, suddenly flew to arms. Forty

thousand horse appeared in the field, and the numbers of the infantry doubled those of the cavalry. The first objects of their avarice were a few cities of the Rhætian frontier; but their hopes soon rising with success, the rapid march of the Alemanni traced a line of devastation from the Danube to the Po.

As the light troops of the Alemanni had spread themselves from the Alps to the Apennine, the incessant vigilance of Aurelian and his officers was exercised in the discovery, the attack, and the pursuit of the numerous detachments. Notwithstanding this desultory war, three considerable battles are mentioned, in which the principal force of both armies was obstinately engaged. The success was various. In the first, fought near Placentia, the Romans received so severe a blow that, according to the expression of a writer extremely partial to Aurelian, the immediate dissolution of the empire was apprehended, but at length, after a dreadful slaughter, the patient firmness of the emperor rallied his troops, and restored, in some degree, the honor of his arms. The second battle was fought near Fano in Umbria; on the spot which, five hundred years before, had been fatal to the brother of Hannibal. Thus far the successful Germans had advanced along the Æmilian and Flaminian way, with a design of sacking the defenseless mistress of the world. But Aurelian, who, watchful for the safety of Rome, still hung on their rear, found in this place the decisive moment of giving them a total and irretrievable defeat. The flying remnant of their host was exterminated in a third and last battle near Pavia; and Italy was delivered from the inroads of the Alemanni.

The victory of Claudius over the Goths, and the success of Aurelian against the Alemanni, had already restored to the arms of Rome their ancient superiority over the barbarous nations of the North. To chastise domestic tyrants, and to reunite the dismembered parts of the empire, was a task reserved for the second of those warlike emperors. Though he was acknowledged by the senate and people, the frontiers of Italy, Africa, Illyricum, and Thrace, confined the limits of his reign. Gaul, Spain, and Britain, Egypt, Syria, and Asia Minor, were still possessed by two rebels, who alone, out of so numerous a list, had hitherto escaped the dangers of their situation; Tetricus governor of the peaceful province of Aquitaine and Zenobia, the celebrated Queen of Palymra and the East.

Aurelian had no sooner secured the person and provinces of Tetricus than he turned his arms against Zenobia. She claimed her descent from the Macedonian kings of Egypt, equalled in beauty her ancestor Cleopatra, and far surpassed that princess in chastity and valor. Zenobia was esteemed the most lovely as well as the most heroic of her sex. She was of a dark complexion (for in speaking of a lady these trifles become important). Her teeth were of a pearly whiteness, and her large black

Pagan priest dressed in high conical shaped hats lighting the sacrificial fire. (Frescoes from Dura Europos, Syria)

eyes sparkled with uncommon fire, tempered by the most attractive sweetness. Her voice was strong and harmonious. Her manly understanding was strengthened and adorned by study. She was not ignorant of the Latin tongue, but possessed in equal perfection of the Greek, the Syriac, and the Egyptian languages. She had drawn up for her own use an epitome of oriental history, and familiarity compared the beauties of Homer and Plato under the tuition of the sublime Longinus.

When Aurelian passed over into Asia, against an adversary whose sex alone could render her an object of contempt, his presence restored obedience to the province of Bithynia, already shaken by the arms and intrigues of Zenobia. Advancing at the head of his legions, he accepted the submission of Ancyra, and was admitted into Tyana, after an obstinate siege, by the help of a perfidious citizen.

Zenobia would have ill deserved her reputation had she indolently permitted the emperor of the West to approach within an hundred miles of her capital. The fate of the East was decided in two great battles; so similar in almost every circumstance, that we can scarcely distinguish them from each other, except by observing that the first was fought near Antioch, and the second near Emesa. After the defeat of Emesa, Zenobia found it impossible to collect a third army. As far as the frontier of Egypt, the nations subject to her empire had joined the standard of the conqueror, who detached Probus, the bravest of his generals, to possess himself of the Egyptian provinces. Palmyra was the last resource of the widow of Odenathus. She retired within the walls of her capital, made every preparation for a vigorous resistance, and declared, with the intrepidity of a heroine, that the last moment of her reign and of her life should be the same.

In his march over the sandy desert between Emesa and Palmyra, the emperor Aurelian was perpetually harassed by the Arabs; nor could he always defend his army, and especially his baggage, from those flying troops of active and daring robbers, who watched the moment of surprise, and eluded the slow pursuit of the legions. The siege of Palmyra was an object far more difficult and important, and the emperor, who, with incessant vigor, pressed the attacks in person, was himself wounded with a dart. 'The Roman people,' says Aurelian, in an original letter, 'speak with contempt of the war which I am waging against a woman. They are ignorant both of the character and of the power of Zenobia. It is impossible to enumerate her warlike preparations, of stones, of arrows, and of every species of missile weapons. Every part of the walls is provided with two or three *balistæ*, and artificial fires are thrown from her military engines. The fear of punishment has armed her with a desperate courage. Yet still I trust in the protecting deities of Rome, who have hitherto been favorable to all my undertakings.' Doubtful, however, of the protection of the gods, and of the event of the siege, Aurelian judged it more prudent to offer terms of an advantageous capitulation; to the queen, a splendid retreat; to the citizens, their ancient privileges. His proposals were obstinately rejected, and the refusal was accompanied with insult.

The firmness of Zenobia was supported by the hope that in a very short time famine would compel the Roman army to repass the desert; and by the reasonable expectation that the kings of the East, and particularly the Persian monarch, would arm in the defense of their most natural ally. But fortune and the perseverance of Aurelian overcame every obstacle. The death of Sapor, which happened about this time, distracted the councils of Persia, and the inconsiderable succors that attempted to relieve Palmyra were easily intercepted either by the arms or the liberality of the emperor. From every part of Syria a regular succession of convoys safely arrived in the camp, which was increased by the return of Probus with his victorious troops from the conquest of Egypt. It was then that Zenobia resolved to fly. She mounted the fleetest of her dromedaries, and had already reached the banks of the Euphrates, about sixty miles from Palmyra, when she was overtaken by the pursuit of Aurelian's light horse, seized and brought back a captive to the feet of the emperor.

Aurelian might now congratulate the senate, the people, and himself, that, in little more than three years, he had restored universal peace and order to the Roman world.

Since the foundation of Rome no general had more nobly deserved a triumph than Aurelian; nor was a triumph ever celebrated with superior pride and magnificence. The pomp was opened by twenty elephants, four royal tigers, and above two hundred of the most curious animals from every climate of the North, the East, and the South. They were followed by sixteen hundred gladiators, devoted to the cruel amusement of the amphitheater. The wealth of Asia, the arms and ensigns of so many conquered nations, and the magnificent plate and wardrobe of the Syrian queen, were disposed in exact symmetry or artful disorder. The ambassadors of the most remote parts of the earth, of Æthiopia, Arabia, Persia, Bactriana, India, and China, all remarkable by their rich or singular dresses, displayed the fame and power of the Roman emperor, who exposed likewise to the public view the presents that he had received, and particularly a great number of crowns of gold, the offerings of grateful cities.

So long and so various was the pomp of Aurelian's triumph that, although it opened with the dawn of day, the slow majesty of the procession ascended not the Capitol before the ninth hour; and it was already dark when the emperor returned to the palace. The festival was protracted by theatrical representations, the games of the circus, the hunting of wild beasts, combats of gladiators, and naval engagements. Liberal donatives were distributed to the army and people, and several institutions, agreeable or beneficial to the city, contributed to perpetrate the glory of Aurelian.

The arms of Aurelian had vanquished the foreign and domestic foes of the republic. We are assured that, by his salutary rigor, crimes and factions, mischievous arts and pernicious connivance, the luxuriant growth of a feeble and oppressive government, were eradicated throughout the Roman world. But if we attentively reflect how much swifter is the progress of corruption than its cure, and if we remember that the years abandoned to public disorders exceeded the months allotted to the martial reign of Aurelian, we must confess that a few short intervals of peace were insufficient for the arduous work of reformation.

It was observed by one of the most sagacious of the Roman princes, that the talents of his predecessor Aurelian were better suited to the command of an army than to the government of an empire. His own secretary, whom he had accused of extortion, conspired against him, and, he was felled by the hand of Mucapor, a general whom he had always loved and trusted. He died regretted by the army, detested by the senate, but universally acknowledged as a warlike and fortunate prince, the useful though severe reformer of a degenerate state.

Detail of the great triumphal arch, Palmyra, Syria.

CHAPTER TEN

Conduct of the army and senate after the death of Aurelian – reigns of Tacitus, Probus, Carus and his son

[AD 275–285]

SUCH was the unhappy condition of the Roman emperors, that, whatever might be their conduct, their fate was commonly the same. A life of pleasure or virtue, of severity or mildness, of indolence or glory, alike led to an untimely grave; and almost every reign is closed by the same disgusting repetition of treason and murder. The death of Aurelian, however, is remarkable by its extraordinary consequences. The legions admired, lamented, and revenged their victorious chief. The artifice of his perfidious secretary was discovered and punished. The deluded conspirators attended the funeral of their injured sovereign with sincere or well-feigned contrition, and submitted to the unanimous resolution of the military order, which was signified by the following epistle: 'The brave and fortunate armies to the senate and people of Rome – The crime of one man, and the error of many, have deprived us of the late emperor Aurelian. May it please you, venerable lords and fathers! to place him in the number of the gods, and to appoint a successor whom your judgement shall

The contention that ensued is one of the best attested but most improbable events in the history of mankind? The troops, as if satiated with the exercise of power, again conjured the senate to invest one of its own body with the Imperial purple. The senate still persisted in its refusal; the army in its request. The reciprocal offer was pressed and rejected at least three times, and, whilst the obstinate modesty of either party was resolved to receive a master from the hands of the other, eight months insensibly elapsed; an amazing period of tranquil anarchy, during which the Roman world remained without a sovereign, without an usurper, and without a sedition. The generals and magistrates appointed by Aurelian continued to execute their ordinary functions; and it is observed that a proconsul of Asia was the only considerable person removed from his office in the whole course of the interregnum.

On the twenty-fifth of September, near eight months after the murder of Aurelian, the consul convoked an assembly of the senate, and reported the doubtful and dangerous situation of the empire. He

Left: Pont-du-Gard, the Roman aqueduct built in the first century BC by Agrippa, 300m long and 50m high, to carry water into Nîmes. This three-tiered aqueduct is one of the most spectacular feats of Roman engineering.

Left: Roman road over Wheeldale Moor, North Yorkshire. Swift means of transport for the militia and the civil population were facilitated by a network of trunk roads which spread out from Rome across the Empire. Like the aqueducts, these were often constructed by soldiers who, apart from their military duties, were employed as architects and engineers.

declare worthy of the Imperial purple! None of those whose guilt or misfortune have contributed to our loss shall ever reign over us.' The Roman senators heard, without surprise, that another emperor had been assassinated in his camp; they secretly rejoiced in the fall of Aurelian; but the modest and dutiful address of the legions, when it was communicated in full assembly by the consul, diffused the most pleasing astonishment. Such honors as fear and perhaps esteem could extort they liberally poured forth on the memory of their deceased sovereign. Such acknowledgments as gratitude could inspire they returned to the faithful armies of the republic, who entertained so just a sense of the legal authority of the senate in the choice of an emperor. Yet, notwithstanding this flattering appeal, the most prudent of the assembly declined exposing their safety and dignity to the caprice of an armed multitude. The strength of the legions was, indeed, a pledge of their sincerity, since those who may command are seldom reduced to the necessity of dissembling; but could it naturally be expected that a hasty repentance would correct the inveterate habits of fourscore years? Should the soldiers relapse into their accustomed seditions, their insolence might disgrace the majesty of the senate and prove fatal to the object of its choice. Motives like these dictated a decree by which the election of a new emperor was referred to the suffrage of the military order.

slightly insinuated that the precarious loyalty of the soldiers depended on the chance of every hour and of every accident; but he represented, with the most convincing eloquence, the various dangers that might attend any farther delay in the choice of an emperor. Intelligence, he said, was already received that the Germans had passed the Rhine and occupied some of the strongest and most opulent cities of Gaul. The ambition of the Persian king kept the East in perpetual alarms; Egypt, Africa, and Illyricum were exposed to foreign and domestic arms; and the levity of Syria would prefer even a female scepter to the sanctity of the Roman laws. The consul then, addressing himself to Tacitus, the first of the senators, required his opinion on the important subject of a proper candidate for the vacant throne.

If we can prefer personal merit to accidental greatness, we shall esteem the birth of Tacitus more truly noble than that of kings. He claimed his descent from the philosophic historian whose writing will instruct the last generations of mankind. The senator Tacitus was then seventy-five years of age. The long period of his innocent life was adorned with wealth and honors. He had twice been invested with the consular dignity, and enjoyed with elegance and sobriety his ample patrimony of between two and three millions sterling. The experience of so many princes, whom he had esteemed or endured, from the vain follies of Elagabalus to the useful rigor of Aurelian, taught him to form a just estimate of the duties, the dangers, and the temptations of their sublime station. From the assiduous study of his immortal ancestor he derived the knowledge of the Roman constitution and of human nature. The voice of the people had already named Tacitus as the citizen the most worthy of empire.

As soon as the tumult of acclamations subsided, Tacitus attempted to decline the dangerous honor, and to express his wonder that they should elect his age and infirmities to succeed the martial vigor of Aurelian.

The reluctance of Tacitus, and it might possibly be sincere, was encountered by the affectionate obstinacy of the senate. Five hundred voices repeated at once, in eloquent confusion, that the greatest of the Roman princes, Numa, Trajan, Hadrian, and the Antonines, had ascended the throne in a very advanced season of life; that the mind, not the body, a sovereign, not a soldier, was the object of their choice; and that they expected from him no more than to guide by his wisdom the valor of the legions.

While the deceased emperor was making preparations for a second expedition into the East, he had negotiated with the Alani, a Scythian people, who pitched their tents in the neighborhood of the lake Mæotis. These barbarians, allured by presents and subsidies, had promised to invade Persia with a numerous body of light cavalry. They were faithful to their engagements; but when they arrived on the Roman frontier Aurelian was already dead, the design of the Persian war was at least suspended, and the generals who, during the interregnum, exercised a doubtful authority, were unprepared either to receive or to oppose them. Provoked by such treatment, which they considered as trifling and perfidious, the Alani had recourse to their own valor for their payment and revenge; and as they moved with the usual swiftness of Tartars, they had soon spread themselves over the provinces of Pontus, Cappadocia, Cilicia, and Galatia. The legions who, from the opposite shores of the Bosphorus, could almost distinguish the flames of the cities and villages, impatiently urged their general to lead them against the invaders. The conduct of Tacitus was suitable to his age and

Scenes of the Nile showing a detail of a funeral procession. (Roman mosaic from Palestrina, I BC–AD I)

The Graeco-Roman Temple
of Philae, Egypt.

station. He convinced the barbarians of the faith, as well as of the power, of the empire. Great numbers of the Alani, appeased by the punctual discharge of the engagements which Aurelian had contracted with them, relinquished their booty and captives, and quietly retreated to their own deserts beyond the Phasis. Against the remainder, who refused peace, the Roman emperor waged, in person, a successful war. Seconded by an army of brave and experienced veterans, in a few weeks he delivered the provinces of Asia from the terror of the Scythian invasion.

But the glory and life of Tacitus were of short duration. Transported in the depth of winter from the soft retirement of Campania to the foot of Mount Caucasus, he sunk under the unaccustomed hardships of a military life. The fatigues of the body were aggravated by the cares of the mind. For a while the angry and selfish passions of the soldiers had been suspended by the enthusiasm of public virtue. They soon broke out with redoubled violence, and raged in the camp, and even in the tent of the aged emperor. It may be doubtful whether the soldiers imbrued their hands in the blood of this innocent prince. It is certain that their insolence was the cause of his death. He expired at Tyana in Cappadocia, after a reign of only six months and about twenty days.

The eyes of Tacitus were scarcely closed before his brother Florianus showed himself unworthy to reign by the hasty usurpation of the purple, without expecting the approbation of the senate. The reverence for the Roman constitution, which yet influenced the camp and the provinces, was sufficiently strong to dispose them to censure, but not to provoke them to oppose, the precipitate ambition of Florianus. The discontent would have evaporated in idle murmurs, had not the general of the East, the heroic Probus, boldly declared himself the avenger of the senate. The contest, however, was still unequal; nor could the most able leader, at the head of the effeminate troops of Egypt and Syria, encounter, with any hopes of victory, the legions of Europe, whose irresistible strength appeared to support the brother of Tacitus. But the fortune and activity of Probus triumphed over every obstacle. The hardy veterans of his rival, accustomed to cold climates, sickened and consumed away in the sultry heats of Cilicia, where the summer proved remarkably unwholesome. Their numbers were diminished by frequent desertion, the passes of the mountains were feebly defended; Tarsus opened its gates; and the soldiers of Florianus, when they had permitted him to enjoy the Imperial title about three months, delivered the empire from civil war by the easy sacrifice of a prince whom they despised.

His acknowledged merit, and the success of his arms against Florianus, left him without an enemy or a competitor. Yet, if we may credit his own professions, very far from being desirous of the empire, he had accepted it with the most sincere reluctance. The reign of Probus corresponded with this fair beginning. The senate was permitted to direct the civil administration of the empire. Their faithful general asserted the honor of the Roman arms, and often laid at their feet crowns of gold and barbaric trophies, the fruits of his numerous victories. Yet, whilst he gratified their vanity, he must secretly have despised their indolence and weakness. Though it was every moment in

their power to repeal the disgraceful edict of Gallienus, the proud successors of the Scipios patiently acquiesced in their exclusion from all military employments. They soon experienced that those who refuse the sword must renounce the scepter.

The strength of Aurelian had crushed on every side the enemies of Rome. After his death they seemed to revive with an increase of fury and of numbers. They were again vanquished by the active vigor of Probus, who, in a short reign of about six years, equalled the fame of ancient heroes, and restored peace and order to every province of the Roman world.

But the most important service which Probus rendered to the republic was the deliverance of Gaul, and the recovery of seventy flourishing cities oppressed by the barbarians of Germany, who, since the death of Aurelian, had ravaged that great province with impunity. The deliverance of Gaul is reported to have cost the lives of four hundred thousand of the invaders; a work of labor to the Romans, and of expense to the emperor, who gave a piece of gold for the head of every barbarian. But as the fame of warriors is built on the destruction of human kind, we may naturally suspect that the sanguinary account was multiplied by the avarice of the soldiers, and accepted without any very severe examination by the liberal vanity of Probus.

Since the expedition of Maximin, the Roman generals had confined their ambition to a defensive war against the nations of Germany, who perpetually pressed on the frontiers of the empire. The more daring Probus pursued his Gallic victories, passed the Rhine, and displayed his invincible eagles on the banks of the Elbe and the Neckar. He was fully convinced that nothing could reconcile the minds of the barbarians to peace, unless they experienced in their own country the calamities of war. Germany, exhausted by the ill success of the last emigration, was astonished by his presence. Nine of the most considerable princes repaired to his camp, and fell prostrate at his feet. Such a treaty was humbly received by the Germans as it pleased the conqueror to dictate.

Among the useful conditions of peace imposed by Probus on the vanquished nations of Germany was the obligation of supplying the Roman army with sixteen thousand recruits, the bravest and most robust of their youth. The emperor dispersed them through all the provinces, and distributed this dangerous reinforcement, in small bands of fifty or sixty each, among the national troops; judiciously observing that the aid which the republic derived from the barbarians should be felt but not seen.

The arms of Probus had now suppressed all the foreign and domestic enemies of the state. His mild but steady administration confirmed the re-establishment of the public tranquillity; nor was there left in the provinces a hostile barbarian, a tyrant, or even a robber, to revive the memory of past disorders. It was time that the emperor should revisit Rome, and celebrate his own glory and the general happiness. The triumph due to the valor of Probus was conducted with a magnificence suitable to his fortune; and the people, who had so lately admired the trophies of Aurelian, gazed with equal pleasure on those of his heroic successor.

The military discipline which reigned in the camps of Probus was less cruel than that of Aurelian, but it was equally rigid and exact.

But in the persecution of a favorite scheme, the best of men, satisfied with the rectitude of their intentions, are subject to forget the bounds of moderation; nor did Probus himself sufficiently consult the patience and disposition of his fierce legionaries. The dangers of the military profession seem only to be compensated by a life of pleasure and idleness; but if the duties of the soldier are incessantly aggravated by the labors of the peasant, he will at last sink under the intolerable burden or shake it off with indignation. The imprudence of Probus is said to have inflamed the discontent of his troops. More attentive to the interests of mankind than to those of the army, he expressed the vain hope that, by the establishment of universal peace, he should soon abolish the necessity of a standing and mercenary force. The un-guarded expression proved fatal to him. In one of the hottest days of summer, as he severely urged the unwholesome labor of draining the marshes of Sirmium, the soldiers, impatient of fatigue, on a sudden threw down their tools, grasped their arms, and broke out into a furious mutiny. The emperor, conscious of his danger, took refuge in a lofty tower constructed for the purpose of surveying the progress of the work. The tower was instantly forced, and a thousand swords were plunged at once into the bosom of the unfortunate Probus. The rage of the troops subsided as soon as it had been gratified. They then lamented their fatal rashness, forgot the severity of the emperor whom they had massacred, and hastened to perpetuate, by an honorable monument, the memory of his virtues and victories.

When the legions had indulged their grief and repentance for the death of Probus, their unanimous consent declared Carus, his Prætorian præfect, the most deserving of the Imperial throne. Notwithstanding the severe justice which he exercised against the assassins of Probus, to whose favor and esteem he was highly indebted, he could not escape the suspicion of being accessory to a deed from whence he derived the principal advantage. He enjoyed, at least before his elevation, an acknowledged character of virtue and abilities; but his austere temper insensibly degenerated into moroseness and cruelty; and the imperfect writers of his life almost hesitate whether they shall not rank him in the number of Roman tyrants. When Carus assumed the purple he was about sixty years of age, and his two sons, Carinus and Numerian, had already attained the season of manhood.

The authority of the senate expired with Probus; nor was the repentance of the soldiers displayed by the same dutiful regard for the civil power which they had testified after the unfortunate death of Aurelian. The election of Carus was decided without expecting the approbation of the senate, and the new emperor contented himself with announcing, in a cold and stately epistle, that he had ascended the vacant throne. A behavior so very opposite to that of his amiable predecessor afforded no favorable presage of the new reign: and the Romans, deprived of power and freedom, asserted their privilege of licentious murmurs.

The Temple of Isis, Aswan, Elephantine Island, Egypt.

It is more than probable that these elegant trifles never reached the ears of a veteran general who, with the consent of the legions, was preparing to execute the long-suspended design of the Persian war. Before his departure for this distant expedition, Carus conferred on his two sons, Carinus and Numerian, the title of Cæsar, and, investing the former with almost an equal share of the Imperial power, directed the young prince first to suppress some troubles which had arisen in Gaul, and afterwards to fix the seat of his residence at Rome, and to assume the government of the Western provinces. The safety of Illyricum was confirmed by a memorable defeat of the Sarmatians; sixteen thousand of those barbarians remained on the field of battle, and the number of captives amounted to twenty thousand. The old emperor, animated with the fame and prospect of victory, pursued his march, in the midst of winter, through the countries of Thrace and Asia Minor, and at length, with his younger son Numerian, arrived on the confines of the Persian monarchy. There, encamping on the summit of a lofty mountain, he pointed out to his troops the opulence and luxury of the enemy whom they were about to invade.

Above: The Roman theater at Pompeii.
Top left: An amusing scene showing the River Nile in flood with hippopotami and alligators. (Mosaic from Palestrina, I BC–AD I)
Bottom left: Roman musicians – pipe and tambourine players from Pompeii. (First century AD, National Archeological Museum, Naples)
Right: Roman actors preparing to go on stage. Note the comic masks on the right. (Mosaic from Pompeii, first century AD)

The successor of Artaxerxes, Varanes, or Bahram, though he had subdued the Segestans, one of the most warlike nations of Upper Asia, was alarmed at the approach of the Romans, and endeavored to retard their progress by a negotiation of peace. His ambassadors entered the camp about sunset, at the time when the troops were satisfying their hunger with a frugal repast. The Persians expressed their desire of being introduced to the presence of the Roman emperor. The conference was conducted with the same disregard of courtly elegance. Carus, taking off a cap which he wore to conceal his baldness, assured the ambassadors that, unless their master acknowledged the superiority of Rome, he would speedily render Persia as naked of trees as his own head was destitute of hair. Notwithstanding some traces of art and preparation, we may discover in this scene the manners of Carus, and the severe simplicity which the martial princes who succeeded Gallienus had already restored in the Roman camps. The ministers of the Great King trembled and retired.

The threats of Carus were not without effect. He ravaged Mesopotamia, cut in pieces whatever opposed his passage, made himself master of the great cities of Seleucia and Ctesiphon (which seem to have surrendered without resistance), and carried his victorious arms beyond the Tigris. He had seized the favorable moment for an invasion. The Persian councils were distracted by domestic factions, and the greater part of their forces were detained on the frontiers of India. Rome and the East received with transport the news of such important advantages. Flattery and hope painted in the most lively colors the fall of Persia, the conquest of Arabia, the submission of Egypt, and a lasting deliverance from the inroads of the Scythian nations. But the reign of Carus was destined to expose the vanity of predictions. They were scarcely uttered before they were contradicted by his death; circumstances that it may be related in a letter from his own secretary to the præfect of the city. 'Carus,' says he, 'our dearest emperor, was confined by sickness to his bed, when a furious tempest arose in the camp. The darkness which overspread the sky was so thick that we could no longer distinguish each other; and the incessant flashes of lightning took from us the knowledge of all that passed in the general confusion. Immediately after the most violent clap of thunder we heard a sudden cry that the emperor was dead; and it soon appeared that his chamberlains, in a rage of grief, had set fire to the royal pavilion, a circumstance which gave rise to the report that Carus was killed by lightning. But, as far as we have been able to investigate the truth, his death was the natural effect of his disorder.'

The vacancy of the throne was not productive of any disturbance. The ambition of the aspiring generals was checked by their mutual fears; and young Numerian, with his absent brother Carinus, were unanimously acknowledged as Roman emperors.

The only merit of the administration of Carinus that history could record, or poetry celebrate, was the uncommon splendor with which, in his own and his brother's name, he exhibited the Roman games of the theater, the circus, and the ampitheater. More than twenty years afterwards, when the courtiers of Diocletian represented to their frugal sovereign the fame and popularity of his munificent predecessor, he acknowledged that the reign of Carinus had indeed been a reign of pleasure. But this vain prodigality, which the prudence of Diocletian might justly despise, was enjoyed with surprise and transport by the Roman people. The oldest of the citizens, recollecting the spectacles of former days, the triumphal pomp of Probus or Aurelian, and the secular games of the emperor Philip, acknowledged that they were all surpassed by the superior magnificence of Carinus.

In the midst of this glittering pageantry, the emperor Carinus, secure of his fortune, enjoyed the acclamations of the people, the flattery of his courtiers, and the songs of the poets, who, for want of a more essential merit, were reduced to celebrate the divine graces of his person. In the same hour, but at the distance of nine hundred miles from Rome, his brother expired; and a sudden revolution transferred into the hands of a stranger the scepter of the house of Carus.

The sons of Carus never saw each other after their father's death. The arrangements which their new situation required were probably deferred till the return of the younger brother to Rome, where a triumph was decreed to the young emperors for the glorious success of

Portrait of a young woman found in a mummy case in a Roman cemetery at Hawwarat in Fayyum, Egypt. (Second century AD, possibly by a Greek painter, British Museum)

the Persian war. It is uncertain whether they intended to divide between them the administration or the provinces of the empire; but it is very unlikely that their union would have proved of any long duration. The jealousy of power must have been inflamed by the opposition of characters. In the most corrupt of times Carinus was unworthy to live: Numerian deserved to reign in a happier period. His affable manners and gentle virtues secured him, as soon as they became known, the regard and affections of the public. He possessed the elegant accomplishments of a poet and orator, which dignify as well as adorn the humblest and the most exalted station. His eloquence, however it was applauded by the senate, was formed not so much on the model of Cicero as on that of the modern declaimers; but in an age very far from being destitute of poetic merit, he contended for the prize with the most celebrated of his contemporaries, and still remained the friend of his rivals; a circumstance which evinces either the goodness of his heart, or the superiority of his genius. But the talents of Numerian were rather of the contemplative than of the active kind. When his father's elevation reluctantly forced him from the shade of retirement, neither his temper nor his pursuits had qualified him for the command of armies. His constitution was destroyed by the hardships of the Persian war; and he had contracted, from the heat of the climate, such a weakness in his eyes, as obliged him, in the course of a long retreat, to confine himself to the solitude and darkness of a tent or litter. The administration of all affairs, civil as well as military, was devolved on Arrius Aper, the Prætorian præfect, who, to the power of his important office, added the honor of being father-in-law to Numerian. The Imperial pavilion was strictly guarded by his most trusty adherents; and during many days Aper delivered to the army the supposed mandates of their invisible sovereign.

It was not till eight months after the death of Carus that the Roman army, returning by slow marches from the banks of the Tigris, arrived on those of the Thracian Bosphorus. The legions halted at Chalcedon in Asia, while the court passed over to Heraclea, on the European side of the Propontis. But a report soon circulated through the camp, at first in secret whispers, and at length in loud clamors, of the emperor's death, and of the presumption of his ambitious minister, who still exercised the sovereign power in the name of a prince who was no more. The impatience of the soldiers could not long support a state of suspense. With rude curiosity they broke into the imperial tent, and discovered only the corpse of Numerian. The gradual decline of his health might have induced them to believe that his death was natural; but the concealment was interpreted as an evidence of guilt, and the measures which Aper had taken to secure his election became the immediate occasion of his ruin. Yet, even in the transport of their rage and grief, the troops observed a regular proceeding, which proves how firmly discipline had been re-established by the martial successors of Gallienus. A general assembly of the army was appointed to be held at Chalcedon, whither Aper was transported in chains, as a prisoner and a criminal. A vacant tribunal was erected in the midst of the camp, and the generals and tribunes formed a great military council. They soon announced to the multitude that their choice had fallen on Diocletian,

commander of the domestics or body-guards, as the person most capable of revenging and succeeding their beloved emperor. The future fortunes of the candidate depended on the chance or conduct of the present hour. Conscious that the station which he had filled exposed him to some suspicions, Diocletian ascended the tribunal, and, made a solemn profession of his own innocence. Then, assuming the tone of a sovereign and a judge, he commanded that Aper should be brought in chains to the foot of the tribunal. 'This man,' said he, 'is the murderer of Numerian'; and without giving him time to enter on a dangerous justification, drew his sword, and buried it in the breast of the unfortunate præfect. A charge supported by such decisive proof was admitted without contradiction, and the legions, with repeated acclamations, acknowledged the justice and authority of the emperor Diocletian.

Before we enter upon the memorable reign of that prince, it will be proper to punish and dismiss the unworthy brother of Numerian. Carinus possessed arms and treasures sufficient to support his legal title to the empire. But his personal vices overbalanced every advantage of birth and situation. The most faithful servants of the father despised the incapacity, and dreaded the cruel arrogance of the son. The hearts of the people were engaged in favor of his rival, and even the senate were inclined to prefer an usurper to a tyrant. The arts of Diocletian inflamed the general discontent; and the winter was employed in secret intrigues and open preparations for a civil war. In the spring the forces of the East and of the West encountered each other in the plains of Margus, a small city of Mæsia, in the neighborhood of the Danube. The troops, so lately returned from the Persian war, had acquired their glory at the expense of health and numbers, nor were they in a condition to contend with the unexhausted strength of the legions of Europe. Their ranks were broken, and, for a moment, Diocletian despaired of the purple and life. But the advantage which Carus had obtained by the valor of his soldiers he quickly lost by the infidelity of his officers. A tribune, whose wife he had seduced, seized the opportunity of revenge, and by a single blow extinguished civil discord in the blood of the adulterer.

Detail of the columns of the Græco-Roman Temple of Philae.

CHAPTER ELEVEN

The reign of Diocletian and his three associates, Maximian, Galerius, and Constantius

general re-establishment of order and tranquillity – the new form of administration –
abdication and retirement of Diocletian and Maximian

[AD 285–313]

As the reign of Diolectian was more illustrious than that of any of his predecessors, so was his birth more abject and obscure. The strong claims of merit and of violence had frequently superseded the ideal prerogatives of nobility; but a distinct line of separation was hitherto preserved between the free and the servile part of mankind. The parents of Diocletian had been slaves in the house of Anulinus, a Roman senator; nor was he himself distinguished by any other name than that which he derived from a small town in Dalmatia, from whence his mother deduced her origin. It is, however, probable that his father obtained the freedom of the family, and that he soon acquired an office of scribe, which was commonly exercised by persons of his condition. Favorable oracles, or rather the consciousness of superior merit, prompted his aspiring son to pursue the profession of arms and the hopes of fortune; and it would be extremely curious to observe the gradation of arts and accidents which enabled him in the end to fulfill those oracles, and to display that merit to the world. Diocletian was successively promoted to the government of Mæsia, the honors of the consulship, and the important command of the guards of the palace. He distinguished his abilities in the Persian war; and after the death of Numerian, the slave, by the confession and judgment of his rivals, was declared the most worthy of the Imperial throne. The malice of religious zeal, while it arraigns the savage fierceness of his colleague Maximian, has affected to cast suspicions on the personal courage of the emperor Diocletian. It would not be easy to persuade us of the cowardice of a soldier of fortune who acquired and preserved the esteem of the legions, as well as the favor of so many warlike princes. Yet even calumny is sagacious enough to discover and to attack the most vulnerable part. The valor of Diocletian was never found inadequate to his duty, or to the occasion; but he appears not to have possessed the daring and generous spirit of a hero, who courts danger and fame, disdains artifice, and boldly challenges the allegiance of his equals. His abilities were useful rather than splendid – a vigorous mind improved by the experience and study of mankind; dexterity and application in business; a judicious mixture of liberality and economy, of mildness and rigor; profound dissimulation under the disguise of military frankness; steadiness to pursue his ends; flexibility to vary his means; and, above all, the great art of submitting his own passions, as well as those of others, to the interest of his ambition, and of coloring his ambition with the most specious pretences of justice and public utility. Like Augustus, Diocletian may be considered as the founder of a new empire. Like the adopted son of Cæsar, he was distinguished as a statesman rather than as a warrior; nor did either of those princes employ force, whenever their purpose could be effected by policy.

The victory of Diocletian was remarkable for its singular mildness. A people accustomed to applaud the clemency of the conqueror, if the usual punishments of death, exile, and confiscation were inflicted with any degree of temper and equity, beheld, with the most pleasing astonishment, a civil war, the flames of which were extinguished in the field of battle. Diocletian received into his confidence Aristobulus, the principal minister of the house of Carus, respected the lives, the fortunes, and the dignity of his adversaries, and even continued in their respective stations the greater number of the servants of Carinus. It is not improbable that motives of prudence might assist the humanity of the artful Dalmatian: of these servants, many had purchased his favor by secret treachery; in others, he esteemed their grateful fidelity to an unfortunate master. The discerning judgment of Aurelian, of Probus, and of Carus, had filled the several departments of the state and army with officers of approved merit, whose removal would have injured the public service, without promoting the interest of the successor. Such a conduct, however, displayed to the Roman world the fairest prospect of the new reign, and the emperor affected to confirm this favorable prepossession by declaring that, among all the virtues of his predecessors, he was the most ambitious of imitating the humane philosophy of Marcus Antoninus.

The first considerable action of his reign seemed to evince his sincerity as well as his moderation. After the example of Marcus, he gave himself a colleague in the person of Maximian, on whom he bestowed at first the title of Cæsar, and afterwards that of Augustus. But the motives of his conduct, as well as the object of his choice, were of a very different nature from those of his admired predecessor. By investing a luxurious youth with the honors of the purple, Marcus had

Left: Marble bust of Diocletian. (Izmir Archeological Museum, Turkey)
Below: Bas relief in porphyry of Diocletian embracing Maximian.
(The Vatican, Rome)

Reconstruction of the Mausoleum at Diocletian's palace near Spalato.
(Mostra Augustea, Rome)

discharged a debt of private gratitude, at the expense, indeed, of the happiness of the state. By associating a friend and fellow-soldier to the favors of government, Diocletian, in a time of public danger, provided for the defense both of the East and of the West. Maximian was born a peasant, and, like Aurelian, in the territory of Sirmium. Ignorant of letters, careless of laws, the rusticity of his appearance and manners still betrayed in the most elevated fortune the meanness of his extraction. War was the only art which he professed. In a long course of service he had distinguished himself on every frontier of the empire; and though his military talents were formed to obey rather than to command, though, perhaps, he never attained the skill of a consummate general, he was capable, by his valor, constancy, and experience, of executing the most arduous undertakings. Notwithstanding the difference of their characters, the two emperors maintained, on the throne, that friendship which they had contracted in a private station. The haughty turbulent spirit of Maximian, so fatal afterwards to himself and to the public peace, was accustomed to respect the genius of Diocletian and confessed the ascendant of reason over brutal violence. From a motive either of pride or superstition, the two emperors assumed the titles, the one of Jovius, the other of Herculius. Whilst the motion of the world (such was the language of their venal orators) was maintained by the all-seeing wisdom of Jupiter, the invincible arm of Hercules purged the earth from monsters and tyrants.

But even the omnipotence of Jovius and Herculius was insufficient to sustain the weight of the public administration. The prudence of Diocletian discovered that the empire, assailed on every side by the barbarians, required on every side the presence of a great army and of an emperor. With this view, he resolved once more to divide his unwieldly power, and, with the inferior title of *Cæsars*, to confer on two generals of approved merit an equal share of the sovereign authority. Galerius, surnamed Armentarius, from his original profession of a herdsman, and Constantius, who from his pale complexion had acquired the denomination of Chlorus, were the two persons invested with the second honors of the Imperial purple. The defense of Gaul, Spain, and Britain was intrusted to Constantius: Galerius was stationed on the banks of the Danube, as the safeguard of the Illyrian provinces. Italy and Africa were considered as the department of Maximian; and for his peculiar portion Diocletian reserved Thrace, Egypt, and the rich countries of Asia.

Notwithstanding the policy of Diocletian, it was impossible to maintain an equal and undisturbed tranquillity during the reign of twenty years, and along a frontier of many hundred miles. Sometimes the barbarians suspended their domestic animosities, and the relaxed vigilance of the garrisons sometimes gave a passage to their strength or dexterity. Whenever the provinces were invaded, Diocletian conducted himself with that calm dignity which he had always affected or possessed; reserved his presence for such occasions as were worthy of his interposition, never exposed his person or reputation to any unnecessary danger, ensured his success by every means that prudence could suggest, and displayed, with ostentation, the consquences of his victory. In wars of a more difficult nature, and more doubtful event, he employed the rough valor of Maximian; and that faithful soldier was content to ascribe his own victories to the wise counsels and auspicious influence of his benefactor. But after the adoption of the two Cæsars, the emperors, themselves retiring to a less laborious scene of action, devolved on their adopted sons the defense of the Danube and of the Rhine. The vigilant Galerius was never reduced to the necessity of vanquishing an army of barbarians on the Roman territory. The brave and active Constantius delivered Gaul from a very furious inroad of the Alemanni; and his victories of Langres and Vindonissa appear to have been actions of considerable danger and merit. As he traversed the open country with a feeble guard, he was encompassed on a sudden by the superior multitude of the enemy. He retreated with difficulty towards Langres; but, in the general consternation, the citizens refused to open their gates, and the wounded prince was drawn up the wall by the means of a rope. But, on the news of his distress, the Roman troops hastened from all sides to his relief, and before the evening he had satisfied his honor and revenge by the slaughter of six thousand Alemanni. From the monuments of those times the obscure traces of several other victories over the barbarians of Sarmatia and Germany might possibly be collected; but the tedious search would not be rewarded either with amusement or with instruction.

The conduct which the emperor Probus had adopted in the disposal of the vanquished was imitated by Diocletian and his associates. The captive barbarians, exchanging death for slavery, were distributed among the provincials, and assigned to those districts (in Gaul, the territories of Amiens, Beauvais, Cambrai, Trèves, Langres, and Troyes, are particularly specified) which had been depopulated by the calamities of war. They were usefully employed as shepherds and husbandmen, but were denied the exercise of arms, except when it was found expedient to enroll them in the military service. Nor did the emperors refuse the property of lands, with a less servile tenure, to such of the barbarians as solicited the protection of Rome. They granted a settlement to several colonies of the Carpi, the Bastarnæ, and the Sarmatians; and, by a dangerous indulgence, permitted them in some measure to retain their national manners and independence. Among the provincials it was a subject of flattering exultation that the barbarian, so lately an object of terror, now cultivated their lands, drove their cattle to the neighboring fair, and contributed by his labor to the public plenty. They congratulated their masters on the powerful accession of subjects and soldiers; but they forgot to observe that multitudes of secret enemies, insolent from favor, or desperate from oppression, were introduced into the heart of the empire.

The arduous work of rescuing the distressed empire from tyrants

Coin of Maximian.
(British Museum, London)

and barbarians had now been completely achieved by a succession of Illyrian peasants. As soon as Diocletian entered into the twenty-fifth year of his reign, he celebrated that memorable era, as well as the success of his arms, by the pomp of a Roman triumph. Maximian, the equal partner of his power, was his only companion in the glory of that day. The two Cæsars had fought and conquered, but the merit of their exploits was ascribed, according to the rigor of ancient maxims, to the auspicious influence of their fathers and emperors. The triumph of Diocletian and Maximian was less magnificent, perhaps, than those of Aurelian and Probus, but in the eyes of posterity this triumph is remarkable by a distinction of a less honorable kind. It was the last that Rome ever beheld. Soon after this period the emperors ceased to vanquish, and Rome ceased to be the capital of the empire.

Diocletian and Maximian were the first Roman princes who fixed, in time of peace, their ordinary residence in the provinces; and their conduct, however it might be suggested by private motives, was justified by very specious considerations of policy. The court of the emperor of the West was, for the most part, established at Milan, whose situation, at the foot of the Alps, appeared far more convenient than that of Rome, for the important purpose of watching the motions of the

The extent of the empire under Diocletian under whose reign the empire was successfully united for a period of twenty years.

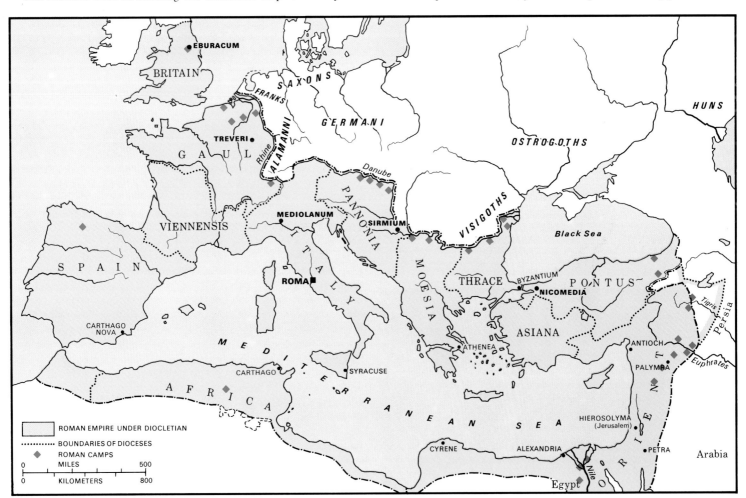

Left: The Senate House (*Curia*) of Diocletian in the Forum, Rome.

Below right: The four tetrarchs: Diocletian and his three colleagues. Diocletian transformed the governmental system into a tetrarchy or four-man rule. (Porphyry sculpture on the facade of St Mark's, Venice, c 300 AD)

barbarians of Germany. Milan soon assumed the splendor of an Imperial city. To rival the majesty of Rome was the ambition likewise of Diocletian, who employed his leisure and the wealth of the East in the embellishment of Nicomedia, a city placed on the verge of Europe and Asia, almost at an equal distance between the Danube and the Euphrates.

The dislike expressed by Diocletian towards Rome and Roman freedom was not the effect of momentary caprice, but the result of the most artful policy. That crafty prince had framed a new system of Imperial government, which was afterwards completed by the family of Constantine; and as the image of the old constitution was religiously preserved in the senate, he resolved to deprive that order of its small remains of power and consideration. We may recollect, about eight years before the elevation of Diocletian, the transient greatness of the ambitious hopes of the Roman senate. As long as that enthusiasm prevailed, many of the nobles imprudently displayed their zeal in the cause of freedom; and after the successors of Probus had withdrawn their countenance from the republican party, the senators were unable

Pagans sacrificing an ox, ram and pig. The state religion of the Romans was rigorously observed by Diocletian under whose administration the Christians were severely persecuted. (Relief from the Decennial Monument in the Roman Forum)

to disguise their impotent resentment. As the sovereign of Italy, Maximian was intrusted with the care of extinguishing this troublesome rather than dangerous spirit, and the task was perfectly suited to his cruel temper. The most illustrious members of the senate, whom Diocletian always affected to esteem, were involved, by his colleague, in the accusation of imaginary plots; and the possession of an elegant villa, or a well-cultivated estate, was interpreted as a convincing evidence of guilt. The camp of the Prætorians, which had so long oppressed, began to protect, the majesty of Rome; and as those haughty troops were conscious of the decline of their power, they were naturally disposed to unite their strength with the authority of the senate. By the prudent measures of Diocletian, the numbers of the Prætorians were insensibly reduced, their privileges abolished, and their place supplied by two faithful legions of Illyricum, who, under the new titles of Jovians and Herculians, were appointed to perform the service of the Imperial guards. But the most fatal though secret wound which the senate received from the hands of Diocletian and Maximian was inflicted by the inevitable operation of their absence. As long as the emperors resided at Rome, that assembly might be oppressed, but it could scarcely be neglected. The successors of Augustus exercised the power of dictating whatever laws their wisdom or caprice might suggest; but those laws were ratified by the sanction of the senate. The model of ancient freedom was preserved in its deliberation and decrees; and wise princes, who respected the prejudices of the Roman people, were in some measure obliged to assume the language and behavior suitable to the general and first magistrate of the republic. In the armies and in the provinces they displayed the dignity of monarchs; and when they fixed their residence at a distance from the capital, they for ever laid aside the dissimulation which Augustus had recommended to his successors. In the exercise of the legislative as well as the executive power, the sovereign advised with his ministers, instead of consulting the great council of the nation. The name of the senate was mentioned with honor till the last period of the empire; the vanity of its members were still flattered with honorary distinctions; but the assembly which had so long been the source, and so long the instrument of power, was respectfully suffered to sink into oblivion. The senate of Rome, losing all connection with the Imperial court and the actual constitution, was left a venerable but useless monument of antiquity on the Capitoline hill.

When the Roman princes had lost sight of the senate and of their ancient capital, they easily forgot the origin and nature of their legal power. The civil offices of consul, of proconsul, of censor, and of tribune, by the union of which it had been formed, betrayed to the people its republican extraction. Those modest titles were laid aside; and if they still distinguished their high station by the appellation of Emperor, or *Imperator*, that word was understood in a new and more dignified sense, and no longer denoted the general of the Roman armies, but the sovereign of the Roman world.

From the time of Augustus to that of Diocletian, the Roman princes, conversing in a familiar manner among their fellow-citizens, were saluted only with the same respect that was usually paid to senators and magistrates. Their principal distinction was the Imperial or military robe of purple; whilst the senatorial garment was marked by a broad, and the equestrian by a narrow, band or stripe of the same honorable color. The pride, or rather the policy, of Diocletian, engaged that artful prince to introduce the stately magnificence of the court of Persia. Diocletian was a man of sense, who, in the course of private as well as public life, had formed a just estimate both of himself and of mankind: nor is it easy to conceive that in substituting the manners of Persia to those of Rome he was seriously actuated by so mean a principle as that of vanity. He flattered himself that an ostentation of splendor and luxury would subdue the imagination of the multitude; that the monarch would be less exposed to the rude license of the people and the soldiers, as his person was secluded from the public view; and that habits of submission would insensibly be productive of sentiments of veneration. Like the modesty affected by Augustus, the state main-

tained by Diocletian was a theatrical representation; but it must be confessed that, of the two comedies, the former was of a much more liberal and manly character than the latter. It was the aim of the one to disguise, and the object of the other to display, the unbounded power which the emperors possessed over the Roman world.

Ostentation was the first principle of the new system instituted by Diocletian. The second was division. He divided the empire, the provinces, and every branch of the civil as well as military administration. He multiplied the wheels of the machine of government, and rendered its operations less rapid but more secure.

He had associated three colleagues in the exercise of the supreme power; and as he was convinced that the abilities of a single man were inadequate to the public defense, he considered the joint administration of four princes not as a temporary expedient, but as a fundamental law of the constitution. It was his intention that the two elder princes should be distinguished by the use of the diadem and the title of *Augusti*; that, as affection or esteem might direct their choice, they should regularly call to their assistance two subordinate colleagues; and that the *Cæsars*, rising in their turn to the first rank, should supply an uninterrupted succession of emperors. The empire was divided into four parts. The East and Italy were the most honorable, the Danube and the Rhine the most laborious stations. The former claimed the presence of the *Augusti*, the latter were intrusted to the administration of the *Cæsars*. The strength of the legions was in the hands of the four partners of sovereignty, and the despair of successively vanquishing four formidable rivals might intimidate the ambition of an aspiring general. In their civil government the emperors were supposed to exercise the undivided power of the monarch, and their edicts, inscribed with their joint names, were received in all the provinces as promulgated by their mutual councils and authority. Notwithstanding these precautions, the political union of the Roman world was gradually dissolved, and a principle of division was introduced, which, in the course of a few years, occasioned the perpetual separation of the eastern and western empires.

It was in the twenty-first year of his reign that Diocletian executed his memorable resolution of abdicating the empire. On the same day, which was the first of May, Maximian, as it had been previously concerted, made his resignation of the Imperial dignity at Milan. As he wished to secure the obedience of Maximian, he exacted from him either a general assurance that he would submit his actions to the authority of his benefactor, or a particular promise that he would descend from the throne whenever he should receive the advice and the example. This engagement, though it was confirmed by the solemnity of an oath before the altar of the Capitoline Jupiter, would have proved a feeble restraint on the fierce temper of Maximian, whose passion was the love of power, and who neither desired peasant tranquillity nor future reputation. But he yielded, however reluctantly, to the ascendant which his wiser colleague had acquired over him, and retired immediately after his abdication to a villa in Lucania, where it was almost impossible that such an impatient spirit could find any lasting tranquillity.

Diocletian, who, from a servile origin, had raised himself to the throne, passed the nine last years of his life in a private condition. Reason had dictated, and content seems to have accompanied, his retreat, in which he enjoyed for a long time the respect of those princes to whom he had resigned the possession of the world. It is seldom that minds long exercised in business have formed any habits of conversing with themselves, and in the loss of power they principally regret the want of occupation. The amusement of letters and of devotion, which afford so many resources in solitude, were incapable of fixing the attention of Diocletian: but he had preserved, or at least he soon recovered, a taste for the most innocent as well as natural pleasures, and his leisure hours were sufficiently employed in building, planting, and gardening. His answer to Maximian is deservedly celebrated. He was solicited by that restless old man to reassume the reins of government and the Imperial purple. He rejected the temptation with a smile of pity, calmly observing, that, if he could show Maximian the cabbages which he had planted with his own hands at Salona, he should no longer be urged to relinquish the enjoyment of happiness for the pursuit of power.

CHAPTER TWELVE

Troubles after the abdication of Diocletian – death of Constantius

elevation of Constantine and Maxentius and Licinius – reunion of the empire under the authority of Constantine

[AD 305–324]

THE balance of power established by Diocletian subsisted no longer than while it was sustained by the firm and dexterous hand of the founder. It required such a fortunate mixture of different tempers and abilities as could be found, or even expected, a second time; two emperors without jealousy, two Cæsars without ambition and the same general interest invariably pursued by four independent princes. The abdication of Diocletian and Maximian was succeeded by eighteen years of discord and confusion. The empire was afflicted by five civil wars; and the remainder of the time was not so much a state of tranquillity as a suspension of arms between several hostile monarchs, who, viewing each other with an eye of fear and hatred, strove to increase their respective forces at the expense of their subjects.

As soon as Diocletian and Maximian had resigned the purple, their station, according to the rules of the new constitution, was filled by the two Cæsars, Constantius and Galerius, who immediately assumed the title of Augustus. The honors of seniority and precedence were allowed to the former of those princes, and he continued under a new appellation to administer his ancient department of Gaul, Spain, and Britain.

After the elevation of Constantius and Galerius to the rank of *Augusti*, two new *Cæsars* were required to supply their place, and to complete the system of the Imperial government. Diocletian was sincerely desirous of withdrawing himself from the world; he considered Galerius, who had married his daughter, as the firmest support of his family and of the empire; and he consented, without reluctance, that his successor should assume the merit as well as the envy of the important nomination. It was fixed without consulting the interest or inclination of the princes of the West. Each of them had a son who was arrived at the age of manhood, and who might have been deemed the most natural candidates for the vacant honor. But the impotent resentment of Maximian was no longer to be dreaded; and the moderate Constantius, though he might despise the dangers, was humanely apprehensive of the calamities, of civil war. The two persons whom Galerius promoted to the rank of Cæsar were much better suited to serve the views of his ambition. The first of these was Daza, or, as he was afterwards called, Maximin, whose mother was the sister of Galerius. He was invested by Diocletian with the purple, exalted to the dignity of Cæsar, and intrusted with the sovereign command of Egypt and Syria. At the same time Severus was sent to Milan to receive from the reluctant hands of Maximian the Cæsarian ornaments and the possession of Italy and Africa. According to the forms of the constitution, Severus acknowledged the supremacy of the western emperor; but he was absolutely devoted to the commands of his benefactor Galerius, who, reserving to himself the intermediate countries from the confines of Italy to those of Syria, firmly established his power over three-fourths of the monarchy. In the full confidence that the approaching death of Constantius would leave him sole master of the Roman world, we are assured that he had arranged in his mind a long succession of future princes, and that he meditated his own retreat from public life after he should have accomplished a glorious reign of about twenty years.

But, within less than eighteen months, two unexpected revolutions overturned the ambitious schemes of Galerius. The hopes of uniting the western provinces to his empire were disappointed by the elevation of Constantine; while Italy and Africa were lost by the successful revolt of Maxentius.

The fame of Constantine has rendered posterity attentive to the most minute circumstances of his life and actions. The place of his birth, as well as the condition of his mother Helena, have been the subject not only of literary but of national disputes. Notwithstanding the recent tradition which assigns for her father a British king, we are obliged to confess that Helena was the daughter of an innkeeper; but at the same time we may defend the legality of her marriage against those who have represented her as the concubine of Constantius. The great Constantine was most probably born at Naissus, in Dacia. He was about eighteen years of age when his father was promoted to the rank of Cæsar. Instead of following Constantius in the West, he remained in the service of Diocletian, signalizing his valor in the wars of Egypt and Persia, and gradually rose to the honorable station of a tribune of the first order. The favor of the people and soldiers, who had named him as a worthy candidate for the rank of Cæsar, served only to exasperate the

Above: Detail from the Arch of Constantine, Rome.
Left: Colossal head of Constantine (Flavius Valerius Constantinus AD 285–337; Roman Emperor AD 306–307).

jealousy of Galerius; and though prudence might restrain him from exercising any open violence, an absolute monarch is seldom at a loss how to execute a sure and secret revenge. Every hour increased the danger of Constantine and the anxiety of his father, who, by repeated letters, expressed the warmest desire of embracing his son. For some time the policy of Galerius supplied him with delays and excuses, but it was impossible long to refuse so natural a request of his associate without maintaining his refusal by arms. The permission of the journey was reluctantly granted, and, whatever precautions the emperor might have taken to intercept a return, the consequences of which he with so much reason apprehended, they were effectually disappointed by the incredible diligence of Constantine. Leaving the palace of Nicomedia in the night, he travelled post through Bithynia, Thrace, Dacia, Pannonia, Italy, and, amidst the joyful acclamations of the people, reached the port of Boulogne in the very moment when his father was preparing to embark for Britain.

The British expedition, and an easy victory over the barbarians of Caledonia, were the last exploits of the reign of Constantius. He ended his life in the Imperial palace of York, fifteen months after he had received the title of Augustus, and almost fourteen months after he had been promoted to the rank of Cæsar. His death was immediately succeeded by the elevation of Constantine. The ideas of inheritance and succession are so very familiar that the generality of mankind consider them as founded not only in reason but in nature itself. Our imagination readily transfers the same principles from private property to public dominion: and whenever a virtuous father leaves behind him a son whose merit seems to justify the esteem, or even the hopes, of the people, the joint influence of prejudice and of affection operates with irresistible weight. The flower of the western armies had followed Constantius into Britain, and the national troops were reinforced by a numerous body of Alemanni, who obeyed the orders of Crocus, one of their hereditary chieftains. The opinion of their own importance, and the assurance that Britain, Gaul, and Spain would acquiesce in their nomination, were diligently inculcated to the legions by the adherents of Constantine. The soldiers were asked whether they could hesitate a moment between the honor of placing at their head the worthy son of their beloved emperor and the ignominy of tamely expecting the arrival of some obscure stranger, on whom it might please the sovereign of Asia to bestow the armies and provinces of the West? It was insinuated to them that gratitude and liberality held a distinguished place among the virtues of Constantine; nor did that artful prince show himself to the troops till they were prepared to salute him with the names of Augustus and Emperor. The throne was the object of his desires; and had he been less actuated by ambition, it was his only means of safety. He was well acquainted with the character and sentiments of Galerius, and sufficiently apprised that, if he wished to live, he must determine to reign. The decent, and even obstinate, resistance which he chose to affect was contrived to justify his usurpation; nor did he yield to the acclamations of the army till he had provided the proper materials for a letter, which he immediately dispatched to the emperor of the East.

Constantine informed him of the melancholy event of his father's death, modestly asserted his natural claim to the succession, and respectfully lamented that the affectionate violence of his troops had not permitted him to solicit the Imperial purple in the regular and constitutional manner. The first emotions of Galerius were those of surprise, disappointment, and rage; and, as he could seldom restrain his passions, he loudly threatened that he would commit to the flames both the letter and the messenger. But his resentment insensibly subsided; and when he recollected the doubtful chance of war, when he had weighed the character and strength of his adversary, he consented to embrace the honorable accommodation which the prudence of Constantine had left open to him.

In his last moments Constantius bequeathed to his eldest son the care of the safety, as well as greatness, of the family.

The ambitious spirit of Galerius was scarcely reconciled to the disappointment of his views upon the Gallic provinces before the unexpected loss of Italy wounded his pride as well as power in a still more sensible part. The long absence of the emperors had filled Rome with discontent and indignation; and the people gradually discovered that the preference given to Nicomedia and Milan was not to be ascribed to the particular inclination of Diocletian, but to the permanent form of government which he had instituted. It was in vain that, a few months after his abdication, his successors dedicated, under his name, those magnificent baths whose ruins still supply the ground as well as the materials for so many churches and convents. The tranquillity of those elegant recesses of ease and luxury was disturbed by the impatient murmurs of the Romans, and a report was insensibly circulated that the sums expended in erecting those buildings would soon be required at their hands. About that time the avarice of Galerius, or perhaps the exigencies of the state, had induced him to make a very strict and rigorous inquisition into the property of his subjects for the purpose of a general taxation, both on their lands and on their persons. A very minute survey appears to have been taken of their real estates; and, wherever there was the slightest suspicion of concealment, torture was very freely employed to obtain a sincere declaration of their personal wealth. The privileges which had exalted Italy above the rank

Left: Coin showing the relief of London by Constantius Chlorus, the father of Constantine. (London Museum)

Right: The battle of Constantine against Maxentius at Milvian Bridge outside Rome, 28 October, AD 312. (Painting by Raphael, 1483–1520 now in the Vatican, Rome)

of the provinces were no longer regarded: and the officers of the revenue already began to number the Roman people, and to settle the proportion of the new taxes. Even when the spirit of freedom had been utterly extinguished, the tamest subjects have sometimes ventured to resist an unprecedented invasion of their property; but on this occasion the injury was aggravated by the insult, and the sense of private interest was quickened by that of national honor. The conquest of Macedonia had delivered the Roman people from the weight of personal taxes. Though they had experienced every form of despotism, they had now enjoyed that exemption near five hundred years; nor could they patiently brook the insolence of an Illyrian peasant, who, from his distant residence in Asia, presumed to number Rome among the tributary cities of his empire. The rising fury of the people was encouraged by the authority, or at least the connivance, of the senate; and the feeble remains of the Prætorian guards, who had reason to apprehend their own dissolution, embraced so honorable a pretense, and declared their readiness to draw their swords in the service of their oppressed country. It was the wish, and it soon became the hope, of every citizen that, after expelling from Italy their foreign tyrants, they should elect a prince who, by the place of his residence, and by his maxims of government, might once more deserve the title of Roman emperor. The name, as well as the situation of Maxentius, determined in his favor the popular enthusiasm.

Maxentius was the son of the emperor Maximian, and he had married the daughter of Galerius. His birth and alliance seemed to offer him the fairest promise of succeeding to the empire; but his vices and incapacity procured him the same exclusion from the dignity of Cæsar which Constantine had deserved by a dangerous superiority of merit. The policy of Galerius preferred such associates as would never disgrace the choice, nor dispute the commands, of their benefactor. An obscure stranger was therefore raised to the throne of Italy, and the son of the late emperor of the West was left to enjoy the luxury of a private fortune in a villa a few miles distant from the capital. The gloomy passions of his soul, shame, vexation, and rage, were inflamed by envy on the news of Constantine's success; but the hopes of Maxentius revived with the public discontent, and he was easily persuaded to unite his personal injury and pretensions with the cause of the Roman people. Two Prætorian tribunes and a commissary of provisions undertook the management of the conspiracy; and, as every order of men was actuated by the same spirit, the immediate event was neither doubtful nor difficult. The præfect of the city and a few magistrates, who maintained their fidelity to Severus, were massacred by the guards; and Maxentius, invested with the Imperial ornaments, was acknowledged, by the applauding senate and people, as the protector of the Roman freedom and dignity. It is uncertain whether Maximian was previously acquainted with the conspiracy; but as soon as the standard of rebellion was erected at Rome, the old emperor broke from the retirement where the authority of Diocletian had condemned him to pass a life of

Coin of Maxentius (Marcus Aurelius Valerius Maxentius c AD 278–312).

melancholy solitude, and concealed his returning ambition under the disguise of paternal tenderness. At the request of his son and of the senate he condescended to reassume the purple. His ancient dignity, his experience, and his fame in arms added strength as well as reputation to the party of Maxentius.

According to the advice, or rather the orders, of his colleague, the emperor Severus immediately hastened to Rome, in the full confidence that, by his unexpected celerity, he should easily suppress the tumult of an unwarlike populace, commanded by a licentious youth. But he found on his arrival the gates of the city shut against him, the walls filled with men and arms, an experienced general at the head of the rebels, and his own troops without spirit or affection. A large body of Moors deserted to the enemy, allured by the promise of a large donative; and, if it be true that they had been levied by Maximian in his African war, preferring the natural feelings of gratitude to the artificial ties of allegiance. Anulinus, the Prætorian præfect, declared himself in favor of Maxentius, and drew after him the most considerable part of the troops accustomed to obey his commands. Rome, according to the expression of an orator, recalled her armies; and the unfortunate Severus, destitute of force and of counsel, retired, or rather fled, with precipitation to Ravenna. Here he might for some time have been safe. The fortifications of Ravenna were able to resist the attempts, and the morasses that surrounded the town were sufficient to prevent the approach, of the Italian army. Thesea, which Severus commanded with a powerful fleet, secured him an inexhaustible supply of provisions, and gave a free entrance to the legions which, on the return of spring, would advance to his assistance from Illyricum and the East. Maximian, who conducted the siege in person, was soon convinced that he might waste his time and his army in the fruitless enterprise, and that he had nothing to hope either from force of famine. With an art more suitable to the character of Diocletian than to his own, he directed his attack not so much against the walls of Ravenna as against the mind of Severus. The treachery which he had experienced disposed that unhappy prince

Left: Roman excavations at Vindolanda, Northumberland.
Below: Corbridge lion: carved figure of a lion known as the Corbridge lion, eating its prey, found at Corbridge, Northumberland.
Bottom: Housesteads Fort, one of the fort for defense garrisons on Hadrian's Wall, Northumberland, England.
Bottom left: Roman excavations at Vindolanda, Northumberland.

Aerial View of Hadrian's Wall. The wall stretched from shore to shore across Britain, guarding the Northern frontier.

to distrust the most sincere of his friends and adherents. The emissaries of Maximian easily persuaded his credulity that a conspiracy was formed to betray the town, and prevailed upon his fears not to expose himself to the discretion of an irritated conqueror, but to accept the faith of an honorable capitulation. He was at first received with humanity and treated with respect. Maximian conducted the captive emperor to Rome, and gave him the most solemn assurances that he had secured his life by the resignation of the purple. But Severus could obtain only an easy death and an Imperial funeral. When the sentence was signified to him, the manner of executing it was left to his own choice; he preferred the favorite mode of the ancients, that of opening his veins; and, as soon as he expired, his body was carried to the sepulcher which had been constructed for the family of Gallienus.

The importance of the occasion called for the presence and abilities of Galerius. At the head of a powerful army collected from Illyricum and the East, he entered Italy, resolved to revenge the death of Severus and to chastise the rebellious Romans; or, as he expressed his intentions, in the furious language of a barbarian, to extirpate the senate, and to destroy the people by the sword. But the skill of Maximian had concerted a prudent system of defense. The invader found every place hostile, fortified, and inaccessible; and though he forced his way as far as Narni, within sixty miles of Rome, his dominion in Italy was confined to the narrow limits of his camp. Sensible of the increasing difficulties of his enterprise, the haughty Galerius made the first advances towards a reconciliation, and dispatched two of his most considerable officers to tempt the Roman princes by the offer of a conference, and the declaration of his paternal regard for Maxentius, who might obtain much more from his liberality than he could hope from the doubtful chance of war. The offers of Galerius were rejected with firmness, his perfidious friendship refused with contempt, and it was not long before he discovered that unless he provided for his safety by a timely retreat, he had some reason to apprehend the fate of Severus. The wealth which the Romans defended against his rapacious tyranny they freely contributed for his destruction. The name of Maximian, the popular arts of his son, the secret distribution of large sums, and the promise of still more liberal rewards, checked the ardor and corrupted the fidelity of the Illyrian legions; and when Galerius at length gave the signal of the retreat, it was with some difficulty that he could prevail on his veterans not to desert a banner which had so often conducted them to victory and honor.

The legions of Galerius exhibited a very melancholy proof of their disposition by the ravages which they committed in their retreat. They murdered, they ravished, they plundered, they drove away the flocks and herds of the Italians; they burned the villages through which they passed, and they endeavored to destroy the country which it had not been in their power to subdue. During the whole march Maxentius hung on their rear, but he very prudently declined a general engagement with those brave and desperate veterans. His father had undertaken a second journey into Gaul, with the hope of persuading Constantine, who had assembled an army on the frontier, to join the pursuit, and to complete the victory. But the actions of Constantine were guided by reason, and not by resentment. He persisted in the wise resolution of maintaining a balance of power in the divided empire, and he no longer hated Galerius when that aspiring prince had ceased to be an object of terror.

The mind of Galerius was the most susceptible of the sterner passions, but it was not, however, incapable of a sincere and lasting friendship. Licinius, whose manners as well as character were not unlike his own, seems to have engaged both his affection and esteem; and as soon as Galerius was invested with the Imperial dignity, he seems to have conceived the design of raising his companion to the same rank with himself. During the short period of his prosperity, he considered the rank of Cæsar as unworthy of the age and merit of the first time, and indeed for the last time, the Roman world was administered by six emperors. In the West, Constantine and Maxentius affected to reverence their father Maximian. In the East, Licinius and Maximin honored with more real consideration their benefactor Galerius. The opposition of interest, and the memory of a recent war, divided the empire into two great hostile powers; but their mutual fears produced an apparent tranquillity, and even a feigned reconciliation, till the death of the elder princes, of Maximian, and more particularly of Galerius, gave a new direction to the views and passions of their surviving associates.

When Maximian had reluctantly abdicated the empire, the venal orators of the times applauded his philosophic moderation. When his ambition excited, or at least encouraged, a civil war, they returned thanks to his generous patriotism, and gently censured that love of ease and retirement which had withdrawn him from the public service. But it was impossible that minds like those of Maximian and his son could long possess in harmony an undivided power. Maxentius considered himself as the legal sovereign of Italy, elected by the Roman senate and people; nor would he endure the control of his father, who arrogantly declared that by *his* name and abilities the rash youth had been established on the throne. The cause was solemnly pleaded before the Prætorian guards; and those troops, who dreaded the severity of the old emperor, espoused the party of Maxentius. The life and freedom of Maximian were, however, respected, and he retired from Italy into Illyricum, affecting to lament his past conduct, and secretly contriving new mischiefs. But Galerius, who was well acquainted with his character, soon obliged him to leave his dominions, and the last refuge of the disappointed Maximian was the court of his son-in-law Constantine. He was received with respect by that artful prince, and with the appearance of filial tenderness by the empress Fausta. That he might remove every suspicion, he resigned the Imperial purple a second time, professing himself at length convinced of the vanity of greatness and ambition. Had he persevered in this resolution, he might have ended his life with less dignity, indeed, than in his first retirement, yet, however, with comfort and reputation. But the near prospect of a throne brought back to his remembrance the state from whence he was fallen, and he resolved, by a desperate effort, either to reign or to perish.

Coin of Licinius (Valerius Licinianus Licinius c AD 250–325).

Licinius, and rather chose to reserve for him the place of Constantius, and the empire of the West. While the emperor was employed in the Italian war, he intrusted his friend with the defense of the Danube; and immediately after his return from that unfortunate expedition he invested Licinius with the vacant purple of Severus, resigning to his immediate command the province of Illyricum. The news of his promotion was no sooner carried into the East, than Maximin, who governed, or rather oppressed, the countries of Egypt and Syria, betrayed his envy and discontent, disdained the inferior name of Cæsar, and, notwithstanding the prayers as well as arguments of Galerius, exacted, almost by violence, the equal title of Augustus. For

The theater of Maxentius, Rome.

The basilica of Maxentius, Rome.

An incursion of the Franks had summoned Constantine, with a part of his army, to the banks of the Rhine; the remainder of the troops were stationed in the southern provinces of Gaul, which lay exposed to the enterprises of the Italian emperor, and a considerable treasure was deposited in the city of Arles. Maximian either craftily invented, or hastily credited, a vain report of the death of Constantine. Without hesitation he ascended the throne, seized the treasure, and, scattering it with his accustomed profusion among the soldiers, endeavored to awake in their minds the memory of his ancient dignity and exploits. Before he could establish his authority, or finish the negotiation which he appears to have entered into with his son Maxentius, the celerity of Constantine defeated all his hopes. On the first news of his perfidy and ingratitude, that prince returned by rapid marches from the Rhine to the Saone, embarked on the last-mentioned river at Châlons, and, at Lyons trusting himself to the rapidity of the Rhone, arrived at the gates of Arles with a military force which it was impossible for Maximian to resist, and which scarcely permitted him to take refuge in the neighboring city of Marseilles. The narrow neck of land which joined that place to the continent was fortified against the besiegers, whilst the sea was open, either for the escape of Maximian, or for the succors of Maxentius, if the latter should choose to disguise his invasion of Gaul under the honorable pretence of defending a distressed, or, as he might allege, an injured father. Apprehensive of the fatal consequences of delay, Constantine gave orders for an immediate assault. A secret but irrevocable sentence of death was pronounced against the usurper; he obtained only the same favor which he had indulged to Severus, and it was published to the world that, oppressed by the remorse of his repeated crimes, he strangled himself with his own hands.

The last years of Galerius were less shameful and unfortunate; and though he had filled with more glory the subordinate station of Cæsar than the superior rank of Augustus, he preserved, till the moment of his death, the first place among the princes of the Roman world. He survived his retreat from Italy about four years; and, wisely relinquishing his views of universal empire, he devoted the remainder of his life to the enjoyment of pleasure and to the execution of some works of public utility, among which we may distinguish the discharging into the Danube the superfluous waters of the lake Pelso, and the cutting down immense forests that encompassed it: an operation worthy of a monarch, since it gave an extensive country to the agriculture of his Pannonian subjects. His death was occasioned by a very painful and lingering disorder. He had no sooner expired in his palace of Nicomedia than the two emperors, who were indebted for their purple to his favor, began to collect their forces, with the intention either of disputing or of dividing the dominions which he had left without a master. They were persuaded, however, to desist from the former design, and to agree in the latter. The provinces of Asia fell to the share of Maximin, and those of Europe augmented the portion of Licinius. The Hellespont and the Thracian Bosphorus formed their mutual boundary, and the banks of those narrow seas, which flowed in the midst of the Roman world, were covered with soldiers, with arms, and with fortifications. The deaths of Maximian and of Galerius reduced the number of emperors to four. The sense of their true interest soon connected Licinius and Constantine; a secret alliance was concluded between Maximin and Maxentius, and their unhappy subjects expected with terror the bloody consequences of their inevitable dissensions, which were no longer restrained by the fear or respect which they had entertained for Galerius.

The virtues of Constantine were rendered more illustrious by the vices of Maxentius. Whilst the Gallic provinces enjoyed as much happiness as the condition of the times was capable of receiving, Italy and Africa groaned under the dominion of a tyrant as contemptible as he was odious.

Above: Roman emperor addressing his troops. (Detail from the Arch of Constantine, Rome)
Right: The Mausoleum of Constantia, the eldest daughter of Constantine who was given in marriage to Licinius. She died in Bithynia in AD 354 and her mausoleum in Via Nomenter, Rome, later became the baptistry of Santa Costanza.

The enterprise was as full of danger as of glory; and the unsuccessful event of two former invasions was sufficient to inspire the most serious apprehensions. The veteran troops who revered the name of Maximian, had embraced in both those wars the party of his son, and were now restrained by a sense of honor, as well as of interest, from entertaining an idea of a second desertion. Maxentius, who considered the Prætorian guards as the firmest defense of his throne, had increased them to their ancient establishment; and they composed, including the rest of the Italians who were enlisted into his service, a formidable body of fourscore thousand men. Forty thousand Moors and Carthaginians had been raised since the reduction of Africa. Even Sicily furnished its proportion of troops; and the armies of Maxentius amounted to one hundred and seventy thousand foot and eighteen thousand horse. The wealth of Italy supplied the expenses of the war; and the adjacent provinces were exhausted to form immense magazines of corn and every other kind of provisions.

The whole force of Constantine consisted of ninety thousand foot and eight thousand horse; and as a defense of the Rhine required an extraordinary attention during the absence of the emperor, it was not in his power to employ above half his troops in the Italian expedition, unless he sacrificed the public safety to his private quarrel. At the head of about forty thousand soldiers, he marched to encounter an enemy whose numbers were at least four times superior to his own.

The celerity of Constantine's march has been compared to the rapid conquest of Italy by the first of the Cæsars; nor is the flattering parallel repugnant to the truth of history, since no more than fifty-eight days elapsed between the surrender of Verona and the final decision of the war. Constantine had always apprehended that the tyrant would consult the dictates of fear, and perhaps of prudence; and that, instead of risking his last hopes in a general engagement, he would shut himself up within the walls of Rome. His ample magazines secured him against the danger of famine; and as the situation of Constantine admitted not of delay, he might have been reduced to the sad necessity of destroying with fire and sword the Imperial city, the noblest reward of his victory, and the deliverance of which had been the motive, or rather indeed the pretense, of the civil war. It was with equal surprise and pleasure that, on his arrival at a place called Saxa Rubra, about nine miles from Rome, he discovered the army of Maxentius prepared to give him battle. Their long front filled a very spacious plain, and their deep array reached to the banks of the Tiber, which covered their rear, and forbade their retreat. We are informed, and we may believe, that Constantine disposed his troops with consummate skill, and that he chose for himself the post of honor and danger. Distinguished by the splendor of his arms, he charged in person the cavalry of his rival; and his irresistible attack determined the fortune of the day. The cavalry of Maxentius was principally composed either of unwieldly cuirassiers or of light Moors and Numidians. They yielded to the vigor of the Gallic horse, which possessed more activity than the one, more firmness than the other. The defeat of the two wings left the infantry without any protection on its flanks, and the undisciplined Italians fled without reluctance from the standard of a tyrant whom they had always hated, and whom they no longer feared. The Prætorians, conscious that their offences were beyond the reach of mercy, were animated by revenge and despair. Notwithstanding their repeated efforts, those brave veterans were unable to recover the victory; they obtained, however, an honorable death; and it was observed that their bodies covered the same ground which had been occupied by their ranks. The confusion then became general, and the dismayed troops of Maxentius, pursued by an implacable enemy, rushed by thousands into the deep and rapid stream of the Tiber. The emperor himself attempted to escape back into the city over the Milvian bridge, but the crowds which pressed together through that narrow passage forced him into the river, where he was immediately drowned by the weight of his armor. His body, which had sunk very deep into the mud, was found with some difficulty the next day. The sight of his head, when it was exposed to the eyes of the people, convinced them of their deliverance, and admonished them to receive with acclamations of loyalty and gratitude the fortunate Constantine, who thus achieved by his valor and ability the most splendid enterprise of his life.

In the use of victory Constantine neither deserved the praise of

Though Constantine might view the conduct of Maxentius with abhorrence, and the situation of the Romans with compassion, we have no reason to presume that he would have taken up arms to punish the one to relieve the other. But the tyrant of Italy rashly ventured to provoke a formidable enemy whose ambition had been hitherto restrained by considerations of prudence rather than by principles of justice. After the death of Maximian, his titles, according to the established custom, had been erased, and his statues thrown down with ignominy. His son, who had persecuted and deserted him when alive, affected to display the most pious regard for his memory, and gave orders that a similar treatment should be immediately inflicted on all the statues that had been erected in Italy and Africa to the honor of Constantine. That wise prince, who sincerely wished to decline a war, with the difficulty and importance of which he was sufficiently acquainted, at first dissembled the insult, and sought for redress by the milder expedients of negotiation, till he was convinced that the hostile and ambitious designs of the Italian emperor made it necessary for him to arm in his own defense. Maxentius, who openly avowed his pretentions to the whole monarchy of the West, had already prepared a very considerable force to invade the Gallic provinces on the side of Rhætia; and though he could not expect any assistance from Licinius, he was flattered with the hope that the legions of Illyricum, allured by his presents and promises, would desert the standard of that prince, and unanimously declare themselves his soldiers and subjects. Constantine no longer hesitated. He had deliberated with caution, he acted with vigor. He gave a private audience to the ambassadors who, in the name of the senate and people, conjured him to deliver Rome from a detested tyrant; and, without regarding the timid remonstrances of his council, he resolved to prevent the enemy, and to carry the war into the heart of Italy.

clemency nor incurred the censure of immoderate rigor. He inflicted the same treatment to which a defeat would have exposed his own person and family, put to death the two sons of the tyrant, and carefully extirpated his whole race. The first time that Constantine honored the senate with his presence he recapitulated his own services and exploits in a modest oration, assured that illustrious order of his sincere regard, and promised to re-establish its ancient dignity and privileges. The grateful senate repaid these unmeaning professions by the empty titles of honor which it was yet in their power to bestow; and, without presuming to ratify the authority of Constantine, they passed a decree to assign him the first rank among the three *Augusti* who governed the Roman world. Games and festivals were instituted to preserve the fame of his victory, and several edifices, raised at the expense of Maxentius, were dedicated to the honor of his successful rival.

Before Constantine marched into Italy he had secured the friendship, or at least the neutrality, of Licinius, the Illyrian emperor. He had promised his sister Constantia in marriage to that prince; but the celebration of the nuptials was deferred till after the conclusion of the war, and the interview of the two emperors at Milan, which was appointed for that purpose, appeared to cement the union of their families and interests. In the midst of the public festivity they were suddenly obliged to take leave of each other. An inroad of the Franks summoned Constantine to the Rhine, and the hostile approach of the sovereign of Asia demanded the immediate presence of Licinius. Maximin had been the secret ally of Maxentius, and, without being discouraged by his fate, he resolved to try the fortune of a civil war. He moved out of Syria, towards the frontiers of Bithynia, in the depth of winter. By extraordinary effort of diligence, he arrived, with a harassed but formidable army, on the banks of the Thracian Bosphorus before the lieutenants of Licinius were appraised of his hostile intentions. Byzantium surrendered to the power of Maximin after a siege of eleven days. He was detained some days under the walls of Heraclea; and he had no sooner taken possession of that city than he was alarmed by the intelligence that Licinius had pitched his camp at the distance of only eighteen miles. After a fruitless negotiation, in which the two princes attempted to seduce the fidelity of each other's adherents, they had recourse to arms. The emperor of the East commanded a disciplined

and veteran army of above seventy thousand men; and Licinius, who had collected about thirty thousand Illyrians, was at first oppressed by the superiority of numbers. His military skill and the firmness of his troops restored the day and obtained a decisive victory. The incredible speed which Maximin exerted in his flight is much more celebrated than his prowess in the battle. Twenty-four hours afterwards he was seen pale, trembling, and without his Imperial ornaments, at Nicomedia, one hundred and sixty miles from the place of his defeat. The wealth of Asia was yet unexhausted; and through the flower of his veterans had fallen in the late action, he had still power, if he could obtain time, to draw very numerous levies from Syria and Egypt. But he survived his misfortune only three or four months. His death, which happened at Tarsus, was variously ascribed to despair, to poison, and to the divine justice. As Maximin was alike destitute of abilities and of virtue, he was lamented neither by the people nor by the soldiers. The provinces of the East, delivered from the terrors of civil war, cheerfully acknowledged the authority of Licinius.

The Roman world was now divided between Constantine and Licinius, the former of whom was master of the West, and the latter of the East. It might perhaps have been expected that the conquerors, fatigued with civil war, and connected by a private as well as public alliance, would have renounced, or at least would have suspended, any farther designs of ambition. And yet a year had scarcely elapsed after the death of Maximin, before the victorious emperors turned their arms against each other.

The first battle was fought near Cibalis, a city of Pannonia, situated on the river Save, about fifty miles above Sirmium. From the inconsiderable forces which in this important contest two such powerful monarchs brought into the field, it may be inferred that the one was suddenly provoked, and that the other was unexpectedly surprised. The emperor of the West had only twenty thousand, and the sovereign of the East no more than five-and-thirty thousand, men. The inferiority of number was, however, compensated by the advantage of the

Below: Castle of Deutz, near Cologne, one of the oldest frontier towns guarding the Rhine. The Castle Deutz was restored under Constantine, c AD 310, in his efforts to contain the border. (Reconstruction, Mostra Augustea)

Above: The Vision of Constantine of the Cross which he was reputed to have seen flash across the sky prior to his victorious battle against Maxentius at Milvian Bridge outside Rome 28 October, AD 312.

ground. Constantine had taken post in a defile about half a mile in breadth, between a steep hill and a deep morass, and in that situation he steadily expected and repulsed the first attack of the enemy. He pursued his success and advanced into the plain. But the veteran legions of Illyricum rallied under the standard of a leader who had been trained to arms in the school of Probus and Diocletian. The missile weapons on both sides were soon exhausted; the two armies, with equal valor, rushed to a closer engagement of swords and spears, and the doubtful contest had already lasted from the dawn of the day to a late hour of the evening, when the right wing, which Constantine led in person, made a vigorous and decisive charge. The judicious retreat of Licinius saved the remainder of his troops from a total defeat; but when he computed his loss, which amounted to more than twenty thousand men, he thought it unsafe to pass the night in the presence of an active and victorious enemy. Abandoning his camp and magazines, he

marched away with secrecy and diligence at the head of the greatest part of his cavalry, and was soon removed beyond the danger of a pursuit. His diligence preserved his wife, his son, and his treasures, which he had deposited at Sirmium. Licinius passed through that city, and, breaking down the bridge on the Save, hastened to collect a new army in Dacia and Thrace. In his flight he bestowed the precarious title of Cæsar on Valens, his general of the Illyrian frontier.

The plain of Mardia in Thrace was the theater of a second battle no less obstinate and bloody than the former. The troops on both sides displayed the same valor and discipline; and the victory was once more decided by the superior abilities of Constantine, who directed a body of five thousand men to gain an advantageous height, from whence, during the heat of the action, they attacked the rear of the enemy, and made a very considerable slaughter. The troops of Licinius, however, presenting a double front, still maintained their ground till the approach of night put an end to the combat, and secured their retreat towards the mountains of Macedonia. The loss of two battles, and of his bravest veterans, reduced the fierce spirit of Licinius to sue for peace.

Left: Roman soldiers besieging a town. (Detail from the Arch of Constantine, Rome)
Bottom left: The Arch of Constantine, Rome.

His ambassador, Mistrianus, was admitted to the audience of Constantine: he expatiated on the common topics of moderation and humanity, which are so familiar to the eloquence of the vanquished; represented in the most insinuating language that the event of the war was still doubtful, while its inevitable calamities were alike pernicious to both the contending parties; and declared that he was authorized to propose a lasting and honorable peace in the name of the *two* emperors his masters. Constantine received the mention of Valens with indignation and contempt. 'It was not for such a purpose,' he sternly replied, 'that we have advanced from the shores of the western ocean in an uninterrupted course of combats and victories, that, after rejecting an ungrateful kinsman, we should accept for our colleague a contemptible slave. The abdication of Valens is the first article of the treaty.' It was necessary to accept this humiliating condition; and the unhappy Valens, after a reign of a few days, was deprived of the purple and of his life. As soon as this obstacle was removed, the tranquillity of the Roman world was easily restored. The successive defeats of Licinius had ruined his forces, but they had displayed his courage and abilities. His situation was almost desperate, but the efforts of despair are sometimes formidable, and the good sense of Constantine preferred a great and certain advantage to a third trial of the chance of arms. He consented to leave his rival, or, as he again styled Licinius, his friend and brother, in the possession of Thrace, Asia Minor, Syria, and Egypt; but the provinces of Pannonia, Dalmatia, Dacia, Macedonia, and Greece were yielded to the Western empire, and the dominions of Constantine now extended from the confines of Caledonia to the extremity of Peloponnesus. It was stipulated by the same treaty that three royal youths, the sons of the emperors, should be called to the

hopes of the succession. Crispus and the young Constantine were soon afterwards declared Cæsars in the West, while the younger Licinius was invested with the same dignity in the East. In this double proportion of honors, the conqueror asserted the superiority of his arms and power.

The reconciliation of Constantine and Licinius, though it was embittered by resentment and jealousy, by the remembrance of recent injuries, and by the apprehension of future dangers, maintained, however, above eight years, the tranquillity of the Roman world. As a very regular series of the Imperial laws commences about this period, it would not be difficult to transcribe the civil regulations which employed the leisure of Constantine. But the most important of his institutions are intimately connected with the new system of policy and religion, which was not perfectly established till the last and peaceful years of his reign.

The civil administration was sometimes interrupted by the military defense of the empire. Crispus, a youth of the most amiable character, who had received with the title of Cæsar the command of the Rhine, distinguished his conduct as well as valor in several victories over the Franks and Alemanni, and taught the barbarians of that frontier to dread the eldest son of Constantine, and the grandson of Constantius. The emperor himself had assumed the more difficult and important province of the Danube. The Goths, who in the time of Claudius and Aurelian had felt the weight of the Roman arms, respected the power of the empire, even in the midst of its intestine divisions. But the strength of that warlike nation was now restored by a peace of near fifty years; a new generation had arisen, who no longer remembered the misfortunes of ancient days: the Sarmatians of the lake Mæotis followed the Gothic standard either as subjects or as allies, and their united force was poured upon the countries of Illyricum. Campona, Margus, and Bononia, appear to have been the scenes of several memorable sieges and battles; and though Constantine encountered a very obstinate resistance, he prevailed at length in the contest, and the Goths were compelled to purchase an ignominious retreat by restoring the booty and prisoners which they had taken. Nor was this advantage sufficient to satisfy the indignation of the emperor. He resolved to chastise as well as to repulse the insolent barbarians who had dared to invade the territories of Rome. At the head of his legions he passed the Danube, after repairing the bridge which had been constructed by Trajan, penetrated into the strongest recesses of Dacia, and, when he had inflicted a severe revenge, condescended to give peace to the suppliant Goths, on condition that, as often as they were required, they should supply his armies with a body of forty thousand soldiers. Exploits like these were no doubt honorable to Constantine and beneficial to the state; but it may surely be questioned whether they can justify the exaggerated assertion of Eusebius, that all Scythia, as far as the extremity of the North, divided as it was into so many names and nations of the most various and savage manners, had been added by his victorious arms to the Roman empire.

In this exalted state of glory it was impossible that Constantine should any longer endure a partner in the empire. Confiding in the superiority of his genius and military power, he determined, without any previous injury, to exert them for the destruction of Licinius, whose advanced age and unpopular vices seemed to offer a very easy conquest. But the old emperor, awakened by the approaching danger, deceived the expectations of his friends as well as of his enemies. Calling forth the spirit and those abilities by which he had deserved the friendship of Galerius and the Imperial purple, he prepared himself for the contest, collected the forces of the East, and soon filled the plains of Hadrianople with his troops, and the Straits of the Hellespont with his fleet. The troops of Constantine were ordered to rendezvous at Thessalonica; they amounted to above an hundred and twenty thousand horse and foot. Their emperor was satisfied with their martial appearance, and his army contained more soldiers, though fewer men, than that of his eastern competitor. The legions of Constantine were levied in the warlike provinces of Europe; action had confirmed their discipline, victory had elevated their hopes, and there were among them a great number of veterans, who, after seventeen glorious campaigns under the same leader, prepared themselves to deserve an honorable dismission by a last effort of their valor. But the naval preparations of Constantine were in every respect much inferior to those of Licinius. The maritime cities of Greece sent their respective quotas of men and ships to the celebrated harbor of Piræus, and their united forces consisted of no more than two hundred small vessels; a very feeble armament, if it is compared with those formidable fleets which were equipped and maintained by the republic of Athens during the Peloponnesian war. Since Italy was no longer the seat of government, the naval establishments of Misenum and Ravenna had been gradually neglected; and as the shipping and mariners of the empire were supported by commerce rather than by war, it was natural that they should the most abound in the industrious province of Egypt and Asia. It is only surprising that the eastern emperor, who possessed so great a superiority at sea, should have neglected the opportunity of carrying an offensive war into the center of his rival's dominions.

The siege of Byzantium, which was immediately undertaken by Constantine, was attended with great labor and uncertainty. Crispus, the emperor's eldest son, was intrusted with the execution of this daring enterprise, which he performed with so much courage and success, that he deserved the esteem, and most probably excited the jealousy, of his father. The engagement lasted two days; and in the evening of the first, the contending fleets, after a considerable and mutual loss, retired into their respective harbors of Europe and Asia. The second day about noon a strong south wind sprang up, which carried the vessels of Crispus against the enemy; and as the casual advantage was improved by his skillful intrepidity, he soon obtained a complete victory. An hundred and thirty vessels were destroyed, five thousand men were slain, and Amandus, the admiral of the Asiatic fleet, escaped with the utmost difficulty to the shores of Chalcedon. As soon as the Hellespont was open, a plentiful convoy of provisions

Above: The Emperor presiding at a state sacrifice.
Center bottom: Roman soldiers with barbarian captives. (Relief from an earlier monument, inset in the Arch of Constantine)

flowed into the camp of Constantine, who had already advanced the operations of the siege. He constructed artificial mounds of earth of an equal height with the ramparts of Byzantium. The lofty towers which were erected on that foundation galled the besieged with large stones and darts from the military engines, and the battering rams had shaken the walls in several places. If Licinius persisted much longer in the defense, he exposed himself to be involved in the ruin of the place. Before he was surrounded, he prudently removed his person and treasures to Chalcedon in Asia.

The troops of Licinius made head against their conquerors with fruitless but desperate valor, till a total defeat, and the slaughter of five-and-twenty thousand men, irretrievably determined the fate of their leader. The memory of Licinius was branded with infamy, his statues were thrown down, and by a hasty edict, of such mischievous tendency that it was almost immediately corrected, all his laws and all the judicial proceedings of his reign were at once abolished. By this victory of Constantine the Roman world was again united under the authority of one emperor, thirty-seven years after Diocletian had divided his power and provinces with his associate Maximian.

The successive steps of the elevation of Constantine, from his first assuming the purple at York, to the resignation of Licinius at Nicomedia, have been related with some minuteness and precision, not only as the events are in themselves both interesting and important, but still more as they contributed to the decline of the empire by the expense of blood and treasure, and by the perpetual increase, as well of the taxes as of the military establishment. The foundation of Constantinople, and the establishment of the Christian religion, were the immediate and memorable consequences of this revolution.

CHAPTER THIRTEEN

The conduct of the Roman government towards the Christians from the reign of Nero to that of Constantine

[AD 54–313]

IF we seriously consider the purity of the Christian religion, the sanctity of its moral precepts, and the innocent as well as austere lives of the greater number of those who during the first ages embraced the faith of the Gospel, we should naturally suppose that so benevolent a doctrine would have been received with due reverence even by the unbelieving world; that the learned and the polite, however they might deride the miracles, would have esteemed the virtues of the new sect; and that the magistrates, instead of persecuting, would have protected an order of men who yielded the most passive obedience to the laws, though they declined the active cares of war and government. If, on the other hand, we recollect the universal toleration of Polytheism, as it was invariably maintained by the faith of the people, the incredulity of philosophers, and the policy of the Roman senate and emperors, we are at a loss to discover what new offence the Christians had committed, what new provocation could exasperate the mild indifference of antiquity, and what new motives could urge the Roman princes, who beheld without concern a thousand forms of religion subsisting in peace under their gentle sway, to inflict a severe punishment on any part of their subjects who had chosen for themselves a singular but an inoffensive mode of faith and worship.

The religious policy of the ancient world seems to have assumed a more stern and intolerant character to oppose the progress of Christianity. About fourscore years after the death of Christ, his innocent disciples were punished with death by the sentence of a proconsul of the most amiable and philosophic character, and according to the laws of an emperor distinguished by the wisdom and justice of his general administration. The apologies which were repeatedly addressed to the successors of Trajan are filled with the most pathetic complaints that the Christians, who obeyed the dictates and solicited the liberty of conscience, were alone, among all the subjects of the Roman empire, excluded from the common benefits of their auspicious government.

The sectaries of a persecuted religion, depressed by fear, animated with resentment, and perhaps heated by enthusiasm, are seldom in a proper temper of mind calmly to investigate, or candidly to appreciate, the motives of their enemies, which often escape the impartial and discerning view even of those who are placed at a secure distance from the flames of persecution. A reason has been assigned for the conduct of the emperors towards the primitive Christians, which may appear the more specious and probable as it is drawn from the acknowledged genius of Polytheism. It has already been observed that the religious concord of the world was principally supported by the implicit assent and reverence which the nations of antiquity expressed for their respective traditions and ceremonies. It might therefore be expected that they would unite with indignation against any sect or people which should separate itself from the communion of mankind, and, claiming the exclusive possession of divine knowledge, should disdain every form of worship except its own as impious and idolatrous.

Without repeating what has been already mentioned of the reverence of the Roman princes and governors for the temple of Jerusalem, we shall only observe that the destruction of the temple and city was accompanied and followed by every circumstance that could exasperate the minds of the conquerors, and authorize religious persecutions by the most specious arguments of political justice and the public safety. From the reign of Nero to that of Antoninus Pius, the Jews discovered a fierce impatience of the dominion of Rome, which repeatedly broke out in the most furious massacres and insurrections. Humanity is shocked at the recital of the horrid cruelties which they committed in the cities of Egypt, of Cyprus, and of Cyrene, where they dwelt in treacherous friendship with the unsuspecting natives; and we are tempted to applaud the severe retaliation which was exercised by the arms of the legions against a race of fanatics whose dire and credulous superstition seemed to render them the implacable enemies not only of the Roman government, but of human kind. The enthusiasm of the Jews was supported by the opinion that it was unlawful for them to pay taxes to an idolatrous master, and by the flattering promise which they derived from their ancient oracles, that a conquering Messiah would soon arise, destined to break their fetters, and to invest the favorites of heaven with the empire of the earth. It was by announcing himself as their long-expected deliverer, and by calling on all the descendants of Abraham to assert the hope of Israel, that the famous Barchochebas collected a formidable army, with which he resisted during two years the power of the emperor Hadrian.

Left: Bronze statue of Nero (Claudius Caesar Drusus Germanicus AD 37–68; Roman emperor AD 54–68).
Below: Stone set up in honor of Tiberius (Tiberius Claudius Nero 42 BC–AD 37; Roman emperor AD 14–37) by Pontius Pilate, Governor of Judea (c AD 28–37).

St Peter, the Galilean, the first Pope, who was called by Jesus of Nazareth (c 30) to found His Church. (Sixth-century mosaic, Ravenna)

Notwithstanding these repeated provocations, the resentment of the Roman princes expired after the victory, nor were their apprehensions continued beyond the period of war and danger. By the general indulgence of Polytheism, and by the mild temper of Antonius Pius, the Jews were restored to their ancient privileges, and once more obtained the permission of circumcising their children, with the easy restraint that they should never confer on any foreign proselyte that distinguishing mark of the Hebrew race. The numerous remains of that people, though they were still excluded from the precincts of Jerusalem, were permitted to form and to maintain considerable establishments both in Italy and in the provinces, to acquire the freedom of Rome, to enjoy municipal honors, and to obtain at the same time an exemption from the burdensome and expensive offices of society. The moderation or the contempt of the Romans gave a legal sanction to the form of ecclesiastical police which was instituted by the vanquished sect. The patriarch, who had fixed his residence at Tiberias, was empowered to appoint his subordinate ministers and apostles, to exercise a domestic jurisdiction, and to receive from his dispersed brethren an annual contribution. New synagogues were frequently erected in the principal cities of the empire; and the sabbaths, the fasts, and the festivals, which were either commanded by the Mosaic law or enjoined by the traditions of the Rabbis, were celebrated in the most solemn and public manner. Such gentle treatment insensibly assuaged the stern temper of the Jews. Awakened from their dream of prophecy and conquest, they assumed the behavior of peaceable and industrious subjects. Their irreconcilable hatred of mankind, instead of flaming out in acts of blood and violence, evaporated in less dangerous gratifications. They embraced every opportunity of overreaching the idolaters in trade, and they pronounced secret and ambiguous imprecations against the haughty kingdom of Edom.

Since the Jews, who rejected with abhorrence the deities adored by their sovereign and by their fellow-subjects, enjoyed, however, the free exercise of their unsocial religion, there must have existed some other cause which exposed the disciples of Christ to those severities from which the posterity of Abraham was exempt. The difference between them is simple and obvious, but, according to the sentiments of antiquity, it was of the highest importance. The Jews were a *nation*, the Christians were a *sect*: and if it was natural for every community to respect the sacred institutions of their neighbors, it was incumbent on them to persevere in those of their ancestors. The voice of oracles, the precepts of philosophers, and the authority of the laws, unanimously

enforced this national obligation. By their lofty claim of superior sanctity the Jews might provoke the Polytheists to consider them as an odious and pure race. By disdaining the intercourse of other nations they might deserve their contempt. The laws of Moses might be for the most part frivolous or absurd; yet, since they had been received during many ages by a large society, his followers were justified by the example of mankind, and it was universally acknowledged that they had a right to practice what it would have been criminal in them to neglect. But this principle, which protected the Jewish synagogue, afforded not any favor or security to the primitive church. By embracing the faith of the Gospel the Christians incurred the supposed guilt of an unnatural and unpardonable offence. They dissolved the sacred ties of custom and education, violated the religious institutions of their country, and presumptuously despised whatever their fathers had believed as true or had reverenced as sacred. Nor was this apostasy (if we may use the expression) merely of a partial or local kind; since the pious deserter who withdrew himself from the temples of Egypt or Syria would equally disdain to seek an asylum in those of Athens or Carthage. Every Christian rejected with contempt the superstitions of his family, his city, and his province. The whole body of Christians unanimously refused to hold any communion with the gods of Rome, of the empire, and of mankind. It was in vain that the oppressed believer asserted the inalienable rights of conscience and private judgment. Though his situation might excite the pity, his arguments could never reach the understanding, either of the philosophic or of the believing part of the Pagan world. To their apprehensions it was no less a matter of surprise that any individuals should entertain scruples against complying with the established mode of worship than if they had conceived a sudden abhorrence to the manners, the dress, or the language of their native country.

The surprise of the Pagans was soon succeeded by resentment, and the most pious of men were exposed to the unjust but dangerous imputation of impiety. Malice and prejudice concurred in representing the Christians as a society of atheists, who, by the most daring attack on the religious constitution of the empire, had merited the severest animadversion of the civil magistrate.

The personal guilt which every Christian had contracted, in thus preferring his private sentiment to the national religion, was aggravated in a very high degree by the number and union of the criminals. It is well known, that Roman policy viewed with the utmost jealousy and distrust any association among its subjects; and that the privileges of

The Levantine features of St Paul of Tarsus (c AD 62–64) who, with amazing energy, established Christian Churches in the cities of the Empire.

The Amphitheater of St Perpetua and St Felicitas, Carthage, the site of the martyrdom of a young Christian noblewoman and her slave girl.

private corporations, though formed for the most harmless or beneficial purposes, were bestowed with a very sparing hand. The religious assemblies of the Christians, who had separated themselves from the public worship, appeared of a much less innocent nature: they were illegal in their principle, and in their consequences might become dangerous; nor were the emperors conscious that they violated the laws of justice, when, for the peace of society, they prohibited those secret and sometimes nocturnal meetings. The pious disobedience of the Christians made their conduct, or perhaps their designs, appear in a much more serious and criminal light.

The precautions with which the disciples of Christ performed the offices of religion were at first dictated by fear and necessity; but they were continued from choice. By imitating the awful secrecy which reigned in the Eleusinian mysteries, the Christians had flattered themselves that they should render their sacred institutions more respectable in the eyes of the Pagan world. But the event, as it often happens to the operations of subtile policy, deceived their wishes and their expectations. It was concluded that they only concealed what they would have blushed to disclose. Their mistaken prudence afforded an opportunity for malice to invent, and for suspicious credulity to believe, the horrid tales which described the Christians as the most wicked of human kind.

By the wise dispensation of Providence a mysterious veil was cast over the infancy of the church, which, till the faith of the Christians was matured, and their numbers were multiplied, served to protect them not only from the malice but even from the knowledge of the Pagan world. The slow and gradual abolition of the Mosaic ceremonies afforded a safe and innocent disguise to the more early proselytes of the Gospel. As they were for the greater part of the race of Abraham, they were distinguished by the peculiar mark of circumcision, offered up their devotions in the Temple of Jerusalem till its final destruction, and received both the Law and the Prophets as the genuine inspirations of the Deity. The Gentile converts who by a spiritual adoption had been associated to the hope of Israel, were likewise confounded under the garb and appearance of Jews; and as the Polytheists paid less regard to articles of faith than to the external worship, the new sect, which carefully concealed, or faintly announced, its future greatness and ambition, was permitted to shelter itself under the general toleration which was granted to an ancient and celebrated people in the Roman empire. It was not long, perhaps, before the Jews themselves, animated with a fiercer zeal and a more jealous faith, perceived the gradual separation of their Nazarene brethren from the doctrine of the synagogue: and they would gladly have extinguished the dangerous heresy in the blood of its adherents. But the decrees of Heaven had already disarmed their malice; and though they might sometimes exert the licentious privilege of sedition, they no longer possessed the administration of criminal justice; nor did they find it easy to infuse into the calm breast of a Roman magistrate the rancor of their own zeal and prejudice. The provincial governors declared themselves ready to listen to any accusation that might affect the public safety; but as soon as they were informed that it was a question not of facts but of words, a dispute relating only to the interpretation of the Jewish laws and prophecies, they deemed it unworthy of the majesty of Rome seriously to discuss the obscure differences which might arise among a barbarous and superstitious people. The innocence of the first Christians was protected by ignorance and contempt; and the tribunal of the Pagan magistrate often proved their most assured refuge against the fury of the synagogue.

During a long period, from the death of Christ to that memorable rebellion, we cannot discover any traces of Roman intolerance, unless they are to be found in the sudden, the transient, but the cruel persecution, which was exercised by Nero against the Christians of the capital, thirty-five years after the former, and only two years before the latter, of those great events. The character of the philosophic historian, to whom we are principally indebted for the knowledge of this singular transaction, would alone be sufficient to recommend it to our most attentive consideration.

In the tenth year of the reign of Nero the capital of the empire was afflicted by a fire which raged beyond the memory or example of former ages. The monuments of Grecian art and of Roman virtue, the trophies of the Punic and Gallic wars, the most holy temples, and the most splendid palaces were involved in one common destruction. Of the fourteen regions or quarters into which Rome was divided, four only subsisted entire, three were levelled with the ground, and the remaining seven, which had experienced the fury of the flames, displayed a melancholy prospect of ruin and desolation. The vigilance of government appears not to have neglected any of the precautions which might alleviate the sense of so dreadful a calamity. The Imperial gardens were thrown open to the distressed multitude, temporary buildings were

Right: Agape feast: a small
group of friends celebrating
the Eucharist. (Wall-painting
from the Catacomb of
St Calista, Rome)
Bottom: A favorite motif,
particularly of Frankish
Christians, was that of Daniel
in the Lion's Den, here
engraved in a fourth-century
reliquary casket.

erected for their accommodation, and a plentiful supply of corn and provisions was distributed at a very moderate price. The most generous policy seemed to have dictated the edicts which regulated the disposition of the streets and the construction of private houses; and, as it usually happens in an age of prosperity, the conflagration of Rome, in the course of a few years, produced a new city, more regular and more beautiful than the former. But all the prudence and humanity affected by Nero on this occasion were insufficient to preserve him from the popular suspicion. Every crime might be imputed to the assassin of his wife and mother; nor could the prince who prostituted his person and dignity on the theater be deemed incapable of the most extravagant folly. The voice of rumor accused the emperor as the incendiary of his own capital; and, as the most incredible stories are the best adapted to the genius of an enraged people, it was gravely reported, and firmly believed, that Nero, enjoying the calamity which he had occasioned,

amused himself with singing to his lyre the destruction of ancient Troy. To divert a suspicion which the power of despotism was unable to suppress, the emperor resolved to substitute in his own place some fictitious criminals. 'With this view (continues Tacitus) he inflicted the most exquisite tortures on those men who, under the vulgar appellation of Christians, were already branded with deserved infamy. The confessions of those who were seized discovered a great multitude of their accomplices, and they were all convicted, not so much for the crime of setting fire to the city as for their hatred of human kind. They died in torments, and their torments were embittered by insult and derision. Some were nailed on crosses; others sewn up in the skins of wild beasts, and exposed to the fury of dogs; others again, smeared over with combustible materials, were used as torches to illuminate the darkness of the night. The gardens of Nero were destined for the melancholy spectacle, which was accompanied with a horse-race, and honored with

the presence of the emperor, who mingled with the populace in the dress and attitude of a charioteer. The guilt of the Christians deserved indeed the most exemplary punishment, but the public abhorrence was changed into commiseration, from the opinion that those unhappy wretches were sacrificed, not so much to the public welfare as to the cruelty of a jealous tyrant. Those who survey with a curious eye the revolutions of mankind may observe that the gardens and circus of Nero on the Vatican, which were polluted with the blood of the first Christians, have been rendered still more famous by the triumph and by the abuse of the persecuted religion. On the same spot a temple, which far surpasses the ancient glories of the Capitol, has been since erected by the Christian Pontiffs, who, deriving their claim of universal dominion from an humble fisherman of Galilee, have succeeded to the throne of the Cæsars, given laws to the barbarian conquerors of Rome, and extended their spiritual jurisdiction from the coast of the Baltic to the shores of the Pacific Ocean.

It is somewhat remarkable that the flames of war consumed almost at the same time the Temple of Jerusalem and the Capitol of Rome; and it appears no less singular that the tribute which devotion had destined to the former should have been converted by the power of an assaulting victor to restore and adorn the splendor of the latter. The emperors levied a general capitation tax on the Jewish people; and although the sum assessed on the head of each individual was inconsiderable, the use for which it was designed, and the severity with which it was exacted, were considered as an intolerable grievance. Since the officers of the revenue extended their unjust claim to many persons who were strangers to the blood or religion of the Jews, it was impossible that the Christians, who had so often sheltered themselves under the shade of the synagogue, should now escape this rapacious persecution. Anxious as they were to avoid the slightest infection of idolatory, their conscience forbade them to contribute to the honor of that dæmon who had assumed the character of the Capitoline Jupiter. As a very numerous though declining party among the Christians still adhered to the law of Moses, their efforts to dissemble their Jewish origin were detected by the decisive test of circumcision; nor were the Roman magistrates at leisure to inquire into the difference of their religious tenets. Among the Christians who were brought to the tribunal of the emperor, or, as it seems more probable, before that of the procurator of Judæa, two persons are said to have appeared, distinguished by their extraction, which was more truly noble than that of the greatest monarchs. These were the grandsons of St Jude the apostle, who himself was the brother of Jesus Christ. Their natural pretensions to the throne of David might perhaps attract the respect of the people, and excite the jealousy of the governor; but the meanness of their garb and the simplicity of their answers soon convinced him that they were neither desirous nor capable of disturbing the peace of the Roman empire. They frankly confessed their royal origin, and their near relation to the Messiah, but they disclaimed any temporal views, and professed that his kingdom, which they devoutly expected, was purely of a spiritual and angelic nature. When they were examined concerning their fortune and occupation, they showed their hands hardened with daily labor, and declared that they derived their whole subsistence from the cultivation of a farm near the village of Cocaba, of the extent of about twenty-four English acres, and of the value of nine thousand drachms, or three hundred pounds sterling. The grandsons of St Jude were dismissed with compassion and contempt.

But although the obscurity of the house of David might protect them from the suspicions of a tyrant, the present greatness of his own family alarmed the pusillanimous temper of Domitian, which could only be appeased by the blood of those Romans whom he either feared, or hated, or esteemed. Of the two sons of his uncle Flavius Sabinus, the elder was soon convicted of treasonable intentions, and the younger, who bore the name of Flavius Clemens, was indebted for his safety to his want of courage and ability. The emperor for a long time distinguished so harmless a kinsman by his favor and protection, bestowed on him his own niece Domitilla, adopted the children of that marriage to the hope of the succession, and invested their father with the honors of the consulship. But he had scarcely finished the term of his annual magistracy, when on a slight pretense he was condemned and executed; Domitilla was banished to a desolate island on the coast of Campania;

and sentences either of death or of confiscation were pronounced against a great number of persons who were involved in the same accusation. The guilt imputed to their charge was that of *Atheism* and *Jewish manners;* a singular association of ideas, which cannot with any propriety be applied except to the Christians, as they were obscurely and imperfectly viewed by the magistrates and by the writers of that period. On the strength of so probable an interpretation, and too eagerly admitting the suspicions of a tyrant as an evidence of their honorable crime, the church has placed both Clemens and Domitilla among its first martyrs, and has branded the cruelty of Domitian with the name of the second persecution. But this persecution (if it deserves that epithet) was of no long duration. A few months after the death of Clemens and the banishment of Domitilla, Stephen, a freedman belonging to the latter, who had enjoyed the favor, but who had not surely embraced the faith, of his mistress, assassinated the emperor in his palace. The memory of Domitian was condemned by the senate; his acts were rescinded; his exiles recalled; and under the gentle administration of Nerva, while the innocent were restored to their rank and fortunes, even the most guilty either obtained pardon or escaped punishment.

About ten years afterwards, under the reign of Trajan, the younger Pliny was intrusted by his friend and master with the government of Bithynia and Pontus. He soon found himself at a loss to determine by what rule of justice or of law he should direct his conduct in the execution of an office the most repugnant to his humanity. Pliny had never assisted at any judicial proceedings against the Christians, with whose name alone he seems to be acquainted; and he was totally uninformed with regard to the nature of their guilt, the method of their conviction, and the degree of their punishment. In this perplexity he had recourse to his usual expedient, of submitting to the wisdom of Trajan an impartial, and, in some respects, a favorable account of the new superstition, requesting the emperor that he would condescend to resolve his doubts and to instruct his ignorance. The life of Pliny had been employed in the acquisition of learning, and in the business of the world. Since the age of nineteen he had pleaded with distinction in the tribunals of Rome, filled a place in the senate, had been invested with the honors of the consulship, and had formed very numerous connections with every order of men, both in Italy and in the provinces. From *his* ignorance therefore we may derive some useful information. We may assure ourselves that when he accepted the government of Bithynia there were no general laws or decrees of the senate in force

Christians with their arms uplifted in prayer. (Restored wall-painting from Lullingstone Villa, Kent c AD 350. The chapel formed part of the villa.)

against the Christians; that neither Trajan nor any of his virtuous predecessors, whose edicts were received into the civil and criminal jurisprudence, had publicly declared their intentions concerning the new sect; and that, whatever proceedings had been carried on against the Christians, there were none of sufficient weight and authority to establish a precedent for the conduct of a Roman magistrate.

The answer of Trajan, to which the Christians of the succeeding age have frequently appealed, discovers as much regard for justice and humanity as could be reconciled with his mistaken notions of religious policy. Instead of displaying the implacable zeal of an Inquisitor, anxious to discover the most minute particles of heresy, and exulting in the number of his victims, the emperor expresses much more solicitude to protect the security of the innocent than to prevent the escape of the guilty. He acknowledges the difficulty of fixing any general plan; but he lays down two salutary rules, which often afforded relief and support to the distressed Christians. Though he directs the magistrates to punish such persons as are legally convicted, he prohibits them, with a very human inconsistency, from making any inquiries concerning the supposed criminals. Nor was the magistrate allowed to proceed on every kind of information. Anonymous charges the emperor rejects, as too repugnant to the equity of his government; and he strictly requires, for the conviction of those to whom the guilt of Christianity is imputed, the positive evidence of a fair and open accuser.

Notwithstanding the general rules established for the conviction and punishment of the Christians, the fate of those sectaries, in an extensive and arbitrary government, must still, in a great measure, have depended on their own behavior, the circumstances of the times, and the temper of their supreme as well as subordinate rulers. Zeal might sometimes provoke, and prudence might sometimes avert or assuage, the superstitious fury of the Pagans. A variety of motives might dispose the provincial governors either to enforce or to relax the execution of the laws; and of these motives the most forcible was their regard not only for the public edicts, but for the secret intentions of the emperor, a glance from whose eye was sufficient to kindle or to extinguish the flames of persecution. As often as any occasional severities were exercised in the different parts of the empire, the primitive Christians lamented and perhaps magnified their own sufferings; but the celebrated number of *ten* persecutions has been determined by the ecclesiastical writers of the fifth century, who possessed a more distinct view of the prosperous or adverse fortunes of the church from the age of Nero to that of Diocletian. The ingenious parallels of the *ten* plagues of Egypt, and of the *ten* horns of the Apocalypse, first suggested this calculation to their minds; and in their application of the faith of

Coin of the Emperor Nero (London Museum).

prophecy to the truth of history they were careful to select those reigns which were indeed the most hostile to the Christian cause. But these transient persecutions served only to revive the zeal and to restore the discipline of the faithful; and the moments of extraordinary rigor were compensated by much longer intervals of peace and security. The indifference of some princes and the indulgence of others permitted the Christians to enjoy, though not perhaps a legal, yet an actual and public toleration of their religion.

The Apology of Tertullian contains two very ancient, very singular, but at the same time very suspicious instances of Imperial clemency; the edicts published by Tiberius and by Marcus Antoninus, and designed not only to protect the innocence of the Christians, but even to proclaim those stupendous miracles which had attested the truth of their doctrine. The first of these examples is attended with some difficulties which might perplex a skeptical mind. We are required to believe *that* Pontius Pilate informed the emperor of the unjust sentence of death which he had pronounced against an innocent, and, as it appeared, a divine person; and that, without acquiring the merit, he exposed himself to the danger, of martyrdom; *that* Tiberius, who avowed his contempt for all religion, immediately conceived the design of placing the Jewish Messiah among the gods of Rome; *that* his servile senate ventured to disobey the commands of their master; *that* Tiberius, instead of resenting their refusal, contented himself with protecting the Christians from the severity of the laws, many years before such laws were enacted or before the church had assumed any distinct name or existence; and lastly, *that* the memory of this extraordinary transaction was preserved in the most public and authentic records, which escaped the knowledge of the historians of Greece and Rome, and were only visible to the eyes of an African Christian, who composed his Apology one hundred and sixty years after the death of Tiberius. The edict of Marcus Antonius is supposed to have been the effect of his devotion and gratitude for the miraculous deliverance which he had obtained in the Marcomannic war. The distress of the legions, the seasonable tempest of rain and hail, of thunder and of lightning, and the dismay and defeat of the barbarians, have been celebrated by the eloquence of several Pagan writers. If there were any Christians in that army, it was natural that they should ascribe some merit to the fervent prayers which, in the moment of danger, they had offered up for their own and the public safety. But we are still assured by monuments of brass and marble, by the Imperial medals, and by the Antonine column, that neither the prince nor the people entertained any sense of this signal obligation, since they unanimously attribute their deliverance to the providence of Jupiter, and to the interposition of Mercury. During the whole course of his reign Marcus despised the Christians as a philosopher, and punished them as a sovereign.

By a singular fatality, the hardships which they had endured under the government of a virtuous prince immediately ceased on the accession of a tyrant; and as none except themselves had experienced the injustice of Marcus, so they alone were protected by the lenity of Commodus. The celebrated Marcia, the most favored of his concubines, and who at length contrived the murder of her Imperial lover, entertained a singular affection for the oppressed church; and though it was impossible that she could reconcile the practice of vice with the precepts of the Gospel, she might hope to atone for the frailties of her sex and profession by declaring herself the patroness of the Christians. Under the gracious protection of Marcia they passed in safety the thirteen years of a cruel tyranny; and when the empire was established in the house of Severus, they formed a domestic but more honorable connection with the new court. The emperor was persuaded that, in a dangerous sickness, he had derived some benefit, either spiritual or physical, from the holy oil with which one of his slaves had anointed him. He always treated with peculiar distinction several persons of both sexes who had embraced the new religion. The nurse as well as the preceptor of Caracalla were Christians; and if that young prince ever betrayed a sentiment of humanity, it was occasioned by an incident which however trifling, bore some relation to the cause of Christianity. Under the reign of Severus the fury of the populace was checked; the rigor of ancient laws was for some time suspended; and the provincial governors were satisfied with receiving an annual present from the churches within their jurisdiction, as the price, or as the reward, of their

Relief on the font at Timgad, Africa.

moderation. The controversy concerning the precise time of the celebration of Easter armed the bishops of Asia and Italy against each other, and was considered as the most important business of this period of leisure and tranquillity. Nor was the peace of the church interrupted till the increasing numbers of proselytes seem at length to have attracted the attention, and to have alienated the mind, of Severus. With the design of restraining the progress of Christianity, he published an edict, which, though it was designed to effect only the new converts, could not be carried into strict execution without exposing to danger and punishment the most zealous of their teachers and missionaries. In this mitigated persecution we may still discover the indulgent spirit of Rome and of Polytheism, which so readily admitted every excuse in favor of those who practiced the religious ceremonies of their fathers.

But the laws which Severus had enacted soon expired with the authority of that emperor; and the Christians, after this accidental tempest, enjoyed a calm of thirty-eight years. Till this period they had usually held their assemblies in private houses and sequestered places. They were now permitted to erect and consecrate convenient edifices for the purpose of religious worship; to purchase lands, even at Rome itself, for the use of the community; and to conduct the elections of their ecclesiastical ministers in so public, but at the same time in so exemplary a manner, as to deserve the respectful attention of the Gentiles. This long repose of the church was accompanied with dignity. The reigns of those princes who derived their extraction from the Asiatic provinces proved the most favorable to the Christians; the eminent persons of the sect, instead of being reduced to implore the protection of a slave or concubine, were admitted into the palace in the honorable characters of priests and philosophers; and their mysterious doctrines, which were already diffused among the people, insensibly attracted the curiosity of their sovereign. When the empress Mamæa passed through Antioch, she expressed a desire of conversing with the celebrated Origen, the fame of whose piety and learning was spread over the East. Origen obeyed so flattering an invitation, and, though he could not expect to succeed in the conversion of an artful and ambitious woman, she listened with pleasure to his eloquent exhortations, and honorably dismissed him to his retirement in Palestine. The sentiments of Mamæa were adopted by her son Alexander, and the philosophic devotion of that emperor was marked by a singular but injudicious regard for the Christian religion. In his domestic chapel he placed the statues of Abraham, of Orpheus, of Apollonius, and of Christ, as an honor justly due to those respectable sages who had instructed mankind in the various modes of addressing their homage to the supreme and universal Deity. A purer faith, as well as worship, was openly professed and practiced among his household. Bishops, perhaps for the first time, were seen at court; and, after the death of Alexander, when the inhuman Maximin discharged his fury on the favorites and servants of his unfortunate benefactor, a great number of Christians, of every rank, and of both sexes, were involved in the promiscuous massacre, which, on their account, has improperly received the name of Persecution.

Notwithstanding the cruel disposition of Maximin, the effects of his resentment against the Christians were of a very local and temporary nature, and the pious Origen, who had been proscribed as a devoted victim, was still reserved to convey the truths of the Gospel to the ear of monarchs. He addressed several edifying letters to the emperor Philip, to his wife, and to his mother, and as soon as that prince, who was born in the neighborhood of Palestine, had usurped the Imperial scepter, the Christians acquired a friend and a protector. The public and even partial favor of Philip towards the sectaries of the new religion, and his constant reverence for the ministers of the church, gave some color to the suspicion, which prevailed in his own times, that the emperor himself was become a convert to the faith; and afforded some grounds for a fable which was afterwards invented, that he had been purified by confession and penance from the guilt contracted by the murder of his innocent predecessor. The fall of Philip introduced, with the change of masters, a new system of government, so oppressive to the Christians, that their former condition, ever since the time of Domitian, was represented as a state of perfect freedom and security, if compared with the rigorous treatment which they experienced under the short reign of Decius. The virtues of that prince will scarcely allow us to suspect that he was actuated by a mean resentment against the favorites of his predecessor and it is more reasonable to believe that, in the prosecution of his general design to restore the purity of Roman manners, he was desirous of delivering the empire from what he condemned as a recent and criminal superstition. The bishops of the most considerable cities were removed by exile or death: the vigilance of the magistrates prevented the clergy of Rome during sixteen months from proceeding to a new election; and it was the opinion of the Christians that the emperor would more patiently endure a competitor for the purple than a bishop in the capital. Were it possible to suppose that the penetration of Decius had discovered pride under the disguise of humility, or that he could foresee the temporal dominion which might insensibly arise from the claims of spiritual authority, we might be less surprised that he should consider the successors of St Peter as the most formidable rivals to those of Augustus.

The administration of Valerian was distinguished by a levity and inconstancy ill suited to the gravity of the *Roman Censor*. In the first part of his reign he surpassed in clemency those princes who had been suspected of an attachment to the Christian faith. In the last three years and a half, listening to the insinuations of a minister addicted to the superstitions of Egypt, he adopted the maxims, and imitated the severity, of his predecessor Decius. The accession of Gallienus, which increased the calamities of the empire, restored peace to the church; and the Christians obtained the free exercise of their religion by an edict addressed to the bishops, and conceived in such terms as seemed to acknowledge their office and public character. The ancient laws, without being formally repealed, were suffered to sink into oblivion; and (excepting only some hostile intentions which are attributed to the emperor Aurelian) the disciples of Christ passed above forty years in a state of prosperity, far more dangerous to their virtue than the severest trials of persecution.

Amidst the frequent revolutions of the empire the Christians still flourished in peace and prosperity; and notwithstanding a celebrated era of martyrs has been deduced from the accession of Diocletian, the new system of policy, introduced and maintained by the wisdom of that prince, continued, during more than eighteen years, to breathe the mildest and most liberal spirit of religious toleration.

Notwithstanding this seeming security, an attentive observer might discern some symptoms that threatened the church with a more violent persecution than any which she had yet endured. The zeal and rapid progress of the Christians awakened the Polytheists from their supine indifference in the cause of those deities whom custom and education had taught them to revere.

Although the policy of Diocletian and the humanity of Constantius inclined them to preserve inviolate the maxims of toleration, it was soon discovered that their two associates, Maximian and Galerius, entertained the most implacable aversion for the name and religion of the Christians.

After the success of the Persian war had raised the hopes and the reputation of Galerius, he passed a winter with Diocletian in the palace of Nicomedia; and the fate of Christianity became the object of their secret consultations. The experienced emperor was still inclined to pursue measures of lenity; and though he readily consented to exclude the Christians from holding any employments in the household or the army, he urged in the strongest terms the danger as well as cruelty of shedding the blood of those deluded fanatics. The Christians (it might speciously be alleged), renouncing the gods and the institutions of Rome, had constituted a distinct republic, which might yet be suppressed before it had acquired any military force.

The general edict of persecution was published; and though Diocletian, still averse to the effusion of blood, had moderated the fury of Galerius, who proposed that every one refusing to offer sacrifice should immediately be burnt alive, the penalties inflicted on the obstinacy of the Christians might be deemed sufficiently rigorous and effectual. It was enacted that their churches, in all the provinces of the empire, should be demolished to their foundations; and the punishment of death was denounced against all who should presume to hold any secret assemblies for the purpose of religious worship. The philosophers, who now assumed the unworthy office of directing the blind zeal of persecution, had diligently studied the nature and genius of the Christian religion; and as they were not ignorant that the speculative doctrines of the faith were supposed to be contained in the writings of the prophets, of the evangelists, and of the apostles, they most probably suggested the order that the bishops and presbyters should deliver all their sacred books into the hands of the magistrates; who were commanded, under the severest penalties, to burn them in a public and solemn manner. By the same edict, the property of the church was at once confiscated; and the several parts of which it might consist were either sold to the highest bidder, united to the Imperial domain, bestowed on the cities and corporations, or granted to the solicitations of rapacious courtiers. After taking such effectual measures to abolish the worship and to dissolve the government of the Christians, it was thought necessary to subject to the most intolerable hardships the condition of those perverse individuals who should still reject the religion of nature, of Rome, and of their ancestors. Persons of a liberal birth were declared incapable of holding any honors or employments; slaves were for ever deprived of the hopes of freedom; and the whole body of the people were put out of the protection of the law. The judges were authorized to hear and to determine every action that was brought against a Christian. But the Christians were not permitted to complain of any injury which they themselves had suffered; and thus those unfortunate sectaries were exposed to the severity, while they were excluded from the benefits, of public justice. This new species of martyrdom, so painful and lingering, so obscure and ignominious, was, perhaps, the most proper to weary the constancy of the faithful: nor can it be doubted that the passions and interest of mankind were disposed on this occasion to second the designs of the emperors. But the policy of a well-ordered government must sometimes have interposed in behalf of the oppressed Christians; nor was it possible for the Roman princes entirely to remove the apprehension of punishment, or to connive at every act of fraud and violence, without exposing their own authority and the rest of their subjects to the most alarming dangers.

This edict was scarcely exhibited to the public view, in the most conspicuous place of Nicomedia, before it was torn down by the hands of a Christian, who expressed at the same time, by the bitterest invectives, his contempt as well as abhorrence for such impious and tyrannical governors. His offence, according to the mildest laws,

Roman funerary mosaic, showing the Christian Chi-Rho symbol.
(From Sousse, Tunisia, fourth century AD)

amounted to treason, and deserved death. And if it be true that he was a person of rank and education, those circumstances could serve only to aggravate his guilt. He was burnt, or rather roasted, by a slow fire; and his executioners, zealous to revenge the personal insult which had been offered to the emperors, exhausted every refinement of cruelty, without being able to subdue his patience, or to alter the steady and insulting smile which, in his dying agonies, he still preserved in his countenance. The Christians, though they confessed that his conduct had not been strictly conformable to the laws of prudence, admired the divine fervor of his zeal; and the excessive commendations which they lavished on the memory of their hero and martyr contributed to fix a deep impression of terror and hatred in the mind of Diocletian.

His fears were soon alarmed by the view of a danger from which he very narrowly escaped. Within fifteen days the palace of Nicomedia, and even the bedchamber of Diocletian, were twice in flames; and though both times they were extinguished without any material damage, the singular repetition of the fire was justly considered as an evident proof that it had not been the effect of chance or negligence. The suspicion naturally fell on the Christians; and it was suggested, with some degree of probability, that those desperate fanatics, provoked by their present sufferings, and apprehensive of impending calamities, had entered into a conspiracy with their faithful brethren, the eunuchs of the palace, against the lives of two emperors whom they detested as the irreconcilable enemies of the church of God. Jealousy and resentment prevailed in every breast, but especially in that of Diocletian. A great number of persons, distinguished either by the offices which they had filled or by the favor which they had enjoyed, were thrown into prison. Every mode of torture was put in practice, and the court, as well as city, was polluted with many bloody executions. But as it was found impossible to extort any discovery of this mysterious transaction, it seems incumbent on us either to presume the innocence, or to admire the resolution, of the sufferers. A few days afterwards Galerius hastily withdrew himself from Nicomedia, declaring that, if he delayed his departure from that devoted palace, he should fall a sacrifice to the rage of the Christians. The ecclesiastical historians, from whom alone we derive a partial and imperfect knowledge of this persecution, are at a loss how to account for the fears and danger of the emperors. Two of these writers, a prince and a rhetorician, were eyewitnesses of the fire of Nicomedia. The one ascribes it to lightning and the divine wrath, the other affirms that it was kindled by the malice of Galerius himself.

As the edict against the Christians was designed for a general law of the whole empire, and as Diocletian and Galerius, though they might not wait for the consent, were assured of the concurrence, of the Western princes, it would appear more consonant to our ideas of policy that the governors of all the provinces should have received secret instructions to publish, on one and the same day, this declaration of war within their respective departments. It was at least to be expected that the convenience of the public highways and established posts would have enabled the emperors to transmit their orders with the utmost dispatch from the palace of Nicomedia to the extremities of the Roman world; and that they would not have suffered fifty days to elapse before the edict was published in Syria, and nearly four months before it was signified to the cities of Africa. This delay may perhaps be imputed to the cautious temper of Diocletian, who had yielded a reluctant consent to the measures of persecution, and who was desirous of trying the experiment under his more immediate eye before he gave way to the disorders and discontent which it must inevitably occasion in the distant provinces. At first, indeed, the magistrates were restrained from the effusion of blood; but the use of every other severity was permitted, and even recommended to their zeal; nor could the Christians, though they cheerfully resigned the ornaments of their churches, resolve to interrupt their religious assemblies, or to deliver their sacred books to the flames.

Diocletian had no sooner published his edicts against the Christians than, as if he had been desirous of committing to other hands the work of persecution, he divested himself of the Imperial purple. The character and situation of his colleagues and successors sometimes urged them to enforce, and sometimes inclined them to suspend, the execution of these rigorous laws; nor can we acquire a just and distinct idea

The theme of Christ as the Good Shepherd was a popular theme which predominated throughout the early centuries of Christian art.

The provinces of Italy and Africa experienced a short but violent persecution. The rigorous edicts of Diocletian were strictly and cheerfully executed by his associate Maximian, who had long hated the Christians, and who delighted in acts of blood and violence. In the autumn of the first year of the persecution the two emperors met at Rome to celebrate their triumph; several oppressive laws appear to have issued from their secret consultations, and the diligence of the magistrates was animated by the presence of their sovereigns. After Diocletian had divested himself of the purple, Italy and Africa were administered under the name of Severus, and were exposed, without defense, to the implacable resentment of his master Galerius. Among the martyrs of Rome, Adauctus deserves the notice of posterity. He was of a noble family in Italy, and had raised himself, through the successive honors of the palace, to the important office of treasurer of the private demesnes. Adauctus is the more remarkable for being the only person of rank and distinction who appears to have suffered death during the whole course of this general persecution.

The revolt of Maxentius immediately restored peace to the churches of Italy and Africa, and the same tyrant who oppressed every other class of his subjects showed himself just, humane, and even partial, toward the afflicted Christians. He depended on their gratitude and affection, and very naturally presumed that the injuries which they had suffered, and the dangers which they still apprehended, from his most inveterate enemy, would secure the fidelity of a party already considerable by their numbers and opulence.

The sanguinary temper of Galerius, the first and principal author of the persecution, was formidable to those Christians whom their misfortunes had placed within the limits of his dominions. When Galerius had obtained the supreme power and the government of the East, he indulged in their fullest extent his zeal and cruelty, not only in the provinces of Thrace and Asia, which acknowledged his immediate jurisdiction, but in those of Syria, Palestine, and Egypt, where Maximin gratified his own inclination by yielding a rigorous obedience to the stern commands of his benefactor.

The frequent disappointments of his ambitious views, the experience of six years of persecution, and the salutary reflections which a lingering and painful distemper suggested to the mind of Galerius, at length convinced him that the most violent efforts of despotism are insufficient to extirpate a whole people, or to subdue their religious prejudices. Desirous of repairing the mischief that he had occasioned, he published in his own name, and in those of Licinius and Constantine, a general edict of toleration.

But this treacherous calm was of short duration; nor could the Christians of the East place any confidence in the character of their sovereign. Cruelty and superstition were the ruling passions of the soul of Maximin. The former suggested the means, the latter pointed out the objects, of persecution. The Asiatic Christians had everything to dread from the severity of a bigoted monarch. But a few months had scarcely elapsed before the edicts published by the two Western emperors obliged Maximin to suspend the prosecution of his designs: the civil war which he so rashly undertook against Licinius employed all his attention; and the defeat and death of Maximin soon delivered the church from the last and most implacable of her enemies.

Early Christian ivory casket showing scenes of the Passion, c AD 400.

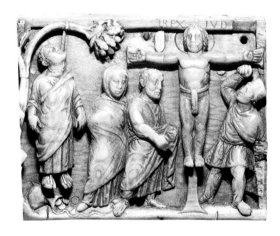

of this important period of ecclesiastical history unless we separately consider the state of Christianity, in the different parts of the empire, during the space of ten years which elapsed between the first edicts of Diocletian and the final peace of the church.

The mild and humane temper of Constantius was averse to the oppression of any part of his subjects. The principal offices of his palace were exercised by Christians. He loved their persons, esteemed their fidelity, and entertained not any dislike to their religious principles. But as long as Constantius remained in the subordinate station of Cæsar, it was not in his power openly to reject the edicts of Diocletian, or to disobey the commands of Maximian. His authority contributed, however, to alleviate the sufferings which he pitied and abhorred. He consented with reluctance to the ruin of the churches, but he ventured to protect the Christians themselves from the fury of the populace and from the rigor of the laws. The provinces of Gaul (under which we may probably include those of Britain) were indebted for the singular tranquillity which they enjoyed to the gentle interposition of their sovereign. The elevation of Constantius to the supreme and independent dignity of Augustus gave a free scope to the exercise of his virtues, and the shortness of his reign did not prevent him from establishing a system of toleration of which he left the precept and the example to his son Constantine. His fortunate son, from the first moment of his accession declaring himself the protector of the church, at length deserved the appellation of the first emperor who publicly professed and established the Christian religion.

Foundation of Constantinople – political system of Constantine and his successors – military discipline – the finances

[AD 300–500]

THE unfortunate Licinius was the last rival who opposed the greatness, and the last captive who adorned the triumph, of Constantine. After a tranquil and prosperous reign the conqueror bequeathed to his family the inheritance of the Roman empire; a new capital, a new policy, and a new religion; and the innovations which he established have been embraced and consecrated by succeeding generations.

After the defeat and abdication of Licinius his victorious rival proceeded to lay the foundations of a city destined to reign in future times the mistress of the East, and to survive the empire and religion of Constantine. As he gradually reached the summit of prosperity and the decline of life, he began to meditate the design of fixing in a more permanent situation the strength as well as majesty of the throne. In the choice of an advantageous situation he preferred the confines of Europe and Asia; to curb with a powerful arm the barbarians who dwelt between the Danube and the Tanais; to watch with an eye of jealousy the conduct of the Persian monarch, who indignantly supported the yoke of an ignominious treaty. With these views Diocletian had selected and embellished the residence of Nicomedia: but the memory of Diocletian was justly abhorred by the protector of the church; and Constantine was not insensible to the ambition of founding a city which might perpetuate the glory of his own name. During the late operations of the war against Licinius he had sufficient opportunity to contemplate, both as a soldier and as a statesman, the incomparable position of Byzantium; and to observe how strongly it was guarded by nature against an hostile attack, while it was accessible on every side to the benefits of commercial intercourse.

The master of the Roman world, who aspired to erect an eternal monument of the glories of his reign, could employ in the prosecution of that great work the wealth, the labor, and all that yet remained of the genius, of obedient millions. Some estimate may be formed of the expense bestowed with Imperial liberality on the foundation of Constantinople by the allowance of about two millions five hundred thousand pounds for the construction of the walls, the porticoes, and the aqueducts.

But we should deviate from the design of this history if we attempted minutely to describe the different buildings or quarters of the city. It may be sufficient to observe that whatever could adorn the dignity of a great capital, or contribute to the benefit or pleasure of its numerous inhabitants, was contained within the walls of Constantinople. A particular description, composed about a century after its foundation, enumerates a capitol or school of learning, a circus, two theaters, eight public and one hundred and fifty-three private baths, fifty-two porticoes, five granaries, eight aqueducts or reservoirs of water, four spacious halls for the meetings of the senate or courts of justice, fourteen churches, fourteen palaces, and four thousand three hundred and eighty-eight houses which, for their size or beauty, deserved to be distinguished from the multitude of plebeian habitations.

In less than a century Constantinople disputed with Rome itself the pre-eminence of riches and numbers. New piles of buildings, crowded together with too little regard to health or convenience, scarcely allowed the intervals of narrow streets for the perpetual throng of men, of horses, and of carriages. The allotted space of ground was insufficient to contain the increasing people, and the additional foundations, which on either side were advanced into the sea, might alone have composed a very considerable city.

The foundation of a new capital is naturally connected with the establishment of a new form of civil and military administration. The distinct view of the complicated system of policy introduced by Diocletian, improved by Constantine, and completed by his immediate successors, may not only amuse the fancy by the singular picture of a great empire, but will tend to illustrate the secret and internal causes of its rapid decay.

Left: Bronze head of Constantine. (National Museum of Belgrade)
Below: Tax collectors. (Bas relief from Noviomagus, Trier, Trier Museum)

CONSTANTINE'S ADMINISTRATION

Thirteen years after the Edict of Milan, Constantine (Flavius Valerius Aurelius Constantius 274–337 AD) removed the seat of the Empire to Byzantium, a city which had been famous during the time of the Greeks, and renamed it Constantinople. The city was a naturally fortified harbor surrounded on two sides by sea and on a third by mountains.

The move had profound repercussions for his people. A new city required a new civil and military administration. The civil service of the state grew correspondingly large and unwieldly and the expense placed intolerable burdens on the people, precipitating an economic crisis which was to reach its climax with the loss of the Roman colonies during the waves of barbarian invasions in the fifth century.

The policies of Diocletian were continued during the reign of Constantine. The consuls who had gained their power through democratic elections were reduced to puppet figures appointed yearly by Constantine and they retained only the pageantry of their office.

The powerful Prætorian guards were deprived of their role as guardians of the Emperor's person and on leaving the field were appointed as civil magistrates.

The civil and military administration of the provinces was made separate. The governors since the time of Augustus had wielded powers almost equivalent to those of the Emperor. In time of war they had been the military commanders and in time of peace they presided over the civil administration and the courts of justice. Constantine appointed two men for the two offices.

The policy secured his own safety at the expense of the provinces which were left at the mercy of the barbarians since the two governors were as unlikely to unite in the defense of the province as they were to conspire against his person.

In the system of policy introduced by Augustus, the governors, those at least of the Imperial provinces, were invested with the full powers of the sovereign himself. Ministers of peace and war, the distribution of rewards and punishments depended on them alone, and they successively appeared on their tribunal in the robes of civil magistracy, and in complete armor at the head of the Roman legions. The influence of the revenue, the authority of law, and the command of a military force, concurred to render their power supreme and absolute; and whenever they were tempted to violate their allegiance, the loyal province which they involved in their rebellion was scarcely sensible of any change in its political state. From the time of Commodus to the reign of Constantine near one hundred governors might be enumerated, who, with various success, erected the standard of revolt; and though the innocent were too often sacrificed, the guilty might be sometimes prevented, by the suspicious cruelty of their master. To secure his throne and the public tranquillity from these formidable servants, Constantine resolved to divide the military from the civil administration, and to establish, as a permanent and professional distinction, a practice which had been adopted only as an occasional expedient. The supreme jurisdiction exercised by the Prætorian præfects over the armies of the empire was transferred to the two *masters general* whom he instituted, the one for the *cavalry*, the other for the *infantry*; and though each of

Above: A consul's triumphal procession in Rome from the Basilica of Junius Bassus in the Palazzo Vecchio, Florence. (Marble inlay, fourth century AD)
Right: Vintage scene showing Roman slaves gathering grape harvest. (Detail of the mosaic from the vault of the Church of Santa Costanza, Rome, fourth century AD)

they received a liberal allowance sufficient to maintain one hundred and ninety servants and one hundred and fifty-eight horses. They were strictly prohibited from interfering in any matter which related to the administration of justice or the revenue; but the command which they exercised over the troops of their department was independent of the authority of the magistrates. About the same time that Constantine gave a legal sanction to the ecclesiastical order, he instituted in the Roman empire the nice balance of the civil and the military powers. The emulation, and sometimes the discord, which reigned between two professions of opposite interests and incompatible manners, was productive of beneficial and of pernicious consequences. It was seldom to be expected that the general and the civil governor of a province should either conspire for the disturbance, or should unite for the service, of their country. While the one delayed to offer the assistance which the other disdained to solicit, the troops very frequently remained without orders or without supplies, the public safety was betrayed, and the defenseless subjects were left exposed to the fury of the barbarians. The divided administration, which had been formed by Constantine, relaxed the vigor of the state, while it secured the tranquility of the monarch.

The memory of Constantine has been deservedly censured for another innovation which corrupted military discipline, and prepared the ruin of the empire. The nineteen years which preceded his final victory over Licinius had been a period of license and intestine war. The rivals who contended for the possession of the Roman world had withdrawn the greatest part of their forces from the guard of the general frontier; and the principal cities which formed the boundary of their respective dominions were filled with soldiers, who considered their countrymen as their most implacable enemies. After the use of these internal garrisons had ceased with the civil war, the conqueror wanted either wisdom or firmness to revive the severe discipline of Diocletian, and to suppress a fatal indulgence which habit had endeared and almost confirmed to the military order. From the reign of Constantine a popular and even legal distinction was admitted between the *Palatines* and the *Borderers;* the troops of the court, as they were improperly styled, and the troops of the frontier. The former, elevated by the superiority of their pay and privileges, were permitted, except in the extraordinary emergencies of war, to occupy their tranquil stations in the heart of the provinces. The most flourishing cities were oppressed by the intolerable weight of quarters. The soldiers insensibly forgot the virtues of their profession, and contracted only the vices of civil life. They were either degraded by the industry of mechanic trades, or enervated by the luxury of baths and theaters. They soon became careless of their martial exercises, curious in their diet and apparel, and, while they inspired terror to the subjects of the empire, they trembled at the hostile approach of the barbarians. The chain of fortifications which Diocletian and his colleagues had extended along the banks of the great rivers was no longer maintained with the same care, or defended with the same vigilance. The numbers which still remained under the name of the troops of the frontier might be sufficient for the ordinary defense. But their spirit was degraded by the humiliating reflection that *they,* who were exposed to the hardships and dangers of a

these *illustrious* officers was more peculiarly responsible for the discipline of those troops which were under his immediate inspection, they both indifferently commanded in the field the several bodies, whether of horse or foot, which were united in the same army. Their number was soon doubled by the division of the East and West; and as separate generals of the same rank and title were appointed on the four important frontiers of the Rhine, of the Upper and the Lower Danube, and of the Euphrates, the defense of the Roman empire was at length committed to eight masters general of the cavalry and infantry. Under their orders, thirty-five military commanders were stationed in the provinces: three in Britain, six in Gaul, one in Spain, one in Italy, five on the Upper and four on the Lower Danube, in Asia eight, three in Egypt, and four in Africa. The titles of *counts* and *dukes,* by which they were properly distinguished, have obtained in modern languages so very different a sense that the use of them may occasion some surprise. But it should be recollected that the second of those appellations is only a corruption of the Latin word which was indiscriminately applied to any military chief. All these provincial generals were therefore *dukes;* but no more than ten among them were dignified with the rank of *counts* or companions, a title of honor, or rather of favor, which had been recently invented in the court of Constantine. A gold belt was the ensign which distinguished the office of the counts and dukes; and, besides their pay,

perpetual warfare, were rewarded only with about two-thirds of the pay and emoluments which were lavished on the troops of the court. Even the bands or legions that were raised the nearest to the level of those unworthy favorites were in some measure disgraced by the title of honor which they were allowed to assume. It was in vain that Constantine repeated the most dreadful menaces of fire and sword against the Borderers who should dare to desert their colors, to connive at the inroads of the barbarians, or to participate in the spoil. The mischiefs which flow from injudicious counsels are seldom removed by the application of partial severities: and though succeeding princes labored to restore the strength and numbers of the frontier garrisons, the empire, till the last moment of its dissolution, continued to languish under the mortal wound which had been so rashly or so weakly inflicted by the hand of Constantine.

The same timid policy, of dividing whatever is united, of reducing whatever is eminent, of dreading every active power, and of expecting that the most feeble will prove the most obedient, seems to pervade the institutions of several princes and particularly those of Constantine. The martial pride of the legions, whose victorious camps had so often been the scene of rebellion, was nourished by the memory of their past exploits, and the consciousness of their actual strength. As long as they maintained their ancient establishment of six thousand men, they subsisted, under the reign of Diocletian, each of them singly, a visible and important object in the military history of the Roman empire. A few years afterwards these gigantic bodies were shrunk to a very diminutive size; and when *seven* legions, with some auxiliaries, defended the city of Amida against the Persians, the total garrison, with the inhabitants of both sexes, and the peasants of the deserted country, did not exceed the number of twenty thousand persons. From this fact, and from similar examples, there is reason to believe that the constitution of the legionary troops, to which they partly owed their valor and discipline, was dissolved by Constantine; and that the bands of Roman infantry, which still assumed the same names and the same

honors, consisted only of one thousand or fifteen hundred men. The conspiracy of so many separate detachments, each of which was awed by the sense of its own weakness, could easily be checked; and the successors of Constantine might indulge their love of ostentation, by issuing their orders to one hundred and thirty-two legions, inscribed on the muster-roll of their numerous armies. The remainder of their troops was distributed into several hundred cohorts of infantry, and squadrons of cavalry. Their arms, and titles, and ensigns were calculated to inspire terror, and to display the variety of nations who marched under the Imperial standard. And not a vestige was left of that severe simplicity which, in the ages of freedom and victory, had distinguished the line of battle of a Roman army from the confused host of an Asiatic monarch. A more particular enumeration, drawn from the *Notitia*, might exercise the diligence of an antiquary; but the historian will content himself with observing that the number of permanent stations or garrisons established on the frontiers of the empire amounted to five hundred and eighty-three; and that, under the successors of Constantine, the complete force of the military establishment was computed at six hundred and forty-five thousand soldiers. An effort so prodigious surpassed the wants of a more ancient and the faculties of a later period.

In the various states of society armies are recruited from very different motives. Barbarians are urged by the love of war; the citizens of a free republic may be prompted by a principle of duty; the subjects, or at least the nobles, of a monarchy are animated by a sentiment of honor; but the timid and luxurious inhabitants of a declining empire must be allured into the service by the hopes of profit, or compelled by the dread of punishment. The resources of the Roman treasury were exhausted by the increase of pay, by the repetition of donatives, and by the invention of new emoluments and indulgences, which, in the opinion of the provincial youth, might compensate the hardships and dangers of a military life. Yet, although the stature was lowered, although slaves, at least by a tacit connivance, were indiscriminately received into the ranks, the insurmountable difficulty of procuring a regular and adequate supply of volunteers obliged the emperors to adopt more effectual and coercive methods. The lands bestowed on the veterans, as the free reward of their valor, were henceforwards granted under a condition which contains the first rudiments of the feudal tenures—that their sons, who succeeded to the inheritance, should devote themselves to the profession of arms as soon as they attained the age of manhood; and their cowardly refusal was punished by the loss of honor, of fortune, or even of life. But as the annual growth of the sons of the veterans bore a very small proportion to the demands of the service, levies of men were frequently required from the provinces, and every proprietor was obliged either to take up arms, or to procure a substitute, or to purchase his exemption by the payment of a heavy fine. The sum of forty-two pieces of gold, to which it was *reduced*, ascertains the exorbitant price of volunteers, and the reluctance with which the government admitted of this alternative. Such was the horror for the profession of a soldier which had affected the minds of the degenerate Romans that many of the youth of Italy and the provinces chose to cut off the fingers of their right hand to escape from being pressed into the service; and this strange expedient was so commonly practiced as to deserve the severe animadversion of the laws, and a peculiar name in the Latin language.

The introduction of barbarians into the Roman armies became every day more necessary. The most daring of the Scythians, of the Goths, and of the Germans, who delighted in war, and who found it more profitable to defend than to ravage the provinces, were enrolled not only in the auxiliaries of their respective nations, but in the legions themselves, and among the most distinguished of the Palatine troops.

The perpetual intercourse between the court and the provinces was facilitated by the construction of roads and the institution of posts. But these beneficial establishments were accidentally connected with a pernicious and intolerable abuse. Two or three hundred *agents* or messengers were employed, under the jurisdiction of the master of the offices, to announce the names of the annual consuls, and the edicts or victories of the emperors. They insensibly assumed the license of reporting whatever they could observe of the conduct either of magistrates or of private citizens; and were soon considered as the eyes of the monarch and the scourge of the people. Under the warm influence of a feeble reign they multiplied to the incredible number of ten thousand, disdained the mild though frequent admonitions of the laws, and exercised in the profitable management of the posts a rapacious and insolent oppression. These official spies, who regularly corresponded with the palace, were encouraged, by favor and reward, anxiously to watch the progress of every treasonable design, from the faint and latent symptoms of disaffection, to the actual preparation of an open revolt. Their careless or criminal violation of truth and justice was covered by the consecrated mask of zeal; and they might securely aim their poisoned arrows at the breast of the guilty or the innocent, who had provoked their resentment, or refused to purchase their silence.

These evils, however terrible they may appear, were confined to the smaller number of Roman subjects whose dangerous situation was in some degree compensated by the enjoyment of those advantages, either of nature or of fortune, which exposed them to the jealousy of the monarch. The obscure millions of a great empire have much less to dread from the cruelty than from the avarice of their masters; and *their* humble happiness is principally affected by the grievance of excessive

Left: Cloth merchants in a drapery store. (The Uffizzi Gallery, Florence)
Right: Goatherd milking his goat. Taxes were collected in kind in the form of produce from the fat of the land. (Relief from a sarcophagus, Museo Nazionale, Rome)

CONSTANTINE'S LAND TAX
During the reign of Constantine the massive building programs in Constantinople which the building of a new palace and city entailed and the establishment of a new imperial government gave rise to an iniquitous land tax which was exacted either in gold or in kind. As the system was easily open to abuse and corruption was rife, small landowners were often reduced to poverty and forced to abandon their holdings. The agriculture of the country was effectively ruined and 70 years after Constantine's reign the once flourishing and fertile plain of Campania had been reduced to an uncultivated desert.

Vintage scene showing Roman slaves gathering in the grape harvest.
(Detail from a mosaic from the vault of the Church of Santa Costanza
in Rome, fourth century AD)

taxes, which, gently pressing on the wealthy, descend with accelerated weight on the meaner and more indigent classes of society.

The execution of these laws (which it would be tedious to pursue in their minute and intricate detail) consisted of two distinct operations: the resolving the general imposition into its constituent parts, which were assessed on the provinces, the cities, and the individuals of the Roman world; and the collecting the separate contributions of the individuals, the cities, and the provinces, till the accumulated sums were poured into the Imperial treasuries. But as the account between the monarch and the subject was perpetually open, and as the renewal of the demand anticipated the perfect discharge of the preceding obligation, the weighty machine of the finances was moved by the same hands round the circle of its yearly revolution. The whole landed property of the empire (without excepting the patrimonial estates of the monarch) was the object of ordinary taxation. The lands were measured by surveyors, who were sent into the provinces; their nature, whether arable or pasture, or vineyards or woods, was distinctly reported; and an estimate was made of their common value from the average produce of five years. The numbers of slaves and of cattle constituted an essential part of the report; an oath was administered to the proprietors which bound them to disclose the true state of their affairs; and their attempts to prevaricate, or elude the intention of the legislator, were severely watched, and punished as a capital crime, which included the double guilt of treason and sacrilege. A large portion of the tribute was paid in money; and of the current coin of the empire, gold alone could be legally accepted. The remainder of the taxes, according to the proportions determined by the annual indiction, was furnished in a manner still more direct, and still more oppressive. According to the different nature of lands, their real produce in the various articles of wine or oil, corn or barley, wood or iron, was transported by the labor or at the expense of the provincials to the Imperial magazines, from whence they were occasionally distributed, for the use of the court, of the army, and of the two capitals, Rome and Constantinople. The commissioners of the revenue were so frequently obliged to make considerable purchases, that they were strictly prohibited from allowing any compensation, or from receiving in money the value of those supplies which were exacted in kind. In the primitive simplicity of small communities this method may be well adapted to collect the almost voluntary offerings of the people; but it is at once

susceptible of the utmost latitude and of the utmost strictness, which in a corrupt and absolute monarchy must introduce a perpetual contest between the power of oppression and the arts of fraud. The agriculture of the Roman provinces was insensibly ruined, and, in the progress of despotism, which tends to disappoint its own purpose, the emperors were obliged to derive some merit from the forgiveness of debts, or the remission of tributes, which their subjects were utterly incapable of paying. According to the new division of Italy, the fertile and happy province of Campania, the scene of the early victories and of the delicious retirements of the citizens of Rome, extended between the sea and the Apennine from the Tiber to the Silarus. Within sixty years after the death of Constantine, and on the evidence of an actual survey, an exemption was granted in favor of three hundred and thirty thousand English acres of desert and uncultivated land, which amounted to one-eighth of the whole surface of the province. As the footsteps of the barbarians had not yet been seen in Italy, the cause of this amazing desolation, which is recorded in the laws, can be ascribed only to the administration of the Roman emperors.

These general taxes were imposed and levied by the absolute authority of the monarch; but the occasional offerings of the *coronary gold* still retained the name and semblance of popular consent. It was an ancient custom that the allies of the republic, who ascribed their safety or deliverance to the success of the Roman arms, and even the cities of Italy, who admired the virtues of their victorious general, adorned the pomp of his triumph by their voluntary gifts of crowns of gold, which, after the ceremony, were consecrated in the temple of Jupiter, to remain a lasting monument of his glory to future ages. The progress of zeal and flattery soon multiplied the number, and increased the size, of these popular donations; and the triumph of Cæsar was enriched with two thousand eight hundred and twenty-two massy crowns, whose weight amounted to twenty thousand four hundred and fourteen pounds of gold. This treasure was immediately melted down by the prudent dictator, who was satisfied that it would be more serviceable to his soldiers than to the gods: his example was imitated by his successors; and the custom was introduced of exchanging these splendid ornaments for the more acceptable present of the current gold coin of the empire. The spontaneous offering was at length exacted as the debt of duty and, instead of being confined to the occasion of a triumph, it was supposed to be granted by the several cities and provinces of the monarchy as often as the emperor condescended to announce his accession, his consulship, the birth of a son, the creation of a Cæsar, a victory over the barbarians, or any other real or imaginary event which graced the annals of his reign. The peculiar free gift of the senate of Rome was fixed by custom at sixteen hundred pounds of gold, or about sixty-four thousand pounds sterling. The oppressed subjects celebrated their own felicity that their sovereign should graciously consent to accept this feeble but voluntary testimony of their loyalty and gratitude.

A people elated by pride, or soured by discontent, is seldom qualified to form a just estimate of their actual situation. The subjects of Constantine were incapable of discerning the decline of genius and manly virtue, which so far degraded them below the dignity of their ancestors; but they could feel and lament the rage of tyranny, the relaxation of discipline, and the increase of taxes. The impartial historian, who acknowledges the justice of their complaints, will observe some favorable circumstances which tended to alleviate the misery of their condition. The threatening tempest of barbarians, which so soon subverted the foundations of Roman greatness, was still repelled, or suspended, on the frontiers. The arts of luxury and literature were cultivated, and the elegant pleasures of society were enjoyed, by the inhabitants of a considerable portion of the globe. The forms, the pomp, and the expense of the civil administration contributed to restrain the irregular license of the soldiers; and although the laws were violated by power, or perverted by subtlety, the sage principles of the Roman jurisprudence preserved a sense of order and equity unknown to the despotic governments of the East. The rights of mankind might derive some protection from religion and philosophy; and the name of freedom, which could no longer alarm, might sometimes admonish, the successors of Augustus, that they did not reign over a nation of Slaves or Barbarians.

Right: Gold medallion of Constantine: the gold *aureus,* universally known as the *solidus* was regarded in much the same way as the dollar is today. (British Museum)
Left: Head of Constantine on a Roman bronze coin of AD 306.

Roman Villas

Roman towns were beautifully laid out. Often they were planned in the shape of a pentagon or rectangle such as that of the Roman British Silchester – the remains of which can still be seen. Great attention was paid to careful drainage and an efficient sewage system. The *Cloaca maxima*, the main sewage pipe in Rome, is still functional today.

Talented engineers, the Romans constructed aqueducts which provided fresh running water to supply public and private houses, where baths and bath houses of greater complexity than we know them today played a major part in the everyday life of the Roman citizen. The Public Baths such as those at Caracalla outside Rome, or Hadrian's Villa in Tivoli or at Bath, England were designed as much for social gatherings as for personal cleanliness. The same was true of the bath house which was such an integral part of every private villa. The Roman would enter the first room, the dressing room. Emerging, the bather would then pass through a series of rooms filled with hot air. The *Tepidarium* contained a fairly warm bath and was followed by the *Caldarium* which contained a hot bath and often a bath of cold water to splash down with before passing out of the 'bathing' areas. In the massage room attendants would massage and scrape the body with strigils and anoint it with oils and unguents. A final cold plunge in the *Frigidarium* completed the bathing process.

Below: Model of the Roman Palace at Fishbourne, Dorset. Built in 75 AD the palace is one of the most exciting archeological finds of the Roman period in Britain.

Above: 'The Canopus' or water garden of Hadrian's Villa at Tivoli showing the dining hall (triclinium) in the form of a underground grotto at the far end.

Below: Detail from the Dolphin mosaic of the Palace of Fishbourne, 75 AD.

Right: The garden courtyard of the House of the Stags, Pompeii. The houses of the wealthy citizens were often constructed round a courtyard or series of courtyards such as this.
Below: The flour mills at Ostia. The holes in each mill were for shafts which it is believed were turned by donkeys.

Perhaps the most complex and intriguing baths were built by Hadrian at his villa in Tivoli. Here the Great Poikile fashioned after the Poikile in Greece provided a great outer bath or swimming pool and was probably surrounded by a chariot race course. For private reflection, the Emperor built himself a *Théâtre d'eau* – a small circular pool surrounded by walls and a movable bridge which allowed access to a central island on which he built himself a library, dining quarters, and a bedroom. Steps from this led down to the bath house. This *Théâtre d'eau* was subsequently to inspire the garden architecture of many of the most famous of Renaissance Italian villas.

Hadrian's villa also provides one of the most well-preserved sites of a Roman villa on the grand scale. The gardens were constructed as a place of entertainment and again the use of water in the form of lakes and watercourses is one of the overall themes linking each section to the other. Perhaps the most spectacular of these is the Canopus; Hadrian used this as a splendid outdoor dining room or *triclinium*. Inspired by the Egyptian temple to Seramis at Alexandria, it was designed around a long lake, and at the far end of this lake in what seems to be a hollow grotto was the dining room. Water cascaded over the rocks above and gurgled in rivulets passing reclining guests as they ate.

Left: Fragments of black and white geometric mosaic. (The Palace of Fishbourne, 75 AD)
Right: The *thermopolae* or local wine bar at Ostia, where hot mulled wine, a favorite drink of the Romans, would have been served. (Third century AD)

Right: The tall cypresses among the ruins of Hadrian's Villa at Tivoli. The garden was composed of a series of gardens and large sumptuous buildings inspired by his travels abroad.
Below: Enlarged detail of Neptune with his trident astride a dolphin. (Detail from the Dolphin mosaic, the Palace of Fishbourne, second century AD)

Above: Seahorse. (Detail from the Dolphin mosaic, the Palace of Fishbourne)

Right: The aqueduct of Claudius, Rome.

Right: The reclining figure of Venus. (Wall-painting from the garden courtyard of the House of the Marine, Venus, Pompeii, first century AD)

Extreme right, top: The Roman Bath at Bath, Avon. The baths were used almost as much for social gatherings as for personal cleanliness.

Below: The elegiac remains of the Nymphæum in the House of Neptune and Amphitrite, Herculaneum. Lacking a garden, the cool shaded grotto was used as a retreat during the heat of the day. The idea of the nymphaeum inspired many of the later Italian gardens of the Renaissance.

Although Hadrian, Pliny (Gaius Pluvius Secundus AD 23–79) and Domitian (Titus Flavius Domitianus AD 51–96) were noted for their sumptuous villas and gardens on a grand scale, the average Roman villa would have been simpler in construction. It was generally built around a courtyard on two levels, and the bath house would be set slightly to one side. Plans and ruins of such villas can be most easily seen at Pompeii or Herculaneum, where the whole of these two small trading towns have been preserved intact following the eruption of Vesuvius in AD 79. Rooms have been perfectly preserved. Intricate frescoes of great delicacy of detail adorn the walls of the interiors, doors have been left half open and hastily prepared meals lie half eaten on

tables, jewelry lies abandoned and exquisitely sculptured statues stand bereft.

From these eloquent ruins one can obtain a clear picture of the life of the times – a tavern bar, or kitchen with its raised brick-covered fire and cooking utensils and pottery recreate in an intimate way, the household and life styles of the ordinary people. The slender columns of the forum silhouetted against the skyline and the circular levels of the amphitheater evoke the public life around which the town revolved.

Mosaics used in floor decoration for the important reception rooms of each house fill in the colorful story of religious ceremonies or popular gladatorial fights.

Right above: A garden of pomegranate trees. (Wall-painting from the Villa of the Empress Livia at Prima Porta, Rome, Museo Nazionale, Rome)
Left: Garden scene painted on the wall of an open-air court in the House of the Marine Venus, Pompeii.

CHAPTER FIFTEEN

Character of Constantine – death of Constantine

division of the Empire among his three sons – tragic deaths of Constantine the Younger and Constans – usurpation of Magnentius – civil war – victory of Constantius

[AD 324–353]

THE character of the prince who removed the seat of empire, and introduced important changes into the civil and religious constitution of his country, has fixed the attention, and divided the opinions, of mankind. By the grateful zeal of the Christians the deliverer of the church has been decorated with every attribute of a hero, and even of a saint; while the discontent of the vanquished party has compared Constantine to the most abhorred of those tyrants who, by their vice and weakness, dishonored the Imperial purple. But it would soon appear that the vain attempt to blend such discordant colors, and to reconcile such inconsistent qualities, must produce a figure monstrous rather than human, unless it is viewed in its proper and distinct lights by a careful separation of the different periods of the reign of Constantine.

The person, as well as the mind, of Constantine had been enriched by nature with her choicest endowments. His stature was lofty, his countenance majestic, his deportment graceful; his strength and activity were displayed in every manly exercise, and, from his earliest youth to a very advanced season of life, he preserved the vigor of his constitution by a strict adherence to the domestic virtues of chastity and temperance. In the dispatch of business his diligence was indefatigable; and the active powers of his mind were almost continually exercised in reading, writing, or meditating, in giving audience to ambassadors, and in examining the complaints of his subjects. Even those who censured the propriety of his measures were compelled to acknowledge that he possessed magnanimity to conceive, and patience to execute, the most arduous designs, without being checked either by the prejudices of education or by the clamors of the multitude. In the field he infused his own intrepid spirit into the troops, whom he conducted with the talents of a consummate general; and to his abilities, rather than to his fortune, we may ascribe the signal victories which he obtained over the foreign and domestic foes of the republic.

Had Constantine fallen on the banks of the Tiber, or even in the plains of Hadrianople, such is the character which, with a few exceptions, he might have transmitted to posterity. But the conclusion of his reign (according to the moderate and indeed tender sentence of a writer of the same age) degraded him from the rank which he had acquired among the most deserving of the Roman princes. The general peace which he maintained during the last fourteen years of his reign was a period of apparent splendor rather than of real prosperity; and the old age of Constantine was disgraced by the opposite yet reconcilable vices of rapaciousness and prodigality. The accumulated treasures found in the palaces of Maxentius and Licinius were lavishly consumed; the various innovations introduced by the conqueror were attended with an increasing expense; the cost of his buildings, his court, and his festivals required an immediate and plentiful supply; and the oppression of the people was the only fund which could support the magnificence of the sovereign. His unworthy favorites, enriched by the boundless liberality of their master, usurped with impunity the privilege of rapine and corruption. A secret but universal decay was felt in every part of the public administration, and the emperor himself, though he still retained the obedience, gradually lost the esteem, of his subjects. The dress and manners which, towards the decline of life, he chose to effect, served only to degrade him in the eyes of mankind. The Asiatic pomp which had been adopted by the pride of Diocletian assumed an air of softness and effeminacy in the person of Constantine. He is represented with false hair of various colors, laboriously arranged by the skillful artists of the times; a diadem of a new and more expensive fashion; a profusion of gems and pearls, of collars and bracelets; and a variegated flowing robe of silk, most curiously embroidered with flowers of gold.

The same fortune which so invariably followed the standard of Constantine seemed to secure the hopes and comforts of his domestic life. The emperor had been twice married. Minervina, the obscure but lawful object of his youthful attachment, had left him only one son, who was called Crispus. By Fausta, the daughter of Maximian, he had three daughters, and three sons known by the kindred names of Constantine, Constantius, and Constans. The unambitious brothers of the great Constantine, Julius Constantius, Dalmatius, and Hannibalianus, were permitted to enjoy the most honorable rank and the most affluent fortune that could be consistent with a private station.

Crispus, the eldest son of Constantine, and the presumptive heir of the empire is represented by impartial historians as an amiable and accomplished youth. The care of his education, or at least of his studies, was intrusted to Lactantius, the most eloquent of the Christians; a preceptor admirably qualified to form the taste and to excite the virtues of his illustrious disciple. At the age of seventeen Crispus was invested with the title of Cæsar, and the administration of the Gallic provinces, where the inroads of the Germans gave him an early occasion of signalizing his military prowess. In the civil war which broke out soon afterwards, the father and son divided their powers; and this history has already celebrated the valor as well as conduct displayed by the latter in forcing the straits of the Hellespont, so obstinately defended by the superior fleet of Licinius. This naval victory contributed to determine

Left: Bust of Magnentius the Usurper, Emperor 350–353. (Fourth-century AD, Vienne, France)
Below: Emperor Constantius II (Flavius Julius Constantius 317–61; Roman Emperor 340–361).

Left: Fourth-century imperial family, portrait on gold glass, set in a reliquary cross. (Museo Cristiano, Brescia, Italy)
Right: Samian bowl. (Fourth-century, British, London Museum)

the event of the war, and the names of Constantine and of Crispus were united in the joyful acclamations of their eastern subjects, who loudly proclaimed that the world had been subdued, and was now governed by an emperor endowed with every virtue, and by his illustrious son, a prince beloved of Heaven, and the lively image of his father's perfections. The public favor, which seldom accompanies old age, diffused its luster over the youth of Crispus. He deserved the esteem and he engaged the affections of the court, the army, and the people.

This dangerous popularity soon excited the attention of Constantine, who, both as a father and as a king, was impatient of an equal. Instead of attempting to secure the allegiance of his son by the generous ties of confidence and gratitude, he resolved to prevent the mischiefs which might be apprehended from dissatisfied ambition. An edict of Constantine, published about this time, manifestly indicates his real or affected suspicions that a secret conspiracy had been formed against his person and government. By all the allurements of honors and rewards he invites informers of every degree to accuse, without exception, his magistrates or ministers, his friends or his most intimate favorites, protesting, with a solemn asseveration, that he himself will listen to the charge, that he himself will revenge his injuries; and concluding with a prayer, which discovers some apprehension of danger, that the providence of the Supreme Being may still continue to protect the safety of the emperor and of the empire.

The informers who complied with so liberal an invitation were sufficiently versed in the arts of courts to select the friends and adherents of Crispus as the guilty persons; nor is there any reason to distrust the veracity of the emperor, who had promised an ample measure of revenge and punishment. The policy of Constantine maintained, however, the same appearances of regard and confidence towards a son whom he began to consider as his most irreconcilable enemy. Medals were struck with the customary vows for the long and auspicious reign of the young Cæsar; and as the people, who were not admitted into the secrets of the palace, still loved his virtues and respected his dignity, a poet, who solicits his recall from exile, adores with equal devotion the majesty of the father and that of the son. The time was now arrived for celebrating the august ceremony of the twentieth year of the reign of Constantine, and the emperor, for that purpose, removed his court from Nicomedia to Rome, where the most splendid preparations had been made for his reception. Every eye and every tongue affected to express their sense of the general happiness, and the veil of ceremony and dissimulation was drawn for a while over the darkest designs of revenge and murder. In the midst of the festival the unfortunate Crispus was apprehended by order of the emperor, who laid aside the tenderness of a father without assuming the equity of a judge. The examination was short and private; and as it was thought decent to conceal the fate of the young prince from the eyes of the Roman people, he was sent under a strong guard to Pola, in Istria, where, soon afterwards, he was put to death, either by the hand of the executioner or by the more gentle operation of poison.

By the death of Crispus the inheritance of the empire seemed to devolve on the three sons of Fausta, who have been already mentioned under the names of Constantine, of Constantius, and of Constans. These young princes were successively invested with the title of Cæsar, and the dates of their promotion may be referred to the tenth, the twentieth, and the thirtieth years of the reign of their father. This conduct, though it tended to multiply the future masters of the Roman world, might be excused by the partiality of paternal affection; but it is not so easy to understand the motives of the emperor, when he endangered the safety both of his family and of his people by the unnecessary elevation of his two nephews, Dalmatius and Hannibalianus. The former was raised, by the title of Cæsar, to an equality with his cousins. In favor of the latter, Constantine invented the new and singular appellation of *Nobilissimus*, to which he annexed the flattering distinction of a robe of purple and gold.

The whole empire was deeply interested in the education of these five youths, the acknowledged successors of Constantine. His destined successors had the misfortune of being born and educated in the Imperial purple. Incessantly surrounded with a train of flatterers, they passed their youth in the enjoyment of luxury and the expectation of a throne; not would the dignity of their rank permit them to descend from that elevated station from whence the various characters of human nature appear to wear a smooth and uniform aspect. The

indulgence of Constantine admitted them, at a very tender age, to share the administration of the empire; and they studied the art of reigning, at the expense of the people intrusted to their care. The younger Constantine was appointed to hold his court in Gaul; and his brother Constantius exchanged that department, the ancient patrimony of their father, for the more opulent, but less martial, countries of the East. Italy, the Western Illyricum, and Africa, were accustomed to revere Constans, the third of his sons, as the representative of the great Constantine. He fixed Dalmatius on the Gothic frontier, to which he annexed the government of Thrace, Macedonia, and Greece. The city of Cæsarea was chosen for the residence of Hannibalianus; and the provinces of Pontus, Cappadocia, and the Lesser Armenia, were designed to form the extent of his new kingdom. For each of these princes a suitable establishment was provided. A just proportion of guards, of legions, and of auxiliaries, was allotted for their respective dignity and defense. The ministers and generals who were placed about their persons were such as Constantine could trust to assist, and even to control, these youthful sovereigns in the exercise of their delegated power. As they advanced in years and experience, the limits of their authority were insensibly enlarged: but the emperor always reserved for himself the title of Augustus; and while he showed the *Cæsars* to the armies and provinces, he maintained every part of the empire in equal obedience to its supreme head. The tranquillity of the last fourteen years of his reign was scarcely interrupted by the contemptible in-surrection of a camel-driver in the island of Cyprus, or by the active part which the policy of Constantine engaged him to assume in the wars of the Goths and Sarmatians.

At the mature age of sixty-four, after a short illness, Constantine ended his memorable life at the palace of Aquyrion, in the suburbs of Nicomedia, whither he had retired for the benefit of the air, and with the hope of recruiting his exhausted strength by the use of the warm baths. The excessive demonstrations of grief, or at least of mourning, surpassed whatever had been practiced on any former occasion.

The voice of the dying emperor had recommended the care of his funeral to the piety of Constantius; and that prince, by the vicinity of his eastern station, could easily prevent the diligence of his brothers, who resided in their distant governments of Italy and Gaul. As soon as he had taken possession of the palace of Constantinople, his first care was to remove the apprehensions of his kinsmen, by a solemn oath which he pledged for their security. His next employment was to find some specious pretence which might release his conscience from the obligation of an imprudent promise. The arts of fraud were made subservient to the designs of cruelty; and a manifest forgery was attested by a person of the most sacred character. From the hands of the bishop of Nicomedia, Constantius received a fatal scroll, affirmed to be the genuine testament of his father; in which the emperor expressed his suspicions that he had been poisoned by his brothers; and conjured his sons to revenge his death, and to consult their own safety, by the punishment of the guilty. Whatever reasons might have been alleged by these unfortunate princes to defend their life and honor against so incredible an accusation, they were silenced by the furious clamors of the soldiers, who declared themselves, at once, their enemies, their judges, and their executioners. The spirit, and even the forms, of legal proceedings were repeatedly violated in a promiscuous massacre; which involved the two uncles of Constantius, seven of his cousins, of whom Dalmatius and Hannibalianus were the most illustrious, the Patrician Optatus, who had married a sister of the late emperor, and the præfect Ablavius, whose power and riches had inspired him with some hopes of obtaining the purple. Of so numerous a family, Gallus and Julian alone, the two youngest children of Julius Constantius, were saved from the hand of the assassins, till their rage, satiated with slaughter, had in some measure subsided.

Silver bowl with a domed lid. (Mildenhall Treasure, fourth-century, British Museum, London)

The massacre of the Flavian race was succeeded by a new division of the provinces, which was ratified in a personal interview of the three brothers. Constantine, the eldest of the Cæsars, obtained, with a certain pre-eminence of rank, the possession of the new capital, which bore his own name and that of his father. Thrace and the countries of the East were allotted for the patrimony of Constantius; and Constans was acknowledged as the lawful sovereign of Italy, Africa, and the western Illyricum. The armies submitted to their hereditary right, and they condescended, after some delay, to accept from the Roman senate the title of *Augustus*. When they first assumed the reins of government, the eldest of these princes was twenty-one, the second twenty, and the third only seventeen, years of age.

During the long period of the reign of Constantius the provinces of the East were afflicted by the calamities of the Persian war. The irregular incursions of the light troops alternately spread terror and devastation beyond the Tigris and beyond the Euphrates, from the gates of Ctesiphon to those of Antioch, and this active service was performed by the Arabs of the desert, who were divided in their interest and affections, some of their independent chiefs being enlisted in the party of Sapor, while others had engaged their doubtful fidelity to the emperor. The more grave and important operations of the war were conducted with equal vigor; and the armies of Rome and Persia encountered each other in nine bloody fields, in two of which Constantius himself commanded in person.

Whatever advantages might attend the arms of Sapor in the field, though nine repeated victories diffused among the nations the fame of his valor and conduct, he could not hope to succeed in the execution of his designs while the fortified towns of Mesopotamia, and, above all, the strong and ancient city of Nisibis, remained in the possession of the Romans. Notwithstanding the disappointment of his hopes and the loss of more than twenty thousand men, Sapor still pressed the reduction of Nisibis with an obstinate firmness which could have yielded only to the necessity of defending the eastern provinces of Persia against a formidable invasion of the Massagetæ. Alarmed by this intelligence, he hastily relinquished the siege, and marched with rapid diligence from the banks of the Tigris to those of the Oxus. The danger and difficulties of the Scythian war engaged him soon afterwards to conclude, or at least to observe, a truce with the Roman emperor, which was equally grateful to both princes, as Constantius himself, after the deaths of his two brothers, was involved, by the revolutions of the West, in a civil contest which required and seemed to exceed the most vigorous exertion of his undivided strength.

After the partition of the empire three years had scarcely elapsed before the sons of Constantine seemed impatient to convince mankind that they were incapable of contenting themselves with the dominions which they were unqualified to govern. The eldest of those princes soon complained that he was defrauded of his just proportion of the spoils of their murdered kinsmen; and though he might yield to the superior

Pewter jug and bowl.
(Fourth-century AD, London Museum)

Silver medallion of
Magnentius. (British
Museum, London)

guilt and merit of Constantius, he exacted from Constans the cession of the African provinces, as an equivalent for the rich countries of Macedonia and Greece which his brother had acquired by the death of Dalmatius. The want of sincerity which Constantine experienced in a tedious and fruitless negotiation exasperated the fierceness of his temper, and he eagerly listened to those favorites who suggested to him that his honor, as well as his interest, was concerned in the prosecution of the quarrel. At the head of a tumultuary band, suited for rapine rather than for conquest, he suddenly broke into the dominions of Constans, by the way of the Julian Alps, and the country round Aquileia felt the first effects of his resentment. The measures of Constans, who then resided in Dacia, were directed with more prudence and ability. On the news of his brother's invasion he detached a select and disciplined body of his Illyrian troops, proposing to follow them in person with the remainder of his forces. But the conduct of his lieutenants soon terminated the unnatural contest. By the artful appearances of flight, Constantine was betrayed into an ambuscade, which had been concealed in a wood, where the rash youth, with a few attendants, was surprised, surrounded, and slain. His body, after it had been found in the obscure stream of the Alsa, obtained the honors of an Imperial sepulcher, but his provinces transferred their allegiance to the conqueror, who, refusing to admit his elder brother Constantius to any share in these new acquisitions, maintained the undisputed possession of more than two-thirds of the Roman empire.

The fate of Constans himself was delayed about ten years longer, and the revenge of his brother's death was reserved for the more ignoble hand of a domestic traitor. The pernicious tendency of the system introduced by Constantine was displayed in the feeble administration of his sons, who, by their vices and weakness, soon lost the esteem and affections of their people. Magnentius, an ambitious soldier, who was himself of barbarian extraction, was encouraged by the public discontent to assert the honor of the Roman name. By his secrecy and diligence he entertained some hopes of surprising the person of Constans, who was pursuing in the adjacent forest his favorite amusement of hunting, or perhaps some pleasures of a more private and criminal nature. The rapid progress of fame allowed him, however, an instant for flight, though the desertion of his soldiers and subjects deprived him of the power of resistance. Before he could reach a seaport in Spain, where he intended to embark, he was overtaken near Helena, at the foot of the Pyrenees, by a party of light cavalry, whose chief, regardless of the sanctity of a temple, executed his commission by the murder of the son of Constantine.

As soon as the death of Constans had decided this easy but important revolution, the example of the court of Autun was imitated by the provinces of the West. The authority of Magnentius was acknowledged through the whole extent of the two great præfectures of Gaul and Italy; and the usurper prepared, by every act of oppression, to collect a treasure which might discharge the obligation of an immense donative and supply the expenses of a civil war.

The intelligence of these important events, which so deeply affected the honor and safety of the Imperial house, recalled the arms of Constantius from the inglorious prosecution of the Persian war. He recommended the care of the East to his lieutenants, and afterwards to his cousin Gallus, whom he raised from a prison to a throne, and marched towards Europe, with a mind agitated by the conflict of hope and fear, of grief and indignation. On his arrival at Heraclea in Thrace, the emperor gave audience to the ambassadors of Magnentius. These deputies were instructed to soothe the resentment, and to alarm the fears, of Constantius. They were empowered to offer him the friendship and alliance of the western princes, to cement their union by a double marriage—of Constantius with the daughter of Magnentius, and of Magnentius himself with the ambitious Constantina—and to acknowledge in the treaty the pre-eminence of rank which might justly be claimed by the emperor of the East. Should pride and mistaken piety urge him to refuse these equitable conditions, the ambassadors were ordered to expatiate on the inevitable ruin which must attend his rashness, if he ventured to provoke the sovereigns of the West to exert their superior strength, and to employ against him that valor, those abilities, and those legions, to which the house of Constantine had been indebted for so many triumphs. Such propositions and such arguments appeared to deserve the most serious attention; the answer of Constantius was deferred till the next day; and as he had reflected on the importance of justifying a civil war in the opinion of the people, he thus addressed his council, who listened with real or affected credulity: 'Last night,' said he, 'after I retired to rest, the shade of the great Constantine, embracing the corpse of my murdered brother, rose before my eyes; his well-known voice awakened me to revenge, forbade me to despair of the republic, and assured me of the success and immortal glory which would crown the justice of my arms.' The authority of such a vision, or rather of the prince who alleged it, silenced every doubt, and excluded all negotiation.

Such was the conduct, and such perhaps was the duty, of the brother of Constans towards the perfidious usurper of Gaul.

The tyrant advanced by rapid marches to encounter Constantius, at the head of a numerous army, composed of Gauls and Spaniards, of Franks and Saxons; of those provincials who supplied the strength of the legions, and of those barbarians who were dreaded as the most formidable enemies of the republic. The fertile plains of the Lower Pannonia, between the Drave, the Save, and the Danube, presented a spacious theater; and the operations of the civil war were protracted during the summer months by the skill or timidity of the combatants. Constantius had declared his intention of deciding the quarrel in the fields of Cibalis, a name that would animate his troops by the remembrance of the victory which, on the same auspicious ground, had been obtained by the arms of his father Constantine. Yet, by the impregnable fortifications with which the emperor encompassed his camp, he appeared to decline rather than to invite a general engagement. It was the object of Magnentius to tempt or to compel his adversary to relinquish this advantageous position; and he employed with that view the various marches, evolutions, and stratagems which the knowledge of the art of war could suggest to an experienced officer. During the greater part of the summer the tyrant of Gaul showed himself master of the field. The troops of Constantius were harassed and dispirited.

Directing his march towards Mursa, Magnentius set fire to the gates, and, by a sudden assault, had almost scaled the walls of the town. The vigilance of the garrison extinguished the flames; the approach of Constantius left him no time to continue the operations of the siege; and the emperor soon removed the only obstacle that could embarrass his motions, by forcing a body of troops which had taken post in an adjoining amphitheater. The signal victory which Constantius obtained is attributed to the arms of his cavalry. His cuirassiers are described as so many massy statues of steel, glittering with their scaly armor, and breaking with their ponderous lances the firm array of the Gallic legions. As soon as the legions gave way, the lighter and more active squadrons of the second line rode sword in hand into the intervals and completed the disorder. In the meanwhile, the huge bodies of the Germans were exposed almost naked to the dexterity of the Oriental archers; and whole troops of those barbarians were urged by anguish and despair to precipitate themselves into the broad and rapid stream of the Drave. The number of the slain was computed at fifty-four thousand men. The tyrant seems to have displayed the virtues of a general and of a soldier till the day was irrecoverably lost, and his camp in the possession of the enemy. Magnentius then consulted his safety, and, throwing away the Imperial ornaments, escaped with some difficulty from the pursuit of the light horse, who incessantly followed his rapid flight from the banks of Drave to the foot of the Julian Alps.

CHAPTER SIXTEEN

Constantius as sole Emperor – elevation and death of Gallus – danger and elevation of Julian – victories of Julian in Gaul

[AD 351–360]

THE divided provinces of the empire were again united by the victory of Constantius; but as that feeble prince was destitute of personal merit either in peace or war; as he feared his generals, and distrusted his ministers; the triumph of his arms served only to establish the reign of the *eunuchs* over the Roman world. They multiplied in the palaces of his degenerate sons, and insensibly acquired the knowledge, and at length the direction, of the secret councils of Constantius. Of these slaves the most distinguished was the chamberlain Eusebius, who ruled the monarch and the palace with such absolute sway, that Constantius, according to the sarcasm of an impartial historian, possessed some credit with this haughty favorite.

At length, the emergencies of the state compelled the emperor, or rather his eunuchs, to invest Gallus, in the twenty-fifth year of his age, with the title of Cæsar, and to cement this political connection by his marriage with the princess Constantia. After a formal interview, in which the two princes mutually engaged their faith never to undertake anything to the prejudice of each other, they repaired without delay to their respective stations. Constantius continued his march towards the West, and Gallus fixed his residence at Antioch; from whence, with a delegated authority, he administered the five great dioceses of the eastern præfecture. In this fortunate change, the new Cæsar was not unmindful of his brother Julian, who obtained the honors of his rank, the appearances of liberty, and the restitution of an ample patrimony.

The writers the most indulgent to the memory of Gallus, and even Julian himself, though he wished to cast a veil over the frailties of his brother, are obliged to confess that the Cæsar was incapable of reigning. The cruelty of Gallus was sometimes displayed in the undissembled violence of popular or military executions: and was sometimes disguised by the abuse of law and the forms of judicial proceedings. The private houses of Antioch, and the palaces of public resort, were besieged by spies and informers; and the Cæsar himself, concealed in a plebeian habit, very frequently condescended to assume that odious character. Every apartment of the palace was adorned with the instruments of death and torture, and a general consternation was diffused through the capital of Syria. But he forgot that he was depriving himself of his only support, the affection of the people; while he furnished the malice of his enemies with the arms of truth, and afforded the emperor the fairest pretense of exacting the forfeit of his purple and of his life.

But as it still appeared dangerous to arrest Gallus in his capital, the slow and safer arts of dissimulation were practiced with success. The frequent and pressing epistles of Constantius were filled with professions of confidence and friendship, exhorting the Cæsar to discharge the duties of his high station, to relieve his colleague from a part of the public cares, and to assist the West by his presence, his counsels, and his arms.

After a long delay the reluctant Cæsar set forward on his journey to the Imperial court. At Petovio in Pannonia in the close of the evening he was arrested, ignominiously stripped of the ensigns of Cæsar, and hurried away to Pola, in Istria, a sequestered prison, which had been so recently polluted with royal blood. The Cæsar sunk under the weight of shame and guilt, confessed all the criminal actions and all the treasonable designs with which he was charged. The emperor was easily convinced that his own safety was incompatible with the life of his cousin: the sentence of death was signed, dispatched, and executed; and the nephew of Constantine, with his hands tied behind his back, was beheaded in prison, like the vilest malefactor.

Besides the reigning emperor, Julian alone survived of all the numerous posterity of Constantius Chlorus. The misfortune of his royal birth involved him in the disgrace of Gallus. From his retirement in the happy country of Ionia he was conveyed, under a strong guard, to the court of Milan, where he languished above seven months in the continual apprehension of suffering the same ignominious death which was daily inflicted, almost before his eyes, on the friends and adherents of his persecuted family. Julian most devoutly ascribes his miraculous deliverance to the protection of the gods, who had exempted his innocence from the sentence of destruction pronounced by their justice against the impious house of Constantine. As the most effectual instrument of their providence, he gratefully acknowledges the steady and generous friendship of the empress Eusebia, a woman of beauty and merit, who, by the ascendant which she had gained over the mind of her husband, counterbalanced in some measure the powerful conspiracy of the eunuchs. By the intercession of his patroness Julian was admitted into the Imperial presence: he pleaded his cause with a decent freedom; he was heard with favor; and, notwithstanding the efforts of his enemies, who urged the danger of sparing an avenger of the blood of Gallus, the milder sentiment of Eusebia prevailed in the council. But the effects of a second interview were dreaded by the eunuchs; and Julian was advised to withdraw for a while into the neighborhood of Milan, till the emperor thought proper to assign the city of Athens for the place of his honorable exile.

Left: Titus Flavius, cavalry general. (Fourth century AD, Germany)
Below: Early Christian jewelry – gold mount with scenes of a lion hunt, 51mm, c AD 350. (British Museum)

While his hours were passed in studious retirement, the empress, resolute to achieve the generous design which she had undertaken, was not unmindful of the care of his fortune. The death of the late Cæsar had left Constantius invested with the sole command, and oppressed by the accumulated weight, of a mighty empire. Before the wounds of civil discord could be healed, the provinces of Gaul were overwhelmed by a deluge of barbarians. The Sarmatians no longer respected the barrier of the Danube. The impunity of rapine had increased the boldness and numbers of the wild Isaurians; those robbers descended from their craggy mountains to ravage the adjacent country, and had even presumed, though without success, to besiege the important city of Seleucia, which was defended by a garrison of three Roman legions. Above all, the Persian monarch, elated by victory, again threatened the peace of Asia; and the presence of the emperor was indispensably required both in the West and in the East. For the first time Constantius sincerely acknowledged that his single strength was unequal to such an extent of care and of dominion. Insensible to the voice of flattery, which assured him that his all-powerful virtue and celestial fortune would still continue to triumph over every obstacle, he listened with complacency to the advice of Eusebia, which gratified his indolence, without offending his suspicious pride. As she perceived that the remembrance of Gallus dwelt on the emperor's mind, she artfully turned his attention to the opposite characters of the two brothers, which from their infancy had been compared to those of Domitian and of Titus. She accustomed her husband to consider Julian as a youth of a mild, unambitious disposition, whose allegiance and gratitude might be secured by the gift of the purple, and who was qualified to fill with honor a subordinate station, without aspiring to dispute the commands or to shade the glories of his sovereign and benefactor. After an obstinate though secret struggle, the opposition of the favorite eunuchs submitted to the ascendancy of the empress; and it was resolved that Julian, after celebrating his nuptials with Helena, sister of Constantius, should be appointed, with the title of Cæsar, to reign over the countries beyond the Alps.

Under these melancholy circumstances, an inexperienced youth was appointed to save and to govern the provinces of Gaul, or rather, as he expresses it himself, to exhibit the vain image of Imperial greatness. The retired scholastic education of Julian, in which he had been more conversant with books than with arms, with the dead than with the living, left him in profound ignorance of the practical arts of war and government; and when he awkwardly repeated some military exercise which it was necessary for him to learn, he exclaimed with a sigh, 'O Plato, Plato, what a task for a philosopher!'

Immediately after Julian had received the purple at Milan he was sent into Gaul with a feeble retinue of three hundred and sixty soldiers. In his march from Autun, through the heart of the Gallic provinces, Julian embraced with ardor the earliest opportunity of signalizing his courage. The aspect of their young prince revived the drooping spirit of the soldiers, and they marched from Rheims in search of the enemy with a confidence which had almost proved fatal to them. The Alemanni, familiarized to the knowledge of the country, secretly collected their scattered forces, and, seizing the opportunity of a dark and rainy day, poured with unexpected fury on the rear-guard of the Romans. Before the inevitable disorder could be remedied, two legions were destroyed; and Julian was taught by experience that caution and vigilance are the most important lessons of the art of war. In a second and more successful action he recovered and established his military fame. The power of the enemy was yet unbroken; and the Cæsar had no sooner separated his troops, and fixed his own quarters at Sens, in the center of Gaul, than he was surrounded and besieged by a numerous host of Germans. Reduced in this extremity to the resources of his own mind, he displayed a prudent intrepidity which compensated for all the deficiencies of the place and garrison; and the barbarians, at the end of thirty days, were obliged to retire with disappointed rage.

The Alemanni meanwhile prepared to chastise the Roman youth who presumed to dispute the possession of that country which they claimed as their own by the right of conquest and of treaties. They employed three days, and as many nights, in transporting over the Rhine their military powers. The fierce Chnodomar, shaking the ponderous javelin which he had victoriously wielded against the brother of Magnentius, led the van of the barbarians, and moderated by his experience the martial ardor which his example inspired. He was followed by six other kings, by ten princes of regal extraction, by a long train of high-spirited nobles, and by thirty-five thousand of the bravest warriors of the tribes of Germany. The confidence derived from the view of their own strength was increased by the intelligence which they received from a deserter, that the Cæsar, with a feeble army of thirteen thousand men, occupied a post about one-and-twenty miles from their camp of Strasburg. With this inadequate force Julian resolved to seek and to encounter the barbarian host; and the chance of a general action was preferred to the tedious and uncertain operation of separately engaging the dispersed parties of the Alemanni. The Romans marched in close order, and in two columns; the cavalry on the right, the infantry on the left; and the day was so far spent when they appeared in sight of the enemy, that Julian was desirous of deferring the battle till the next morning, and of allowing his troops to recruit their exhausted strength by the necessary refreshments of sleep and food. Yielding, however, with some reluctance, to the clamors of the soldiers, and even to the opinion of his council, he exhorted them to justify by their valor the eager impatience which, in case of a defeat, would be universally branded with the epithets of rashness and presumption. The trumpets sounded, the military shout was heard through the field, and the two armies rushed with equal fury to the charge, The Caesar, who conducted in person his right wing, depended on the dexterity of his archers and the weight of his cuirassiers. But his ranks were instantly broken by an irregular mixture of light-horse and of light-infantry, and he had the mortification of beholding the flight of six hundred of his most renowned cuirassiers. The fugitives were stopped and rallied by the presence and authority of Julian, who, careless of his own safety, threw himself before them, and, urging every motive of shame and honor, led them back against the victorious enemy. The conflict between the two lines of infantry was obstinate and bloody. The Germans possessed the superiority of strength and stature, the Romans that of discipline and temper; and as the barbarians who served under the standard of the empire united the respective advantages of both parties, their strenuous efforts, guided by a skillful leader, at length determined the event of the day. The Romans lost four tribunes, and two hundred and forty-three soldiers, in this memorable battle of Strasburg, so glorious to the Cæsar, and so salutary to the afflicted provinces of Gaul.

Roman betrothal ring worked in gold in the shape of clasped right hands. (Third–fourth century AD)

A silver scrinium circular casket for storing receptacles for five different unguents. The design is typical of the work of the late decadent classical period. (Fourth century AD, Rome)

Six thousand of the Alemanni were slain in the field, without including those who were drowned in the Rhine, or transfixed with darts whilst they attempted to swim across the river. Chnodomar himself was surrounded and taken prisoner, with three of his brave companions, who had devoted themselves to follow in life or death the fate of their chieftain. Julian received him with military pomp in the council of his officers; and expressing a generous pity for the fallen state, dissembled his inward contempt for the abject humiliation of his captive. Instead of exhibiting the vanquished king of the Alemanii as a grateful spectacle to the cities of Gaul, he respectfully laid at the feet of the emperor this splendid trophy of his victory. Chnodomar experienced an honorable treatment: but the impatient barbarian could not long survive his defeat, his confinement, and his exile.

As soon as the valor and conduct of Julian had secured an interval of peace, he applied himself to a work more congenial to his humane and philosophic temper. The cities of Gaul, which had suffered from the inroads of the barbarians, he diligently repaired; and seven important posts, between Mentz and the mouth of the Rhine, are particularly mentioned as having been rebuilt and fortified by the order of Julian. The vanquished Germans had submitted to the just but humiliating condition of preparing and conveying the necessary materials. The active zeal of Julian urged the prosecution of the work, and such was the spirit which he had diffused among the troops that the auxiliaries themselves, waiving their exemption from any duties of fatigue, contended in the most servile labors with the diligence of the Roman soldiers. It was incumbent on the Cæsar to provide for the subsistence as well as for the safety of the inhabitants and of the garrisons. The desertion of the former, and the mutiny of the latter, must have been the fatal and inevitable consequences of famine. The tillage of the provinces of Gaul had been interrupted by the calamities of war; but the scanty harvests of the continent were supplied, by his paternal care, from the plenty of the adjacent island. Six hundred large barques, framed in the forest of the Ardennes, made several voyages to the coast of Britain; and returning from thence, laden with corn, sailed up the Rhine, and distributed their cargoes to the several towns and fortresses along the banks of the river. The arms of Julian had restored a free and secure navigation, which Constantius had offered to purchase at the expense of his dignity, and of a tributary present of two thousand pounds of silver. The emperor parsimoniously refused to his soldiers the sums which he granted with a lavish and trembling hand to the barbarians. The dexterity, as well as the firmness of Julian, was put to a severe trial, when he took the field with a discontented army, which had already served two campaigns without receiving any regular pay or any extraordinary donative.

The precarious and dependent situation of Julian displayed his virtues and concealed his defects. The young hero who supported, in Gaul, the throne of Constantius, was not permitted to reform the vices of the government; but he had courage to alleviate or to pity the distress of the people. Unless he had been able to revive the martial spirit of the Romans, or to introduce the arts of industry and refinement among their savage enemies, he could not entertain any rational hopes of securing the public tranquillity, either by the peace or conquest of Germany. Yet the victories of Julian suspended for a short time the inroads of the barbarians, and delayed the ruin of the Western Empire.

CHAPTER SEVENTEEN

The effects of the conversion of Constantine – establishment of the Christian Catholic Church

the Arian controversy – distracted state of the Church and Empire under Constantine and his sons

[AD 306–348]

THE public establishment of Christianity may be considered as one of the most important and domestic revolutions which excite the most lively curiosity, and afford the most valuable instruction. The victories and the civil policy of Constantine no longer influence the state of Europe; but a considerable portion of the globe still retains the impression which it received from the conversion of that monarch; and the ecclesiastical institutions of his reign are still connected, by an indissoluble chain, with the opinions, the passions, and the interests of the present generation.

Whatever symptoms of Christian piety might transpire in the discourses or actions of Constantine, he persevered till he was near forty years of age in the practice of the established religion; and the same conduct which in the court of Nicomedia might be imputed to his fear, could be ascribed only to the inclination or policy of the sovereign of Gaul. His liberality restored and enriched the temples of the gods; the medals which issued from his Imperial mint are impressed with the figures and attributes of Jupiter and Apollo, of Mars and Hercules; and his filial piety increased the council of Olympus by the solemn apotheosis of his father Constantius. But the devotion of Constantine was more peculiarly directed to the genius of the Sun, the Apollo of Greek and Roman mythology; and he was pleased to be represented with the symbols of the God of Light and Poetry. The unerring shafts of that deity, the brightness of his eyes, his laurel wreath, immortal beauty, and elegant accomplishments, seem to point him out as the patron of a young hero. The altars of Apollo were crowned with the votive offerings of Constantine; and the credulous multitude were taught to believe that the emperor was permitted to behold with mortal eyes the visible majesty of their tutelar deity; and that, either waking or in a vision, he was blessed with the auspicious omens of a long and victorious reign. The Sun was universally celebrated as the invincible guide and protector of Constantine; and the Pagans might reasonably expect that the insulted god would pursue with unrelenting vengeance the impiety of his ungrateful favorite.

As long as Constantine exercised a limited sovereignty over the provinces of Gaul, his Christian subjects were protected by the authority, and perhaps by the laws, of a prince who wisely left to the gods the care of vindicating their own honor. If we may credit the assertion of Constantine himself, he had been an indignant spectator of the savage cruelties which were inflicted, by the hands of Roman soldiers, on those citizens whose religion was their only crime. In the East and in the West he had seen the different effects of severity and indulgence; and as the former was rendered still more odious by the example of Galerius, his implacable enemy, the latter was recommended to his imitation by the authority and advice of a dying father. The son of Constantius, immediately suspended or repealed the edicts of persecution, and granted the free exercise of their religious ceremonies to all those who had already professed themselves members of the church. They were soon encouraged to depend on the favor as well as on the justice of their sovereign, who had imbibed a secret and sincere reverence for the name of Christ, and for the God of the Christians.

About five months after the conquest of Italy, the emperor made a solemn and authentic declaration of his sentiments by the celebrated edict of Milan, which restored peace to the catholic church. In the personal interview of the two western princes, Constantine, by the ascendant of genius and power, obtained the ready concurrence of his colleague, Licinius; the union of their names and authority disarmed the fury of Maximin; and, after the death of the tyrant of the East, the edict of Milan was received as a general and fundamental law of the Roman world.

The irresistible power of the Roman emperors was displayed in the important and dangerous change of the national religion. The terrors of a military force silenced the faint and unsupported murmurs of the Pagans, and there was reason to expect that the cheerful submission of the Christian clergy, as well as people, would be the result of conscience and gratitude. It was long since established as a fundamental maxim of the Roman constitution, that every rank of citizens was alike subject to the laws, and that the care of religion was the right as well as duty of the civil magistrate. Constantine and his successors could not easily persuade themselves that they had forfeited, by their conversion, any branch of the Imperial prerogatives, or that they were incapable of giving laws to a religion which they had protected and embraced. The emperors still continued to exercise a supreme jurisdiction over the ecclesiastical order; and the sixteenth book of the Theodosian code represents, under a variety of titles, the authority which they assumed in the government of the catholic church.

The edict of Milan secured the revenue as well as the peace of the church. The Christians not only recovered the lands and houses of which they had been stripped by the persecuting laws of Diocletian, but they acquired a perfect title to all the possessions which they had hitherto enjoyed by the connivance of the magistrate. As soon as Christianity became the religion of the emperor and the empire, the national clergy might claim a decent and honorable maintenance: and the payment of an annual tax might have delivered the people from the more oppressive tribute which superstition imposes on her votaries. But as the wants and expenses of the church increased with her prosperity, the ecclesiastical order was still supported and enriched by the voluntary oblations of the faithful. Eight years after the edict of Milan, Constantine granted to all his subjects the free and universal permission of bequeathing their fortunes to the holy catholic church;

Left: Head believed to be that of Christ. (Mosaic from St Mary's, Hinton, Devon, fourth century, British Museum)
Below: Eleventh-century interpretation of the Baptism of Constantine.

CONSTANTINE AND THE EDICT OF MILAN

In 313 Constantine (Flavius Valerius Aurelius Constantinus 274–337 AD) adopted Christianity as the official religion of the Roman Empire and under the Edict of Milan the Christians were ceded rights to inherit and dispose of property as they wished. They were entitled to elect their own church government whose prelates nonetheless remained under the jurisdiction of the Emperor.

Unfortunately, the universal toleration of Christianity had no sooner been decreed than the Church and Empire were split by the factions rising out of the Donatist and Arian heresies. The former were confined to Africa but the latter inflamed the entire domain which remained in a bitter debate until Constantine intervened by convening the Council of Nice, in which he pronounced himself in favor of the Nicene Creed. This was the orthodox dogma of Christianity.

Arianism was linked with the neo-Platonist belief in the Logos and held that Christ was not consubstantial with God the Father but rather that He was the first of his created creatures. But the conflict continued long after his reign involving the ruins of emperors and prelates, embroiling the blood of martyrs for two centuries. The disputes were at least in part political rather than theological, Arianism being particularly popular among the northern peoples.

and their devout liberality, which during their lives was checked by luxury or avarice, flowed with a profuse stream at the hour of their death. The wealthy Christians were encouraged by the example of their sovereign.

The grateful applause of the clergy has consecrated the memory of a prince who indulged their passions and promoted their interest. Constantine gave them security, wealth, honors, and revenge; and the support of the orthodox faith was considered as the most sacred and important duty of the civil magistrate. The edict of Milan, the great charter of toleration, had confirmed to each individual of the Roman world the privilege of choosing and professing his own religion. But this inestimable privilege was soon violated: with the knowledge of truth the emperor imbibed the maxims of persecution; and the sects which dissented from the catholic church were afflicted and oppressed by the triumph of Christianity.

The complaints and mutual accusations which assailed the throne of Constantine, as soon as the death of Maxentius had submitted

Africa to his victorious arms, were ill adapted to edify an imperfect proselyte. He learned with surprise that the provinces of that great country, from the confines of Cyrene to the Columns of Hercules, were distracted with religious discord. The schism of the Donatists was confined to Africa; the more diffusive mischief of the Trinitarian controversy successively penetrated into every part of the Christian world. The attention of the prince and people was attracted by this theological dispute; and the decision, at the end of six years, was referred to the authority of the council of Nice.

The unhappy spirit of discord which pervaded the provinces of the East interrupted the triumph of Constantine; but the emperor continued for some time to view with cool and careless indifference the object of the dispute. As he was yet ignorant of the difficulty of appeasing the quarrels of theologians, he addressed to the contending parties, to Alexander and to Arius, a moderating epistle; which may be ascribed with far greater reason to the untutored sense of a soldier and statesman than to the dictates of any of his episcopal counselors. The presence of the monarch swelled the importance of the debate; his attention multiplied the arguments; and he exposed his person with a patient intrepidity which animated the valor of the combatants. Notwithstanding the applause which has been bestowed on the eloquence and sagacity of Constantine, a Roman general, whose religion might be still a subject of doubt, and whose mind had not been enlightened either by study or by inspiration, was indifferently qualified to discuss, in the Greek language, a metaphysical question, or an article of faith. But the credit of his favorite Osius, who appears to have presided in the council of Nice, might dispose the emperor in favor of the orthodox party; and a well-timed insinuation, that the same Eusebius of Nicomedia, who now protected the heretic, had lately assisted the tyrant, might exasperate him against their adversaries. The Nicene creed was ratified by Constantine; and his firm declaration, that those who resisted the divine judgment of the synod must prepare themselves for an immediate exile, annihilated the murmurs of a feeble opposition. The impious Arius was banished into one of the remote provinces of Illyricum; his person and disciples were branded, by law, with the odious name of Porphyrians; his writings were condemned to the flames, and a capital punishment was denounced against those in whose possession they should be found. The emperor had now imbibed the spirit of controversy, and the angry sarcastic style of his edicts was designed to inspire his subjects with the hatred which he had conceived against the enemies of Christ.

While the flames of the Arian controversy consumed the vitals of the empire, the African provinces were infested by their peculiar enemies, the savage fanatics who, under the name of *Circumcellions*, formed the strength and scandal of the Donatist party.

The divisions of Christianity suspended the ruin of *Paganism;* and the holy war against the infidels was less vigorously prosecuted by princes and bishops who were more immediately alarmed by the guilt and danger of domestic rebellion. The extirpation of *idolatry* might have been justified by the established principles of intolerance: but the hostile sects, which alternately reigned in the Imperial court, were mutually apprehensive of alienating, and perhaps exasperating, the minds of a powerful, though declining faction. Every motive of authority and fashion, of interest and reason, now militated on the side of Christianity; but two or three generations elapsed before their victorious influence was universally felt. The religion which had so long and so lately been established in the Roman empire was still revered by a numerous people, less attached indeed to speculative opinion than to ancient custom. The honors of the state and army were indifferently bestowed on all the subjects of Constantine and Constantius; and a considerable portion of knowledge and wealth and valor was still engaged in the service of polytheism. The superstition of the senator and of the peasant, of the poet and the philosopher, was derived from very different causes, but they met with equal devotion in the temples of the gods. Their zeal was insensibly provoked by the insulting triumph of a proscribed sect; and their hopes were revived by the well-grounded confidence that the presumptive heir of the empire, a young and valiant hero, who had delivered Gaul from the arms of the barbarians, had secretly embraced the religion of his ancestors.

Left: The Council of Constantinople, convened a few years after the Council of Nice, which ratified the Nicene Creed. (Ms of St Gregory of Nazianus, ninth century AD, Bibliothèque Nationale)
Right: (top) Orthodox Christians escaping persecution by boat and (below) Arians setting fire to an Orthodox Church. (Ms of St Gregory of Nazianus, ninth century AD, Bibliothèque Nationale, Paris)

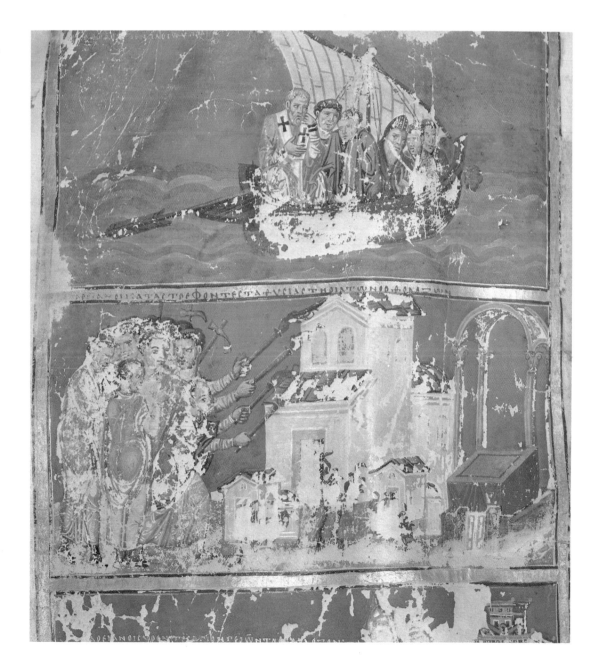

CHAPTER EIGHTEEN

Julian is declared Emperor by the legion of Gaul – his march and success – the death of Constantius – civil administration of Julian

[AD 360–361]

WHILE the Romans languished under the ignominious tyranny of eunuchs and bishops, the praises of Julian were repeated with transport in every part of the empire, except in the palace of Constantius. The voice of malicious folly was at length silenced by the shouts of victory; the conqueror of the Franks and Alemanni could no longer be painted as an object of contempt; and the monarch himself was meanly ambitious of stealing from his lieutenant the honorable reward of his labors. In the letters crowned with laurel, which, according to ancient custom, were addressed to the provinces, the name of Julian was omitted. 'Constantius had made his dispositions in person; *he* had signalized his valor in the foremost ranks; *his* military conduct had secured the victory; and the captive king of the barbarians was presented to *him* on the field of battle,' from which he was at that time distant above forty days' journey. So extravagant a fable was incapable, however, of deceiving the public credulity, or even of satisfying the pride of the emperor himself. Secretly conscious that the applause and favor of the Romans accompanied the rising fortunes of Julian, his discontented mind was prepared to receive the subtle poison of those artful sycophants who colored their mischievous designs with the fairest appearances of truth and candor. Instead of depreciating the merits of Julian, they acknowledged, and even exaggerated, his popular fame, superior talents, and important services. But they darkly insinuated that the virtues of the Cæsar might instantly be converted into the most dangerous crimes, if the inconstant multitude should prefer their inclinations to their duty; or if the general of a victorious army should be tempted from his allegiance by the hopes of revenge and independent greatness. The personal fears of Constantius were interpreted by his council as a laudable anxiety for the public safety; while in private, he disguised the sentiments of hatred and envy which he had secretly conceived for the inimitable virtues of Julian.

The apparent tranquillity of Gaul, and the imminent danger of the eastern provinces, offered a specious pretense for the design which was artfully concerted by the Imperial ministers. They resolved to disarm the Cæsar; to recall those faithful troops who guarded his person and dignity; and to employ, in a distant war against the Persian monarch, the hardy veterans who had vanquished, on the banks of the Rhine, the fiercest nations of Germany. While Julian used the laborious hours of his winter quarters at Paris in the administration of power, he was surprised by the hasty arrival of a tribune and a notary, with positive orders from the emperor, which *they* were directed to execute, and *he* was commanded not to oppose. Constantius signified his pleasure that four entire legions – the Celtæ and Petulants, the Heruli and the Batavians – should be separated from the standard of Julian, under which they had acquired their fame and discipline; that in each of the remaining bands three hundred of the bravest youths should be selected; and that this numerous detachment, the strength of the Gallic army, should instantly begin their march, and exert their utmost diligence to arrive, before the opening of the campaign, on the frontiers of Persia. The Cæsar foresaw and lamented the consequences of this fatal mandate. Most of the auxiliaries, who engaged their voluntary service, had stipulated that they should never be obliged to pass the Alps. The public faith of Rome, and the personal honor of Julian, had been pledged for the observance of this condition. Such an act of treachery and oppression would destroy the confidence, and excite the resentment, of the independent warriors of Germany.

After a painful conflict, Julian was compelled to acknowledge that obedience was the virtue of the most eminent subject, and that the sovereign alone was entitled to judge of the public welfare. He issued the necessary orders for carrying into execution the commands of Constantius; a part of the troops began their march for the Alps; and the detachments from the several garrisons moved toward their respective places of assembly. They advanced with difficulty through the trembling and affrighted crowds of provincials, who attempted to excite their pity by silent despair or loud lamentations; while the wives of the soldiers, holding their infants in their arms, accused the desertion of their husbands in the mixed language of grief, of tenderness, and of indignation. This scene of general distress afflicted the humanity of the Cæsar; he granted a sufficient number of post-wagons to transport the wives and families of the soldiers, endeavored to alleviate the hardships which he was constrained to inflict, and increased by the most laudable arts his own popularity and the discontent of the exiled troops. The grief of an armed multitude is soon converted into rage; their licentious murmurs, which every hour were communicated from tent to tent with more boldness and effect, prepared their minds for the most daring acts of sedition; and by the connivance of their tribunes a seasonable libel was secretly dispersed, which painted in lively colors the disgrace of the Cæsar, the oppression of the Gallic army, and the feeble vices of the tyrant of Asia. The servants of Constantius were alarmed by the progress of this dangerous spirit. They pressed the Cæsar to hasten the departure of the troops; but they imprudently rejected the honest and judicious advice of Julian, who proposed that they should not march through Paris, and suggested the danger of a last interview.

As soon as the approach of the troops was announced, the Cæsar went out to meet them, and ascended his tribunal, which had been erected in a plain before the gates of the city. The soldiers, who were apprehensive of offending their general by an indecent clamor, or of belying their sentiments by false and venal acclamations, maintained an obstinate silence; and, after a short pause, were dismissed to their

Left: Julian the Apostate (Flavius Claudius Julianus, c 331–63; Roman Emperor 361–63). (The Louvre, Paris)
Below: A pagan sacrifice. (Miniature of Dido sacrificing from the Vatican *Aeneid*, fourth century)

quarters. The principal officers were entertained by the Cæsar, who professed in the warmest language of friendship, his desire and his inability to reward, according to their deserts, the brave companions of his victories. They retired from the feast full of grief and perplexity; and lamented the hardship of their fate, which tore them from their beloved general and their native country. The only expedient which could prevent their separation was boldly agitated and approved; the popular resentment was insensibly molded into a regular conspiracy; their just reasons of complaint were heightened by passion, and their passions were inflamed by wine, as on the eve of their departure the troops were indulged in licentious festivity. At the hour of midnight the impetuous multitude, with swords, and bows, and torches in their hands, rushed into the suburbs; encompassed the palace; and, careless of future dangers, pronounced the fatal and irrevocable words, JULIAN AUGUSTUS! Prudence as well as loyalty inculcated the propriety of resisting their treasonable designs, and of preparing for his oppressed virtue the excuse of violence. But the soldiers, who were conscious of their guilt, chose rather to depend on the gratitude of Julian than on the

Left: Julian the Apostate presiding at a conference. Once in power Julian who disliked the complicated and corrupt set-up of the government of Constantius, inaugurated a program of public reform. (Painting by E Armitage RA)

Left: The Amphitheater at Pergamon. Pergamon was a center of classical learning visited by Julian and his cousin Gallus while he was still a student.
Right: Mosaic of Christ from the vault of the Church of Santa Costanza, Rome. (Fourth century AD)

Below: Bearded statue of Homer. The study of the Classics continued for Christians and pagans alike – Julian in particular turned to the ancient Hellenistic culture for inspiration. (From Herculaneum, first century AD)

clemency of the emperor. Their zeal was insensibly turned into impatience, and their impatience into rage. The inflexible Cæsar sustained, till the third hour of the day, their prayers, their reproaches, and their menaces; nor did he yield till he had been repeatedly assured that, if he wished to live, he must consent to reign. He was exalted on a shield in the presence and amidst the unanimous acclamations of the troops; a rich military collar, which was offered by chance, supplied the want of a diadem; the ceremony was concluded by the promise of a moderate donative; and the new emperor, overwhelmed with real or affected grief, retired into the most secret recesses of his apartment.

Although he was firmly resolved to maintain the station which he had assumed, he was still desirous of saving his country from the calamities of civil war, of declining a contest with the superior forces of Constantius, and of preserving his own character from the reproach of perfidy and ingratitude.

The negotiations of peace were accompanied and supported by the most vigorous preparations for war. The army, which Julian held in readiness for immediate action, was recruited and augmented by the disorders of the times. The cruel persecution of the faction of Magnentius had filled Gaul with numerous bands of outlaws and robbers. They cheerfully accepted the offer of a general pardon from a prince whom they could trust, submitted to the restraints of military discipline, and retained only their implacable hatred to the person and government of Constantius.

The ambassadors of Julian had been instructed to execute with the utmost diligence their important commission. But in their passage through Italy and Illyricum they were detained by the tedious and affected delays of the provincial governors; they were conducted by slow journeys from Constantinople to Cæsarea in Cappadocia; and when at length they were admitted to the presence of Constantius, they found that he had already conceived, from the dispatches of his own officers, the most unfavorable opinion of the conduct of Julian and of the Gallic army. The letters were heard with impatience; the trembling messengers were dismissed with indignation and contempt; and the looks, the gestures, the furious language of the monarch, expressed the disorder of his soul. The domestic connection which might have reconciled the brother and the husband of Helena, was recently dissolved by the death of that princess, whose pregnancy had been several times fruitless, and was at last fatal to herself. The empress Eusebia had preserved, to the last moment of her life, the warm, and even jealous, affection which she had conceived for Julian; and her mild influence might have moderated the resentment of a prince who, since her death, was abandoned to his own passions, and to the arts of his eunuchs. But the terror of a foreign invasion obliged him to suspend the punishment of a private enemy; he continued his march towards the confines of Persia, and thought it sufficient to signify the conditions which might entitle Julian and his guilty followers to the clemency of their offended sovereign. He required that the presumptuous Cæsar should expressly renounce the appellation and rank of Augustus which he had accepted from the rebels; that he should descend to his former station of a limited and dependant minister; that he should vest the powers of the state and army in the hands of those officers who were appointed by the Imperial court.

The hopes of Julian depended much less on the number of his troops than on the celerity of his motions. In the execution of a daring enterprise he availed himself of every precaution, as far as prudence could suggest; and where prudence could no longer accompany his steps, he trusted the event to valor and to fortune. In the neighborhood of Basel he assembled and divided his army. One body, which consisted of ten thousand men, was directed, under the command of Nevitta, general of the cavalry, to advance through the midland parts of Rhætia and Noricum. A similar division of troops, under the orders of Jovius and Jovinus, prepared to follow the oblique course of the highways through the Alps and the northern confines of Italy. The instructions to the generals were conceived with energy and precision: to hasten their march in close and compact columns, which, according to the disposition of the ground, might readily be changed into any order of battle; to secure themselves against the surprises of the night by strong posts and vigilant guards; to prevent resistance by their unexpected arrival; to elude examination by their sudden departure; to spread the opinion of their strength, and the terror of his name; and to join their sovereign under the walls of Sirmium. For himself Julian had reserved a more difficult and extraordinary part. He selected three thousand brave and active volunteers, resolved, like their leader, to cast behind them every hope of a retreat; at the head of this faithful band he fearlessly plunged into the recesses of the Marcian, or Black Forest, which conceals the sources of the Danube; and, for many days, the fate of Julian was unknown to the world.

The intelligence of the march and rapid progress of Julian was speedily transmitted to his rival, who, by the retreat of Sapor, had obtained some respite from the Persian war. Disguising the anguish of his soul under the semblance of contempt, Constantius professed his intention of returning into Europe, and of giving chase to Julian; for he never spoke of this military expedition in any other light than that of a hunting party.

But the humanity of Julian was preserved from the cruel alternative which he pathetically laments of destroying or of being himself destroyed: and the seasonable death of Constantius delivered the Roman empire from the calamities of civil war. The last of the sons of Constantine may be dismissed from the world with the remark that he had inherited the defects, without the abilities, of his father. Before Con-

stantius expired, he is said to have named Julian for his successor; nor does it seem improbable that his anxious concern for the fate of a young and tender wife, whom he left with child, may have prevailed in his last moments over the harsher passions of hatred and revenge. Eusebius and his guilty associates made a faint attempt to prolong the reign of the eunuchs by the election of another emperor; but their intrigues were rejected with disdain by an army which now abhorred the thought of civil discord; and two officers of rank were instantly dispatched to assure Julian that every sword in the empire would be drawn for his service. The military designs of that prince, who had formed three different attacks against Thrace, were prevented by this fortunate event. Without shedding the blood of his fellow-citizens, he escaped the dangers of a doubtful conflict, and acquired the advantages of a complete victory. Impatient to visit the place of his birth and the new capital of the empire, he advanced from Naissus through the mountains of Hæmus and the cities of Thrace. When he reached Heraclea, at the distance of sixty miles, all Constantinople was poured forth to receive him; and he made his triumphal entry amidst the dutiful acclamations of the soldiers, the people, and the senate. Julian, in the thirty-second year of his age, acquired the undisputed possession of the Roman empire.

Philosophy had instructed Julian to compare the advantages of action and retirement; but the elevation of his birth and the accidents of his life never allowed him the freedom of choice. He might perhaps sincerely have preferred the groves of the Academy and the society of Athens; but he was constrained, at first by the will, and afterwards by the injustice of Constantius, to expose his person and fame to the dangers of Imperial greatness; and to make himself accountable to the world and to posterity for the happiness of millions. Julian recollected with terror the observation of his master Plato, that the government of our flocks and herds is always committed to beings of a superior species; and that the conduct of nations requires and deserves the celestial powers of the Gods or of the Genii. From this principle he justly concluded that the man who presumes to reign should aspire to the perfection of the divine nature; that he should purify his soul from her mortal and terrestrial part; that he should extinguish his appetites, enlighten his understanding, regulate his passions, and subdue the wild beast which, according to the lively metaphor of Aristotle, seldom fails to ascend the throne of a despot. The throne of Julian, which the death of Constantius fixed on an independent basis, was the seat of reason, of virtue, and perhaps of vanity. He despised the honors, renounced the

Left: The Hadrianic Library at Ephesus where Julian pursued his classical studies. (Reconstruction, first century AD, Mosta Augustea, Rome)
Below: Head of a philosopher, Aquilea.

The basilica of Constantine where Constantius II (Flavius Julius Constantius AD 317–61; Roman emperor 337–61) was buried.

pleasures, and discharged with incessant diligence the duties of his exalted station. The luxury of the palace excited the contempt and indignation of Julian, who usually slept on the ground, who yielded with reluctance to the indispensable calls of nature, and who placed his vanity not in emulating, but in despising the pomp of royalty.

By the total extirpation of a mischief which was magnified even beyond its real extent, he was impatient to relieve the distress and to appease the murmurs of the people, who support with less uneasiness the weight of taxes if they are convinced that the fruits of their industry are appropriated to the service of the state. But in the execution of this salutary work Julian is accused of proceeding with too much haste and inconsiderable severity. By a single edict he reduced the palace of Constantinople to an immense desert, and dismissed with ignominy the whole train of slaves and dependants, without providing any just, or at least benevolent, exceptions for the age, the services, or the poverty of the faithful domestics of the Imperial family. Such indeed was the temper of Julian, who seldom recollected the fundamental maxim of Aristotle, that true virtue is placed at an equal distance between the opposite vices. The splendid and effeminate dress of the Asiatics, the curls and paint, the collars and bracelets, which had appeared so ridiculous in the person of Constantine, were consistently rejected by his philosophic successor. But, with the fopperies, Julian affected to renounce the decencies of dress; and seemed to value himself for his neglect of the laws of cleanliness. In a satirical performance, which was designed for the public eye, the emperor descants with pleasure, and even pride, on the length of his nails and the inky blackness of his hands; protests that, although the greatest part of his body was covered with hair, the use of the razor was confined to his head alone; and celebrates with visible complacency the shaggy and *populous* beard which he fondly cherished, after the example of the philosophers of Greece. Had Julian consulted the simple dictates of reason, the first magistrate of the Romans would have scorned the affectation of Diogenes, as well as that of Darius.

But the work of public reformation would have remained imperfect if Julian had only corrected the abuses, without punishing the crimes, of his predecessor's reign. The chamberlain Eusebius, who had so long abused the favor of Constantius, expiated, by an ignominious death, the insolence, the corruption, and cruelty of his servile reign.

The numerous army of spies, of agents, and informers enlisted by Constantius to secure the repose of one man, and to interrupt that of millions, was immediately disbanded by his generous successor. Julian was slow in his suspicions, and gentle in his punishments; and his contempt of treason was the result of judgment, of vanity, and of courage.

Julian was not insensible of the advantages of freedom. From his studies he had imbibed the spirit of ancient sages and heroes. He sincerely abhorred the system of oriental despotism which Diocletian, Constantine, and the patient habits of four score years, had established in the empire. A motive of superstition prevented the execution of the design which Julian had frequently meditated, of relieving his head from the weight of a costly diadem; but he absolutely refused the title of *Dominus* or Lord, a word which was grown so familiar to the ears of the Romans, that they no longer remembered its servile and humiliating origin. The behavior of Julian was uniformly supported. During the games of the Circus, he had, imprudently or designedly, performed the manumission of a slave in the presence of the consul. The moment he was reminded that he had trespassed on the jurisdiction of *another* magistrate, he condemned himself to pay a fine of ten pounds of gold, and embraced this public occasion of declaring to the world that he was subject, like the rest of his fellow-citizens, to the laws, and even to the forms, of the republic. The spirit of his administration, and his regard for the place of his nativity, induced Julian to confer on the senate of Constantinople the same honors, privileges, and authority which were still enjoyed by the senate of ancient Rome. A legal fiction was introduced and gradually established, that one half of the national council had migrated into the East, and the despotic successors of Julian, accepting the title of Senators, acknowledged themselves the members of a respectable body which was permitted to represent the majesty of the Roman name. From Constantinople the attention of the monarch was extended to the municipal senates of the provinces. He abolished, by repeated edicts, the unjust and pernicious exemptions which had withdrawn so many idle citizens from the service of their country; and by imposing an equal distribution of public duties, he restored the strength, the splendor, or, according to the glowing expression of Libanius, the soul of the expiring cities of his empire.

The generality of princes, if they were stripped of their purple and cast naked into the world, would immediately sink to the lowest rank of society, without a hope of emerging from their obscurity. But the personal merit of Julian was, in some measure, independent of his fortune. Whatever had been his choice of life, by the force of intrepid courage, lively wit, and intense application, he would have obtained, or at least he would have deserved, the highest honors of his profession, and Julian might have raised himself to the rank of minister or general of the state in which he was born a private citizen. If the jealous caprice of power had disappointed his expectations; if he had prudently declined the paths of greatness, the employment of the same talents in studious solitude would have placed beyond the reach of kings his present happiness and his immortal fame. When we inspect with minute, or perhaps malevolent, attention the portrait of Julian, something seems wanting to the grace and perfection of the whole figure. His genius was less powerful and sublime than that of Cæsar, nor did he possess the consummate prudence of Augustus. The virtues of Trajan appear more steady and natural, and the philosophy of Marcus is more simple and consistent. Yet Julian sustained adversity with firmness, and prosperity with moderation. After an interval of one hundred and twenty years from the death of Alexander Severus, the Romans beheld an emperor who made no distinction between his duties and his pleasures, who labored to relieve the distress and to revive the spirit of his subjects, and who endeavored always to connect authority with merit, and happiness with virtue. Even faction, and religious faction, was constrained to acknowledge the superiority of his genius in peace as well as in war, and to confess, with a sigh, that the aspostate Julian was a lover of his country, and that he deserved the empire of the world.

The basilica of Constantine. (From the painting by the architect G Wightwich reproduced as a lithograph by J M Baynes)

CHAPTER NINETEEN

The apostasy and religion of Julian – his attempts to restore pagan worship – his artful persecution of the Christians

[AD 351–363]

THE character of Apostate has injured the reputation of Julian; and the enthusiasm which clouded his virtues has exaggerated the real and apparent magnitude of his faults. Our partial ignorance may represent him as a philosophic monarch, who studied to protect, with an equal hand, the religious factions of the empire, and to allay the theological fever which had inflamed the minds of the people from the edicts of Diocletian to the exile of Athanasius. A more accurate view of the character and conduct of Julian will remove this favorable pre-possession for a prince who did not escape the general contagion of the times. We enjoy the singular advantage of comparing the pictures which have been delineated by his fondest admirers and his implacable enemies. The actions of Julian are faithfully related by a judicious and candid historian, the impartial spectator of his life and death. The unanimous evidence of his contemporaries is confirmed by the public and private declarations of the emperor himself; and his various writings express the uniform tenor of his religious sentiments, which policy would have prompted him to dissemble rather than to affect. A devout and sincere attachment for the gods of Athens and Rome constituted the ruling passion of Julian; the powers of an enlightened understanding were betrayed and corrupted by the influence of superstitious prejudice; and the phantoms which existed only in the mind of the emperor had a real and pernicious effect on the government of the empire. The vehement zeal of the Christians, who despised the worship, and overturned the altars, of those fabulous deities, engaged their votary in a state of irreconcilable hostility with a very numerous party of his subjects; and he was sometimes tempted, by the desire of victory or the shame of a repulse, to violate the laws of prudence, and even of justice. The triumph of the party which he deserted and opposed has fixed a stain of infamy on the name of Julian; and the unsuccessful apostate has been overwhelmed with a torrent of pious invectives, of which the signal was given by the sonorous trumpet of Gregory Nazianzen. The interesting nature of the events which were crowded into the short reign of this active emperor deserves a just and circumstantial narrative. His motive, his counsels, and his actions, as far as they are connected with the history of religion, will be the subject of the present chapter.

The cause of his strange and fatal apostasy may be derived from the early period of his life when he was left an orphan in the hands of the murderers of his family. The names of Christ and of Constantius, the ideas of slavery and of religion, were soon associated in a youthful imagination, which was susceptible of the most lively impressions. The care of his infancy was intrusted to Eusebius, bishop of Nicomedia, who was related to him on the side of his mother; and till Julian reached the twentieth year of his age, he received from his Christian preceptors the education not of a hero but of a saint. The emperor, less jealous of a heavenly than of an earthly crown, contented himself with the imperfect character of a catechumen, while he bestowed the advantages of baptism on the nephews of Constantine. They were even admitted to the inferior offices of the ecclesiastical order; and Julian publicly read the Holy Scripture in the church of Nicomedia.

He was educated in the Lesser Asia, amidst the scandals of the Arian controversy. The fierce contests of the Eastern bishops, the incessant alterations of their creeds, and the profane motives which appeared to actuate their conduct, insensibly strengthened the prejudice of Julian that they neither understood nor believed the religion for which they so fiercely contended. Instead of listening to the proofs of Christianity with that favorable attention which adds weight to the most respectable evidence, he heard with suspicion, and disputed with obstinacy and acuteness, the doctrines for which he already entertained an invincible aversion. Julian always declared himself the advocate of Paganism, under the specious excuse that, in the defense of the weaker cause, his learning and ingenuity might be more advantageously exercised and displayed.

The Christians, who beheld with horror and indignation the apostacy of Julian, had much more to fear from his power than from his arguments. Instructed by history and reflection, Julian was persuaded that, if the diseases of the body may sometimes be cured by salutary violence, neither steel nor fire can eradicate the erroneous opinions of the mind. The reluctant victim may be dragged to the foot of the altar; but the heart still abhors and disclaims the sacrilegious act of the hand. Religious obstinacy is hardened and exasperated by oppression; and, as soon as the persecution subsides, those who have yielded are restored as penitents, and those who have resisted are honored as saints and martyrs. If Julian adopted the unsuccessful cruelty of Diocletian and his colleagues, he was sensible that he should stain his memory with the name of tyrant, and add new glories to the catholic church, which had

Left: The Goddess of Plenty. (Vienne, France)
Below: The Greek Philosopher, Plato (c 427–347 BC) from whom Julian drew his inspiration.

derived strength and increase from the severity of the Pagan magistrates. Actuated by these motives, and apprehensive of disturbing the repose of an unsettled reign, Julian surprised the world by an edict which was not unworthy of a statesman or a philosopher. He extended to all the inhabitants of the Roman world the benefits of a free and equal toleration; and the only hardship which he inflicted on the Christians was to deprive them of the power of tormenting their fellow-subjects, whom they stigmatized with the odious titles of idolators and heretics. The Pagans received a gracious permission, or rather an express order, to open all their temples; and they were at once delivered from the oppressive laws and arbitrary vexations which they had sustained under the reign of Constantine and of his sons. At the same time, the bishops and clergy who had been banished by the Arian monarch were recalled from exile, and restored to their respective churches; the Donatists, the Novatians, the Macedonians, the Eunomians, and those who, with a more prosperous fortune, adhered to the doctrine of the council of Nice. Julian, who understood and derided their theological disputes, invited to the palace the leaders of the hostile sects, that he might enjoy the agreeable spectacle of their furious encounters. The clamor of controversy sometimes provoked the emperor to exclaim, 'Hear me! the Franks have heard me, and the Alemanni'; but he soon discovered that he was now engaged with more obstinate and implacable enemies; and though he exerted the powers of oratory to persuade them to live in concord, or at least in peace, he was perfectly satisfied, before he dismissed them from his presence, that he had nothing to dread from the union of the Christians. The impartial Ammianus has ascribed this affected clemency to the desire of fomenting the intestine divisions of the church; and the insidious design of undermining the foundations of Christianity was inseparably connected with the zeal which Julian professed to restore the ancient religion of the empire.

Julian still continued to maintain the freedom of religious worship, without distinguishing whether this universal toleration proceeded from his justice or his clemency. He affected to pity the unhappy Christians, who were mistaken in the most important object of their lives; but his pity was degraded by contempt, his contempt was embittered by hatred; and the sentiments of Julian were expressed in a style of sarcastic wit, which inflicts a deep and deadly wound whenever it issues from the mouth of a sovereign. As he was sensible that the Christians gloried in the name of their Redeemer, he countenanced, and perhaps enjoined, the use of the less honorable appellation of Galilæans. He declared that, by the folly of the Galilæans, whom he describes as a sect of fanatics, contemptible to men and odious to the

gods, the empire had been reduced to the brink of destruction; and he insinuates in a public edict that a frantic patient might sometimes be cured by salutary violence. An ungenerous distinction was admitted into the mind and counsels of Julian, that, according to the difference of their religious sentiments, one part of his subjects deserved his favor and friendship, while the other was entitled only to the common benefits that his justice could not refuse to an obedient people. According to a principle pregnant with mischief and oppression, the emperor transferred to the pontiffs of his own religion the management of the liberal allowances from the public revenue which had been granted to the church by the piety of Constantine and his sons. But the will of the legislator was not exempt from prejudice and passion; and it was the object of the insidious policy of Julian to deprive the Christians of all the temporal honors and advantages which rendered them respectable in the eyes of the world.

A just and severe censure has been inflicted on the law which prohibited the Christians from teaching the arts of grammar and rhetoric. The motives alleged by the emperor to justify this partial and oppressive measure might command, during his lifetime, the silence of slaves and the applause of flatterers. Julian abuses the ambiguous meaning of a word which might be indifferently applied to the language and the religion of the Greeks: he contemptuously observes that the men who exalt the merit of implicit faith are unfit to claim or to enjoy the advantages of science; and he vainly contends that, if they refuse to adore the gods of Homer and Demosthenes, they ought to content themselves with expounding Luke and Matthew in the churches of the Galilæans. As soon as the resignation of the more obstinate teachers had established the unrivalled dominion of the Pagan sophists, Julian invited the rising generation to resort with freedom to the public schools, in a just confidence that their tender minds would receive the impressions of literature and idolatry. If the greatest part of the Christian youth should be deterred by their own scruples, or by those of their parents, from accepting this dangerous mode of instruction, they must, at the same time, relinquish the benefits of a liberal education. Julian had reason to expect that, in the space of a few years, the church would relapse into its primæval simplicity, and that the theologians, who possessed an adequate share of the learning and eloquence of the age, would be succeeded by a generation of blind and ignorant fanatics, incapable of defending the truth of their own principles, or of exposing the various follies of Polytheism.

The most effectual instrument of oppression with which they were armed was the law that obliged the Christians to make full and ample

JULIAN THE APOSTATE

Julian (Flavius Claudius Julianus c331–63) was brought up amidst the troubles of the Arian controversy and although he had been given a Christian upbringing he seems to have turned to the ancient philosophers for inspiration. During his reign he attempted to re-establish paganism by using a subtle form of persecution. The pagan priests were reinstated with state salaries and the Christians were banned from teaching in schools with the hope that by the second generation all children would be brought up under the influence of pagan precepts. In addition Christians were also ordered to repay the cost of the rebuilding of the temples which they had destroyed. Not unnaturally they were unable to do so and Julian's policies enflamed discontent right across the provinces.

Above: Bacchanalian orgy. (Relief from a sarcophagus)
Left: Wall-painting of an anatomy lesson from the catacombs of the Hypogeum, Via Latina. (Rome, fourth century AD)

satisfaction for the temples which they had destroyed under the preceding reign. The zeal of the triumphant church had not always expected the sanction of the public authority; and the bishops, who were secure of impunity, had often marched at the head of their congregations to attack and demolish the fortresses of the prince of darkness. The authors of the injury had neither the ability nor the inclination to discharge this accumulated demand: and the impartial wisdom of a legislator would have been displayed in balancing the adverse claims and complaints by an equitable and temperate arbitration. But the whole empire, and particularly the East, was thrown into confusion by the rash edicts of Julian; and the Pagan magistrates, inflamed by zeal and revenge, abused the rigorous privilege of the Roman law, which substitutes, in the place of his inadequate property, the person of the insolvent debtor.

I have endeavored faithfully to represent the artful system by which Julian proposed to obtain the effects, without incurring the guilt or reproach, of persecution. But if the deadly spirit of fanaticism perverted the heart and understanding of a virtuous prince, it must, at the same time, be confessed, that the *real* sufferings of the Christians were inflamed and magnified by human passions and religious enthusiasm. The meekness and resignation which had distinguished the primitive disciples of the Gospel was the object of the applause, rather than of the imitation, of their successors. The Christians, who had now possessed above forty years the civil and ecclesiastical government of the empire, had contracted the insolent vices of prosperity, and the habit of believing that the saints alone were entitled to reign over the earth. The Christians considered Julian as a cruel and crafty tyrant, who suspended the execution of his revenge till he should return victorious from the Persian war. They expected that, as soon as he had triumphed over the foreign enemies of Rome, he would lay aside the irksome mask of dissimulation; that the amphitheaters would stream with the blood of hermits and bishops; and that the Christians who still persevered in the profession of the faith would be deprived of the common benefits of nature and society. Every calumny that could wound the reputation of the Apostate was credulously embraced by the fears and hatred of his adversaries; and their indiscreet clamors provoked the temper of a sovereign whom it was their duty to respect, and their interest to flatter. They still protested that prayers and tears were their only weapons against the impious tyrant, whose head they devoted to the justice of offended Heaven. But they insinuated, with sullen resolution, that their submission was no longer the effect of weakness; and that, in the imperfect state of human virtue, the patience which is founded on principle may be exhausted by persecution. It is impossible to determine how far the zeal of Julian would have prevailed over his good sense and humanity; but, if we seriously reflect on the strength and spirit of the church, we shall be convinced that, before the emperor could have extinguished the religion of Christ, he must have involved his country in the horrors of a civil war.

CHAPTER TWENTY

Residence of Julian at Antioch

his successful expedition against the Persians – passage of the Tigris – the retreat and
death of Julian – election of Jovian – he saves the Roman army by a disgraceful treaty
[AD 314–390]

IN the cool moments of reflection, Julian preferred the useful and benevolent virtues of Antoninus; but his ambitious spirit was inflamed by the glory of Alexander, and he solicited, with equal ardor, the esteem of the wise and the applause of the multitude. In the season of life when the powers of the mind and body enjoy the most active vigor, the emperor, who was instructed by the experience and animated by the success of the German war, resolved to signalize his reign by some more splendid and memorable achievement. The ambassadors of the East, from the continent of India and the isle of Ceylon, had respectfully saluted the Roman purple. The nations of the West esteemed and dreaded the personal virtues of Julian both in peace and war. He despised the trophies of a Gothic victory, and was satisfied that the rapacious barbarians of the Danube would be restrained from any future violation of the faith of treaties by the terror of his name and the additional fortifications with which he strengthened the Thracian and Illyrian frontiers. The successor of Cyrus and Artaxerxes was the only rival whom he deemed worthy of his arms, and he resolved, by the final conquest of Persia, to chastise the haughty nation which had so long resisted and insulted the majesty of Rome. As soon as the Persian monarch was informed that the throne of Constantius was filled by a prince of a very different character, he condescended to make some artful or perhaps sincere overtures towards a negotiation of peace. But the pride of Sapor was astonished by the firmness of Julian, who sternly declared that he would never consent to hold a peaceful conference among the flames and ruins of the cities of Mesopotamia, and who added, with a smile of contempt, that it was needless to treat by ambassadors, as he himself had determined to visit speedily the court of Persia. The impatience of the emperor urged the diligence of the military preparations. The generals were named, a formidable army was destined for this important service, and Julian, marching from Constantinople through the provinces of Asia Minor, arrived at Antioch about eight months after the death of his predecessor. His ardent desire to march into the heart of Persia was checked by the indispensable duty of regulating the state of the empire, by his zeal to revive the worship of the gods, and by the advice of his wisest friends, who represented the necessity of allowing the salutary interval of winter quarters to restore the exhausted strength of the legions of Gaul and the discipline and spirit of the Eastern troops. Julian was persuaded to fix, till the ensuing spring, his residence at Antioch, among a people maliciously disposed to deride and to censure the delays of their sovereign.

The martial impatience of Julian urged him to take the field in the beginning of the spring, and he dismissed, with contempt and reproach, the senate of Antioch, who accompanied the emperor beyond the limits of their own territory, to which he was resolved never to return.

Hierapolis, situated almost on the banks of the Euphrates, had been appointed for the general rendezvous of the Roman troops, who immediately passed the great river on a bridge of boats which was previously constructed. If the inclinations of Julian had been similar to those of his predecessor, he might have wasted the active and important season of the year in the circus of Samosata or in the churches of Edessa. But as the war-like emperor, instead of Constantius, had chosen Alexander for his model, he advanced without delay to Carrhæ, a very ancient city of Mesopotamia, at the distance of fourscore miles from Hierapolis.

The army of Julian, the most numerous that any of the Cæsars had ever led against Persia, consisted of sixty-five thousand effective and well-disciplined soldiers. The veteran bands of cavalry and infantry, of Romans and barbarians, had been selected from the different provinces, and a just pre-eminence of loyalty and valor was claimed by the hardy Gauls, who guarded the throne and person of their beloved prince. A formidable body of Scythian auxiliaries had been transported from another climate, and almost from another world, to invade a distant country of whose name and situation they were ignorant. The love of rapine and war allured to the Imperial standard several tribes of Saracens, or roving Arabs, whose service Julian had commanded, while he sternly refused the payment of the accustomed subsidies. The broad channel of the Euphrates was crowded by a fleet of eleven hundred ships, destined to attend the motions and to satisfy the wants of the Roman army. The military strength of the fleet was composed of fifty armed galleys, and these were accompanied by an equal number of flat-bottomed boats, which might occasionally be connected into the form of temporary bridges. The rest of the ships, partly constructed of timber and partly covered with raw hides were laden with an almost inexhaustible supply of arms and engines, of utensils and provisions.

From the moment that the Romans entered the enemy's country, the country of an active and artful enemy, the order of march was disposed in three columns. The strength of the infantry, and consequently of the whole army, was placed in the center, under the peculiar command of their master-general Victor. On the right, the brave Nevitta led a column of several legions along the banks of the Euphrates, and almost always in sight of the fleet. The left flank of the army was protected by the column of cavalry. The ordinary post of Julian was at the head of the center column, but, as he preferred the duties of a general to the state of a monarch, he rapidly moved, with a small escort of light

Left: Gold dinar of the Sassanian King Sapor II (AD 309–379).
(British Museum, London)
Below: Sassanian silver depicting a hunt. (First–fifth century AD)

Roman battering ram (top) suspended, ready for attack and (bottom) covered with a defensive tower known as the toise of the ram. (Old French print)

cavalry, to the front, the rear, the flanks, wherever his presence could animate or protect the march of the Roman army. The country which they traversed from the Chaboras to the cultivated lands of Assyria may be considered as a part of the desert of Arabia, a dry and barren waste, which could never be improved by the most powerful arts of human industry.

The fields of Assyria were devoted by Julian to the calamities of war; and the philosopher retaliated on a guiltless people the acts of rapine and cruelty which had been committed by their haughty master in the Roman provinces. Two cities of Assyria presumed to resist the arms of a Roman emperor; and they both paid the severe penalty of their rashness. At the distance of fifty miles from the royal residence of Ctesiphon, Perisabor, or Anbar, held the second rank in the province: a city, large, populous, and well fortified, surrounded with a double wall, almost encompassed by a branch of the Euphrates, and defended by the valor of a numerous garrison. The exhortations of Hormisdas were repulsed with contempt; and the ears of the Persian prince were wounded by a just reproach, that, unmindful of his royal birth, he conducted an army of strangers against his king and country. The Assyrians maintained their loyalty by a skillful as well as vigorous defense, till the lucky stroke of a battering-ram having opened a large breach by shattering one of the angles of the wall, they hastily retired into the fortifications of the interior citadel. The soldiers of Julian rushed impetuously into the town, and, after the full gratification of every military appetite, Perisabor was reduced to ashes; and the engines which assaulted the citadel were planted on the ruins of the smoking houses.

The city, or rather fortress, of Maogamalcha, which was defended by sixteen large towers, a deep ditch, and two strong and solid walls of brick and bitumen, appears to have been constructed at the distance of eleven miles, as the safeguard of the capital of Persia. The emperor, apprehensive of leaving such an important fortress in his rear, immediately formed the siege of Maogamalcha. The fortifications were razed to the ground; and not a vestige was left that the city of Maogamalcha had ever existed. The neighborhood of the capital of Persia was adorned with three stately palaces, laboriously enriched with every production that could gratify the luxury and pride of an Eastern monarch. The pleasant situation of the gardens along the banks of the Tigris was improved, according to the Persian taste, by the symmetry of flowers, fountains, and shady walks: and spacious parks were enclosed for the reception of the bears, lions, and wild boars, which were maintained at a considerable expense for the pleasure of the royal chase.

The park-walls were broken down, the savage game was abandoned to the darts of the soldiers, and the palaces of Sapor were reduced to ashes, by the command of the Roman emperor.

The successful valor of Julian had triumphed over all the obstacles that opposed his march to the gates of Ctesiphon. But the reduction, or even the siege, of the capital of Persia was still at a distance. Twenty miles to the south of Bagdad, and on the eastern bank of the Tigris, the curiosity of travellers has observed some ruins of the palaces of Ctesiphon, which in the time of Julian was a great and populous city. The name and glory of the adjacent Seleucia were for ever extinguished; and the only remaining quarter of that Greek colony had resumed, with the Assyrian language and manners, the primitive appellation of Coche. Coche was situate on the western side of the Tigris; but it was naturally considered as a suburb of Ctesiphon, with which we may suppose it to have been connected by a permanent bridge of boats. Near the ruins of Seleucia the camp of Julian was fixed, and secured by a ditch and rampart against the sallies of the numerous and enterprising garrison of Coche.

The Romans, after sending up a military shout, advanced in measured steps to the animating notes of martial music; launched their formidable javelins, and rushed forwards with drawn swords to deprive the barbarians, by a closer onset, of the advantage of their missile weapons. The whole engagement lasted above twelve hours; till the gradual retreat of the Persians was changed into a disorderly flight, of which the shameful example was given by the principal leaders and the Surenas himself. They were pursued to the gates of Ctesiphon; and the conquerors might have entered the dismayed city, if the general, Victor, who was dangerously wounded with an arrow, had not conjured them to desist from a rash attempt, which must be fatal if it were not successful. On *their* side the Romans acknowledged the loss of only seventy-five men; while they affirmed that the barbarians had left on the field of battle two thousand five hundred, or even six thousand, of their bravest soldiers. The spoil was such as might be expected from the riches and luxury of an Oriental camp; large quantities of silver and gold, splendid arms and trappings, and beds and tables of massive silver. The victorious emperor distributed, as the rewards of valor, some honorable gifts, civic, and mural, and naval crowns; which he, and perhaps he alone, esteemed more precious than the wealth of Asia. A solemn sacrifice was offered to the god of war, but the appearances of the victims threatened the most inauspicious events; and Julian soon discovered, by less ambiguous signs, that he had now reached the term of his prosperity.

While the Persians beheld from the walls of Ctesiphon the desolation of the adjacent country, Julian cast many an anxious look towards the North, in full expectation that, as he himself had victoriously penetrated to the capital of Sapor, the march and junction of his lieutenants, Sebastian and Procopius, would be executed with the same courage and diligence. His expectations were disappointed by the treachery of the Armenian king, who permitted, and most probably directed, the desertion of his auxiliary troops from the camp of the Romans; and by the dissensions of the two generals, who were incapable of forming or executing any plan for the public service. When the emperor had relinquished the hope of this important reinforcement, he condescended to hold a council of war, and approved, after a full debate, the sentiment of those generals who dissuaded the siege of Ctesiphon, as a fruitless and pernicious undertaking. It is not easy for us to conceive by what arts of fortification a city thrice besieged and taken by the predecessors of Julian could be rendered impregnable against an army of sixty thousand Romans, commanded by a brave and experienced general, and abundantly supplied with ships, provisions, battering engines and military stores. But we may rest assured, from the love of glory, and contempt of danger, which formed the character of Julian, that he was not discouraged by any trivial or imaginary obstacles. At the very time when he declined the siege of Ctesiphon, he rejected, with obstinacy and disdain, the most flattering offers of a negotiation of peace.

The honor, as well as interest, of Julian, forbade him to consume his time under the impregnable walls of Ctesiphon; and as often as he defied the barbarians, who defended the city, to meet him on the open plain, they prudently replied that, if he desired to exercise his valor, he

might seek the army of the Great King. He felt the insult, and he accepted the advice. Instead of confining his servile march to the banks of the Euphrates and Tigris, he resolved to imitate the adventurous spirit of Alexander, and boldly to advance into the inland provinces, till

Above: The ruins at the site of Sapor's palace at Ctesiphon, Iraq, besieged by Julian in AD 363.
Left: Sapor II hunting deer. (Diameter 18cm, fourth century, British Museum, London)
Right: Sassanian silver bowl engraved with a pheasant. (Height 8.5cm, fourth–fifth century AD, British Museum, London)

he forced his rival to contend with him, perhaps in the plains of Arbela, for the empire of Asia. He destroyed in a single hour the whole navy, which had been transported above five hundred miles, at so great an expense of toil, of treasure, and of blood. Twelve, or, at the most, twenty-two, small vessels were saved, to accompany, on carriages, the march of the army, and to form occasional bridges for the passage of the rivers. A supply of twenty days' provisions was reserved for the use of the soldiers; and the rest of the magazines, with a fleet of eleven hundred vessels, which rode at anchor in the Tigris, were abandoned to the flames by the absolute command of the emperor. Yet there are not wanting some specious, and perhaps solid, reasons, which might justify the resolution of Julian. The navigations of the Euphrates never ascended above Babylon, nor that of the Tigris above Opis. The distance of the last-mentioned city from the Roman camp was not very considerable; and Julian must soon have renounced the vain and impracticable

thought surprising that the Genius of the empire should once more appear before him, covering with a funereal veil his head and his horn of abundance, and slowly retiring from the Imperial tent. The monarch started from his couch, and, stepping forth to refresh his wearied spirits with the coolness of the midnight air, he beheld a fiery meteor, which shot athwart the sky, and suddenly vanished. Julian was convinced that he had seen the menacing countenance of the god of war; the council which he summoned, of Tuscan Haruspices, unanimously pronounced that he should abstain from action; but, on this occasion, necessity and reason were more prevalent than superstition; and the trumpets sounded at the break of day. The army marched through a hilly country; and the hills had been secretly occupied by the Persians. Julian led the van with the skill and attention of a consummate general; he was alarmed by the intelligence that his rear was suddenly attacked. The heat of the weather had tempted him to lay aside his cuirass; but he snatched a shield from one of his attendants, and hastened, with a sufficient reinforcement, to the relief of the rear guard. A similar danger recalled the intrepid prince to the defense of the front; and, as he galloped between the columns, the center of the left was attacked, and almost overpowered, by a furious charge of the Persian cavalry and elephants. This huge body was soon defeated by the well-timed evolution of the light infantry, who aimed their weapons, with dexterity and effect, against the backs of the horsemen, and the legs of the elephants. The barbarians fled: and Julian, who was foremost in every danger, animated the pursuit with his voice and gestures. His trembling guards, scattered and oppressed by the disorderly throng of friends and enemies, reminded their fearless sovereign that he was without armor; and conjured him to decline the fall of the impending ruin. As they exclaimed, a cloud of darts and arrows was discharged from the flying squadrons; and a javelin, after razing the skin of his arm, transpierced the ribs, and fixed in the inferior part of the liver. Julian attempted to draw the deadly weapon from his side; but his fingers were cut by the

Mobile attack tower fitted with a drawbridge for assaulting town walls. (Old French print)

attempt of forcing upwards a great fleet against the stream of a rapid river, which in several places was embarrassed by natural or artificial cataracts. The power of sails and oars was insufficient; it became necessary to tow the ships against the current of the river; the strength of twenty thousand soldiers was exhausted in this tedious and servile labor; and if the Romans continued to march along the banks of the Tigris, they could only expect to return home without achieving any enterprise worthy of the genius or fortune of their leader. If, on the contrary, it was advisable to advance into the inland country, the destruction of the fleet and magazines was the only measure which could save that valuable prize from the hands of the numerous and active troops which might suddenly be poured from the gates of Ctesiphon. Had the arms of Julian been victorious, we should now admire the conduct as well as the courage of a hero who, by depriving his soldiers of the hopes of a retreat, left them only the alternative of death or conquest.

The visionary conquests of Hyrcania and India, which had so long amused, now tormented, the mind of Julian. Conscious that his own imprudence was the cause of the public distress, he anxiously balanced the hopes of safety or success without obtaining a satisfactory answer either from gods or men. At length, as the only practicable measure, he embraced the resolution of directing his steps towards the banks of the Tigris, with the design of saving the army by a hasty march to the confines of Corduene, a fertile and friendly province, which acknowledged the sovereignty of Rome. The desponding troops obeyed the signal of the retreat, only seventy days after they had passed the Chaboras with the sanguine expectation of subverting the throne of Persia.

While Julian struggled with the almost insuperable difficulties of his situation, the silent hours of the night were still devoted to study and contemplation. Whenever he closed his eyes in short and interrupted slumbers, his mind was agitated with painful anxiety: nor can it be

Gold coin showing bearded head of the Emperor Julian.
(British Museum)

sharpness of the steel, and he fell senseless from his horse. His guards flew to his relief; and the wounded emperor was gently raised from the ground, and conveyed out of the tumult of the battle into an adjacent tent.

The first words that Julian uttered, after his recovery from the fainting fit into which he had been thrown by loss of blood, were expressive of his martial spirit. He called for his horse and arms, and was impatient to rush into the battle. His remaining strength was exhausted by the painful effort; and the surgeons, who examined his wound, discovered the symptoms of approaching death. He employed the awful moments with the firm temper of a hero and a sage; the philosophers who had accompanied him in this fatal expedition compared the tent of Julian with the prison of Socrates; and the spectators, whom duty, or friendship, or curiosity, had assembled round his couch,

Roman soldiers besieging a walled city. (Nineteenth-century print)

listened with respectful grief to the funeral oration of their dying emperor. The efforts which he made, of mind as well as body, most probably hastened his death. His wound began to bleed with fresh violence: his respiration was embarrassed by the swelling of the veins: he called for a draught of cold water, and, as soon as he had drunk it, expired without pain, about the hour of midnight. Such was the end of that extraordinary man, in the thirty-second year of his age, after a reign of one year and about eight months from the death of Constantius. In his last moments he displayed, perhaps with some ostentation, the love of virtue and of fame, which had been the ruling passions of his life.

The triumph of Christianity, and the calamities of the empire, may, in some measure, be ascribed to Julian himself, who had neglected to secure the future execution of his designs by the timely and judicious nomination of an associate and successor. But the royal race of Constantius Chlorus was reduced to his own person; and if he entertained any serious thoughts of investing with the purple the most worthy among the Romans, he was diverted from his resolution by the difficulty of the choice, the jealousy of power, the fear of ingratitude, and the natural presumption of health, of youth, and of prosperity. His unexpected death left the empire without a master, and without an heir, in a state of perplexity and danger which, in the space of fourscore years, had never been experienced, since the election of Diocletian. While they debated, a few voices saluted Jovian, who was no more than *first* of the domestics, with the names of Emperor and Augustus. The tumultuary acclamation was instantly repeated by the guards who surrounded the tent, and passed, in a few minutes, to the extremities of the line. The new prince, astonished with his own fortune, was hastily invested with the Imperial ornaments, and received an oath of fidelity from the generals, whose favor and protection he so lately solicited. The strongest recommendation of Jovian was the merit of his father, Count Varronian, who enjoyed, in honorable retirement, the fruit of his long services. In the obscure freedom of a private station, the son indulged his taste for wine and women; yet he supported, with credit, the character of a Christian and a soldier. Without being conspicuous for any of the ambitious qualifications which excite the admiration and envy of mankind, the comely person of Jovian, his cheerful temper, and familiar wit, had gained the affection of his fellow-soldiers; and the generals of both parties acquiesced in a popular election which had not been conducted by the arts of their enemies. The pride of this unexpected elevation was moderated by the just apprehension that the same day might terminate the life and reign of the new emperor. The pressing voice of necessity was obeyed without delay; and the first orders issued by Jovian, a few hours after his predecessor had expired, were to prosecute a march which could alone extricate the Romans from their actual distress.

In this hopeless situation, the fainting spirits of the Romans were revived by the sound of peace. The transient presumption of Sapor had vanished: he observed, with serious concern, that, in the repetition of doubtful combats, he had lost his most faithful and intrepid nobles, his bravest troops, and the greatest part of his train of elephants: and the experienced monarch feared to provoke the resistance of despair, the vicissitudes of fortune, and the unexhausted powers of the Roman empire, which might soon advance to relieve, or to revenge, the successor of Julian. The Surenas himself, accompanied by another satrap, appeared in the camp of Jovian, and declared that the clemency of his sovereign was not averse to signify the conditions on which he would consent to spare and to dismiss the Cæsar with the relics of his captive army. The hopes of safety subdued the firmness of the Romans; the emperor was compelled, by the advice of his council and the cries of the soldiers, to embrace the offer of peace; and the præfect Sallust was immediately sent, with the general Arinthæus, to understand the pleasure of the Great King.

Sapor enjoyed the glory and the fruits of his victory; and this ignominious peace has justly been considered as a memorable era in the decline and fall of the Roman empire. The predecessors of Jovian had sometimes relinquished the dominion of distant and unprofitable provinces; but, since the foundation of the city, the genius of Rome, the god Terminus, who guarded the boundaries of the republic, had never retired before the sword of a victorious enemy.

CHAPTER TWENTY-ONE

The government and death of Jovian – election of Valentian

who associates his brother Valens and makes the final division of the Eastern and
Western Empires – the death of Valentinian – his two sons, Gratian and Valentian II
succeed to the Western Empire

[AD 343–384]

THE death of Julian had left the public affairs of the empire in a very doubtful and dangerous situation. The Roman army was saved by an inglorious, perhaps a necessary treaty; and the first moments of peace were consecrated by the pious Jovian to restore the domestic tranquillity of the church and state. As soon as he ascended the throne he transmitted a circular epistle to all the governors of provinces, in which he confessed the divine truth and secured the legal establishment of the Christian religion. The insidious edicts of Julian were abolished, the ecclesiastical immunities were restored and enlarged, and Jovian condescended to lament that the distress of the times obliged him to diminish the measure of charitable distributions. The Christians were unanimous in the loud and sincere applause which they bestowed on the pious successor of Julian; but they were still ignorant what creed or what synod he would choose for the standard of orthodoxy, and the peace of the church immediately revived those eager disputes which had been suspended during the season of persecution. But his attachment to the Nicene Creed was at length discovered and declared by the reverence which he expressed for the *celestial* virtues of the great Athanasius.

The slightest force, when it is applied to assist and guide the natural descent of its object, operates with irresistible weight; and Jovian had the good fortune to embrace the religious opinions which were supported by the spirit of the times, and the zeal and numbers of the most powerful sect. Under his reign Christianity obtained an easy and lasting victory; and as soon as the smile of royal patronage was withdrawn, the genius of Paganism, which had been fondly raised and cherished by the arts of Julian, sunk irrecoverably in the dust. In many cities the temples were shut or deserted; the philosophers, who had abused their transient favor, thought it prudent to shave their beards and disguise their profession; and the Christians rejoiced that they were now in a condition to forgive or to revenge the injuries which they had suffered under the preceding reign. The consternation of the Pagan world was dispelled by a wise and gracious edict of toleration, in which Jovian explicitly declared that, although he should severely punish the sacrilegious rites of magic, his subjects might exercise, with freedom and safety, the ceremonies of the ancient worship.

In the space of seven months the Roman troops, who were now returned to Antioch, had performed a march of fifteen hundred miles, in which they had endured all the hardships of war, of famine, and of climate. Notwithstanding their services, their fatigues, and the approach of winter, the timid and impatient Jovian allowed only to the men and horses a respite of six weeks. The emperor could not sustain the indiscreet and malicious raillery of the people of Antioch. He was impatient to possess the palace of Constantinople, and to prevent the ambition of some competitor who might occupy the vacant allegiance of Europe. However his journey was interrupted by his sudden death. The cause of his death was variously understood. By some it was ascribed to the consequences of an indigestion, occasioned either by the quantity of the wine or the quality of the mushrooms which he had swallowed in the evening. According to others, he was suffocated in his sleep by the vapor of charcoal, which extracted from the walls of the apartment the unwholesome moisture of the fresh plaster. But the want of a regular inquiry into the death of a prince whose reign and person were soon forgotten appears to have been the only circumstance which countenanced the malicious whispers of poison and domestic guilt.

After the death of Jovian the throne of the Roman world remained ten days without a master until he was succeeded by Valentinian. Valentinian was the son of Count Gratian, a native of Cibalis, in Pannonia, who from an obscure condition had raised himself, by matchless strength and dexterity, to the military commands of Africa and Britain, from which he retired with an ample fortune and suspicious integrity. The rank and services of Gratian contributed, however, to smooth the first steps of the promotion of his son, and afforded him an early opportunity of displaying those solid and useful qualifications which raised his character above the ordinary level of his fellow-soldiers. The person of Valentinian was tall, graceful, and majestic. His manly countenance, deeply marked with the impression of sense and spirit, inspired his friends with awe, and his enemies with fear; and, to second the efforts of his undaunted courage, the son of Gratian had inherited the advantages of a strong and healthy constitution. By the habits of chastity and temperance, which restrain the appetites and invigorate the faculties, Valentinian preserved his own and the public esteem. The avocations of a military life had diverted his youth from the elegant pursuits of literature; he was ignorant of the Greek language and the arts of rhetoric; but, as the mind of the orator was never disconcerted by timid perplexity, he was able, as often as the occasion prompted him, to deliver his decided sentiments with bold and ready elocution. The laws of martial discipline were the only laws that he had studied, and he was soon distinguished by the laborious diligence and inflexible severity with which he discharged and enforced the duties of the camp. In the time of Julian he provoked the danger of

Left: A fortified gateway and town wall. (Reconstruction drawing)
Below: Silver bowl found at Mildenhall, Suffolk. The treasure is believed to have belonged to a Roman nobleman attached to the Imperial court. (Fourth century AD)

disgrace by the contempt which he publicly expressed for the reigning religion; and it should seem, from his subsequent conduct, that the indiscreet and unseasonable freedom of Valentinian was the effect of military spirit rather than of Christian zeal. He was pardoned, however, and still employed by a prince who esteemed his merit, and in the various events of the Persian war he improved the reputation which he had already acquired on the banks of the Rhine. The celerity and success with which he executed an important commission recommended him to the favor of Jovian, and to the honorable command of the second *school*, or company, of Targeteers of the domestic guards. In the march from Antioch he had reached his quarters at Ancyra, when he was unexpectedly summoned, without guilt and without intrigue, to assume, in the forty-third year of his age, the absolute government of the Roman empire.

The emperor, who suppressed his displeasure without altering his intention, slowly proceeded from Nice to Nicomedia and Constantinople. In one of the suburbs of that capital, thirty days after his own elevation, he bestowed the title of Augustus on his brother Valens: and as the boldest patriots were convinced that their opposition, without being serviceable to their country, would be fatal to themselves, the declaration of his absolute will was received with silent submission. Valens was now in the thirty-sixth year of his age, but his abilities had never been exercised in any employment, military or civil, and his character had not inspired the world with any sanguine expectations. He possessed, however, one quality which recommended him to Valentinian, and preserved the domestic peace of the empire: a

devout and grateful attachment to his benefactor, whose superiority of genius, as well as of authority, Valens humbly and cheerfully acknowledged in every action of his life.

In the castle or palace of Mediana, only three miles from Naissus, they executed the solemn and final division of the Roman empire. Valentinian bestowed on his brother the rich præfecture of the *East*, from the Lower Danube to the confines of Persia; whilst he reserved for his immediate government the warlike præfectures of *Illyricum, Italy*, and *Gaul*, from the extremity of Greece to the Caledonian rampart, and from the rampart of Caledonia to the foot of Mount Atlas. The provincial administration remained on its former basis, but a double supply of generals and magistrates was required for two councils and two courts; the division was made with a just regard to their peculiar merit and situation, and seven master-generals were soon created either of the cavalry or infantry. When this important business had been amicably transacted, Valentinian and Valens embraced for the last time. The emperor of the West established his temporary residence at Milan, and the emperor of the East returned to Constantinople to assume the dominion of fifty provinces.

When Tacitus describes the deaths of the innocent and illustrious Romans who were sacrificed to the cruelty of the first Cæsars, the art of the historian, or the merit of the sufferers, excites in our breasts the most lively sensations of terror, of admiration, and of pity. The coarse and undistinguished pencil of Ammianus has delineated his bloody figures with tedious and disgusting accuracy. But as our attention is no longer engaged by the contrast of freedom and servitude, of recent

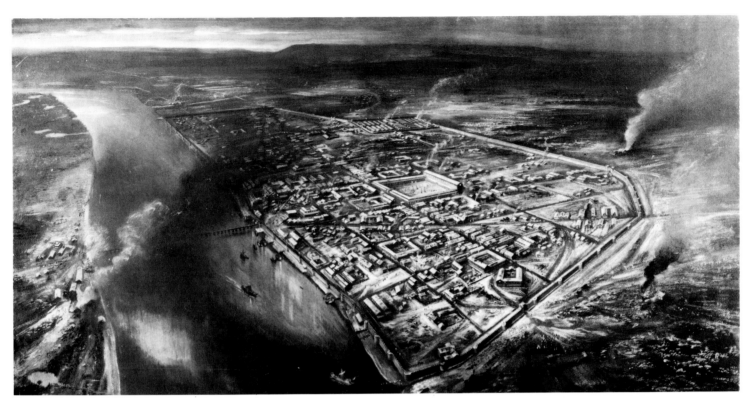

Above: Aerial view of London (Londinium) delivered from barbarian raiders by Theodosius (Flavius Theodosius c AD 346–95; Roman Emperor AD 379–95) in whom the defense and recovery of Britain had been entrusted. (Reconstruction drawing by Alan Sorrell, London Museum)

Left: Guard post along the frontier wall. Note the ditch (*vallum*). Valentian (Flavius Valentianus AD 321–75; Roman Emperor AD 364–75) fortified the frontiers and garrisons throughout the Empire. His generals were particularly active in Britain which was subject to sporadic attacks by the Picts and Saxons. (Reconstruction drawing by Alan Sorrell, London Museum)

greatness and of actual misery, we should turn with horror from the frequent executions which disgraced, both at Rome and Antioch, the reign of the two brothers. Valens was of a timid, and Valentinian of a choleric, disposition. In the government of his household, or of his empire, slight, or even imaginary offences – a hasty word, a casual omission, an involuntary delay – were chastised by a sentence of immediate death. The expressions which issued the most readily from the mouth of the emperor of the West were, 'Strike off his head;' 'Burn him alive;' 'Let him be beaten with clubs till he expires;' and his most favored ministers soon understood that, by a rash attempt to dispute or suspend the execution of his sanguinary commands, they might involve themselves in the guilt and punishment of disobedience.

But in the calmer moments of reflection, when the mind of Valens was not agitated by fear, or that of Valentinian by rage, the tyrant resumed the sentiments, or at least the conduct, of the father of his country. The dispassionate judgment of the Western emperor could clearly perceive, and accurately pursue, his own and the public interest; and the sovereign of the East, who imitated with equal docility the various examples which he received from his elder brother, was sometimes guided by the wisdom and virtue of the præfect Sallust. Both princes invariably retained, in the purple, the chaste and temperate simplicity which had adorned their private life; and, under their reign, the pleasures of the court never cost the people a blush or a sigh. They gradually reformed many of the abuses of the times of Constantius; judiciously adopted and improved the designs of Julian and his successor; and displayed a style and spirit of legislation which might inspire posterity with the most favorable opinion of their character and government. Valentinian condemned the exposition of new-born infants, and established fourteen skillful physicians, with stipends and privileges, in the fourteen quarters of Rome. The good sense of an illiterate soldier founded an useful and liberal institution for the education of youth, and the support of declining science. It was his intention that the arts of rhetoric and grammar should be taught, in the Greek and Latin languages, in the metropolis of every province; and as the size and dignity of the school was usually proportioned to the importance of the city, the academies of Rome and Constantinople claimed a just and singular pre-eminence. The fragments of the literary edicts of Valentinian imperfectly represent the school of Constantinople, which was gradually improved by subsequent regulations. That school consisted of thirty-one professors in different branches of learning. One philosopher and two lawyers; five sophists and ten grammarians for the Greek, and three orators and ten grammarians for the Latin tongue; besides seven scribes, or, as they were then styled, antiquarians, whose laborious pens supplied the public library with fair and correct copies of the classic writers. The rule of conduct which was prescribed to the students is the more curious, as it affords the first outlines of the form and discipline of a modern university. It was required that they should bring proper certificates from the magistrates of their native province. Their names, professions, and places of abode, were regularly entered in a public register. The studious youths were severely prohibited from wasting their time in feasts or in the theater; and the term of their education was limited to the age of twenty. The præfect of the city was empowered to chastise the idle and refractory by stripes or expulsion; and he was directed to make an annual report to the master of the offices, that the knowledge and abilities of the scholars might be usefully applied to the public service. The institutions of Valentinian contributed to secure the benefits of peace and plenty; and the cities were guarded by the establishment of the *Defensors;* freely elected as the tribunes and advocates of the people, to support their rights, and to expose their grievances, before the tribunals of the civil magistrates, or even at the foot of the Imperial throne. The finances were diligently administered by two princes who had been so long accustomed to the rigid economy of a private fortune; but in the receipt and application of the revenue, a discerning eye might observe some difference between the government of the East and of the West. Valens was persuaded that royal liberality can be supplied only by public oppression, and his ambition never aspired to secure, by their actual distress, the future strength and prosperity of his people. Instead of increasing the weight of taxes, which in the space of forty years had been gradually doubled, he reduced, in the first years of his reign, one-fourth of the tribute of the East. Valentinian appears to have been less attentive and less anxious to relieve the burthens of his people. He might reform the abuses of the fiscal administration; but he exacted, without scruple, a very large share of the private property; as he was convinced that the revenues which supported the luxury of individuals would be much more advantageously employed for the defense and improvement of the state. The subjects of the East, who enjoyed the present benefit, applauded the indulgence of their prince. The solid, but less splendid, merit of Valentinian was felt and acknowledged by the subsequent generation.

But the most honorable circumstance of the character of Valentinian is the firm and temperate impartiality which he uniformly preserved in an age of religious contention. His strong sense, unenlightened, but uncorrupted, by study, declined, with respectful indifference, the subtle questions of theological debate. The government of the *Earth* claimed his vigilance, and satisfied his ambition; and while he remembered that he was the disciple of the church, he never forgot that he was the sovereign of the clergy. Under the reign of an apostate, he had signalized his zeal for the honor of Christianity: he allowed to his subjects the privilege which he had assumed for himself; and they

Saxon graves found at Old Hexham, Northumberland.

might accept with gratitude and confidence the general toleration which was granted by a prince addicted to passion, but incapable of fear or of disguise. The Pagans, the Jews, and all the various sects which acknowledged the divine authority of Christ, were protected by the laws from arbitrary power or popular insult; nor was any mode of worship prohibited by Valentinian, except those secret and criminal practices which abused the name of religion for the dark purposes of vice and disorder.

When the suffrage of the generals and of the army committed the scepter of the Roman empire to the hands of Valentinian, his reputation in arms, his military skill and experience, and his rigid attachment to the forms as well as spirit of ancient discipline, were the principal motives of their judicious choice. The eagerness of the troops, who pressed him to nominate his colleague, was justified by the dangerous situation of public affairs; and Valentinian himself was conscious that the abilities of the most active mind were unequal to the defense of the distant frontiers of an invaded monarchy. As soon as the death of Julian had relieved the barbarians from the terror of his name, the most sanguine hopes of rapine and conquest excited the nations of the East, of the North, and of the South. Their inroads were often vexatious, and sometimes formidable; but, during the twelve years of the reign of Valentinian, his firmness and vigilance protected his own dominions; and his powerful genius seemed to inspire and direct the feeble counsels of his brother.

Under the reign of Valentinian the maritime provinces of Gaul were afflicted by the Saxons and Britain by the Scots and Picts. A military count was stationed for the defense of the sea-coast, or Armorican limit; and that officer, who found his strength or his abilities unequal to the task, implored the assistance of Severus, master-general of the infantry. The Saxons, surrounded and outnumbered, were forced to relinquish their spoil, and to yield a select band of their tall and robust youth to serve in the Imperial armies. They stipulated only a safe and honorable retreat; and the condition was readily granted by the Roman general, who meditated an act of perfidy, imprudent as it was inhuman, while a Saxon remained alive and in arms to revenge the fate of his countrymen. The premature eagerness of the infantry, who were secretly posted in a deep valley, betrayed the ambuscade; and they would perhaps have fallen the victims of their own treachery, if a large body of cuirassiers, alarmed by the noise of the combat, had not hastily advanced to extricate their companions, and to overwhelm the undaunted valor of the Saxons. Some of the prisoners were saved from the edge of the sword to shed their blood in the amphitheater; and the orator Symmachus complains that twenty-nine of those desperate savages, by strangling themselves with their own hands, had disappointed the amusement of the public. Yet the polite and philosophic citizens of Rome were impressed with the deepest horror when they were informed that the Saxons consecrated to the gods the tithe of their *human* spoil; and that they ascertained by lot the objects of the barbarous sacrifice.

Six years after the death of Constantine the destructive inroads of the Scots and Picts required the presence of his youngest son, who reigned in the Western empire. Constans visited his British dominions: but we may form some estimate of the importance of his achievements by the language of panegyric, which celebrates only his triumph over the elements, or, in other words, the good fortune of a safe and easy passage from the port of Boulogne to the harbor of Sandwich. The calamities which the afflicted provincials continued to experience from foreign war and domestic tyranny were aggravated by the feeble and corrupt administration of the eunuchs of Constantius; and the transient relief which they might obtain from the virtues of Julian was soon lost by the absence and death of their benefactor. The hostile tribes of the North, who detested the pride and power of the King of the World, suspended their domestic feuds; and the barbarians of the land and sea, the Scots, the Picts, and the Saxons, spread themselves, with rapid and irresistible fury, from the wall of Antonius to the shores of Kent.

Every messenger who escaped across the British Channel conveyed the most melancholy and alarming tidings to the ears of Valentinian, and the emperor was soon informed that the two military commanders of the province had been surprised and cut off by the barbarians. Severus, count of the domestics, was hastily dispatched, and as sud-

The bridal casket of Seconda and Projecta. With the new affluence it became customary to exchange ornate gifts such as this engraved silver bridal casket, c AD 379–389.

denly recalled, by the court of Trèves. The representations of Jovinus served only to indicate the greatness of the evil, and, after a long and serious consultation, the defense, or rather the recovery, of Britain was intrusted to the abilities of the brave Theodosius. The exploits of that general, the father of a line of emperors, have been celebrated, with peculiar complacency, by the writers of the age; but his real merit deserved their applause, and his nomination was received, by the army and province, as a sure presage of approaching victory. He seized the favorable moment of navigation, and securely landed the numerous and veteran bands of the Heruli and Batavians, the Jovians and the Victors. In his march from Sandwich to London, Theodosius defeated several parties of the barbarians, released a multitude of captives, and, after distributing to his soldiers a small portion of the spoil, established the fame of disinterested justice by the restitution of the remainder to the rightful proprietors. The citizens of London, who had almost despaired of their safety, threw open their gates, and, as soon as Theodosius had obtained from the court of Trèves the important aid of a military lieutenant and a civil governor, he executed with wisdom and vigor the laborious task of the deliverance of Britain. The vagrant soldiers were recalled to their standard, an edict of amnesty dispelled the public apprehensions, and his cheerful example alleviated the rigor of martial discipline. The scattered and desultory warfare of the barbarians, who infested the land and sea, deprived him of the glory of a signal victory; but the prudent spirit and consummate art of the Roman general were displayed in the operations of two campaigns, which successively rescued every part of the province from the hands of a cruel and rapacious enemy. The splendor of the cities and the security of the fortifications were diligently restored by the paternal care of Theodosius, who with a strong hand confined the trembling Caledonians to the northern angle of the island, and perpetuated, by the name and settlement of the new province of *Valentia*, the glories of the reign of Valentinian.

The ignominious treaty which saved the army of Jovian had been faithfully executed on the side of the Romans; and as they had solemnly renounced the sovereignty and alliance of Armenia and Iberia, those tributary kingdoms were exposed, without protection, to the arms of the Persian monarch. Sapor entered the Armenian territories at the head of a formidable host of cuirassiers, of archers, and of mercenary foot; but it was the invariable practice of Sapor to mix war and negotiation, and to consider falsehood and perjury as the most powerful instruments of regal policy. He affected to praise the prudent and moderate conduct of the king of Armenia; and the unsuspicious Tiranus was persuaded, by the repeated assurances of insidious friendship, to deliver his person into the hands of a faithless and cruel enemy. In the midst of a splendid entertainment, he was bound in chains of silver, as an honor due to the blood of that Arsacides; and, after a short confinement in the Tower of Oblivion at Ecbatana, he was released from the miseries of life, either by his own dagger or by that of an assassin. The kingdom of Armenia was reduced to the state of a Persian province; the administration was shared between a distinguished satrap and a favorite eunuch; and Sapor marched, without delay, to subdue the martial spirit of the Iberians. Sauromaces, who reigned in that country by the permission of the emperors, was expelled by a superior force, and, as an insult on the majesty of Rome, the king of kings placed a diadem on the head of his abject vassal Aspacuras. The city of Artogerassa was the only place of Armenia which presumed to resist the effort of his arms. The treasure deposited in that strong fortress tempted the avarice of Sapor; but the danger of Olympias, the wife or widow of the Armenian king, excited the public compassion and animated the desperate valor of her subjects and soldiers. The Persians were surprised and repulsed under the walls of Artogerassa by a bold and well-concerted sally of the besieged. But the forces of Sapor were continually renewed and increased; the hopeless courage of the garrison was exhausted; the strength of the walls yielded to the assault; and the proud conqueror, after wasting the rebellious city with fire and sword, led away captive an unfortunate queen, who, in a more auspicious hour, had been the destined bride of the son of Constantine. Yet if Sapor already triumphed in the easy conquest of two dependent kingdoms, he

soon felt that a country is unsubdued as long as the minds of the people are actuated by an hostile and contumacious spirit. The satraps, whom he was obliged to trust, embraced the first opportunity of regaining the affection of their countrymen, and of signalizing their immortal hatred to the Persian name. Since the conversion of the Armenians and Iberians, those nations considered the Christians as the favorites, and the Magians as the adversaries, of the Supreme Being; the influence of the clergy over a superstitious people was uniformly exerted in the cause of Rome; and as long as the successors of Constantine disputed with those of Artaxerxes the sovereignty of the intermediate provinces, the religious connection always threw a decisive advantage into the scale of the empire. A numerous and active party acknowledged Para, the son of Tiranus, as the lawful sovereign of Armenia, and his title to the throne was deeply rooted in the hereditary succession of five hundred years. By the unanimous consent of the Iberians, the country was equally divided between the rival princes; and Aspacuras, who owed his diadem to the choice of Sapor, was obliged to declare that his regard for his children, who were detained as hostages by the tyrant, was the only consideration which prevented him from openly renouncing the alliance of Persia. The emperor Valens, who respected the obligations of the treaty, and who was apprehensive of involving the East in a dangerous war, ventured, with slow and cautious measures, to support the Roman party in the kings of Iberia and Armenia. Twelve legions established the authority of Sauromaces on the banks of the Cyrus. The Euphrates was protected by the valor of Arintheus. A powerful army, under the command of Count Trajan, and of Vadomair king of the Alemanni, fixed their camp on the confines of Armenia. But they were strictly enjoined not to commit the first hostilities, which might be understood as a breach of the treaty; and such was the implicit obedience of the Roman general, that they retreated, with exemplary patience, under a shower of Persian arrows, till they had clearly acquired a just title to an honorable and legitimate victory. Yet these appearances of war insensibly subsided in a vain and tedious negotiation. The contending parties supported their claims by mutual reproaches of perfidy and ambition; and it should seem that the original treaty was expressed in very obscure terms, since they were reduced to the necessity of making their inconclusive appeal to the partial testimony of the generals of the two nations who had assisted at the negotiations. The invasion of the Goths and Huns, which soon afterwards shook the foundations of the Roman empire, exposed the provinces of Asia to the arms of Sapor. But the declining age, and perhaps the infirmities of the monarch, suggested new maxims of tranquillity and moderation. His death, which happened in the full maturity of a reign of seventy years, changed in a moment the court and councils of Persia, and their attention was most probably engaged by domestic troubles and the distant efforts of a Carmanian war. The remembrance of ancient injuries was lost in the enjoyment of peace. The kingdoms of Armenia and Iberia were permitted, by the mutual though tacit consent of both empires, to resume their doubtful neutrality. In the first years of the reign of Theodosius, a Persian embassy arrived at Constantinople to excuse the unjustifiable measures of the former reign, and to offer, as the tribute of friendship, or even of respect, a splendid present of gems, of silk, and of Indian elephants.

The emperor of the West, who had resigned to his brother the command of the Lower Danube, reserved for his immediate care the defense of the Rhætian and Illyrian provinces, which spread so many hundred miles along the greatest of the European rivers. The active policy of Valentinian was continually employed in adding new fortifications to the security of the frontier: but the abuse of this policy provoked the just resentment of the barbarians. The Quadi complained that the ground for an intended fortress had been marked out on their territories, and their complaints were urged with so much reason and moderation, that Equitius, master-general of Illyricum, consented to suspend the prosecution of the work till he should be more clearly informed of the will of his sovereign. This fair occasion of injuring a rival, and of advancing the fortune of his son, was eagerly embraced by the inhuman Maximin, the præfect, or rather tyrant of Gaul. The

passions of Valentinian were impatient of control, and he credulously listened to the assurances of his favorite, that, if the government of Valeria, and the direction of the work, were intrusted to the zeal of his son Marcellinus, the emperor should no longer be importuned with the audacious remonstrances of the barbarians. The subjects of Rome, and the natives of Germany, were insulted by the arrogance of a young and worthless minister, who considered his rapid elevation as the proof and reward of his superior merit. He affected, however, to receive the modest application of Gabinius, king of the Quadi, with some attention and regard; but this artful civility concealed a dark and bloody design, and the credulous prince was persuaded to accept the pressing invitation of Marcellinus. I am at a loss how to vary the narrative of similar crimes; or how to relate that, in the course of the same year, but in remote parts of the empire, the inhospitable table of two Imperial generals was stained with the royal blood of two guests and allies, inhumanly murdered by their order, and in their presence. The fate of Gabinius, and of Para, was the same: but the cruel death of their sovereign was resented in a very different manner by the servile temper of the Armenians and the free and daring spirit of the Germans. The Quadi were much declined from that formidable power which, in the time of Marcus Antoninus, had spread terror to the gates of Rome. But they still possessed arms and courage; their courage was animated by despair, and they obtained the usual reinforcement of the cavalry of their Sarmatian allies. They invaded Pannonia in the season of harvest, unmercifully destroyed every object of plunder which they could not easily transport, and either disregarded or demolished the empty fortifications. The princess Constantia, the daughter of the emperor Constantius, and the granddaughter of the great Constantine, very narrowly escaped. That royal maid, who had innocently supported the revolt of Procopius, was now the destined wife of the heir of the Western empire. She traversed the peaceful province with a splendid and unarmed train. Her person was saved from danger, and the republic from disgrace, by the active zeal of Messalla, governor of the provinces. As soon as he was informed that the village where she stopped only to dine was almost encompassed by the barbarians, he hastily placed her in his own chariot, and drove full speed till he reached the gates of Sirmium, which were at the distance of six-and-twenty miles. Even Sirmium might not have been secure if the Quadi and Sarmatians had diligently advanced during the general consternation of the magistrates and people. Their delay allowed Probus, the Prætorian præfect, sufficient time to recover his own spirits and to revive the courage of the citizens. He skillfully directed their strenuous efforts to repair and strengthen the decayed fortifications, and procured the seasonable and effectual assistance of a company of archers to protect the capital of the Illyrian provinces. Disappointed in their attempts against the walls of Sirmium, the indignant barbarians turned their arms against the master-general of the frontier, to whom they unjustly attributed the murder of their king. Equitius could bring into the field nor more than two legions, but they contained the veteran strength of the Mæsian and Pannonian bands. The obstinacy with which they disputed the vain honors of rank and precedency was the cause of their destruction, and, while they acted with separate forces and divided councils, they were surprised and slaughtered by the active vigor of the Sarmatian horse. The success of this invasion provoked the emulation of the bordering tribes, and the province of Mæsia would infallibly have been lost if young Theodosius, the duke or military commander of the frontier, had not signalized, in the defeat of the public enemy, an intrepid genius worthy of his illustrious father and of his future greatness.

The mind of Valentinian, who then resided at Trèves, was deeply affected by the calamities of Illyricum, but the lateness of the season suspended the execution of his designs till the ensuing spring. He marched in person, with a considerable part of the forces of Gaul, from the banks of the Moselle; and to the suppliant ambassadors of the Sarmatians, who met him on the way, he returned a doubtful answer, that as soon as he reached the scene of action he should examine and pronounce. But the haughty monarch was incapable of the magnanimity which dares to acknowledge a fault. He forgot the provocation, remembered only the injury, and advanced into the country of the Quadi with an insatiate thirst of blood and revenge. The extreme

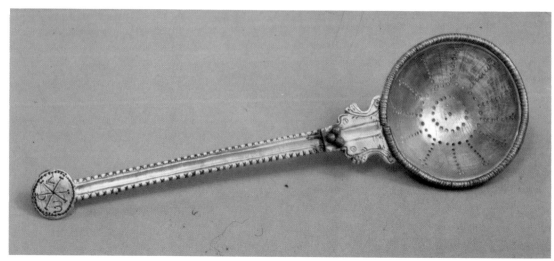

Above: Head of Neptune or Oceanus, the Roman sea-god. (Detail from the center of a great dish, part of the Mildenhall Treasure, fourth century, British Museum)
Right: Silver strainer decorated with the Chi-Rho symbol. (Length 20.2cm, part of the Water Newton Treasure, fourth century AD, British Museum, London)

devastation and promiscuous massacre of a savage war were justified in the eyes of the emperor, and perhaps in those of the world, by the cruel equity of retaliation; and such was the discipline of the Romans, and the consternation of the enemy, that Valentinian repassed the Danube without the loss of a single man. As he had resolved to complete the destruction of the Quadi by a second campaign, he fixed his winter-quarters at Bregetio, on the Danube, near the Hungarian city of Presburg. While the operations of war were suspended by the severity of the weather, the Quadi made an humble attempt to deprecate the wrath of their conqueror. The answer of the emperor left them but little to hope from his clemency or compassion. His eyes, his voice, his color, his gestures, expressed the violence of his ungoverned fury; and while his whole frame was agitated with convulsive passion a large blood-vessel suddenly burst in his body, and Valentinian fell speechless into the arms of his attendants. Their pious care immediately concealed his situation from the crowd, but in a few minutes the emperor of the West expired in an agony of pain, retaining his senses till the last, and struggling, without success, to declare his intentions to the generals and ministers who surrounded the royal couch. Valentinian was about fifty-four years of age, and he wanted only one hundred days to accomplish the twelve years of his reign.

The polygamy of Valentinian is seriously attested by an ecclesiastical historian. But we may be assured, from the evidence of reason as well as history, that the two marriages of Valentinian with Severa and with Justina were *successively* contracted, and that he used the ancient permission of divorce, which was still allowed by the laws, though it was condemned by the church. Severa was the mother of Gratian, who seemed to unite every claim which could entitle him to the undoubted succession of the Western empire. At the death of his father the royal youth was in the seventeenth year of his age, and his virtues already justified the favorable opinion of the army and people. But Gratian resided, without apprehension, in the palace of Trèves, whilst at the distance of many hundred miles Valentinian suddenly expired in the camp of Bregetio. On the sixth day after the death of Valentinian, the infant prince of the same name, who was only four years old, was

shown, in the arms of his mother, to the legions, and solemnly invested, by military acclamation, with the titles and ensigns of supreme power. The impending dangers of a civil war were seasonably prevented by the wise and moderate conduct of the emperor Gratian. He cheerfully accepted the choice of the army, declared that he should always consider the son of Justina as a brother, not as a rival, and advised the empress, with her son Valentinian, to fix their residence at Milan, in the fair and peaceful province of Italy, while he assumed the more arduous command of the countries beyond the Alps. Gratian dissembled his resentment till he could safely punish or disgrace the authors of the conspiracy; and though he uniformly behaved with tenderness and regard to his infant colleague, he gradually confounded, in the administration of the Western empire, the office of a guardian with the authority of a sovereign. The government of the Roman world was exercised in the united names of Valens and his two nephews; but the feeble emperor of the East, who succeeded to the rank of his elder brother, never obtained any weight or influence in the councils of the West.

Top right: Faceted silver bowl. (Diameter 19cm, the Water Newton Treasure, fourth century AD)
Right: Silver platter decorated with dancing bacchanalian figures. (The Mildenhall Treasure, fourth century AD, British Museum)
Below: Silver jug. (Height 20.3cm, the Water Newton Treasure, fourth century AD)

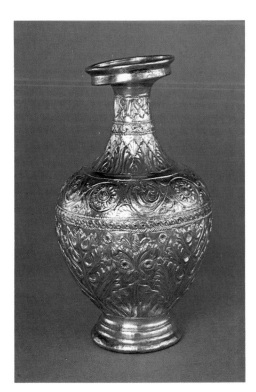

CHAPTER TWENTY-TWO

Progress of the Huns from China to Europe

flight of the Goths – defeat and death of Valens – Gratian and the Eastern Empire –
peace and settlement of the Goths

[AD 365–395]

IN the second year of the reign of Valentian and Valens, on the morning of the twenty-first day of July, the greatest part of the Roman world was shaken by a violent and destructive earthquake. The impression was communicated to the waters; the shores of the Mediterranean were left dry by the sudden retreat of the sea; great quantities of fish were caught with the hand; large vessels were stranded on the mud; and curious spectator amused his eye, or rather his fancy, by contemplating the various appearance of valleys and mountains which had never since the formation of the globe been exposed to the sun. But the tide soon returned with the weight of an immense and irresistible deluge, which was severely felt on the coasts of Sicily, of Dalmatia, of Greece, and of Egypt, large boats were transported and lodged on the roofs of houses, or at the distance of two miles from the shore; the people with the habitations were swept away by the waters; and the city of Alexandria annually commemorated the fatal day on which fifty thousand persons had lost their lives in the inundation. This calamity, the report of which was magnified from one province to another astonished and terrified the subjects of Rome and their affrighted imagination enlarged the real extent of a momentary evil. They recollected the preceding earthquakes, which had subverted the cities of Palestine and Bithynia; they considered these alarming strokes as the prelude only of still more dreadful calamities; and their fearful vanity was disposed to confound the symptoms of a declining empire and a sinking world. Without presuming to discuss the truth or propriety of these lofty speculations, the historian may content himself with an observation, which seems to be justified by experience, that man has much more to fear from the passions of his fellow-creatures than from the convulsions of the elements. In the disastrous period of the fall of the Roman empire, which may justly be dated from the reign of Valens, the happiness and security of each individual were personally attacked, and the arts and labors of ages were rudely defaced by the barbarians of Scythia and Germany. The invasion of the Huns precipitated on the provinces of the West the Gothic nation, which advanced, in less than forty years, from the Danube to the Atlantic, and opened a way, by the success of their arms, to the inroads of so many hostile tribes more savage than themselves. The original principle of motion was concealed in the remote countries of the North, and the curious observation of the pastoral life of the Scythians or Tartars will illustrate the latent cause of these destructive emigrations.

The Huns, who under the reign of Valens threatened the empire of Rome, had been formidable, in a much earlier period, to the empire of China. Their ancient, perhaps their original, seat was an extensive, though dry and barren, tract of country immediately on the north side of the great wall. But the valor of the Huns had extended the narrow limits of their dominions; and their rustic chiefs, who assumed the appellation of *Tanjou*, gradually became the conquerors and the sovereigns of a formidable empire bounded by the natural barriers of the ocean on the East. The submission of so many distant nations might flatter the pride of the Tanjou; but the valor of the Huns could be rewarded only by the enjoyment of the wealth and luxury of the empire of the South. In the third century before the Christian era, a wall of

fifteen hundred miles in length was constructed, to defend the frontiers of China against the inroads of the Huns; but this stupendous work, which holds a conspicuous place in the map of the world, has never contributed to the safety of an unwarlike people. The cavalry of the Tanjou frequently consisted of two or three hundred thousand men, formidable by the matchless dexterity with which they managed their bows and their horses; by their hardy patience in supporting the inclemency of the weather; and by the incredible speed of their march.

They spread themselves at once over the face of the country; and their rapid impetuosity surprised, astonished, and disconcerted the grave and elaborate tactics of a Chinese army. A regular payment of money and silk was stipulated as the condition of a temporary and precious peace; and the wretched expedient of disguising a real tribute under the names of a gift or subsidy was practiced by the emperors of China as well as by those of Rome.

But their pride was humbled, and their progress was checked, by the arms and policy of Vouti, the fifth emperor of the powerful dynasty of the Han. His lieutenants penetrated many hundred miles into the country of the Huns. In those boundless deserts, where it is impossible to form magazines, and difficult to transport a sufficient supply of provisions, the armies of Vouti were repeatedly exposed to intolerable hardships: and, of one hundred and forty thousand soldiers who marched against the barbarians, thirty thousand only returned in safety to the feet of their master. These losses, however, were compensated by splendid and decisive success. The Chinese generals improved the superiority which they derived from the temper of their arms, their chariots of war, and the service of their Tartar auxiliaries. The camp of the Tanjou was surprised in the midst of sleep and intemperance; and, though the monarch of the Huns bravely cut his way through the ranks of the enemy, he left above fifteen thousand of his subjects on the field of battle. Yet this signal victory, which was preceded and followed by many bloody engagements, contributed much less to the destruction of the power of the Huns than the effectual policy which was employed to detach the tributary nations from their obedience. Intimidated by the arms or allured by the promises, of Vouti and his successors, the most considerable tribes, both of the East and of the West, disclaimed the authority of the Tanjou. While some acknowledged themselves the allies or vassals of the empire, they all became the implacable enemies of the Huns.

The desertion of his subjects, and the perplexity of a civil war, at length compelled the Tanjou himself to renounce the dignity of an independent sovereign, and the freedom of a warlike and high-spirited nation. He was received at Sigan, the capital of the monarchy, by the troops, the mandarins, and the emperor himself, with all the honors that could adorn and disguise the triumph of Chinese vanity. He performed, on his knees, the duty of a respectful homage to the emperor of China; pronounced, in his own name, and in the name of his successors, a perpetual oath of fidelity; and gratefully accepted a seal, which was bestowed as the emblem of his regal dependence. After this humiliating submission, the Tanjous sometimes departed from their allegiance, and seized the favorable moments of war and rapine; but the monarchy of the Huns gradually declined, till it was broken, by civil dissension, into two hostile and separate kingdoms. One of the princes of the nation was urged by fear and ambition to retire towards the south with eight hordes, which composed between forty and fifty thousand families. He obtained, with the title of Tanjou, a convenient territory

Theodosius, later known as Theodosius the Great, appointed by the Emperor Gratian (Flavius Gratianus AD 359–383; Roman Emperor AD 367–83) as his colleague following the death of Valens in AD 378. (Detail from the Silver Missorum of Theodosius, fourth century AD, Academy of History, Madrid)

on the verge of the Chinese provinces; and his constant attachment to the service of the empire was secured by weakness and the desire of revenge. From the time of this fatal schism, the Huns of the north continued to languish about fifty years, till they were oppressed on every side by their foreign and domestic enemies, particularly the Sienpi.

Thereafter above one hundred thousand persons, the poorest, indeed, and the most pusillanimous of the people, were contented to remain in their native country, to renounce their peculiar name and origin, and to mingle with their conquerors. Fifty-eight hordes, about two hundred thousand men, ambitious of a more honorable servitude, retired towards the south, implored the protection of the emperors of China, and were permitted to inhabit and to guard the extreme frontiers of the province of Chansi and the territory of Ortous. But the most warlike and powerful tribes of the Huns maintained in their adverse fortune the undaunted spirit of their ancestors. The western world was open to their valor, and they resolved, under the conduct of their hereditary chieftains, to discover and subdue some remote country which was still inaccessible to the arms of the Sienpi and to the laws of China. The course of their emigration soon carried them beyond the mountains of Imaus and the limits of the Chinese geography; but *we* are able to distinguish the two great divisions of these formidable exiles, which directed their march towards the Oxus and towards the Volga. The first of these colonies established their dominion in the fruitful and extensive plains of the Sogdiana, on the eastern side of the Caspian, where they preserved the name of Huns, with the epithet of Euthalites or Nephthalites. Their vicinity to the provinces of Persia involved them in frequent and bloody contests with the power of that monarchy. The

second division of their countrymen, the Huns who gradually advanced towards the northwest, were exercised by the hard ships of a colder climate and a more laborious march. Necessity compelled them to exchange the silks of China for the furs of Siberia.

It is impossible to fill the dark interval of time which elapsed after the Huns of the Volga were lost in the eyes of the Chinese, and before they showed themselves to those of the Romans. There is some reason, however, to apprehend that the same force which had driven them from their native seats still continued to impel their march towards the frontiers of Europe. But one cannot suppress the very natural suspicion *that* the Huns of the North derived a considerable reinforcement from the ruin of the dynasty of the South, which, in the course of the third century, submitted to the dominion of China; *that* the bravest warriors marched away in search of their free and adventurous countrymen; *and* that, as they had been divided by prosperity, they were easily reunited by the common hardships of their adverse fortune. The Huns, with their flocks and herds, their wives and children, their dependents and allies, were transported to the West of the Volga, and united they boldly advanced to invade the country of the Alani, a pastoral people, who occupied, or wasted, an extensive tract of the deserts of Scythia. On the banks of the Tanais the military power of the Huns and the Alani encountered each other. The Huns prevailed. The king of the Alani was slain; and the remains of the vanquished nation were dispersed by the ordinary alternative of flight or submission. A colony of exiles found a secure refuge in the mountains of Caucasus, between the Euxine and the Caspian, where they still preserve their name and their independence. But the greatest part of the nation of the Alani embraced the offers of an honorable and advantageous union; and the Huns, who esteemed the valor of their less fortunate enemies, proceeded, with an increase of numbers and confidence, to invade the limits of the Gothic empire.

The waves of the barbarian migrations and invasions which eventually overwhelmed the Empire, culminating in the sack of Rome in AD 410 and the final fall of the West in AD 476.

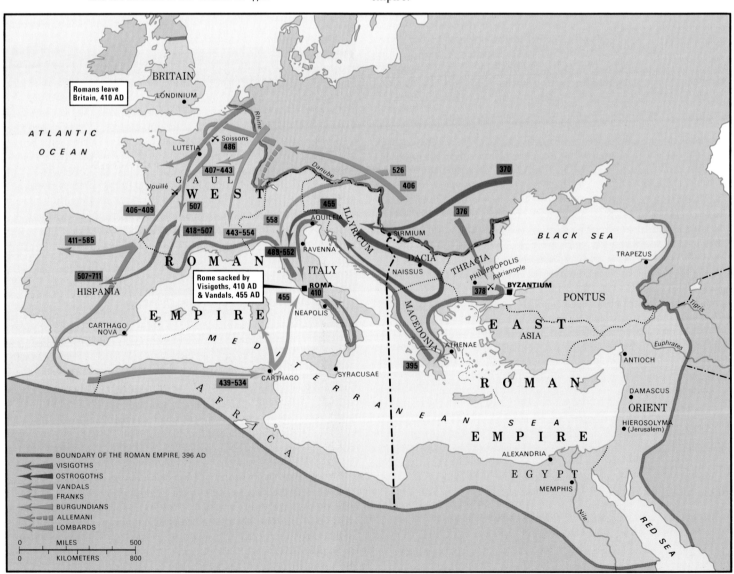

Sixth-century AD Allemanic helmet but of southeast European origin which probably came to the Allemani by means of the battlefield.

The great Hermanric, whose dominions extended from the Baltic to the Euxine, enjoyed, in the full maturity of age and reputation, the fruit of his victories, when he was alarmed by the formidable approach of an host of unknown enemies. Against these enemies, Hermanric prepared to exert the united forces of the Gothic state.

But the hopes and measures of the Judge of the Visigoths were soon disappointed by the trembling impatience of the dismayed country-men, who were persuaded by their fears that the interposition of the Danube was the only barrier that could save them from the rapid pursuit and invincible valor of the barbarians of Scythia. Under the command of Fritigern and Alavivus, the body of the nation hastily advanced to the banks of the great river, and implored the protection of the Roman emperor of the East.

He was informed that the North was agitated by a furious tempest; that the irruption of the Huns, an unknown and monstrous race of savages, had subverted the power of the Goths; and that the suppliant multitudes of the warlike nation, whose pride was now humbled in the dust, covered a space of many miles along the banks of the river. With outstretched arms and pathetic lamentations they loudly deplored their past misfortunes and their present danger; acknowledged that their only hope of safety was in the clemency of the Roman government. The emperor of the East was no longer guided by the wisdom and authority of his elder brother, whose death happened towards the end of the preceding year; and as the distressful situation of the Goths required an instant and peremptory decision, he was deprived of the favorite resource of feeble and timid minds, who consider the use of dilatory and ambiguous measures as the most admirable efforts of consummate prudence. The prayers of the Goths were granted, and orders were immediately dispatched to the civil and military governors of the Thracian diocese to make the necessary preparations for the passage and subsistence of a great people. The liberality of the emperor was accompanied, however, with two harsh and rigorous conditions, which

prudence might justify on the side of the Romans, but which distress alone could extort from the indignant Goths. Before they passed the Danube they were required to deliver their arms, and it was insisted that their children should be taken from them and dispersed through the provinces of Asia, where they might be civilized by the arts of education, and serve as hostages to secure the fidelity of their parents.

A large fleet of vessels, of boats, and of canoes, was provided; many days and nights they passed and repassed with indefatigable toil. And if we can venture to add the just proportion of women, of children, and of slaves, the whole mass of people which composed this formidable emigration must have amounted to near a million of persons. The children of the Goths, those at least of a distinguished rank, were separated from the multitude. They were conducted without delay to the distant seats assigned for their residence and education; and as the numerous train of hostages or captives passed through the cities, their gay and splendid apparel, their robust and martial figure, excited the surprise and envy of the provincials. But the stipulation, the most offensive of the Goths and the most important to the Romans, was shamefully eluded. The barbarians, who considered their arms as the ensigns of honor and the pledges of safety, were disposed to offer a price which the lust or avarice of the Imperial officers was easily tempted to accept. To preserve their arms, the haughty warriors consented, with some reluctance, to prostitute their wives or their daughters; the charms of a beauteous maid, or a comely boy, secured the connivance of the inspectors, who sometimes cast an eye of covetousness on the fringed carpets and linen garments of their new allies, or who sacrificed their duty to the mean consideration of filling their farms with cattle and their houses with slaves. The Goths, with arms in their hands, were permitted to enter the boats; and, when their strength was collected on the other side of the river, the immense camp which was spread over the plains and the hills of the Lower Mæsia assumed a threatening and even

Barbarian cavalryman carrying a small round shield. (Probably eighth-century AD German origin)

On the death of Valens (Flavius Valens c AD 328–78, Roman Emperor AD 364–78) at the Battle of Hadrianople Gratian inherited the throne of the Eastern Empire. Gratian was pious, temperate and brave, but his fondness for the frivolous pursuits of hunting and his persecution of the pagans alienated his troops; he was defeated in battle by the popular usurper Maximus at Paris and put to death at Lyons.
Left: Hunters carrying their bag of game. (Mosaic from the Royal Villa at Armerina, Sicily, late third century AD)
Right: Boar hunt. (Mosaic from the Royal Villa at Armerina, Sicily, late third century AD)

hostile aspect. The leaders of the Ostrogoths, Alatheus and Saphrax, the guardians of their infant king, appeared soon afterwards on the northern banks of the Danube, and immediately dispatched their ambassadors to the court of Antioch to solicit, with the same professions of allegiance and gratitude, the same favor which had been granted to the suppliant Visigoths. The absolute refusal of Valens suspended their progress, and discovered the repentance, the suspicions, and the fears of the Imperial council.

An undisciplined and unsettled nation of barbarians required the firmest temper and the most dexterous management. The daily subsistence of near a million of extraordinary subjects could be supplied only by constant and skillful diligence, and might continually be interrupted by mistake or accident. At this important crisis the military government of Thrace was exercised by Lupicinus and Maximus, in whose venal minds the slightest hope of private emolument outweighed every consideration of public advantage, and whose guilt was only alleviated by their incapacity of discerning the pernicious effects of their rash and criminal administration. Instead of obeying the orders of their sovereign, and satisfying, with decent liberality, the demands of the Goths, they levied an ungenerous and oppressive tax on the wants of the hungry barbarians. The vilest food was sold at an extravagant price, and in the room of wholesome and substantial provisions, the markets were filled with the flesh of dogs and of unclean animals who had died of disease. To obtain the valuable acquisition of a pound of bread, the Goths resigned the possession of an expensive though serviceable slave, and a small quantity of meat was greedily purchased with ten pounds of a precious but useless metal. When their property was exhausted, they continued this necessary traffic by the sale of their sons and daughters. The barbarians beheld around them the wealth and plenty of a fertile province, in the midst of which they suffered the intolerable hardships of artificial famine. But the means of relief, and even of revenge, were in their hands, since the rapaciousness of their tyrants had left to an injured people the possession and the use of arms. The clamors of a multitude, untaught to disguise their sentiments, announced the first symptoms of resistance, and alarmed the timid and guilty minds of Lupicinus and Maximus. Those crafty ministers, who

substituted the cunning of temporary expedients to the wise and salutary counsels of general policy, attempted to remove the Goths from their dangerous station on the frontiers of the empire, and to disperse them, in separate quarters of cantonment, through the interior provinces. As they were conscious how ill they had deserved the respect or confidence of the barbarians, they diligently collected from every side a military force that might urge the tardy and reluctant march of a people who had not yet renounced the title or the duties of Roman subjects. But the generals of Valens, while their attention was solely directed to the discontented Visigoths, imprudently disarmed the ships and the fortifications which constituted the defense of the Danube. The fatal oversight was observed and improved by Alatheus and Saphrax, who anxiously watched the favorable moment of escaping from the pursuit of the Huns. By the help of such rafts and vessels as could be hastily procured, the leaders of the Ostrogoths transported, without opposition, their king and their army, and boldly fixed an hostile and independent camp on the territories of the empire.

Under the name of Judges, Alavivus and Fritigern were the leaders of the Visigoths in peace and war; and the authority which they derived from their birth was ratified by the free consent of the nation. In a season of tranquillity their power might have been equal as well as their rank; but, as soon as their countrymen were exasperated by hunger and oppression, the superior abilities of Fritigern assumed the military command. Sensible of the benefits which would result from the union of the Gothic powers under the same standard, he secretly cultivated the friendship of the Ostrogoths; and while he professed an implicit obedience to the orders of the Roman generals, he proceeded by slow marches towards Marcianopolis, the capital of the Lower Mæsia, about seventy miles from the banks of the Danube. On that fatal spot the flames of discord and mutual hatred burst forth into a dreadful conflagration. The generals of the Goths were saluted by the fierce and joyful acclamations of the camp; war was instantly resolved, and the resolution was executed without delay.

The weak and guilty Lupicinus, who had dared to provoke, who had neglected to destroy, and who still presumed to despise his formidable enemy, marched against the Goths, at the head of such a military force as could be collected on this sudden emergency. The barbarians expected his approach about nine miles from Marcianopolis; and on this occasion the talents of the general were found to be of more prevailing efficacy than the weapons and discipline of the troops. The valor of the Goths was so ably directed by the genius of Fritigern, that they broke, by a close and vigorous attack, the ranks of the Roman legions. Lupicinus left his arms and standards, his tribunes and his bravest soldiers, on the field of battle; and their useless courage served only to protect the ignominious flight of their leader. 'That successful day put an end to the distress of the barbarians and the security of the Romans: from that day the Goths, renouncing the precarious condition of strangers and exiles, assumed the character of citizens and masters, claimed an absolute dominion over the possessors of land, and held, in their own right, the northern provinces of the empire, which are bounded by the Danube.' Such are the words of the Gothic historian Jornandes de Rebus Geticis, who celebrates, with rude eloquence, the glory of his countrymen. But the dominion of the barbarians was exercised only for the purposes of rapine and destruction. The report of the Gothic

victory was soon diffused over the adjacent country; and while it filled the minds of the Romans with terror and dismay, their own hasty imprudence contributed to increase the forces of Fritigern and the calamities of the province. Some time before the great emigration a numerous body of Goths, under the command of Suerid and Colias, had been received into the protection and service of the empire. They were encamped under the walls of Hadrianople: but the ministers of Valens were anxious to remove them beyond the Hellespont, at a distance from the dangerous temptation which might so easily be communicated by the neighborhood and the success of their countrymen. The respectful submission with which they yielded to the order of their march might be considered as a proof of their fidelity; and their moderate request of a sufficient allowance of provisions and of a delay of only two days was expressed in the most dutiful terms. But the first magistrate of Hadrianople, incensed by some disorders which had been committed at his country-house, refused this indulgence; and arming against them the inhabitants and manufacturers of a populous city, he urged, with hostile threats, their instant departure. The barbarians

Coin of the Emperor Valentian II (Flavius Valentinianus AD 321–75; Roman Emperor AD 364–75) half-brother of Gratian.

who lay encamped in the spacious and fertile meadows near the most southern of the six mouths of the Danube. Their camp was surrounded by the usual fortification of wagons; and the barbarians, secure within the vast circle of the enclosure, enjoyed the fruits of their valor and the spoils of the province. In the midst of riotous intemperance, the watchful Fritigern observed the motions and penetrated the designs of the Romans. He perceived that the numbers of the enemy were continually increasing; and, as he understood their intention of attacking his rear as soon as the scarcity of forage should oblige him to remove his camp, he recalled to their standard his predatory detachments, which covered the adjacent country. As soon as they descried the flaming beacons they obeyed with incredible speed the signal of their leader; the

stood silent and amazed till they were exasperated by the insulting clamors and missile weapons of the populace: but when patience or contempt was fatigued, they crushed the undisciplined multitude, inflicted many a shameful wound on the backs of their flying enemies, and despoiled them of the splendid armor which they were unworthy to bear. The resemblance of their sufferings and their actions soon united this victorious detachment to the nation of the Visigoths; the troops of Colias and Suerid expected the approach of the great Fritigern, ranged themselves under his standard, and signalized their ardor in the siege of Hadrianople. But the resistance of the garrison informed the barbarians that in the attack of regular fortifications the efforts of unskillful courage are seldom effectual. Their general acknowledged his error, raised the siege, declared that 'he was at peace with stone walls,' and revenged his disappointment on the adjacent country. He accepted with pleasure the useful reinforcement of hardy workmen who labored in the gold-mines of Thrace for the emolument and under the lash of an unfeeling master: and these new associates conducted the barbarians through the secret paths to the most sequestered places, which had been chosen to secure the inhabitants, the cattle, and the magazines of corn. With the assistance of such guides nothing could remain impervious or inaccessible: resistance was fatal; flight was impracticable; and the patient submission of helpless innocence seldom found mercy from the barbarian conqueror. In the course of these depredations a great number of the children of the Goths, who had been sold into captivity, were restored to the embraces of their afflicted parents; but these tender interviews, which might have revived and cherished in their minds some sentiments of humanity, tended only to stimulate their native fierceness by the desire of revenge. They listened with eager attention to the complaints of their captive children, who had suffered the most cruel indignities from the lustful or angry passions of their masters, and the same cruelties, the same indignities, were severely retaliated on the sons and daughters of the Romans.

The imprudence of Valens and his ministers had introduced into the heart of the empire a nation of enemies; but the Visigoths might even yet have been reconciled by the manly confession of past errors and the sincere performance of former engagements. But on this occasion alone Valens was brave; and his unseasonable bravery was fatal to himself and to his subjects. He declared his intention of marching from Antioch to Constantinople, to subdue this dangerous rebellion; and, as he was not ignorant of the difficulties of the enterprise, he solicited the assistance of his nephew, the emperor Gratian, who commanded all the forces of the West. In a council of war, which was influenced by pride rather than by reason, it was resolved to seek and to encounter the barbarians,

camp was filled with the martial crowd of barbarians; their impatient clamors demanded the battle, and their tumultuous zeal was approved and animated by the spirit of their chiefs. While the trumpets sounded to arms, the undaunted courage of the Goths was confirmed by the mutual obligation of a solemn oath; and, as they advanced to meet the enemy, the rude songs which celebrated the glory of their forefathers were mingled with their fierce and dissonant outcries, and opposed to the artificial harmony of the Roman shout. Some military skill was displayed by Fritigern to gain the advantage of a commanding eminence; but the bloody conflict, which began and ended with the light,

was maintained on either side by the personal and obstinate efforts of strength, valor, and agility. And when the two armies, at a late hour of the evening, retreated to their respective camps, neither of them could claim the honors or the effects of a decisive victory.

The Imperial generals, whose army would have been consumed by the repetition of such a contest, embraced the more rational plan of destroying the barbarians by the wants and pressure of their own multitudes. They prepared to confine the Visigoths in the narrow angle of land between the Danube, the desert of Scythia, and the mountains of Hæmus, till their strength and spirit should be insensibly wasted by the inevitable operation of famine. The design was prosecuted with some conduct and success; the barbarians had almost exhausted their

The Fury of the Goths. (Painting by Paul Ivanovitz)

Above: Boar hunt. (Mosaic from Carthage, Tunisia, fourth century AD)
Right: Hunters bring back captive animals. (Mosaic from the Royal Villa, Piazza Armerina, Sicily, late third century AD)

own magazines and the harvests of the country; and the diligence of Saturninus, the master-general of the cavalry, was employed to improve the strength and to contract the extent of the Roman fortifications. His labors were interrupted by the alarming intelligence that new swarms of barbarians had passed the unguarded Danube, either to support the cause or to imitate the example of Fritigern. The just apprehension that he himself might be surrounded and overwhelmed by the arms of hostile and unknown nations, compelled Saturninus to relinquish the siege of the Gothic camp.

The emperor Valens, who at length had removed his court and army from Antioch, was received by the people of Constantinople as the author of the public calamity. Before he had reposed himself ten days in the capital he was urged by the licentious clamors of the Hippodrome to march against the barbarians whom he had invited into his dominions: and the citizens, who are always brave at a distance from any real danger, declared, with confidence, that if they were supplied with arms, *they* alone would undertake to deliver the province from the ravages of an insulting foe. The vain reproaches of an ignorant multitude hastened the downfall of the Roman empire: provoking the desperate rashness of Valens, who did not find, either in his reputation or in his mind, any motives to support with firmness the public contempt. He was soon persuaded by the successful achievements of his lieutenants to despise the power of the Goths, who, by the diligence of Fritigern, were now collected in the neighborhood of Hadrianople. The march of the Taifalæ had been intercepted by the valiant Frigerid; the king of those licentious barbarians was slain in battle; and the suppliant captives were sent into distant exile to cultivate the lands of Italy, which were assigned for their settlement in the vacant territories of Modena and Parma. The exploits of Sebastian, who was recently engaged in the service of Valens, and promoted to the rank of master-general of the infantry, were still more honorable to himself, and useful to the republic. He obtained the permission of selecting three hundred soldiers from each of the legions, and this separate detachment soon acquired the spirit of discipline and the exercise of arms, which were almost forgotten under the reign of Valens. By the vigor and conduct of

Tenth-century portrayal of a Hunnish battle.

Sebastian, a large body of the Goths was surprised in their camp; and the immense spoil which was recovered from their hands filled the city of Hadrianople and the adjacent plain. The splendid narratives which the general transmitted of his own exploits alarmed the Imperial court by the appearance of superior merit; and though he cautiously insisted on the difficulties of the Gothic war, his valor was praised, his advice was rejected; and Valens, who listened with pride and pleasure to the flattering suggestions of the eunuchs of the palace, was impatient to seize the glory of an easy and assured conquest. His army was strengthened by a numerous reinforcement of veterans; and his march from Constantinople to Hadrianople was conducted with so much military skill that he prevented the activity of the barbarians, who designed to occupy the intermediate defiles, and to intercept either the troops themselves or their convoys of provisions. The camp of Valens, which he pitched under the walls of Hadrianople, was fortified, according to the practice of the Romans, with a ditch and rampart; and a most important council was summoned to decide the fate of the emperor and of the empire. The party of reason and of delay was strenuously maintained by Victor, who had corrected, by the lessons of experience, the native fierceness of the Sarmatian character; while Sebastian, with the flexible and obsequious eloquence of a courtier, represented every precaution and every measure that implied a doubt of immediate victory as unworthy of the courage and majesty of their invincible monarch. The ruin of Valens was precipitated by the deceitful arts of Fritigern and the prudent admonitions of the emperor of the West. The advantages of negotiating in the midst of war were perfectly understood by the general of the barbarians; and a Christian ecclesiastic was dispatched, as the holy minister of peace, to penetrate and to perplex the councils of the enemy. The misfortunes, as well as the provocations, of the Gothic nation were forcibly and truly described by their ambassador, who protested, in the name of Fritigern, that he was still disposed to lay down his arms, or to employ them only in the defense of the empire, if he could secure for his wandering countrymen a tranquil settlement on the waste lands of Thrace, and a sufficient allowance of corn and cattle. But he added, in a whisper of confidential friendship, that the exasperated barbarians were averse to these reasonable conditions; and that Fritigern was doubtful whether he could accomplish the conclusion of the treaty unless he found himself supported by the presence and terrors of an Imperial army. About the same time, Count Richomer returned from the West to announce the defeat and submission of the Alemañni; to inform Valens that his nephew advanced by rapid marches at the head of the veteran and victorious legions of Gaul; and to request, in the name of Gratian and of the republic, that every dangerous and decisive measure might be suspended till the junction of the two emperors should ensure the success of the Gothic war. But the feeble sovereign of the East was actuated only by the fatal illusions of pride and jealousy. He disdained the importunate advice; he rejected the humiliating aid; he secretly compared the ignominious, at least the inglorious, period of his own reign with the fame of a beardless youth; and Valens rushed into the field to erect his imaginary trophy before the

diligence of his colleague could usurp any share of the triumph.

On the 9 August, a day which has deserved to be marked among the most inauspicious of the Roman calendar, the emperor Valens, leaving, under a strong guard, his baggage and military treasure, marched from Hadrianople to attack the Goths, who were encamped about twelve miles from the city. By some mistakes of the orders, or some ignorance of the ground, the right wing or column of cavalry arrived in sight of the enemy whilst the left was still at a considerable distance; the soldiers were compelled, in the sultry heat of summer, to precipitate their pace; and the line of battle was formed with tedious confusion and irregular delay. The Gothic cavalry had been detached to forage in the adjacent country; and Fritigern still continued to practice his customary arts. He dispatched messengers of peace, made proposals, required hostages, and wasted the hours, till the Romans, exposed without shelter to the burning rays of the sun, were exhausted by thirst, hunger, and intolerable fatigue. The emperor was persuaded to send an ambassador to the Gothic camp; the zeal of Richomer, who alone had courage to accept the dangerous commission, was applauded; and the count of the domestics, adorned with the splendid ensigns of his dignity, had proceeded some way in the space between the two armies when he was suddenly recalled by the alarm of battle. The hasty and imprudent attack was made by Bacurius the Iberian, who commanded a body of archers and targeteers: and, as they advanced with rashness, they

Barbarian weapons found in the grave of a Frankish warrior (period of the Great Migrations).

retreated with loss and disgrace. In the same moment the flying squadrons of Alatheus and Saphrax, whose return was anxiously expected by the general of the Goths, descended like a whirlwind from the hills, swept across the plain, and added new terrors to the tumultuous but irresistible charge of the barbarian host. The event of the battle of Hadrianople, so fatal to Valens and to the empire, may be described in a few words: the Roman cavalry fled; the infantry was abandoned, surrounded, and cut in pieces. The most skillful evolutions, the firmest courage, are scarcely sufficient to extricate a body of foot encompassed on an open plain by superior numbers of horse; but the troops of Valens, oppressed by the weight of the enemy and their own fears, were crowded into a narrow space, where it was impossible for them to extend their ranks, or even to use, with effect, their swords and javelins. In the midst of tumult, of slaughter, and of dismay, the emperor, deserted by his guards, and wounded, as it was supposed, with an arrow, sought protection among the Lancearii and the Mattiarii, who still maintained their ground with some appearance of order and firmness. His faithful generals, Trajan and Victor, who perceived his danger, loudly exclaimed that all was lost unless the person of the emperor could be saved. Some troops, animated by their exhortation, advanced to his relief: they found only a bloody spot, covered with a heap of broken arms and mangled bodies, without being able to discover their unfortunate prince either among the living or the dead. Their search could not indeed be successful, if there is any truth in the circumstances with which some historians have related the death of the emperor. By the care of his attendants, Valens was removed from the field of battle to a neighboring cottage, where they attempted to dress his wound and to provide for his future safety. But this humble retreat was instantly surrounded by the enemy; they tried to force the door; they were provoked by a discharge of arrows from the roof; till at length, impatient of delay, they set fire to a pile of dry faggots, and consumed the cottage with the Roman emperor and his train. Valens perished in the flames; and a youth, who dropped from the window, alone escaped, to attest the melancholy tale and to inform the Goths of the inestimable prize which they had lost by their own rashness. Above two-thirds of the Roman army were destroyed: and the darkness of the night was esteemed a very favorable circumstance, as it served to conceal the flight of the multitude, and to protect the more orderly retreat of Victor and Richomer, who alone, amidst the general consternation, maintained the advantage of calm courage and regular discipline.

The pride of the Goths was elated by this memorable victory; but their avarice was disappointed by the mortifying discovery that the richest part of the Imperial spoil had been within the walls of Hadrianople. They hastened to possess the reward of their valor; but they were encountered by the remains of a vanquished army with an intrepid resolution, which was the effect of their despair and the only hope of their safety. After the hasty and impolitic massacre of three hundred deserters, an act of justice extremely useful to the discipline of the Roman armies, the Goths indignantly raised the siege of Hadrianople. The scene of war and tumult was instantly converted into a silent solitude; the multitude suddenly disappeared; the secret paths of the woods and mountains were marked with the footsteps of the trembling fugitives.

Whatever may have been the just measure of the calamities of Europe, there was reason to fear that the same calamities would soon extend to the peaceful countries of Asia.

The emperor Gratian, after a delay caused by the rising of the Alemanni in Gaul, was far advanced on his march towards the plains of Hadrianople when he was informed, at first by the confused voice of fame, and afterwards by the more accurate reports of Victor and Richomer, that his impatient colleague had been slain in battle, and that two-thirds of the Roman army were exterminated by the sword of the victorious Goths. Whatever resentment the rash and jealous vanity of his uncle might deserve, the resentment of a generous mind is easily subdued by the softer emotions of grief and compassion; and even the sense of pity was soon lost in the serious and alarming consideration of the state of the republic. Gratian was too late to assist, he was too weak to revenge, his unfortunate colleague; and the valiant and modest youth felt himself unequal to the support of a sinking world. The death of Valens had left the East without a sovereign and it was the wish of Gratian to bestow the purple as the reward of virtue. His choice was declared in favor of an exile, whose father, only three years before, had suffered, under the sanction of *his* authority, an unjust and ignominious

Detail of a barbarian captive woman. (Trajan's Column)

Weapons and utensils found in a barbarian grave.

death, the great Theodosius. Five months after the death of Valens the emperor Gratian produced before the assembled troops *his* colleague and *their* master, who, after a modest, perhaps a sincere resistance, was compelled to accept, amidst the general acclamations, the diadem, the purple, and the equal title of Augustus. The provinces of Thrace, Asia, and Egypt, over which Valens had reigned, were resigned to the administration of the new emperor; but as he was specially intrusted with the conduct of the Gothic war, the Illyrian præfecture was dismembered, and the two great dioceses of Dacia and Macedonia were added to the dominions of the Eastern empire.

The fabric of a mighty state, which has been reared by the labors of successive ages, could not be overturned by the misfortune of a single day, if the fatal power of the imagination did not exaggerate the real measure of the calamity. The loss of forty thousand Romans, who fell in the plains of Hadrianople, might have been soon recruited in the populous provinces of the East, which contained so many millions of inhabitants. But the effects which were produced by the Battle of Hadrianople on the minds of the barbarians and of the Romans, extended the victory of the former, and the defeat of the latter, far beyond the limits of a single day. A Gothic chief was heard to declare, with insolent moderation, that, for his own part, he was fatigued with slaughter; but that he was astonished how a people who fled before him like a flock of sheep could still presume to dispute the possession of their treasures and provinces. The same terrors which the name of the Huns had spread among the Gothic tribes were inspired, by the formidable name of the Goths, among the subjects and soldiers of the Roman empire. If Theodosius, hastily collecting his scattered forces, had led them into the field to encounter a victorious enemy, his army would have been vanquished by their own fears; and his rashness could not have been excused by the chance of success. But the *great* Theodosius, an epithet which he honorably deserved on this momentous occasion, conducted himself as the firm and faithful guardian of the republic. He fixed his headquarters at Thessalonica, the capital of the Macedonian diocese; from whence he could watch the irregular motions of the barbarians, and direct the operations of his lieutenants, from the gates of Constantinople to the shores of the Hadriatic. The fortifications and garrisons of the cities were strengthened. From these secure stations his troops were encouraged to make frequent sallies on the barbarians, who infested the adjacent country; and, as they were seldom allowed to engage, without some decisive superiority, either of ground or of numbers, their enterprises were, for the most part, successful; and they were soon convinced, by their own experience, of the possibility of vanquishing their *invincible* enemies. The detachments of these separate garrisons were gradually united into small armies; the same cautious measures were pursued, according to an extensive and well-concerted plan of operations; the events of each day added strength and spirit to the Roman arms; and the artful diligence of the emperor, who circulated the most favorable reports of the success of the war, contributed to subdue the pride of the barbarians, and to animate the hopes and courage of his subjects.

The deliverance and peace of the Roman provinces was the work of prudence, rather than of valor: the prudence of Theodosius was seconded by fortune; and the emperor never failed to seize, and to improve, every favorable circumstance. As long as the superior genius of Fritigern preserved the union and directed the motions of the barbarians, their power was not inadequate to the conquest of a great empire. The death of that hero, the predecessor and master of the renowned Alaric, relieved an impatient multitude from the intolerable yoke of discipline and discretion. The barbarians, who had been restrained by his authority, abandoned themselves to the dictates of their passions; and their passions were seldom uniform or consistent. An army of conquerors was broken into many disorderly bands of savage robbers; and their blind and irregular fury was not less pernicious to themselves than to their enemies. Their mischievous disposition was shown in the destruction of every object which they wanted strength to remove, or taste to enjoy; and they often consumed, with improvident rage, the harvests, or the granaries, which soon afterwards became necessary for their own subsistence. A spirit of discord arose among the independent tribes and nations, which had been united only by the bands of a loose and voluntary alliance and the officers of Theodosius were instructed to purchase, with liberal gifts and promises, the retreat or service of the discontented party. In the hands of a skillful politician the most different means may be successfully applied to the same ends; and the peace of the empire, which had been forwarded by the divisions, was accomplished by the reunion of the Gothic nation. Athanaric, who had been a patient spectator of these extraordinary events, was at length driven, by the chance of arms, from the dark recesses of the woods of Caucaland. He no longer hesitated to pass the Danube; and a very considerable part of the subjects of Fritigern, who already felt the inconveniences of anarchy, were easily persuaded to acknowledge for their king a Gothic Judge, whose birth they respected, and whose abilities they had frequently experienced. But age had chilled the daring spirit of Athanaric; and instead of leading his people to the field of battle and victory, he wisely listened to the fair proposal of an honorable and advantageous treaty. Theodosius, who was acquainted with the merit and power of his new ally, condescended to meet him at the distance of several miles from Constantinople; and entertained him in the Imperial city, with the confidence of a friend, and the magnificence of a monarch. 'The barbarian prince observed, with curious attention, the variety of objects which attracted his notice, and at last broke out into a sincere and passionate exclamation of wonder. I now behold (said he) what I never could believe, the glories of this stupendous capital! And as he cast his eyes around, he viewed and he admired the commanding situation of the city, the strength and beauty of the walls and public edifices, the capacious harbor crowded with innumerable vessels, the perpetual concourse of distant nations, and the arms and discipline of the troops. Indeed (continued Athanaric), the emperor of the Romans is a god upon earth; and the presumptuous man who dares to lift his hand against him is guilty of his own blood.' The Gothic king did not long enjoy this splendid and honorable reception; and, as temperance was not the virtue of his nation, it may justly be

suspected that his mortal disease was contracted amidst the pleasures of the Imperial banquets. But the policy of Theodosius derived more solid benefit from the death than he could have expected from the most faithful services of his ally. The funeral of Athanaric was performed with solemn rites in the capital of the East; a stately monument was erected to his memory; and his whole army, won by the liberal courtesy and decent grief of Theodosius, enlisted under the standard of the Roman empire. The submission of so great a body of the Visigoths was productive of the most salutary consequences; and the mixed influence of force, of reason, and of corruption, became every day more powerful and more extensive. Each independent chieftain hastened to obtain a separate treaty, from the apprehension that an obstinate delay might expose *him*, alone and unprotected, to the revenge or justice of the conqueror. The general, or rather the final, capitulation of the Goths, may be dated four years, one month, and twenty-five days, after the defeat and death of the emperor Valens.

Left: Hunters carrying a captured animal. (Mosaic from the Royal Villa at Armerina, Sicily, late third century AD)
Top right: Scenes from the life of St Paul. (Panel from an ivory casket, late fourth century AD, British Museum, London)
Right: Roman funerary mosaic showing the Christian symbols of the fish and anchor. (Early Christian funerary mosaic from the Catacomb of Hermes, Sousse, Tunisia, fourth century AD)

CHAPTER TWENTY-THREE

Character administration and penance of Theodosius – death of Theodosius

[AD 340–397]

THE orator, who may be silent without danger, may praise without difficulty and without reluctance; and posterity will confess that the character of Theodosius might furnish the subject of a sincere and ample panegyric. The wisdom of his laws and the success of his arms rendered his administration respectable in the eyes both of his subjects and of his enemies. He loved and practiced the virtues of domestic life, which seldom hold their residence in the palaces of kings. Theodosius was chaste and temperate; he enjoyed, without excess, the sensual and social pleasures of the table, and the warmth of his amorous passions was never diverted from their lawful objects.

The proud titles of Imperial greatness were adorned by the tender names of a faithful husband, an indulgent father; his uncle was raised, by his affectionate esteem, to the rank of a second parent; Theodosius embraced, as his own, the children of his brother and sister, and the expressions of his regard were extended to the most distant and obscure branches of his numerous kindred. His familiar friends were judiciously selected from among those persons who, in the equal intercourse of private life, had appeared before his eyes without a mask; the consciousness of personal and superior merit enabled him to despise the accidental distinction of the purple, and he proved by his conduct that he had forgotten all the injuries, while he most gratefully remembered all the favors and services which he had received before he ascended the throne of the Roman empire. The serious or lively tone of his conversation was adapted to the age, the rank, or the character of his subjects whom he admitted into his society; and the affability of his manners displayed the image of his mind. Theodosius respected the simplicity of the good and virtuous: every art, every talent, of an useful or even of an innocent nature, was rewarded by his judicious liberality; and, except the heretics, whom he persecuted with implacable hatred, the diffusive circle of his benevolence was circumscribed only by the limits of the human race. The government of a mighty empire may assuredly suffice to occupy the time and the abilities of a mortal; yet the diligent prince, without aspiring to the unsuitable reputation of profound learning, always reserved some moments of his leisure for the instructive amusement of reading. History, which enlarged his experience, was his favorite study. The annals of Rome, in the long period of eleven hundred years, presented him with a various and splendid picture of human life; and it has been particularly observed that, whenever he perused the cruel acts of Cinna, of Marius, or of Sylla, he warmly expressed his generous detestation of those enemies of humanity and freedom. His disinterested opinion of past events was usefully applied as the rule of his own actions, and Theodosius has deserved the singular commendation that his virtues always seemed to expand with his fortune; the season of his prosperity was that of his moderation, and his clemency appeared the most conspicuous after the danger and success of the civil war. The Moorish guards of the tyrant had been massacred in the first heat of the victory, and a small number

of the most obnoxious criminals suffered the punishment of the law. But the emperor showed himself much more attentive to relieve the innocent than to chastise the guilty. The oppressed subjects of the West, who would have deemed themselves happy in the restoration of their lands, were astonished to receive a sum of money equivalent to their losses; and the liberality of the conqueror supported the aged mother and educated the orphan daughters of Maximus. A character thus accomplished might almost excuse the extravagant supposition of the orator Pacatus that, if the elder Brutus could be permitted to revisit the earth, the stern republican would abjure, at the feet of Theodosius, his hatred of kings; and ingeniously confess that such a monarch was the most faithful guardian of the Roman people.

Yet the piercing eye of the founder of the republic must have discerned two essential imperfections, which might, perhaps, have abated his recent love of despotism. The virtuous mind of Theodosius was often relaxed by indolence, and it was sometimes inflamed by passion. In the pursuit of an important object his active courage was capable of the most vigorous exertions; but as soon as the design was accomplished, or the danger was surmounted, the hero sunk into inglorious repose, and, forgetful that the time of a prince is the property of his people, resigned himself to the enjoyment of the innocent but trifling pleasures of a luxurious court. The natural disposition of Theodosius was hasty and choleric; and, in a station where none could resist and few would dissuade the fatal consequence of his resentment, the humane monarch was justly alarmed by the consciousness of his infirmity and of his power. It was the constant study of his life to suppress or regulate the intemperate sallies of passion; and the success of his efforts enhanced the merit of his clemency. But the painful virtue which claims the merit of victory is exposed to the danger of defeat; and the reign of a wise and merciful prince was polluted by an act of cruelty which would stain the annals of Nero or Domitian.

Left: Arcadius (Flavius Arcadius c AD 377–408, Roman Emperor AD 395–423), son of Theodosius I, Emperor of the East. *Below:* Gates of Rome: Porta Appia now known as Saint Sebastian, built by Honorius (Flavius Honorius AD 384–423, Roman Emperor AD 345–423). It was rebuilt by Belisarius and the brick towers added by King Theodoric c AD 500.

Chapter Twenty-Three is concerned with the last years of Theodosius' reign which were torn by the rival factions between Gratian and Maximus in the Eastern and Western Empires. Gratian was addicted to barbarian dress and this together with his inordinate passion for hunting incurred the displeasure of the army, and he was successfully deposed by Maximus. Theodosius attempted to revenge him by placing Valentian on the throne and was in turn deceived by his minister Argobastes who elevated Eugenius to the throne. On the death of Theodosius the empire was left to Honorius and Arcadius. These few passages illustrate the power of the prelates of the time.

The Emperor Theodosius the Great watching the games at his box
at the circus surrounded by his family: the Byzantine Augusti.

The sedition of Thessalonica is ascribed to a more shameful cause, and was productive of much more dreadful consequences. That great city, the metropolis of all the Illyrian provinces, had been protected from the dangers of the Gothic war by strong fortifications and a numerous garrison. Botheric, the general of those troops, and, as it should seem from his name, a barbarian, had among his slaves a beautiful boy, who excited the impure desires of one of the charioteers of the circus. The insolent and brutal lover was thrown into prison by the order of Botheric; and he sternly rejected the importunate clamors of the multitude, who, on the day of the public games, lamented the absence of their favorite, and considered the skill of a charioteer as an object of more importance than his virtue. The resentment of the people was embittered by some previous disputes; and, as the strength of the garrison had been drawn away for the service of the Italian war, the feeble remnant, whose numbers were reduced by desertion, could not save the unhappy general from their licentious fury. Botheric and several of his principal officers were inhumanely murdered; their mangled bodies were dragged about the streets; and the emperor, who then resided at Milan, was surprised by the intelligence of the audacious and wanton cruelty of the people of Thessalonica. The sentence of a dispassionate judge would have inflicted a severe punishment on the authors of the crime; and the merit of Botheric might contribute to exasperate the grief and indignation of his master. The fiery and choleric temper of Theodosius was impatient of the dilatory forms of a judicial inquiry; and he hastily resolved that the blood of his lieutenant should be expiated by the blood of the guilty people. Yet his mind still fluctuated between the counsels of clemency and of revenge; the zeal of the bishops had almost extorted from the reluctant emperor the promise of a general pardon; his passion was again inflamed by the flattering suggestions of his minister Rufinus; and, after Theodosius had dispatched the messengers of death, he attempted, when it was too late, to prevent the execution of his orders. The punishment of a Roman city was blindly committed to the undistinguishing sword of the barbarians; and the hostile preparations were concerted with the dark and perfidious artifice of an illegal conspiracy. The people of Thessalonica were treacherously invited, in the name of their sovereign, to the games of the circus; and such was their insatiate avidity for those amusements that every consideration of fear or suspicion was disregarded by the numerous spectators. As soon as the assembly was complete, the soldiers, who had secretly been posted round the circus, received the signal, not of the races, but of a general massacre. The promiscuous carnage continued three hours, without discrimination of strangers or natives, of age or sex, of innocence or guilt; the most moderate accounts state the number of the slain at seven thousand; and it is affirmed by some writers that more than fifteen thousand victims were sacrificed to the manes of Botheric.

The respectful attachment of the emperor for the orthodox clergy had disposed him to love and admire the character of Ambrose, who united all the episcopal virtues in the most eminent degree.

When Ambrose was informed of the massacre of Thessalonica, his mind was filled with horror and anguish. He retired into the country to indulge his grief and to avoid the presence of Theodosius. But as the archbishop was satisfied that a timid silence would render him the accomplice of his guilt, he represented in a private letter the enormity of the crime, which could only be effaced by the tears of penitence. The episcopal vigor of Ambrose was tempered by prudence; and he contented himself with signifying an indirect sort of excommunication, by the assurance that he had been warned in a vision not to offer the oblation in the name or in the presence of Theodosius, and by the advice that he would confine himself to the use of prayer, without presuming to approach the altar of Christ, or to receive the holy eucharist with those hands that were still polluted with the blood of an innocent people. The emperor was deeply affected, and after he had bewailed the mischievous and irreparable consequences of his rash fury, he proceeded in the accustomed manner to perform his devotions in the great church of Milan. He was stopped in the porch by the archbishop, who, in the tone and language of an ambassador of Heaven, declared to his sovereign that private contribution was not sufficient to atone for a public fault or to appease the justice of the offended Deity. Theodosius humbly represented that, if he had contracted the guilt of homicide, David, the man after God's own heart, had been guilty not only of murder but of adultery. 'You have imitated David in his crime, imitate then his repentance,' was the reply of the undaunted Ambrose. The rigorous conditions of peace and pardon were accepted; and the public penance of the emperor Theodosius has been recorded as one of the most honorable events in the annals of the church.

After the defeat of Eugenius, the merit, as well as the authority, of Theodosius was cheerfully acknowledged by all the inhabitants of the Roman world. The experience of his past conduct encouraged the most pleasing expectations of his future reign; and the age of the emperor, which did not exceed fifty years, seemed to extend the prospect of the public felicity. His death, only four months after his victory, was considered by the people as an unforeseen and fatal event, which destroyed in a moment the hopes of the rising generation. But the indulgence of ease and luxury had secretly nourished the principles of disease. The strength of Theodosius was unable to support the sudden and violent transition from the palace to the camp; and the increasing symptoms of a dropsy announced the speedy dissolution of the emperor. The opinion, and perhaps the interest, of the public had confirmed the division of the Eastern and Western empires; and the two royal youths, Arcadius and Honorius, who had already obtained, from the tenderness of their father, the title of Augustus, were destined to fill the thrones of Constantinople and of Rome. Those princes were not permitted to share the danger and glory of the civil war; but as soon as Theodosius had triumphed over his unworthy rivals, he called his younger son, Honorius, to enjoy the fruits of the victory, and to receive the scepter of the West from the hands of his dying father. The arrival of Honorius at Milan was welcomed by a splendid exhibition of the games of the circus; and the emperor, though he was oppressed by the weight of his disorder, contributed by his presence to the public joy. But the remains of his strength were exhausted by the painful effort which he made to assist at the spectacles of the morning. Honorius supplied, during the rest of the day, the place of his father; and the great Theodosius expired in the ensuing night. Notwithstanding the recent animosities of a civil war, his death was universally lamented. The barbarians, whom he had vanquished, and the churchmen, by whom he had been subdued, celebrated with loud and sincere applause the qualities of the deceased emperor which appeared the most valuable in their eyes. The Romans were terrified by the impending dangers of a feeble and divided administration; and every disgraceful moment of the unfortunate reigns of Arcadius and Honorius revived the memory of their irreparable loss.

If it can be affirmed, with any degree of truth, that the luxury of the Romans was more shameless and dissolute in the reign of Theodosius than in the age of Constantine, perhaps, or of Augustus, the alteration cannot be ascribed to any beneficial improvements which had gradually management of missile weapons, they easily overwhelmed the naked and trembling legions, whose heads and breasts were exposed, without defense, to the arrows of the barbarians. The loss of armies, the destruction of cities, and the dishonor of the Roman name, ineffectually solicited the successors of Gratian to restore the helmets and cuirasses of the infantry. The enervated soldiers abandoned their own and the public defense; and their pusillanimous indolence may be considered as the immediate cause of the downfall of the empire.

Above: Detail of ivory diptych from Constantinople showing a circus. (Hermitage Museum, Leningrad)
Right: Bishop Ambrose (340–397 AD) of Milan, greatly respected by Theodosius, forced the Emperor to do public penance after the massacre at Thessalonica. (Mosaic from the sixth-century AD Church of St Ambrose, Milan)

increased the stock of national riches. A long period of calamity or decay must have checked the industry and diminished the wealth of the people; and their profuse luxury must have been the result of that indolent despair which enjoys the present hour and declines the thoughts of futurity. The uncertain condition of their property discouraged subjects of Theodosius from engaging in those useful and laborious undertakings which require an immediate expense, and promise a slow and distant advantage. The frequent examples of ruin and desolation tempted them not to spare the remains of a patrimony which might, every hour, become the prey of the rapacious Goth. And the mad prodigality which prevails in the confusion of a shipwreck or a siege may serve to explain the progress of luxury amidst the misfortunes and terrors of a sinking nation.

The effeminate luxury, which infected the manners of courts and cities, had instilled a secret and destructive poison into the camps of the legions; and their degeneracy has been marked by the pen of a military writer, who had accurately studied the genuine and ancient principles of Roman discipline. It is the just and important observation of Vegetius, that the infantry was invariably covered with defensive armor from the foundation of the city to the reign of the emperor Gratian. The relaxation of discipline and the disuse of exercise rendered the soldiers less able and less willing to support the fatigues of the service; they complained of the weight of the armor, which they seldom wore; and they successively obtained the permission of laying aside both their cuirasses and their helmets. The heavy weapons of their ancestors, the short sword and the formidable *pilum*, which had subdued the world, insensibly dropped from their feeble hands. As the use of the shield is incompatible with that of the bow, they reluctantly marched into the field, condemned to suffer either the pain of wounds or the ignominy of flight, and always disposed to prefer the more shameful alternative. The cavalry of the Goths, the Huns, and the Alani, had felt the benefits and adopted the use of defensive armor; and, as they excelled in the

CHAPTER TWENTY-FOUR

Final destruction of paganism

[AD 378–420]

THE ruin of Paganism, in the age of Theodosius, is perhaps the only example of the total extirpation of any ancient and popular superstition, and may therefore deserve to be considered as a singular event in the history of the human mind. The Christians, more especially the clergy, had impatiently supported the prudent delays of Constantine and the equal toleration of the elder Valentinian; nor could they deem their conquest perfect or secure as long as their adversaries were permitted to exist. The influence which Ambrose and his brethren had acquired over the youth of Gratian and the piety of Theodosius was employed to infuse the maxims of persecution into the breasts of their Imperial proselytes. Two specious principles of religious jurisprudence were established, from whence they deduced a direct and rigorous conclusion against the subjects of the empire who still adhered to the ceremonies of their ancestors: *that* the magistrate is, in some measure, guilty of the crimes which he neglects to prohibit or to punish; and *that* the idolatrous worship of fabulous deities and real dæmons is the most abominable crime against the supreme majesty of the Creator. The laws of Moses and the examples of Jewish history were hastily, perhaps erroneously, applied by the clergy to the mild and universal reign of Christianity. The zeal of the emperors was excited to vindicate their own honor and that of the Deity; and the temples of the Roman world were subverted about sixty years after the conversion of Constantine.

Paganism was still the constitutional religion of the senate. The hall or temple in which they assembled was adorned by the statue and altar of Victory; a majestic female standing on a globe, with flowing garments, expanded wings, and a crown of laurel in her outstretched hand.

The senators were sworn on the altar of the goddess to observe the laws of the emperor and of the empire; and a solemn offering of wine and incense was the ordinary prelude of their public deliberations. The removal of this ancient monument was the only injury which Constantius had offered to the superstition of the Romans. The altar of Victory was again restored by Julian, tolerated by Valentinian, and once more banished from the senate by the zeal of Gratian. But the emperor yet spared the statues of the gods which were exposed to the public veneration: four hundred and twenty-four temples, or chapels, still remained to satisfy the devotion of the people, and in every quarter of Rome the delicacy of the Christians was offended by the fumes of idolatrous sacrifice.

The filial piety of the emperors themselves engaged them to proceed with some caution and tenderness in the reformation of the eternal city. Those absolute monarchs acted with less regard to the prejudices of the provincials. The pious labor, which had been suspended near twenty years since the death of Constantius, was vigorously resumed, and finally accomplished, by the zeal of Theodosius. While that warlike prince yet struggled with the Goths, not for the glory, but for the safety of the republic, he ventured to offend a considerable party of his subjects, by some acts which might perhaps secure the protection of Heaven, but which must seem rash and unseasonable in the eye of human prudence. The success of his first experiments against the Pagans encouraged the pious emperor to reiterate and enforce his edicts of proscription: the same laws which had been originally published in the provinces of the East, were applied, after the defeat of Maximus, to the whole extent of the Western empire; and every victory of the

Left: A senior sister (*Virgo Maxima*) of the college of Vestal Virgins, priestesses of the oldest Roman divinity Vesta, goddess of the hearth whose fire was brought to Rome by Aeneas with the penates or household gods. (Third century AD, Museo Nazionale, Rome). Under Gratian (Flavius Gratianus AD 359–83; Roman Emperor AD 367–83) the cult of the vestal virgins was abolished – Gratian used the revenue to finance the postal service.
Right: The interior of the Pantheon, Rome. Many of the temples were saved from destruction by being turned into Christian churches and cathedrals such as the Pantheon.

Above: A figure sacrificing from the ivory diptych of the daughter of a fourth-century AD pagan senator.

orthodox Theodosius contributed to the triumph of the Christian and catholic faith. He attacked superstition in her most vital part, by prohibiting the use of sacrifices, which he declared to be criminal as well as infamous; and if the terms of his edicts more strictly condemned the impious curiosity which examined the entrails of the victims, every subsequent explanation tended to involve in the same guilt the general practice of *immolation*, which essentially constituted the religion of the Pagans. As the temples had been erected for the purpose of sacrifice, it was the duty of a benevolent prince to remove from his subjects the dangerous temptation of offending against the laws which he had enacted. A special commission was granted to Cynegius, the Prætorian præfect of the East, and afterwards to the counts Jovius and Gaudentius, two officers of distinguished rank in the West, by which they were directed to shut the temples, to seize or destroy the instruments of idolatry, to abolish the privileges of the priests, and to confiscate the consecrated property for the benefit of the emperor, of the church, or of the army. Here the desolation might have stopped: and the naked edifices, which were no longer employed in the service of idolatry, might have been protected from the destructive rage of fanaticism. Many of those temples were the most splendid and beautiful monuments of Grecian architecture: and the emperor himself was interested not to deface the splendor of his own cities, or to diminish the value of his own possessions. Those stately edifices might be suffered to remain, as so many lasting trophies of the victory of Christ. In the decline of the arts, they might be usefully converted into magazines, manufacturers, or places of public assembly: and perhaps, when the walls of the temple had been sufficiently purified by holy rites, the worship of the true Deity might be allowed to expiate the ancient guilt of idolatry. But as long as they subsisted, the Pagans fondly cherished the secret hope that an auspicious revolution, a second Julian, might again restore the altars of the gods: and the earnestness with which they addressed their

unavailing prayers to the throne increased the zeal of the Christian reformers to extirpate, without mercy, the root of superstition. The laws of the emperors exhibit some symptoms of a milder disposition: but their cold and languid efforts were insufficient to stem the torrent of enthusiasm and rapine, which was conducted, or rather impelled, by the spiritual rulers of the church. In Gaul, the holy Martin, bishop of Tours, marched at the head of his faithful monks to destroy the idols, the temples, and the consecrated trees of his extensive diocese; and, in the execution of this arduous task, the prudent reader will judge whether Martin was supported by the aid of miraculous powers or of carnal weapons.

The temples of the Roman empire were deserted or destroyed; but the ingenious superstition of the Pagans still attempted to elude the laws of Theodosius, by which all sacrifices had been severely prohibited. The inhabitants of the country, whose conduct was less exposed to the eye of malicious curiosity, disguised their *religious* under the appearance of *convivial* meetings. On the days of solemn festivals they assembled in great numbers under the spreading shade of some consecrated trees; sheep and oxen were slaughtered and roasted; and this rural entertainment was sanctified by the use of incense and by the hymns which were sung in honor of the gods. But it was alleged that, as no part of the animal was made a burnt-offering, as no altar was provided to receive the blood, and as the previous oblation of salt cakes and the concluding ceremony of libations were carefully omitted, these festal meetings did not involve the guests in the guilt or penalty of an illegal sacrifice. Whatever might be the truth of the facts or the merit of the distinction, these vain pretences were swept away by the last edict of Theodosius, which inflicted a deadly wound on the superstition of the Pagans. This prohibitory law is expressed in the most absolute and comprehensive terms. 'It is our will and pleasure,' says the emperor, 'that none of our subjects, whether magistrates or private citizens,

Left: Head of a young vestal virgin. (From the Palatine, Museo Nazionale, Rome)
Right: The Temple of Vesta, Rome.

however exalted or however humble may be their rank and condition, shall presume in any city or in any place to worship an inanimate idol by the sacrifice of a guiltless victim.' The act of sacrificing and the practice of divination by the entrails of the victim are declared (without any regard to the object of the inquiry) a crime of high treason against the state, which can be expiated only by the death of the guilty. The rites of Pagan superstition which might seem less bloody and atrocious are abolished as highly injurious to the truth and honor of religion; luminaries, garlands, frankincense, and libations of wine are specially enumerated and condemned; and the harmless claims of the domestic genius, of the household gods, are included in this rigorous proscription. The use of any of these profane and illegal ceremonies subjects the offender to the forfeiture of the house or estate where they have been performed; and if he has artfully chosen the property of another for the scene of his impiety, he is compelled to discharge, without delay, a heavy fine of twenty-five pounds of gold (a rather large sum in the currency of the day). A fine not less considerable is imposed on the connivance of the secret enemies of religion who shall neglect the duty of their respective stations, either to reveal or to punish the guilt of idolatry. Such was the persecuting spirit of the laws of Theodosius, which were repeatedly enforced by his sons and grandsons, with the loud and unanimous applause of the Christian world.

In the cruel reigns of Decius and Diocletian Christianity had been proscribed, as a revolt from the ancient and hereditary religion of the empire; and the unjust suspicions which were entertained of a dark and dangerous faction were in some measure countenanced by the inseparable union and rapid conquests of the catholic church. But the same excuses of fear and ignorance cannot be applied to the Christian emperors, who violated the precepts of humanity and of the Gospel. The experience of ages had betrayed the weakness as well as folly of

Paganism; the light of reason and of faith had already exposed to the greatest part of mankind the vanity of idols; and the declining sect, which still adhered to their worship, might have been permitted to enjoy in peace and obscurity the religious customs of their ancestors. Had the Pagans been animated by the undaunted zeal which possessed the minds of the primitive believers, the triumph of the church must have been stained with blood; and the martyrs of Jupiter and Apollo might have embraced the glorious opportunity of devoting their lives and fortunes at the foot of their altars. But such obstinate zeal was not congenial to the loose and careless temper of Polytheism. If they were sometimes tempted by a sally of passion, or by the hopes of concealment, to indulge their favorite superstition, their humble repentance disarmed the severity of the Christian magistrate, and they seldom refused to atone for their rashness by submitting, with some secret reluctance, to the yoke of the Gospel. The churches were filled with the increasing multitude of these unworthy proselytes, who had conformed, from temporal motives, to the reigning religion; and while they devoutly imitated the postures and recited the prayers of the faithful, they satisfied their conscience by the silent and sincere invocation of the gods of antiquity. If the Pagans wanted patience to suffer, they wanted spirit to resist; and the scattered myriads, who deplored the ruin of the temples, yielded, without a contest, to the fortune of their adversaries. The disorderly opposition of the peasants of Syria and the populace of Alexandria to the rage of private fanaticism was silenced by the name and authority of the emperor.

The generation that arose in the world after the promulgation of the Imperial laws was attracted within the pale of the catholic church: and so rapid, yet so gentle, was the fall of Paganism, that only twenty-eight years after the death of Theodosius the faint and minute vestiges were no longer visible to the eye of the legislator.

Revolt of the Goths – they plunder Greece

two great invasions of Italy by Alaric and Radagasius – they are repulsed by Stilicho –
disgrace and death of Stilicho

[AD 395–408]

THE great Theodosius died in the month of January; and before the end of the winter of the same year, the Gothic nation was in arms. The barriers of the Danube were thrown open; the savage warriors of Scythia issued from their forests; and the uncommon severity of the winter allowed the poet to remark 'that they rolled their ponderous wagons over the broad and icy back of the indignant river.' The unhappy natives of the provinces to the south of the Danube submitted to the calamities which, in the course of twenty years, were almost grown familiar to their imagination; and the various troops of barbarians who gloried in the Gothic name were irregularly spread from the woody shores of Dalmatia to the walls of Constantinople. The Goths were now directed by the bold and artful genius of Alaric. Their renowned leader was descended from the noble race of the Balti, which yielded only to the royal dignity of the Amali: he had solicited the command of the Roman armies; and the Imperial court provoked him to demonstrate the folly of their refusal, and the importance of their loss. Alaric disdained to trample any longer on the prostrate and ruined countries of Thrace and Dacia, and he resolved to seek a plentiful harvest of fame and riches in a province which had hitherto escaped the ravages of war.

The character of the civil and military officers on whom Rufinus had developed the government of Greece confirmed the public suspicion that he had betrayed the ancient seat of freedom and learning to the Gothic invader. The troops which had been posted to defend the straits of Thermopylæ retired, as they were directed, without attempting to disturb the secure and rapid passage of Alaric; and the fertile fields of Phocis and Bœtia were instantly covered by a deluge of barbarians, who massacred the males of an age to bear arms, and drove away the beautiful females, with the spoil and cattle of the flaming villages.

The last hope of a people who could no longer depend on their arms, their gods, or their sovereign, was placed in the powerful assistance of the general of the West; and Stilicho, who had not been permitted to repulse, advanced to chastise the invaders of Greece. A numerous fleet was equipped in the ports of Italy; and the troops, after a short and prosperous navigation over the Ionian Sea, were safely disembarked on the isthmus, near the ruins of Corinth. The woody and mountainous country of Arcadia, the fabulous residence of Pan and the Dryads, became the scene of a long and doubtful conflict between two generals not unworthy of each other. The skill and perseverance of the Roman at length prevailed; and the Goths, after sustaining a considerable loss from disease and desertion, gradually retreated to the lofty mountain of Pholoe, near the sources of the Peneus, and on the frontiers of Elis – a sacred country, which had formerly been exempted from the calamities of war. The camp of the barbarians was immediately besieged; the waters of the river were diverted into another channel; and while they labored under the intolerable pressure of thirst and hunger, a strong line of circumvallation was formed to prevent their escape. After these precautions Stilicho, too confident of victory, retired to enjoy his triumph in the theatrical games and lascivious dances of the Greeks; his soldiers, deserting their standards, spread themselves over the country of their allies, which they stripped of all that had been saved from the rapacious hands of the enemy. Alaric appears to have seized the favorable moment to execute one of those hardy enterprises in which

the abilities of a general are displayed with more genuine luster than in the tumult of a day of battle. To extricate himself from the prison of Peloponnesus it was necessary that he should pierce the entrenchments which surrounded his camp; that he should perform a difficult and dangerous march of thirty miles, as far as the Gulf of Corinth; and that he should transport his troops, his captives, and his spoil, over an arm of the sea, which, in the narrow interval between Rhium and the opposite shore, is at least half a mile in breadth. The operations of Alaric must have been secret, prudent, and rapid, since the Roman general was confounded by the intelligence that the Goths, who had eluded his efforts, were in full possession of the important province of Epirus. This unfortunate delay allowed Alaric sufficient time to conclude the treaty which he secretly negotiated with the ministers of Constantinople. The apprehension of a civil war compelled Stilicho to retire, at the haughty mandate of his rivals, from the dominions of Arcadius; and he respected, in the enemy of Rome, the honorable character of the ally and servant of the emperor of the East.

An edict was published at Constantinople which declared the promotion of Alaric to the rank of master-general of the Eastern Illyricum and the Roman provincials, and the allies who had respected the faith of treaties, were justly indignant that the ruin of Greece and Epirus should be so liberally rewarded. The Gothic conqueror was received as a lawful magistrate in the cities which he had so lately besieged. Armed with this double power, seated on the verge of the two empires, he alternately sold his deceitful promises to the courts of Arcadius and Honorius, till he declared and executed his resolution of invading the dominions of the West. The provinces of Europe which belonged to the Eastern emperor were already exhausted, those of Asia were inaccessible, and the strength of Constantinople had resisted his attack. But he was tempted by the fame, the beauty, the wealth of Italy, which he had twice visited; and he secretly aspired to plant the Gothic standard on the walls of Rome, and to enrich his army with the accumulated spoils of three hundred triumphs.

The scarcity of facts, and the uncertainty of dates, oppose our attempts to describe the circumstances of the first invasion of Italy by the arms of Alaric. His march, perhaps from Thessalonica, through the warlike and hostile country of Pannonia, as far as the foot of the Julian Alps; his passage of those mountains, which were strongly guarded by troops and entrenchments; the siege of Aquileia, and the conquest of the provinces of Istria and Venetia, appear to have employed a considerable time. Unless his operations were extremely cautious and slow, the length of the interval would suggest a probable suspicion that the Gothic king retreated towards the banks of the Danube, and reinforced his army with fresh swarms of barbarians, before he again attempted to penetrate into the heart of Italy.

The emperor Honorius was distinguished, above his subjects, by the pre-eminence of fear as well as of rank. When the sound of war had awakened the young emperor, instead of flying to arms with the spirit, or even the rashness, of his age, he eagerly listened to those timid counsellors who proposed to convey his sacred person and his faithful attendants to some secure and distant station in the provinces of Gaul. Stilicho alone had courage and authority to resist this disgraceful

Left: View of the Acropolis showing the Propylaia and the Nike bastion, Athens, Greece.

Chapter Twenty-Five is taken up with the intrigues of the Eastern and Western courts and the jockeying for power of the ministers Eutropius, Rufinus and the famous General Stilicho, to whose charge Theodosius had entrusted Arcadius and Honorius.

Amphitheater of Verona, Italy.

measure, which would have abandoned Rome and Italy to the barbarians; but as the troops of the palace had been lately detached to the Rhætian frontier, and as the resource of new levies was slow and precarious, the general of the West could only promise that, if the court of Milan would maintain their ground during his absence, he would soon return with an army equal to the encounter of the Gothic king. Stilicho issued his orders to the most remote troops of the West, to advance, by rapid marches, to the defense of Honorius and of Italy. The fortresses of the Rhine were abandoned; and the safety of Gaul was protected only by the faith of the Germans, and the ancient terror of the Roman name. Even the legion which had been stationed to guard the wall of Britain against the Caledonians of the North was hastily recalled. The prudence and vigor of Stilicho were conspicuous on this occasion, which revealed, at the same time, the weakness of the falling empire. The legions of Rome, which had long since languished in the gradual decay of discipline and courage, were exterminated by the Gothic and civil wars; and it was found impossible, without exhausting and exposing the provinces, to assemble an army for the defense of Italy.

When Stilicho seemed to abandon his sovereign in the unguarded palace of Milan, he had probably calculated the term of his absence, the distance of the enemy, and the obstacles that might retard their march. He principally depended on the rivers of Italy, the Adige, the Mincius, the Oglio, and the Addua, which, in the winter or spring, by the fall of rains, or by the melting of the snows, are commonly swelled into broad and impetuous torrents. But the season happened to be remarkably dry; and the Goths could traverse, without impediment, the wide and stony beds, whose center was faintly marked by the course of a shallow stream. The bridge and passage of the Addua were secured by a strong detachment of the Gothic army; and as Alaric approached the walls, or rather the suburbs, of Milan, he enjoyed the proud satisfaction of seeing the emperor of the Romans fly before him. Honorius, accompanied by a feeble train of statesmen and eunuchs, hastily retreated

towards the Alps, with a design of securing his person in the city of Arles, which had been the royal residence of his predecessors. But Honorius had scarcely passed the Po before he was overtaken by the speed of the Gothic cavalry; the urgency of the danger compelled him to seek a temporary shelter within the fortification of Asta, a town of Liguria or Piemont, situated on the banks of the Tanarus. The siege of an obscure place, which contained so rich a prize, and seemed incapable of a long resistance, was instantly formed, and indefatigably pressed, by the king of the Goths. At the head of a chosen and intrepid vanguard, Stilicho swam the stream of the Addua, to gain the time which he must have lost in the attack of the bridge; the passage of the Po was an enterprise of much less hazard and difficulty; and the successful action, in which he cut his way through the Gothic camp under the walls of Asta, revived the hopes and vindicated the honor of Rome. Instead of grasping the fruit of his victory, the barbarian was gradually invested, on every side, by the troops of the West, who successively issued through all the passes of the Alps; his quarters were straitened; his

Exterior of the amphitheater of Verona.

convoys were intercepted; and the vigilance of the Romans prepared to form a chain of fortifications, and to besiege the lines of the besiegers.

Alaric possessed the invincible temper of mind which rises superior to every misfortune, and derives new resources from adversity. After the total defeat of his infantry, he escaped, or rather withdrew, from the field of battle, with the greatest part of his cavalry entire and unbroken. Without wasting a moment to lament the irreparable loss of so many brave companions, he left his victorious enemy to bind in chains the captive images of a Gothic king; and boldly resolved to break through the unguarded passes of the Apennine, to spread desolation over the fruitful face of Tuscany, and to conquer or die before the gates of Rome. The capital was saved by the active and incessant diligence of Stilicho; but he respected the despair of his enemy; and, instead of committing the fate of the republic to the chance of another battle, he proposed to purchase the absence of the barbarians. The spirit of Alaric would have rejected such terms, the permission of a retreat, and the offer of a pension, with contempt and indignation; but he exercised a limited and precarious authority over the independent chieftains who had raised him, for *their* service, above the rank of his equals; they were still less disposed to follow an unsuccessful general, and many of them were tempted to consult their interest by a private negotiation with the minister of Honorius. The king submitted to the voice of his people, ratified the treaty with the empire of the West, and repassed the Po with the remains of the flourishing army which he had led into Italy.

The recent danger to which the person of the emperor had been exposed in the defenseless palace of Milan urged him to seek a retreat in some inaccessible fortress of Italy, where he might securely remain, while the open country was covered by a deluge of barbarians. On the coast of the Hadriatic, about ten or twelve miles from the most southern of the seven mouths of the Po, the Thessalians had founded the ancient colony of Ravenna, which they afterwards resigned to the natives of Umbria.

This advantageous situation was fortified by art and labor; and in the twentieth year of his age the emperor of the West, anxious only for his personal safety, retired to the perpetual confinement of the walls and morasses of Ravenna. The example of Honorius was imitated by his feeble successors, the Gothic kings, and afterwards the Exarchs, who occupied the throne and palace of the emperors; and till the middle of the eighth century Ravenna was considered as the seat of government and the capital of Italy.

The fears of Honorius were not without foundation, nor were his precautions without effect. While Italy rejoiced in her deliverance from the Goths, a furious tempest was excited among the nations of Germany, who yielded to the irresistible impulse that appears to have been gradually communicated from the eastern extremity of the continent of Asia.

The chain of events is interrupted, or rather is concealed, as it passes from the Volga to the Vistula, through the dark interval which separates the extreme limits of the Chinese and of the Roman geography. Yet the North must again have been alarmed and agitated by the invasion of the Huns; and the nations who retreated before them must have pressed with incumbent weight on the confines of Germany. The inhabitants of those regions which the ancients have assigned on the Suevi, the Vandals, and the Burgundians, might embrace the resolution of abandoning to the fugitives of Sarmatia their woods and morasses, or at least of discharging their superfluous numbers on the provinces of the Roman empire. About four years after the victorious Toulun had assumed the title of Khan of the Geougen, another barbarian, the haughty Rhodogast, or Radagaisus, marched from the northern extremities of Germany almost to the gates of Rome, and left the remains of his army to achieve the destruction of the West. The Vandals, the Suevi, and the Burgundians, formed the strength of this mighty host; but the Alani, who had found an hospitable reception in their new seats, added their active cavalry to the heavy infantry of the Germans; and the Gothic adventurers crowded so eagerly to the standard of Radagaisus, that, by some historians, he has been styled the King of the Goths. Twelve thousand warriors, distinguished above the vulgar by their noble birth or their valiant deeds, glittered in the van; and the whole multitude, which was not less than two hundred thousand fighting men, might be increased, by the accession of women, of

The Goths in Italy (painting by Poole, 1807–79). The Goths invaded Italy led by the courageous and clever Alaric. They were eventually turned back at the gates of Rome by Stilicho, the son of Vandal.

children, and of slaves, to the amount of four hundred thousand persons. This formidable emigration issued from the same coast of the Baltic which had poured forth the myriads of the Cimbri and Teutones to assault Rome and Italy in the vigor of the republic.

The correspondence of nations was in that age so imperfect and precarious, that the revolutions of the North might escape the knowledge of the court of Ravenna, till the dark cloud, which was collected along the coast of the Baltic, burst in thunder upon the banks of the Upper Danube. The emperor of the West, if his ministers disturbed his amusements by the news of the impending danger, was satisfied with being the occasion and the spectator of the war. The safety of Rome was intrusted to the counsels and the sword of Stilicho; but such was the feeble and exhausted state of the empire, that it was impossible to restore the fortifications of the Danube, or to prevent by a vigorous effort the invasion of the Germans. The hopes of the vigilant minister of Honorius were confined to the defense of Italy. The thirty legions of Stilicho were reinforced by a large body of barbarian auxiliaries; the faithful Alani were personally attached to his service; and the troops of Huns and of Goths, who marched under the banners of their native princes Huldin and Sarus, were animated by interest and resentment to oppose the ambition of Radagaisus. The king of the confederate Germans passed without resistance the Alps, the Po, and the Apennine; leaving on one hand the inaccessible palace of Honorius securely buried among the marshes of Ravenna, and, on the other, the camp of Stilicho,

The Parthenon, Acropolis, Athens, Greece.

Left: Early Christian jewelry, c AD 400.

Right: Stilicho, the son of a Vandal, was appointed General of the Roman forces by Theodosius and as guardian to his two sons Honorius and Arcadius. For many years he reigned as *de facto* ruler of the Roman Empire. When the Rhine frontier collapsed in AD 406–407 under the hordes of barbarians, he successfully routed the Goths outside Rome, saving the capital from inevitable ruin. He concluded a successful treaty with Alaric who consented to use his troops in service of Rome. However, in spite of his great success his career was ruined by rumors, and he ended his life in disgrace after a rule of almost thirteen years. (Ivory sarcophagus of Stilicho, the Church of St Ambrose, Milan, fifth century AD)

who had fixed his head-quarters at Ticinum, or Pavia, but who seems to have avoided a decisive battle till he had assembled his distant forces. Many cities of Italy were pillaged or destroyed; and the siege of Florence by Radagaisus is one of the earliest events in the history of that celebrated republic, whose firmness checked and delayed the unskillful fury of the barbarians.

Florence was reduced to the last extremity; and the fainting courage of the citizens was supported only by the authority of St. Ambrose, who had communicated in a dream the promise of a speedy deliverance. On a sudden they beheld from their walls the banners of Stilicho, who advanced with his united force to the relief of the faithful city, and who soon marked that fatal spot for the grave of the barbarian host. Conscious that he commanded the *last* army of the republic, his prudence would not expose it in the open field to the headstrong fury of the Germans. The method of surrounding the enemy with strong lines of circumvallation, which he had twice employed against the Gothic king, was repeated on a large scale and with more considerable effect. The imprisoned multitude of horses and men was gradually destroyed by famine rather than by the sword; but the Romans were exposed during the progress of such an extensive work to the frequent attacks of an impatient enemy. The despair of the hungry barbarians would precipitate them against the fortifications of Stilicho; the general might sometimes indulge the ardor of his brave auxiliaries, who eagerly pressed to assault the camp of the Germans; and these various incidents might produce the sharp and bloody conflicts which dignify the narrative of Zosimus and the Chronicles of Prosper and Marcellinus. A seasonable supply of men and provisions had been introduced into the walls of Florence, and the famished host of Radagaisus was in its turn besieged. The proud monarch of so many warlike nations, after the loss of his bravest warriors, was reduced to confide either in the faith of a capitulation, or in the clemency of Stilicho. But the death of the royal captive, who was ignominiously beheaded, disgraced the triumph of Rome and of Christianity; and the short delay of his execution was sufficient to brand the conqueror with the guilt of cool and deliberate cruelty. The famished Germans who escaped the fury of the auxiliaries were sold as slaves, at the contemptible price of as many single pieces of gold; but the difference of food and climate swept away great numbers of those unhappy strangers; and it was observed that the inhuman purchasers, instead of reaping the fruits of their labor, were soon obliged to provide the expense of their interment. Stilicho informed the emperor and the senate of his success, and deserved a second time the glorious title of Deliverer of Italy.

After the defeat of Radagaisus, two parts of the German host, which must have exceeded the number of one hundred thousand men, still remained in arms between the Apennine and the Alps, or between the Alps and the Danube. It is uncertain whether they attempted to revenge the death of their general; but their irregular fury was soon diverted by the prudence and firmness of Stilicho, who opposed their march and facilitated their retreat, who considered the safety of Rome and Italy as the great object of his care, and who sacrificed with too much indifference the wealth and tranquillity of the distant provinces. The barbarians acquired, from the junction of some Pannonian deserters, the knowledge of the country and of the roads, and the invasion of Gaul, which Alaric had designed, was executed by the remains of the great army of Radagaisus.

The victorious confederates pursued their march, and on the last day of the year, in a season when the waters of the Rhine were most probably frozen, they entered without opposition the defenseless provinces of Gaul. This memorable passage of the Suevi, the Vandals, the Alani, and the Burgundians, who never afterwards retreated, may be considered as the fall of the Roman empire in the countries beyond the Alps; and the barriers, which had so long separated the savage and the civilized nations of the earth, were from that fatal moment levelled with the ground.

Adversity had exercised and displayed the genius of Alaric; and the fame of his valor invited to the Gothic standard the bravest of the

barbarian warriors, who, from the Euxine to the Rhine, were agitated by the desire of rapine and conquest. He had deserved the esteem, and he soon accepted the friendship, of Stilicho himself. Renouncing the service of the emperor of the East, Alaric concluded, with the court of Ravenna, a treaty of peace and alliance, by which he was declared master-general of the Roman armies throughout the præfecture of Illyricum; as it was claimed, according to the true and ancient limits, by the minister of Honorius. The execution of the ambitious design, which was either stipulated or implied in the articles of the treaty, appears to have been suspended by the formidable irruption of Radagaisus; and the neutrality of the Gothic king may perhaps be compared to the indifference of Cæsar, who, in the conspiracy of Catiline, refused either to assist or to oppose the enemy of the republic. After the defeat of the Vandals, Stilicho resumed his pretensions to the provinces of the East.

The Lycurgus cup. (Glass cage cup, height 20cm, c AD 400, Italian or Egyptian, British Museum)

Right: Consul presiding over the races. (Detail from the Lampadius diptych, fifth century AD)
Left: Stilicho (Flavius Stilicho, c AD 359–408), the Vandal supreme commander of Rome, with his wife Serena and son Eucharius. (Eburny diptych, c AD 395)
Below: Gold brooch with inscription c AD 450.

But the reign of Stilicho drew towards its end; and the proud minister might perceive the symptoms of his approaching disgrace. He was betrayed by the intrigues of Olympus who artfully insinuated that Stilicho cherished hopes of placing his son on the throne.

About four months after his death an edict was published, in the name of Honorius, to restore the free communication of the two empires, which had been so long interrupted by the *public enemy*. The minister, whose fame and fortune depended on the prosperity of the state, was accused of betraying Italy to the barbarians, whom he repeatedly vanquished at Pollentia, at Verona, and before the walls of Florence. His pretended design of placing the diadem on the head of his son Eucherius could not have been conducted without preparations or accomplices; and the ambitious father would not surely have left the future emperor, till the twentieth year of his age, in the humble station of tribune of the notaries. Even the religion of Stilicho was arraigned by the malice of his rival. The seasonable, and almost miraculous, deliverance was devoutly celebrated by the applause of the clergy, who asserted that the restoration of idols and the persecution of the church would have been the first measure of the reign of Eucherius. The son of Stilicho, however, was educated in the bosom of Christianity, which his father had uniformly professed and zealously supported. Serena had borrowed her magnificent necklace from the statue of Vesta; and the Pagans execrated the memory of the sacrilegious minister, by whose order the Sibylline books, the oracles of Rome, had been committed to the flames. The pride and power of Stilicho constituted his real guilt. An honorable reluctance to shed the blood of his countrymen appears to have contributed to the success of his unworthy rival; and it is the last humiliation of the character of Honorius, that posterity has not condescended to reproach him with his base ingratitude to the guardian of his youth and the support of his empire.

Invasion of Italy by Alaric – Rome is pillaged by the Goths

death of Alaric – the Goths evacuate Italy – Gaul and Spain are occupied by barbarians – independence of Britain

[AD 408–499]

I N the arts of negotiation, as well as in those of war, the Gothic king maintained his superior ascendant over an enemy whose seeming changes proceeded from the total want of counsel and design. From his camp, on the confines of Italy, Alaric attentively observed the revolutions of the palace, watched the progress of faction and discontent, disguised the hostile aspect of a barbarian invader, and assumed the more popular appearance of the friend and ally of the great Stilicho; to whose virtues, when they were no longer formidable, he could pay a just tribute of sincere praise and regret. The pressing invitation of the malcontents, who urged the king of the Goths to invade Italy, was enforced by a lively sense of his personal injuries; and might also speciously complain that the Imperial ministers still delayed and eluded the payment of the four thousand pounds of gold which had been granted by the Roman senate either to reward his services or to appease his fury. His decent firmness was supported by an artful moderation, which contributed to the success of his designs. He required a fair and reasonable satisfaction; but he gave the strongest assurances that, as soon as he had obtained it, he would immediately retire. He refused to trust the faith of the Romans, unless Aëtius and Jason, the sons of two great officers of state, were sent as hostages to his camp: but he offered to deliver in exchange several of the noblest youths of the Gothic nation. The modesty of Alaric was interpreted by the ministers of Ravenna as a sure evidence of his weakness and fear. They disdained either to negotiate a treaty or to assemble an army; and with a rash confidence, derived only from their ignorance of the extreme danger, irretrievably wasted the decisive

Left: The Sack of Rome AD 410 by Alaric, King of the German Visigoths.
Below: Two faces of a silver medallion showing the Emperor Priscus Attalus, the puppet emperor appointed by Alaric following the Sack of Rome.

moments of peace and war. While they expected, in sullen silence, that the barbarians should evacuate the confines of Italy, Alaric, with bold and rapid marches, passed the Alps and the Po; hastily pillaged the cities of Aquileia, Altinum, Concordia, and Cremona, which yielded to his arms; increased his forces by the accession of thirty thousand auxiliaries; and, without meeting a single enemy in the field, advanced as far as the edge of the morass which protected the impregnable residence of the emperor of the West. Instead of attempting the hopeless siege of Ravenna, the prudent leader of the Goths proceeded to Rimini, stretched his ravages along the sea-coast of the Hadriatic, and meditated the conquest of the ancient mistress of the world. An Italian hermit, whose zeal and sanctity were respected by the barbarians themselves, encountered the victorious monarch, and boldly denounced the indignation of Heaven against the oppressors of the earth: but the saint himself was confounded by the solemn asseveration of Alaric that he felt a secret and præternatural impulse, which directed, and even compelled, his march to the gates of Rome. He felt that his genius and his fortune were equal to the most arduous enterprises; and the enthusiasm which he communicated to the Goths insensibly removed the popular and almost superstitious reverence of the nations for the majesty of the Roman name. His troops, animated by the hopes of spoil, followed the course of the Flaminian way, occupied the unguarded passes of the Apennine, descended into the rich plains of Umbria; and, as they lay encamped on the banks of the Clitumnus, might wantonly slaughter and devour the milk-white oxen which had been so long reserved for the use of Roman triumphs. A lofty situation and a seasonable tempest of thunder and lightning preserved the little city of Narni: but the king of the Goths, despising the ignoble prey, still advanced with unabated vigor; and after he had passed through the stately arches, he pitched his camp under the walls of Rome.

Fishing scene. (Mosaic from the *Atriom* of the dining room of the
Roman Villa at Desenzano, Lombardy, mid-fourth century AD)

By a skillful disposition of his numerous forces, who impatiently
watched the moment of an assault, Alaric encompassed the walls,
commanded the twelve principal gates, intercepted all communication
with the adjacent country, and vigilantly guarded the navigation of the
Tiber, from which the Romans derived the surest and most plentiful
supply of provisions. The first emotions of the nobles and of the people
were those of surprise and indignation, that a vile barbarian should dare
to insult the capital of the world; but their arrogance was soon humbled
by misfortune. Perhaps in the person of Serena the Romans might have
respected the niece of Theodosius, the aunt, nay even the adoptive
mother, of the reigning emperor; they abhorred the widow of Stilicho;
and they listened with credulous passion to the tale of calumny which
accused her of maintaining a secret and criminal correspondence with
the Gothic invader. Actuated, or overawed, by the same popular frenzy,
the senate, without requiring any evidence of her guilt, pronounced
the sentence of her death. Serena was ignominiously strangled;
and the infatuated multitude were astonished to find that this cruel
act of injustice did not immediately produce the retreat of the barbarians and the deliverance of the city. That unfortunate city gradually
experienced the distress of scarcity, and at length the horrid calamities
of famine. Many thousands of the inhabitants of Rome expired in their
houses, or in the streets, for want of sustenance; and as the public
sepulchers without the walls were in the power of the enemy, the stench
which arose from so many putrid and unburied carcasses infected the
air; and the miseries of famine were succeeded and aggravated by the
contagion of a pestilential disease. The assurances of speedy and
effectual relief, which were repeatedly transmitted from the court of
Ravenna, supported, for some time, the fainting resolution of the
Romans till at length the despair of any human aid tempted them to
accept the offers of a preternatural deliverance.

The last resource of the Romans was in the clemency, or at least in
the moderation, of the king of the Goths. The senate, who in this
emergency assumed the supreme powers of government, appointed
two ambassadors to negotiate with the enemy. Alaric at length consented to raise the siege, on the immediate payment of five thousand
pounds of gold, of thirty thousand pounds of silver, of four thousand
robes of silk, of three thousand pieces of fine scarlet cloth, and of three
thousand pounds weight of pepper.

At the distance of fourteen centuries we may be satisfied with
relating the military exploits of the conquerors of Rome, without
presuming to investigate the motives of their political conduct. In the
midst of his apparent prosperity, Alaric was conscious, perhaps, of
some secret weakness, some internal defect; or perhaps the moderation
which he displayed was intended only to deceive and disarm the easy
credulity of the ministers of Honorius. The king of the Goths repeatedly declared that it was his desire to be considered as the friend of
peace and of the Romans. Three senators, at his earnest request, were

sent as ambassadors to the court of Ravenna, to solicit the exchange of
hostages and the conclusion of the treaty; and the proposals which he
more clearly expressed during the course of the negotiations could only
inspire a doubt of his sincerity, as they might seem inadequate to the
state of his fortune. The barbarian still aspired to the rank of master-
general of the armies of the West; he stipulated an annual subsidy of
corn and money; and he chose the provinces of Dalmatia, Noricum,
and Venetia for the seat of his new kingdom, which would have
commanded the important communication between Italy and the
Danube. If these modest terms should be rejected, Alaric showed a
disposition to relinquish his pecuniary demands, and even to content
himself with the possession of Noricum; an exhausted and impover-
ished country, perpetually exposed to the inroads of the barbarians of
Germany. But the hopes of peace were disappointed by the weak
obstinacy, or interested views, of the minister Olympius.

The emperor was persuaded to assume a lofty tone of inflexible
dignity, such as neither his situation nor his character could enable him
to support; and a letter, signed with the name of Honorius, was
immediately dispatched to the Prætorian præfect, granting him a free
permission to dispose of the public money, but sternly refusing to
prostitute the military honors of Rome to the proud demands of a
barbarian. This letter was imprudently communicated to Alaric himself; and the Goth, who in the whole transaction had behaved with
temper and decency, expressed in the most outrageous language his
lively sense of the insult so wantonly offered to his person and to his
nation. The conference of Rimini was hastily interrupted; and the
præfect Jovius, on his return to Ravenna, was compelled to adopt, and
even to encourage, the fashionable opinions of the court. By his advice
and example the principal officers of the state and army were obliged to
swear that, without listening in *any* circumstances to *any* conditions of
peace, they would still persevere in perpetual and implacable war
against the enemy of the republic. This rash engagement opposed an
insuperable bar to all future negotiation. The ministers of Honorius
were heard to declare that, if they had only invoked the name of the
Deity, they would consult the public safety, and trust their souls to the
mercy of Heaven: but they had sworn by the sacred head of the emperor
himself; they had touched in solemn ceremony that august seat of
majesty and wisdom; and the violation of their oath would expose them
to the temporal penalties of sacrilege and rebellion.

While the emperor and his court enjoyed with sullen pride the
security of the marshes and fortifications of Ravenna, they abandoned

Animal mosaic showing a tiger chasing an antelope. (Mosaic from the
Roman Villa at Desenzano, Lombardy, fourth century AD)

Ostia, the Port of Rome, showing the Via Decumanus and the theater on the left. (First century BC)

Rome, almost without defense, to the resentment of Alaric. Yet such was the moderation which he still preserved, or affected, that as he moved with his army along the Flaminian way he successively dispatched the bishops of the towns of Italy to reiterate his offers of peace, and to conjure the emperor that he would save the city and its inhabitants from hostile fire and the sword of the barbarians. These impending calamities were however averted, not indeed by the wisdom of Honorius, but by the prudence of humanity of the Gothic king, who employed a milder, though not less effectual, method of conquest. Instead of assaulting the capital he successfully directed his efforts against the *Port* of Ostia, one of the boldest and most stupendous works of Roman magnificence. The accidents to which the precarious subsistence of the city was continually exposed in a winter navigation and an open road had suggested to the genius of the first Cæsar the useful design which was executed under the reign of Claudius. The artificial moles which formed the narrow entrance advanced far into the sea, and

firmly repelled the fury of the waves, while the largest vessels securely rode at anchor within three deep and capacious basins which received the northern branch of the Tiber about two miles from the ancient colony of Ostia. The Roman *Port* insensibly swelled to the size of an episcopal city, where the corn of Africa was deposited in spacious granaries for the use of the capital. As soon as Alaric was in possession of that important place he summoned the city to surrender at discretion; and his demands were enforced by the positive declaration that a refusal, or even a delay, should be instantly followed by the destruction of the magazines on which the life of the Roman people depended. The clamors of that people and the terror of famine subdued the pride of the senate; they listened without reluctance to the proposal of placing a new emperor on the throne of the unworthy Honorius; and the suffrage of the Gothic conqueror bestowed the purple on Attalus, præfect of the city. The grateful monarch immediately acknowledged his protector as master-general of the armies of the West; Adolphus, with the rank of count of the domestics, obtained the custody of the person of Attalus; and the two hostile nations seemed to be united in the closest bands of friendship and alliance.

Coin of Alaric the Visigoth.

The gates of the city were thrown open, and the new emperor of the Romans, encompassed on every side by the Gothic arms, was conducted in tumultuous procession to the palace of Augustus and Trajan. After he had distributed the civil and military dignities among his favorites and followers, Attalus convened an assembly of the senate, before whom, in a formal and florid speech, he asserted his resolution of restoring the majesty of the republic, and of uniting to the empire the provinces of Egypt and the East which had once acknowledged the sovereignty of Rome. Such extravagant promises inspired every reasonable citizen with a just contempt for the character of an unwarlike usurper, whose elevation was the deepest and most ignominious wound which the republic had yet sustained from the insolence of the barbarians. But the populace, with their usual levity, applauded the change of masters. The public discontent was favorable to the rival of Honorius. The first days of the reign of Attalus were fair and prosperous. An officer of confidence was sent with an inconsiderable body of troops to secure the obedience of Africa; the greatest part of Italy submitted to the terror of the Gothic powers; and though the city of Bologna made a vigorous and effectual resistance, the people of Milan, dissatisfied perhaps with the absence of Honorius, accepted with loud acclamations the choice of the Roman senate. At the head of a formidable army, Alaric conducted his royal captive almost to the gates of Ravenna; and a solemn embassy of the principal ministers – of Jovius the Prætorian præfect, of Valens, master of the cavalry and infantry, of the quæstor Potamius, and of Julian, the first of the notaries – was introduced with martial pomp into the Gothic camp. In the name of their sovereign they consented to acknowledge the lawful election of his competitor, and to divide the provinces of Italy and the West between the two emperors. Their proposals were rejected with disdain; and the refusal was aggravated by the insulting clemency of Attalus, who condescended to promise that if Honorius would instantly resign the purple he should be permitted to pass the remainder of his life in the peaceful exile of some remote island.

But there *is* a Providence (such at least was the opinion of the historian Procopius) that watches over innocence and folly, and the pretensions of Honorius to its peculiar care cannot reasonably be disputed. At the moment when his despair, incapable of any wise or manly resolution, meditated a shameful flight, a seasonable reinforcement of four thousand veterans unexpectedly landed in the port of Ravenna. To these valiant strangers, whose fidelity had not been corrupted by the factions of the court, he committed the walls and gates of the city, and the slumbers of the emperor were no longer disturbed by the apprehension of imminent and internal danger. The favorable intelligence which was received from Africa suddenly changed the opinions of men and the state of public affairs. The troops and officers whom Attalus had sent into that province were defeated and slain, and the active zeal of Heraclian maintained his own allegiance and that of his people. The faithful count of Africa transmitted a large sum of money, which fixed the attachment of the Imperial guards; and his vigilance in preventing the exportation of corn and oil introduced famine, tumult, and discontent into the walls of Rome. The failure of the African expedition was the source of mutual complaint and recrimination in the party of Attalus, and the mind of his protector was insensibly alienated from the interest of a prince who wanted spirit to command or docility to obey. In a large plain near Rimini, and in the presence of an innumerable multitude of Romans and barbarians, the wretched Attalus was publicly despoiled of the diadem and purple; and those ensigns of royalty were sent by Alaric as the pledge of peace and friendship to the son of Theodosius. The officers who returned to their duty were reinstated in their employments, and even the merit of a tardy repentance was graciously allowed; but the degraded emperor of the Romans, desirous of life and insensible of disgrace, implored the permission of following the Gothic camp in the train of a haughty and capricious barbarian.

The degradation of Attalus removed the only real obstacle to the conclusion of the peace, and Alaric advanced within three miles of Ravenna to press the irresolution of the Imperial ministers, whose insolence soon returned with the return of fortune. His indignation was kindled by the report that a rival chieftain, that Sarus, the personal enemy of Adolphus, and the hereditary foe of the house of Balti, had been received into the palace. At the head of three hundred followers that fearless barbarian immediately sallied from the gates of Ravenna,

Luxury apartment block at Ostia. By the fourth century AD Ostia had declined in importance and many of the artisan's apartment blocks had been transformed into flats for the well-to-do. (Reconstruction by I Gismondi, Mostra Augustea)

The ruins of the Roman theater at Urbisaglia.

unresisting country. Above four years elapsed from the successful invasion of Italy by the arms of Alaric, to the voluntary retreat of the Goths under the conduct of his successor Adolphus; and, during the whole time, they reigned without control over a country which, in the opinion of the ancients, had united all the various excellences of nature and art.

Whether fame, or conquest, or riches were the object of Alaric, he pursued that object with an indefatigable ardor which could neither be quelled by adversity not satiated by success. No sooner had he reached the extreme land of Italy than he was attracted by the neighboring prospect of a fertile and peaceful island. Yet even the possession of Sicily he considered only as an intermediate step to the important expedition which he already meditated against the continent of Africa. But the whole design was defeated by the premature death of Alaric, which fixed, after a short illness, the fatal term of his conquests. The ferocious character of the barbarians was displayed in the funeral of a hero whose valor and fortune they celebrated with mournful applause.

The personal animosities and hereditary feuds of the barbarians were suspended by the strong necessity of their affairs; and the brave Adolphus, the brother-in-law of the deceased monarch, was unanimously elected to succeed to his throne. The successor of Alaric suspended the operations of war, and seriously negotiated with the Imperial court a treaty of friendship and alliance which was readily accepted by the ministers of Honorius. Adolphus, assuming the character of a Roman general, directed his march from the extremity of Campania to the southern provinces of Gaul. His troops, either by force or agreement, immediately occupied the cities of Narbonne, Toulouse, and Bordeaux; and though they were repulsed by Count Boniface from the walls of Marseilles, they soon extended their quarters from the Mediterranean to the ocean. The oppressed provincials might exclaim that the miserable remnant which the enemy had spared was cruelly ravished by their pretended allies; yet some specious colors were not wanting to palliate or justify the violence of the Goths. The cities of Gaul which they attacked might perhaps be considered as in a state of rebellion against the government of Honorius: the articles of the treaty or the secret instructions of the court might sometimes be alleged in favor of the seeming usurpations of Adolphus; and the guilt of any irregular unsuccessful act of hostility might always be imputed, with an appearance of truth, to the ungovernable spirit of a barbarian host impatient of peace or discipline. The luxury of Italy had been less effectual to soften the temper than to relax the courage of the Goths; and they had imbibed the vices; without imitating the arts and institutions, of civilized society.

Alaric is buried in the river bed at Busento after the Sack of Rome. (Nineteenth-century engraving)

surprised and cut in pieces a considerable body of Goths, re-entered the city in triumph, and was permitted to insult his adversary by the voice of a herald, who publicly declared that the guilt of Alaric had for ever excluded him from the friendship and alliance of the emperor. The crime and folly of the court of Ravenna was expiated a third time by the calamities of Rome. The king of the Goths, who no longer dissembled his appetite for plunder and revenge, appeared in arms under the walls of the capital; and the trembling senate, without any hopes of relief, prepared by a desperate resistance to delay the ruin of their country. But they were unable to guard against the secret conspiracy of their slaves and domestics, who either from birth or interest were attached to the cause of the enemy. At the hour of midnight the Salarian gate was silently opened, and the inhabitants were awakened by the tremendous sound of the Gothic trumpet. Eleven hundred and sixty-three years after the foundation of Rome, the Imperial city, which had subdued and civilized so considerable a part of mankind, was delivered to the licentious fury of the tribes of Germany and Scythia.

The proclamation of Alaric, when he forced his entrance into a vanquished city, discovered, however, some regard for the laws of humanity and religion. He encouraged his troops boldly to seize the rewards of valor, and to enrich themselves with the spoils of a wealthy and effeminate people; but he exhorted them at the same time to spare the lives of the unresisting citizens, and to respect the churches of the apostles St Peter and St Paul as holy and inviolable sanctuaries.

The retreat of the victorious Goths, who evacuated Rome on the sixth day, might be the result of prudence, but it was not surely the effect of fear. At the head of an army emcumbered with rich and weighty spoils, their intrepid leader advanced along the Appian Way into the southern provinces of Italy, destroying whatever dared to oppose his passage, and contenting himself with the plunder of the

Above: Sunset over the ruins of the Capitol viewed from the Forum at
Ostia.
Right: Street scene, Ostia. (Third century AD)

The professions of Adolphus were probably sincere, and his attachment to the cause of the republic was secured by the ascendant which a
Roman princess had acquired over the heart and understanding of the
barbarian king. Placidia, the daughter of the great Theodosius, and of
Galla, his second wife, had received a royal education in the palace of
Constantinople; but the eventful story of her life is connected with the
revolutions which agitated the Western empire under the reign of her
brother Honorius. When Rome was first invested by the arms of Alaric,
Placidia, who was then about twenty years of age, resided in the city;
and her ready consent to the death of her cousin Serena has a cruel and
ungrateful appearance, which, according to the circumstances of he
action, may be aggravated or excused by the consideration of her tender
age. The victorious barbarians detained, either as a hostage or a captive,
the sister of Honorius; but while she was exposed to the disgrace of
following round Italy the motions of a Gothic camp, she experienced,
however, a decent and respectful treatment. The authority of Jornandes, who praises the beauty of Placidia, may perhaps be counterbalanced by the silence, the expressive silence, of her flatterers: yet the
splendor of her birth, the bloom of youth, the elegance of manners, and
the dexterous insinuations which she condescended to employ, made a
deep impression on the mind of Adolphus; and the Gothic king aspired
to call himself the brother of the emperor. The ministers of Honorius
rejected with disdain the proposal of an alliance so injurious to every

sentiment of Roman pride; and repeatedly urged the restitution of Placidia as an indispensable condition of the treaty of peace. But the daughter of Theodosius submitted without reluctance to the desires of the conqueror, a young and valiant prince, who yielded to Alaric in loftiness of stature, but who excelled in the more attractive qualities of grace and beauty. The marriage of Adolphus and Placidia was consummated before the Goths retired from Italy, and the solemn, perhaps the anniversary, day of their nuptials was afterwards celebrated in the house of Ingenuus, one of the most illustrious citizens of Narbonne in Gaul. The bride, attired and adorned like a Roman empress, was placed on a throne of state; and the king of the Goths, who assumed on this occasion the Roman habit, contented himself with a less honorable seat by her side. The nuptial gift, which, according to the custom of his nation, was offered to Placidia, consisted of the rare and magnificent spoils of her country. Fifty beautiful youths, in silken robes, carried a basin in each hand; and one of these basins was filled with pieces of gold, the other with precious stones of an inestimable value. Attalus, so long the sport of fortune and of the Goths, was appointed to lead the chorus of the Hymeneal song; and the degraded emperor might aspire to the praise of a skillful musician. The barbarians enjoyed the insolence of their triumph; and the provincials rejoiced in this alliance, which tempered, by the mild influence of love and reason, the fierce spirit of their Gothic lord.

After the deliverance of Italy from the oppression of the Goths, some secret counsellor was permitted, amidst the factions of the palace, to heal the wounds of that afflicted country. By a wise and humane regulation the eight provinces which had been the most deeply injured – Campania, Tuscany, Picenum, Samnium, Apulia, Calabria, Bruttium, and Lucania – obtained an indulgence of five years; the ordinary tribute was reduced to one-fifth, and even that fifth was destined to restore and support the useful institution of the public posts. By another law the lands which had been left without inhabitants or cultivation were granted, with some diminution of taxes, to the neighbors who should occupy or the strangers who should solicit them; and the new possessors were secured against the future claims of the fugitive proprietors. About the same time a general amnesty was published in the name of Honorius, to abolish the guilt and memory of all the *involuntary* offences which had been committed by his unhappy subjects during the term of the public disorder and calamity. A decent and respectful attention was paid to the restoration of the capital; the citizens were encouraged to rebuild the edifices which had been destroyed or damaged by hostile fire; and extraordinary supplies of corn were imported from the coast of Africa. The crowds that so lately fled before the sword of the barbarians were soon recalled by the hopes of plenty and pleasure; and Albinus, præfect of Rome, informed the court, with some anxiety and surprise, that in a single day he had taken an account of the arrival of fourteen thousand strangers. In less than seven years the vestiges of the Gothic invasion were almost obliterated,

and the city appeared to resume its former splendor and tranquility. The venerable matron replaced her crown of laurel, which had been ruffled by the storms of war, and was still amused in the last moment of her decay with the prophecies of revenge, of victory, and of eternal dominion.

The situation of Spain, separated on all sides from the enemies of Rome, by the sea, by the mountains, and by intermediate provinces, had secured the long tranquillity of that remote and sequestered country. As long as the defense of the mountains was intrusted to the hardy and faithful militia of the country, they successfully repelled the frequent attempts of the barbarians. But no sooner had the national troops been compelled to resign their post to the Honorian bands in the service of Constantine, than the gates of Spain were treacherously betrayed to the public enemy, about ten months before the sack of Rome by the Goths. The greatest part of the Spaniards was even disposed to prefer this new condition of poverty and barbarism to the severe oppressions of the Roman government; yet there were many who still asserted their native freedom, and who refused, more especially in the moutains of Gallicia, to submit to the barbarian yoke.

The important present of the heads of Jovinus and Sebastian had approved the friendship of Adolphus, and restored Gaul to the obedience of his brother Honorius. Peace was incompatible with the situation and temper of the king of the Goths. He readily accepted the

proposal of turning his victorious arms against the barbarians of Spain; the troops of Constantius intercepted his communication with the seaports of Gaul, and gently pressed his march towards the Pyrenees: he passed the mountains, and surprised, in the name of the emperor, the city of Barcelona. The fondness of Adolphus for his Roman bride was not abated by time or possession; and the birth of a son, surnamed, from his illustrious grandsire, Theodosius, appeared to fix him for ever in the interest of the republic. The loss of that infant, whose remains were deposited in a silver coffin in one of the churches near Barcelona, afflicted his parents; but the grief of the Gothic king was suspended by the labors of the field; and the course of his victories was soon interrupted by domestic treason. He had imprudently received into his service one of the followers of Sarus, a barbarian of a daring spirit, but of a diminutive stature, whose secret desire of revenging the death of his beloved patron was continually irritated by the sarcasms of his insolent master. Adolphus was assassinated in the palace of Barcelona; the laws of the succession were violated by a tumultuous faction; and a stranger to the royal race, Singeric, the brother of Sarus himself, was seated on the Gothic throne. The unfortunate Placidia, instead of the respectful compassion which she might have excited in the most savage breasts, was treated with cruel and wanton insult.

But Placidia soon obtained the pleasure of revenge; for the tyrant was assassinated on the seventh day of his usurpation. After the death of Singeric, the free choice of the nation bestowed the Gothic scepter on Wallia, whose warlike and ambitious temper appeared, in the beginning of his reign, extremely hostile to the republic. He marched in arms from Barcelona to the shores of the Atlantic Ocean. Wallia resumed the designs of conquest which had been interrupted by the death of Alaric. However, the winds and waves disappointed the enterprise of the Goths; and the minds of a superstitious people were deeply affected by

Top left: The ruins of Richborough Castle, near Sandwich, Kent, one of the prime Roman sea-port defenses against attacks from Saxon pirates.
Center left: Roman theater at Caerleon, Wales.
Bottom left: The site of the hill-fort known as Maiden Castle, Dorset.
Top right: The Roman bridge at Cordoba, Spain.
Right: The four horsemen of the Apocalypse. (From *Silos Apocalypse,* one of the earliest Spanish manuscripts extant, Ms AD 11695 f102v, AD 1109, British Library Board)

the repeated disasters of storms and shipwrecks. In this disposition, the successor of Adolphus no longer refused to listen to a Roman ambassador, whose proposals were enforced by the real, or supposed, approach of a numerous army, under the conduct of the brave Constantius. A solemn treaty was stipulated and observed and Placidia was honorably restored to her brother, six hundred thousand measures of wheat were delivered to the hungry Goths; and Wallia engaged to draw his sword in the service of the empire. A bloody war was instantly excited among the barbarians of Spain; and the contending princes are said to have addressed their letters, their ambassadors, and their hostages, to the throne of the Western emperor, exhorting him to remain a tranquil spectator of their contest, the events of which must be favorable to the Romans by the mutual slaughter of their common enemies. The Spanish war was obstinately supported, during three campaigns, with desperate valor and various success; and the martial achievements of Wallia diffused through the empire the superior renown of the Gothic hero.

About the same time, in the last years of the reign of Honorius, the GOTHS, the BURGUNDIANS, and the FRANKS, obtained a permanent seat and dominion in the provinces of Gaul.

The odious name of conquerors was softened into the mild and friendly appellation of the *guests* of the Romans; and the barbarians of Gaul, more especially the Goths, repeatedly declared that they were bound to the people by the ties of hospitality, and to the emperor by the duty of allegiance and military service. The title of Honorius and his successors, their laws and their civil magistrates, were still respected in the provinces of Gaul, of which they had resigned the possession to the barbarian allies; and the kings, who exercised a supreme and independent authority over their native subjects, ambitiously solicited the more honorable rank of master-generals of the Imperial armies. Such was the involuntary reverence which the Roman name still impressed on the minds of those warriors who had borne away in triumph the spoils of the Capitol.

Whilst Italy was ravaged by the Goths, and a succession of feeble tyrants oppressed the provinces beyond the Alps, the British island separated itself from the body of the Roman empire. The regular forces which guarded that remote province had been gradually withdrawn; and Britain was abandoned, without defense, to the Saxon pirates and the savages of Ireland and Caledonia. The Britons, reduced to this extremity, no longer relied on the tardy and doubtful aid of a declining monarchy. They assembled in arms, repelled the invaders, and rejoiced in the important discovery of their own strength. Afflicted by similar calamities, and actuated by the same spirit, the Armorican provinces (a name which comprehended the maritime countries of Gaul between the Seine and the Loire) resolved to imitate the example of the neighboring island. The independence of Britain and Armorica was soon confirmed by Honorius himself, the lawful emperor of the West. Armorica, though it could not long maintain the form of a republic, was agitated by frequent and destructive revolts. Britain was irrecoverably lost. But as the emperors wisely acquiesced in the independence of a remote province, the separation was not embittered by the reproach of tyranny or rebellion; and the claims of allegiance and protection were succeeded by the mutual and voluntary offices of national friendship.

CHAPTER TWENTY-SEVEN

Death of Honorius – Valentian III – Emperor of the West – administration of his mother Placidia – Aetius and Boniface – conquests of Africa by the Vandals

[AD 423–455]

DURING a long and disgraceful reign of twenty-eight years, Honorius, emperor of the West, was separated from the friendship of his brother, and afterwards of his nephew, who reigned over the East; and Constantinople beheld, with apparent indifference and secret joy, the calamities of Rome. The strange adventures of Placidia gradually renewed and cemented the alliance of the two empires. The daughter of the great Theodosius had been the captive and the queen of the Goths; she lost an affectionate husband; she was dragged in chains by his insulting assassin; she tasted the pleasure of revenge, and was exchanged, in the treaty of peace, for six hundred thousand measures of wheat. After her return from Spain to Italy, Placidia experienced a new persecution in the bosom of her family. She was averse to a marriage which had been stipulated without her consent; and the brave Constantius, as a noble reward for the tyrants whom he had vanquished, received, from the hand of Honorius himself, the struggling and reluctant hand of the widow of Adolphus. But her resistance ended with the ceremony of the nuptials; nor did Placidia refuse to become the mother of Honoria and Valentinian the Third, or to assume and exercise an absolute dominion over the mind of her grateful husband. Within a few months after the arrival of Placidia a swift messenger announced the death of Honorius, the consequence of a dropsy.

The emperor Theodosius, when he received the news of the victory, interrupted the horse-races; and singing, as he marched through the streets, a suitable psalm, conducted his people from the Hippodrome to the church, where he spent the remainder of the day in grateful devotion.

In a monarchy which, according to various precedents, might be considered as elective, or hereditary, or patrimonial, it was impossible that the intricate claims of female and collateral succession should be clearly defined; and Theodosius, by the right of consanguinity or conquest, might have reigned the sole legitimate emperor of the Romans. For a moment, perhaps, his eyes were dazzled by the prospect of unbounded sway; but his indolent temper gradually acquiesced in the dictates of sound policy. He contented himself with the possession of the East; and wisely relinquished the laborious task of waging a distant and doubtful war against the barbarians beyond the Alps, or of securing the obedience of the Italians and Africans, whose minds were alienated by the irreconcilable difference of language and interest. Instead of listening to the voice of ambition, Theodosius resolved to imitate the moderation of his grandfather, and to seat his cousin Valentinian on the throne of the West.

Valentinian, when he received the title of Augustus, was no more than six years of age; and his long minority was intrusted to the guardian care of a mother who might assert a female claim to the succession of the Western empire. Placidia envied, but she could not equal, the reputation and virtues of the wife and sister of Theodosius; the elegant genius of Eudocia, the wise and successful policy of Pulcheria. The mother of Valentinian was jealous of the power which she was incapable of exercising: she reigned twenty-five years, in the name of her son; and the character of that unworthy emperor gradually countenanced the suspicion that Placidia had enervated his youth by a dissolute education, and studiously diverted his attention from every manly and honorable pursuit. Amidst the decay of military spirit, her armies were commanded by two generals, Aëtius and Boniface, who may be deservedly named as the last of the Romans. Their union might have supported a sinking empire; their discord was the fatal and immediate cause of the loss of Africa. In the melancholy season of her exile and distress, Boniface alone had maintained her cause with unshaken fidelity; and the troops and treasures of Africa had essentially contributed to extinguish the rebellion. The same rebellion had been supported by the zeal and activity of Aëtius, who brought an army of sixty thousand Huns from the Danube to the confines of Italy, for the service of the usurper. The untimely death of John compelled him to accept an advantageous treaty; but he still continued, the subject and the soldier of Valentinian, to entertain a secret, perhaps a treasonable, correspondence with his barbarian allies, whose retreat had been purchased by liberal gifts and more liberal promises. But Aëtius possessed an advantage of singular moment in a female reign: he was present: he besieged with artful and assiduous flattery the palace of Ravenna; disguised his dark designs with the mask of loyalty and friendship; and at length deceived both his mistress and his absent rival, by a subtle conspiracy which a weak woman and a brave man could not easily suspect. He secretly persuaded Placidia to recall Boniface from the government of Africa; he secretly advised Boniface to disobey the Imperial summons: to the one, he represented the order as a sentence of death; to the other, he stated the refusal as a signal of revolt; and when the credulous and unsuspectful count had armed the province in his defense, Aëtius applauded his sagacity in foreseeing the rebellion which his own perfidy had excited. A temperate inquiry into the real motives of Boniface would have restored a faithful servant to his duty and to the republic; but the arts of Aëtius still continued to betray and to inflame, and the count was urged by persecution to embrace the most desperate counsels. The success with which he eluded or repelled the first attacks

Left: A partially restored villa at Carthage, Tunisia. The city was sacked by Genseric the Vandal (c 390–476) in AD 439.
Below: The Villa at Tabarka: this elegant villa took on the form of a fortified house, easy to defend in times of war.

could not inspire a vain confidence that, at the head of some loose disorderly Africans, he should be able to withstand the regular forces of the West, commanded by a rival whose military character it was impossible for him to despise. After some hesitation, the last struggles of prudence and loyalty, Boniface dispatched a trusty friend to the court, or rather to the camp, of Gonderic, king of the Vandals, with the proposal of a strict alliance, and the offer of an advantageous and perpetual settlement.

The prospect of Africa, encouraged the Vandals to accept the invitation which they received from Count Boniface, and the death of Gonderic served only to forward and animate the bold enterprise. In the room of a prince not conspicuous for any superior powers of the mind or body, they acquired his bastard brother, the terrible Genseric; a name which in the destruction of the Roman empire has deserved an equal rank with the names of Alaric and Attila. The vessels which transported the Vandals over the modern Straits of Gibraltar, a channel only twelve miles in breadth, were furnished by the Spaniards, who anxiously wished their departure, and by the African general, who had implored their formidable assistance.

The persecution of the Donatists was an event not less favorable to the designs of Genseric. Genseric, a Christian, but an enemy of the orthodox communion, showed himself to the Donatists as a powerful deliverer, from whom they might reasonably expect the repeal of the odious and oppressive edicts of the Roman emperors. The conquest of Africa was facilitated by the active zeal or the secret favor of a domestic faction; the wanton outrages against the churches and the clergy, of which the Vandals are accused, may be fairly imputed to the fanaticism of their allies; and the intolerant spirit which disgraced the triumph of Christianity contributed to the loss of the most important province of the West.

The court and the people were astonished by the strange intelligence that a virtuous hero, after so many favors and so many services, had renounced his allegiance and invited the barbarians to destroy the province intrusted to his command. The friends of Boniface, who still believed that his criminal behavior might be excused by some honorable motive, solicited, during the absence of Aëtius, a free conference with the Count of Africa; and Darius, an officer of high distinction, was named for the important embassy. In their first interview at Carthage the imaginary provocations were mutually explained, the opposite letters of Aëtius were produced and compared, and the fraud was easily detected. Placidia and Boniface lamented their fatal error, and the count had sufficient magnanimity to confide in the forgiveness of his sovereign, or to expose his head to her future resentment. His repentance was fervent and sincere; but he soon discovered that it was no longer in his power to restore the edifice which he had shaken to its foundations. Carthage and the Roman garrisons returned with their general to the allegiance of Valentinian, but the rest of Africa was still distracted with war and faction; and the inexorable king of the Vandals, disdaining all terms of accommodation, sternly refused to relinquish the possession of his prey. The band of veterans who marched under the standard of Boniface, and his hasty levies of provincial troops, were defeated with considerable loss; the victorious barbarians insulted the open country; and Carthage, Cirta, and Hippo Regius, were the only cities that appeared to rise above the general inundation.

Above: The Mausoleum of Galla Placidia.
Right: Hippo Regius (Numidia), the site of the siege by Aëtius against Genseric in AD 430.

Christ the Good Shepherd. (Mosaic from the vault of the Mausoleum of Galla Placidia, mid-fifth century AD)

The generous mind of Count Boniface was tortured by the exquisite distress of beholding the ruin which he had occasioned, and whose rapid progress he was unable to check. After the loss of a battle he retired into Hippo Regius, where he was immediately besieged by an enemy who considered him as the real bulwark of Africa.

By the skill of Boniface, and perhaps by the ignorance of the Vandals, the siege of Hippo was protracted above fourteen months: the sea was continually open; and when the adjacent country had been exhausted by irregular rapine, the besiegers themselves were compelled by famine to relinquish their enterprise. The importance and danger of Africa were deeply felt by the regent of the West. Placidia implored the assistance of her Eastern ally; and the Italian fleet and army were reinforced by Aspar, who sailed from Constantinople with a powerful armament. As soon as the force of the two empires was united under the command of Boniface, he boldly marched against the Vandals; and the loss of a second battle irretrievably decided the fate of Africa. He embarked with the precipitation of despair, and the people of Hippo were permitted, with their families and effects, to occupy the vacant place of the soldiers, the greatest part of whom were either slain or made prisoners by the Vandals. The count, whose fatal credulity had wounded the vitals of the republic, might enter the palace of Ravenna with some anxiety, which was soon removed by the smiles of Placidia. Boniface accepted with gratitude the rank of patrician and the dignity of master-general of the Roman armies; but he must have blushed at the sight of those medals in which he was represented with the name and attributes of victory. The discovery of his fraud, the displeasure of the empress, and the distinguished favor of his rival, exasperated the haughty and perfidious soul of Aëtius. He hastily returned from Gaul to Italy, with a retinue, or rather with an army, of barbarian followers; and such was the weakness of the government, that the two generals decided their private quarrel in a bloody battle. Boniface was successful; but he received in the conflict a mortal wound from the spear of his adversary, of which he expired within a few days, in such Christian and charitable sentiments that he exhorted his wife, a rich heiress of Spain, to accept Aëtius for her second husband. But Aëtius could not derive any immediate advantage from the generosity of his dying enemy:

he was proclaimed a rebel by the justice of Placidia; and though he attempted to defend some strong fortresses, erected on his patrimonial estate, the Imperial power soon compelled him to retire into Pannonia, to the tents of his faithful Huns. The republic was deprived by their mutual discord of the service of her two most illustrious champions.

It might naturally be expected, after the retreat of Boniface, that the Vandals would achieve without resistance or delay the conquest of Africa. Eight years however elapsed from the evacuation of Hippo to the reduction of Carthage. In the midst of that interval the ambitious Genseric, in the full tide of apparent prosperity, negotiated a treaty of peace, by which he gave his son Hunneric for an hostage, and consented to leave the Western emperor in the undisturbed possession of the three Mauritanias. This moderation, which cannot be imputed to the justice. must be ascribed to the policy, of the conqueror. His throne was encompassed with domestic enemies, who accused the baseness of his birth, and asserted the legitimate claims of his nephews, the sons of Gonderic. Those nephews, indeed, he sacrificed to his safety; and their mother, the widow of the deceased king, was precipitated by his order into the river Ampsaga. But the public discontent burst forth in dangerous and frequent conspiracies; and the warlike tyrant is supposed to have shed more Vandal blood by the hand of the executioner than in the field of battle. The convulsions of Africa, which had favored his attack, opposed the firm establishment of his power; and the various seditions of the Moors and Germans, the Donatists and catholics, continually disturbed or threatened the unsettled reign of the conqueror. These difficulties were gradually subdued by the spirit, the perseverance, and the cruelty of Genseric; who alternately applied the arts of peace and war to the establishment of his African kingdom. He subscribed a solemn treaty, with the hope of deriving some advantage from the term of its continuance and the moment of its violation. The vigilance of his enemies was relaxed by the protestations of friendship which concealed his hostile approach and Carthage was at length surprised by the Vandals, five hundred and eighty-five years after the destruction of the city and republic by the younger Scipio.

CHAPTER TWENTY-EIGHT

Conquests of Attila – invasion of Gaul by Attila – he is repulsed by Aetius and the Visigoths

Attila invades and evacuates Italy – death of Attila, Aetius and Valentian III

[AD 376–455]

THE Western world was oppressed by the Goths and Vandals, who fled before the Huns; but the achievements of the Huns themselves were not adequate to their power and prosperity. Their victorious hordes had spread from the Volga to the Danube; but the public force was exhausted by the discord of independent chieftains; their valor was idly consumed in obscure and predatory excursions; and they often degraded their national dignity, by condescending, for the hopes of spoil, to enlist under the banners of their fugitive enemies. In the reign of ATTILA the Huns again became the terror of the world.

Attila, the son of Mundzuk, deduced his noble, perhaps his regal, descent from the ancient Huns, who had formerly contended with the monarchs of China. His features, according to the observation of a Gothic historian, bore the stamp of his national origin; and the portrait of Attila exhibits the genuine deformity of a modern Calmuck; a large head, a swarthy complexion, small deep-seated eyes, a flat nose, a few hairs in the place of a beard, broad shoulders, and a short square body, of nervous strength, though of a disproportioned form. The haughty step and demeanor of the king of the Huns expressed the consciousness of his superiority above the rest of mankind; and he had a custom of fiercely rolling his eyes, as if he wished to enjoy the terror which he inspired. Yet this savage hero was not inaccessible to pity; his suppliant enemies might confide in the assurance of peace or pardon; and Attila was considered by his subjects as a just and indulgent master. He delighted in war; but, after he had ascended the throne in a mature age, his head, rather than his hand, achieved the conquest of the North, and

Left: Attila the Hun, known as the Scourge of God. (AD 453, medallion from the facade of the Charterhouse of Pavia, Italy)
Below: The Huns of Attila. (After a painting by Checa)

the fame of an adventurous soldier was usefully exchanged for that of a prudent and successful general.

If a line of separation were drawn between the civilized and the savage climates of the globe; between the inhabitants of cities, who cultivated the earth, and the hunters and shepherds, who dwelt in tents, Attila might aspire to the title of supreme and sole monarch of the barbarians. He alone, among the conquerors of ancient and modern times, united the two mighty kingdoms of Germany and Scythia.

In time of peace, the dependent princes, with their national troops, attended the royal camp in regular succession; but when Attila collected his military force, he was able to bring into the field an army of five, or, according to another account, of seven hundred thousand barbarians.

The timid or selfish policy of the Western Romans had abandoned the Eastern empire to the Huns. The loss of armies and the want of discipline or virtue were not supplied by the personal character of the monarch. Theodosius might still affect the style as well as the title of *Invincible Augustus*, but he was reduced to solicit the clemency of Attila, who imperiously dictated these harsh and humiliating conditions of peace.

The emperor Theodosius did not long survive the most humiliating circumstance of an inglorious life. As he was riding or hunting in the neighborhood of Constantinople, he was thrown from his horse into the river Lycus, the spine of his back was injured by the fall; and he expired some days afterwards, in the fiftieth year of his age, and the forty-third of his reign. His sister Pulcheria was unanimously proclaimed empress of the East; the Romans, for the first time, submitted to a female reign. Amidst the general acclamations, the empress did not forget the prejudice and disadvantage to which her sex was exposed; and she wisely

Central nave of the Basilica of Santa Sabina, Rome. (Fifth century)

resolved to prevent their murmurs by the choice of a colleague who would always respect the superior rank and virgin chastity of his wife. She gave her hand to Marcian, a senator, about sixty years of age, and the nominal husband of Pulcheria was solemnly invested with the Imperial purple. The zeal which he displayed for the orthodox creed, as it was established by the council of Chalcedon, would alone have inspired the grateful eloquence of the catholics. But the behavior of Marcian in a private life, and afterwards on the throne, may support a more rational belief that he was qualified to restore and invigorate an empire which had been almost dissolved by the successive weakness of two hereditary monarchs. He was born in Thrace, and educated to the profession of arms; but Marcian's youth had been severely exercised by poverty and misfortune, since his only resource, when he first arrived at Constantinople, consisted in two hundred pieces of gold which he had borrowed of a friend. He passed nineteen years in the domestic and military service of Aspar and his son Ardaburius; followed these powerful generals to the Persian and African wars; and obtained, by their influence, the honorable rank of tribune and senator. His mild disposition and useful talents, without alarming the jealousy, recommended Marcian to the esteem and favor of his patrons; he had seen, perhaps he had felt, the abuses of a venal and oppressive administration; and his own example gave weight and energy to the laws which he promulgated for the reformation of manners.

It was the opinion of Marcian, that war should be avoided as long as it is possible to preserve a secure and honorable peace; but it was likewise his opinion that peace cannot be honorable or secure, if the sovereign betrays a pusillanimous aversion to war. This temperate courage dictated his reply to the demands of Attila, who insolently pressed the payment of the annual tribute. The emperor signified to the barbarians that they must no longer insult the majesty of Rome by the mention of a tribute; that he was disposed to reward, with becoming liberality, the faithful friendship of his allies; but that, if they presumed to violate the public peace, they should feel that he possessed troops, and arms, and resolution, to repel their attacks. The same language, even in the camp of the Huns, was used by his ambassador Apollonius, whose bold refusal to deliver the presents, till he had been admitted to a personal interview, displayed a sense of dignity, and a contempt of danger, which Attila was not prepared to expect from the degenerate Romans. He threatened to chastise the rash successor of Theodosius; but he hesitated, whether he should first direct his invincible arms against the Eastern or the Western empire. But as the barbarian despised, or affected to despise, the Romans of the East, whom he had so often vanquished, he soon declared his resolution of suspending the easy conquest till he had achieved a more glorious and important enterprise. In the memorable invasions of Gaul and Italy, the Huns were naturally attracted by the wealth and fertility of those provinces.

A native of Gaul and a contemporary, the learned and eloquent Sidonius, who was afterwards bishop of Clermont, had made a promise to one of his friends that he would compose a regular history of the war of Attila. If the modesty of Sidonius had not discouraged him from the prosecution of this interesting work, the historian would have related with the simplicity of truth those memorable events to which the poet, in vague and doubtful metaphors, has concisely alluded. The kings and nations of Germany and Scythia, from the Volga perhaps to the Danube, obeyed the warlike summons of Attila. From the royal village in the plains of Hungary his standard moved towards the West, and after a march of seven or eight hundred miles he reached the conflux of the Rhine and the Neckar, where he was joined by the Franks who adhered to his ally, the elder of the sons of Clodion. A troop of light barbarians who roamed in quest of plunder might choose the winter for the convenience of passing the river on the ice, but the innumerable cavalry of the Huns required such plenty of forage and provisions as could be procure only in a milder season; the Hercynian forest supplied materials for a bridge of boats, and the hostile myriads were poured with resistless violence into the Belgic provinces. The consternation of Gaul was universal, and the various fortunes of its cities have been adorned by tradition with martyrdoms and miracles. Troyes was saved by the merits of St Lupus; St Servatius was removed from the world that he might not behold the ruin of Tongres; and the prayers of St Genevieve diverted the march of Attila from the neighborhood of Paris. But as the greatest part of the Gallic cities were alike destitute of saints and soldiers, they were besieged and stormed by the Huns, who practiced, in the example of Metz, their customary maxims of war. They involved in a promiscuous massacre the priests who served at the altar and the infants who, in the hour of danger, had been providently baptized by the bishop; the flourishing city was delivered to the flames, and a solitary chapel of St Stephen marked the place where it formerly stood. From the Rhine and the Moselle, Attila advanced into the heart of Gaul, crossed the Seine at Auxerre, and after a long and laborious march fixed his camp under the walls of Orleans.

The facility with which Attila had penetrated into the heart of Gaul may be ascribed to his insidious policy as well as to the terror of his

arms. His public declarations were skillfully mitigated by his private assurances; he alternately soothed and threatened the Romans and the Goths; and the courts of Ravenna and Toulouse, mutually suspicious of each other's intentions, beheld with supine indifference the approach of their common enemy. Aëtius was the sole guardian of the public safety; but his wisest measures were embarrassed by a faction which, since the death of Placidia, infested the Imperial palace: the youth of Italy trembled at the sound of the trumpet; and the barbarians, who from fear or affection were inclined to the cause of Attila, awaited with doubtful and venal faith the event of the war. The patrician passed the Alps at the head of some troops whose strength and numbers scarcely deserved the name of an army. But on his arrival at Arles or Lyons he was confounded by the intelligence that the Visigoths, refusing to embrace the defense of Gaul, had determined to expect within their own territories the formidable invader whom they professed to despise. The senator Avitus, who after the honorable exercise of the Prætorian præfecture had retired to his estate in Auvergne, was persuaded to accept the important embassy, which he executed with ability and success. He represented to Theodoric that an ambitious conqueror who aspired to the dominion of the earth could be resisted only by the firm and unanimous alliance of the powers whom he labored to oppress. The lively eloquence of Avitus inflamed the Gothic warriors by the description of the injuries which their ancestors had suffered from the Huns, whose implacable fury still pursued them from the Danube to the foot of the Pyrenees. He strenuously urged that it was the duty of every Christian to save from sacrilegious violation the churches of God and the relics of the saints; that it was the interest of every barbarian

Right: The Baptistry, Neoniano. (Fifth century)
Below: Detail of boys fishing. (Mosaic from the Bishop Theodore's Palace at Aquileia, Friuli, Northern Italy, fourth century. Aquileia was sacked by Attila during his invasion of Italy.)

who had acquired a settlement in Gaul to defend the fields and vineyards, which were cultivated for his use, against the desolation of the Scythian shepherds. Theodoric yielded to the evidence of truth, adopted the measure at once the most prudent and the most honorable, and declared that as the faithful ally of Aëtius and the Romans he was ready to expose his life and kingdom for the common safety of Gaul. The Visigoths, who at that time were in the mature vigor of their fame and power obeyed with alacrity the signal of war, prepared their arms and horses, and assembled under the standard of their aged king, who was resolved, with his two eldest sons, Torismond and Theodoric, to command in person his numerous and valiant people. The example of the Goths determined several tribes or nations that seemed to fluctuate between the Huns and the Romans. The indefatigable diligence of the patrician gradually collected the troops of Gaul and Germany, who had formerly acknowledged themselves the subjects or soldiers of the republic, but who now claimed the rewards of voluntary service and the rank of independent allies; the Læti, the Armoricans, the Breones, the Saxons, the Burgundians, the Sarmatians or Alani, the Ripuarians, and the Franks who followed Meroveus as their lawful prince. Such was the various army which, under the conduct of Aëtius and Theodoric, advanced by rapid marches to relieve Orleans, and to give battle to the innumerable host of Attila.

Jonah and the whale. (Mosaic from the Bishop Theodore's Palace)

On their approach the king of the Huns immediately raised the siege, and sounded a retreat to recall the foremost of his troops from the pillage of a city which they had already entered. The valor of Attila was always guided by his prudence; and as he foresaw the fatal consequences of a defeat in the heart of Gaul, he repassed the Seine, and expected the enemy in the plains of Châlons, whose smooth and level surface was adapted to the operations of his Scythian cavalry. But in this tumultuary retreat the vanguard of the Romans and their allies continually pressed, and sometimes engaged, the troops whom Attila had posted in the rear; the hostile columns, in the darkness of the night and the perplexity of the roads, might encounter each other without design; and the bloody conflict of the Franks and Gepidæ, in which fifteen thousand barbarians were slain, was a prelude to a more general and decisive action. The Catalaunian fields spread themselves round Châlons, and extend, according to the vague measurement of Jornandes, to the length of one hundred and fifty, and the breadth of one hundred miles, over the whole province, which is entitled to the appellation of a *champaign* country. This spacious plain was distinguished, however, by some inequalities of ground; and the importance of an height which commanded the camp of Attila was understood and disputed by the two generals. The young and valiant Torismond first occupied the summit; the Goths rushed with irresistible weight on the Huns, who labored to ascend from the opposite side: and the possession of this advantageous post inspired both the troops and their leaders with a fair assurance of victory. Attila immediately formed his order of battle. At the head of his brave and faithful Huns, he occupied in person the center of the line. The nations subject to his empire, the Rugians, the Heruli, the Thuringians, the Franks, the Burgundians, were extended, on either hand, over the ample space of the Catalaunian fields; the right wing was commanded by Ardaric, king of the Gapidæ; and the three valiant brothers who reigned over the Ostrogoths were posted on the left to oppose the kindred tribes of the Visigoths. The disposition of the allies was regulated by a different principle. Sangiban, the faithless king of the Alani, was placed in the center: where his motions might be strictly watched, and his treachery might be instantly punished. Aëtius assumed the command of the left, and Theodoric of the right wing; while Torismond still continued to occupy the heights which appear to have stretched on the flank, and perhaps the rear, of the Scythian army. The nations from the Volga to the Atlantic were assembled on the plain of Châlons; but many of these nations had been divided by faction, or conquest, or emigration; and the appearance of similar arms and ensigns, which threatened each other, presented the image of a civil war.

The Huns, who fought under the eyes of their king, pierced through the feeble and doubtful center of the allies, separated their wings from each other, and wheeling, with a rapid effort, to the left, directed their whole force against the Visigoths. As Theodoric rode along the ranks to animate his troops, he received a mortal stroke from the javelin of Andages, a noble Ostrogoth, and immediately fell from his horse. The wounded king was oppressed in the general disorder and trampled under the feet of his own cavalry. The Visigoths, who had been thrown into confusion by the flight, or defection, of the Alani, gradually restored their order of battle; and the Huns were undoubtedly vanquished, since Attila was compelled to retreat. He had exposed his person with the rashness of a private soldier; but the intrepid troops of the center had pushed forwards beyond the rest of the line; their attack was faintly supported; their flanks were unguarded; and the conquerors of Scythia and Germany were saved by the approach of the night from a total defeat.

Neither the spirit, nor the forces, nor the reputation of Attila were impaired by the failure of the Gallic expedition. In the ensuing spring he repeated his demand of the princess Honoria and her patrimonial treasures. The demand was again rejected or eluded; and the indignant lover immediately took the field, passed the Alps, invaded Italy, and besieged Aquileia with an innumerable host of barbarians. The Huns mounted to the assault with irresistible fury; and the succeeding generation could scarcely discover the ruins of Aquileia. After this dreadful chastisement, Attila pursued his march; and as he passed, the cities of Altinum, Concordia, and Padua were reduced into heaps of stones and ashes. The inland towns, Vicenza, Verona, and Bergamo, were exposed to the rapacious cruelty of the Huns. Milan and Pavia submitted to the loss of their wealth; and applauded the unusual clemency which preserved from the flames the public as well as private buildings, and spared the lives of the captive multitude.

The Italians, who had long since renounced the exercise of arms, were surprised, after forty years' peace, by the approach of a formidable barbarian, whom they abhorred as the enemy of their religion as well as of their republic. Amidst the general consternation, Aëtius alone was incapable of fear; but it was impossible that he should achieve alone and unassisted any military exploits worthy of his former renown. The barbarians who had defended Gaul refused to march to the relief of Italy; and the succours promised by the Eastern emperor were distant and doubtful. Since Aëtius, at the head of his domestic troops, still maintained the field, and harassed or retarded the march of Attila, he never showed himself more truly great than at the time when his conduct was blamed by an ignorant and ungrateful people. If the mind of Valentinian had been susceptible of any generous sentiments, he would have chosen such a general for his example and his guide. But the timid grandson of Theodosius, instead of sharing the dangers, escaped from the sound of war; and his hasty retreat from Ravenna to Rome, from an impregnable fortress to an open capital, betrayed his secret intention of abandoning Italy as soon as the danger should approach his Imperial person. This shameful abdication was suspended, however, by the spirit of doubt and delay which commonly adheres to pusillani-

Right: The extent of the Hunnish empire under Attila (c AD 406–453).
Below: Coin of the Roman Emperor Marcian (Marcianus AD 396–457, Roman Emperor of the East AD 450–57) who challenged and met the attacks of Attila in Italy. (The British Museum, London)

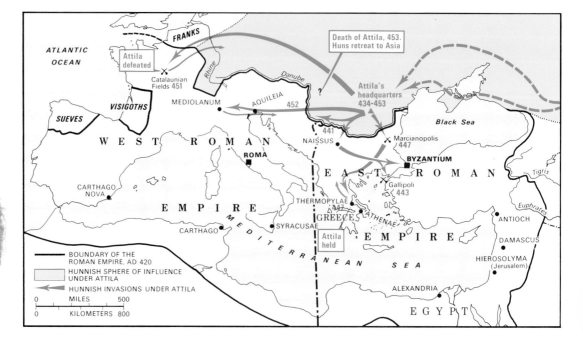

Attila the Hun greeted by Pope Leo the Great (c 390–461) in flowing sacerdotal robes is persuaded to abandon his design of sacking Rome, AD 452. (Painting by Raphael 1483–1520 now in the Vatican, Rome)

mous counsels, and sometimes corrects their pernicious tendency. The Western emperor, with the senate and people of Rome, embraced the more salutary resolution of deprecating, by a solemn and suppliant embassy, the wrath of Attila. This important commission was accepted by Avienus, who, from his birth and riches, his consular dignity, the numerous train of his clients, and his personal abilities, held the first rank in the Roman senate. The specious and artful character of Avienus was admirably qualified to conduct a negotiation either of public or private interest: his colleague Trigetius had exercised the Prætorian præfecture of Italy; and Leo, bishop of Rome, consented to expose his life for the safety of his flock. The genius of Leo was exercised and displayed in the public misfortunes; and he has deserved the appellation of *Great* by the successful zeal with which he labored to establish his opinions and his authority, under the venerable names of orthodox faith and ecclesiastical discipline. The Roman ambassadors were introduced to the tent of Attila, as he lay encamped. The barbarian monarch listened with favorable, and even respectful, attention; and the deliverance of Italy was purchased by the immense ransom or dowry of the princess Honoria. The state of his army might facilitate the treaty and hasten his retreat. Their martial spirit was relaxed by the wealth and indolence of a warm climate. The shepherds of the North, whose ordinary food consisted of milk and raw flesh, indulged themselves too freely in the use of bread, of wine, and of meat prepared and seasoned by the arts of cookery; and the progress of disease revenged in some measure the injuries of the Italians. When Attila declared his resolution of carrying his victorious arms to the gates of Rome, he was admonished by his friends, as well as by his enemies, that Alaric had not long survived the conquest of the eternal city. His mind, superior to real danger, was assaulted by imaginary terrors; nor could he escape the influence of superstition, which had so often been subservient to his designs. The pressing eloquence of Leo, his majestic aspect and sacerdotal robes, excited the veneration of Attila for the spiritual father of the Christians. The apparition of the two apostles of St Peter and St Paul, who menaced the barbarian with instant death if he rejected the prayer of their successor, is one of the noblest legends of ecclesiastical tradition. The safety of Rome might deserve the interposition of celestial beings; and some indulgence is due to a fable which has been represented by the pencil of Raphael and the chisel of Algardi.

Before the king of the Huns evacuated Italy, he threatened to return more dreadful, and more implacable, if his bride, the Princess Honoria, were not delivered to his ambassadors within the term stipulated by the treaty. But he died shortly after returning to his wooden palace beyond the Danube. Yet, in the meanwhile, Attila relieved his tender anxiety, by adding a beautiful maid, whose name was Ildico, to the list of his innumerable wives. Their marriage was celebrated with barbaric pomp and festivity, at his wooden palace beyond the Danube; and the monarch, oppressed with wine and sleep, retired at a late hour from the banquet to the nuptial bed. His attendants continued to respect his pleasures or his repose the greatest part of the ensuing day, till the unusual silence alarmed their fears and suspicions; and, after attempt-

ing to awaken Attila by loud and repeated cries, they at length broke into the royal apartment. They found the trembling bride sitting by the bedside, hiding her face with her veil, and lamenting her own danger, as well as the death of the king, who had expired during the night. His body was solemnly exposed in the midst of the plain, under a silken pavilion; and the chosen squadrons of the Huns, wheeling round in measured evolutions, chanted a funeral song to the memory of a hero, glorious in his life, invincible in his death, the father of his people, the scourge of his enemies, and the terror of the world.

Attila had fondly or superstitiously believed that Irnac, the youngest of his sons, was destined to perpetuate the glories of his race. The character of that prince, who attempted to moderate the rashness of his brother Dengisich, was more suitable to the declining condition of the Huns; and Irnac, with his subject hordes, retired into the heart of the Lesser Scythia. They were soon overwhelmed by a torrent of new barbarians, who followed the same road which their own ancestors had formerly discovered The *Geougen*, or Avares, whose residence is assigned by the Greek writers to the shores of the ocean, impelled the adjacent tribes; till at length the Igours of the North, issuing from the cold Siberian regions which produce the most valuable furs spread themselves over the desert as far as the Borysthenes and the Caspian gates, and finally extinguished the empire of the Huns.

Such an event might contribute to the safety of the Eastern empire under the reign of a prince who conciliated the friendship, without forfeiting the esteem, of the barbarians. But the emperor of the West, the feeble and dissolute Valentinian, who had reached his thirty-fifth year without attaining the age of reason or courage, abused this apparent security to undermine the foundations of his own throne by the murder of the patrician Aëtius; the man who was universally celebrated as the terror of the barbarians and the support of the republic.

The luxury of Rome seems to have attracted the long and frequent visits of Valentinian, who was consequently more despised at Rome than in any other part of his dominions. A republican spirit was insensibly revived in the senate, as their authority, and even their supplies, became necessary for the support of his feeble government. The stately demeanor of an hereditary monarch offended their pride, and the pleasures of Valentinian were injurious to the peace and honor of noble families. The birth of the empress Eudoxia was equal to his own, and her charms and tender affection deserved those testimonies of love which her inconstant husband dissipated in vague and unlawful amors. Petronius Maximus, a wealthy senator of the Anician family, who had been twice consul, was possessed of a chaste and beautiful wife: her obstinate resistance served only to irritate the desires of Valentinian, and he resolved to accomplish them either by stratagem or force. Deep gaming was one of the vices of the court; the emperor, who, by chance or contrivance, had gained from Maximus a considerable sum, uncourteously exacted his ring as a security for the debt, and sent it by a trusty messenger to his wife, with an order in her husband's name that she should immediately attend the empress Eudoxia. The unsuspecting wife of Maximus was conveyed in her litter to the Imperial palace; the emissaries of her impatient lover conducted her to a remote and silent bed-chamber; and Valentinian violated, without remorse, the laws of hospitality. Her tears when she returned home, her deep affliction, and the bitter reproaches against a husband whom she considered as the accomplice of his own shame, excited Maximus to a just revenge; the desire of revenge was stimulated by ambition; and he might reasonably aspire, by the free suffrage of the Roman senate, to the throne of a destested and despicable rival. Valentinian, who supposed that every human breast was devoid like his own of friendship and gratitude, had imprudently admitted among his guards several domestics and followers of Aëtius. Two of these, of barbarian race, were persuaded to execute a sacred and honorable duty by punishing with death the assassin of their patron; and their intrepid courage did not long expect a favorable moment. While Valentinian amused himself in the field of Mars with the spectacle of some military sports, they suddenly rushed upon him with drawn weapons, dispatched the guilty Heraclius, and stabbed the emperor to the heart, without the least opposition from his numerous train, who seemed to rejoice in the tyrant's death. Such was the fate of Valentinian the Third, the last Roman emperor of the family of Theodosius.

CHAPTER TWENTY-NINE

Sack of Rome by Genseric, the Vandal

succession of the last Emperors of the West, Maximus, Avitus, Marjorian, Severus, Anthemius, Olybrius, Glycerius, Nepos, Augustulus – total extinction of the Western Empire – the reign of Odoacer the first barbarian King of Italy

[AD 430–490]

THE loss or desolation of the provinces from the Ocean to the Alps impaired the glory and greatness of Rome: her internal prosperity was irretrievably destroyed by the separation of Africa. The Vandals and Alani, who followed the successful standard of Genseric, had acquired a rich and fertile territory, which stretched along the coast above ninety days' journey from Tangier to Tripoli; but their narrow limits were pressed and confined, on either side, by the sandy desert and the Mediterranean. The discovery and conquest of the Black nations, that might dwell beneath the torrid zone, could not tempt the rational ambition of Genseric; but he cast his eyes towards the sea; he resolved to create a naval power. He immediately equipped a numerous fleet of Vandals and Moors, and cast anchor at the mouth of the Tiber, about three months after the death of Valentinian and the elevation of Maximus to the Imperial throne.

Whatever abilities Maximus might have shown in a subordinate station, he was found incapable of administering an empire: and though he might easily have been informed of the naval preparations which were made on the opposite shores of Africa, he expected with supine indifference the approach of the enemy, without adopting any measures of defense, of negotiation, or of a timely retreat. When the Vandals disembarked at the mouth of the Tiber, the emperor was suddenly roused from his lethargy by the clamors of a trembling and exasperated multitude.

On the third day after the tumult, Genseric boldly advanced from the port of Ostia to the gates of the defenseless city. Instead of a sally of the Roman youth, there issued from the gates an unarmed and venerable procession of the bishop at the head of his clergy. The fearless spirit of Leo, his authority and eloquence, *again* mitigated the fierceness of a barbarian conqueror: the king of the Vandals promised to spare the unresisting multitude, to protect the buildings from fire, and to exempt the captives from torture; and although such orders were neither seriously given, nor strictly obeyed, the mediation of Leo was glorious to himself, and in some degree beneficial to his country. But Rome and its inhabitants were delivered to the licentiousness of the Vandals and Moors. The pillage lasted fourteen days and nights; and all that yet remained of public or private wealth, of sacred or profane treasure, was diligently transported to the vessels of Genseric.

The deaths of Aëtius and Valentinian had relaxed the ties which held the barbarians of Gaul in peace and subordination. The sea-coast was infested by the Saxons; the Alemanni and the Franks advanced from the Rhine to the Seine; and the ambition of the Goths seemed to mediate more extensive and permanent conquests. The emperor Maximus relieved himself, by a judicious choice, from the weight of these distant cares; he silenced the solicitations of his friends, listened to the voice of fame, and promoted a stranger to the general command of the forces in Gaul. Avitus, the stranger whose merit was so nobly rewarded, descended from a wealthy and honorable family in the diocese of Auvergne.

He assumed the military command; the barbarians suspended their fury; and whatever means he might employ, whatever concessions he might be forced to make, the people enjoyed the benefits of actual tranquillity. But the fate of Gaul depended on the Visigoths; and the Roman general, less attentive to his dignity than to the public interest, did not disdain to visit Toulouse in the character of an ambassador. He was received with courteous hospitality by Theodoric, the king of the Goths; but while Avitus laid the foundations of a solid alliance with that powerful nation, he was astonished by the intelligence that the emperor Maximus was slain, and that Rome had been pillaged by the Vandals. A vacant throne, which he might ascend without guilt or danger, tempted his ambition: and the Visigoths were easily persuaded to support his claim by their irresistible suffrage. They loved the person of Avitus; they respected his virtues; and they were not insensible of the advantage, as well as honor, of giving an emperor to the West. The season was now approaching in which the annual assembly of the seven provinces was held at Arles; their deliberations might perhaps be influenced by the presence of Theodoric and his martial brothers; but their choice would naturally incline to the most illustrious of their countrymen. Avitus after a decent resistance, accepted the Imperial diadem from the representatives of Gaul; and his election was ratified by the acclamations of the barbarians and provincials. The formal consent of Marcian, emperor of the East, was solicited and obtained; but the

Left: Detail of a capital, Carthage, Tunisia.
Below: Roman ruin at Sbeitla near the city of Kasserine in the central part of Tunisia.

senate, Rome, and Italy, though humbled by their recent calamities, submitted with a secret murmur to the presumption of the Gallic usurper.

When the king of the Visigoths encouraged Avitus to assume the purple, he offered his person and his forces as a faithful soldier of the republic. The exploits of Theodoric soon convinced the world that he had not degenerated from the warlike virtues of his ancestors. After the establishment of the Goths in Aquitain, and the passage of the Vandals into Africa, the Suevi, who had fixed their kingdom in Gallicia, aspired to the conquest of Spain, and threatened to extinguish the feeble remains of the Roman dominion.

Theodoric carried his victorious arms as far as Merida, the principal town of Lusitania, without meeting any resistance, except from the miraculous powers of St Eulalia; but he was stopped in the full career of success and recalled from Spain before he could provide for the security of his conquests. In his retreat towards the Pyrenees he revenged his disappointment on the country through which he passed; and, in the sack of Polentia and Astorga, he showed himself a faithless ally, as well as a cruel enemy. Whilst the king of the Visigoths fought and vanquished in the name of Avitus, the reign of Avitus had expired; and both the honor and the interest of Theodoric were deeply wounded by the disgrace of a friend whom he had seated on the throne of the Western empire.

Avitus, at a time when the Imperial dignity was reduced to a pre-eminence of toil and danger, indulged himself in the pleasures of Italian luxury: age had not extinguished his amorous inclinations; and he is accused of insulting, with indiscreet and ungenerous raillery, the husbands whose wives he had seduced or violated. But the Romans were not inclined either to excuse his faults or to acknowledge his virtues. The several parts of the empire became every day more alienated from each other; and the stranger of Gaul was the object of popular hatred and contempt. The senate asserted their legitimate claim in the election of an emperor; and their authority, which had been originally derived from the old constitution, was again fortified by the actual weakness of a declining monarchy. Yet even such a monarchy might have resisted the votes of an unarmed senate, if their discontent had not been supported, or perhaps inflamed, by Count Ricimer, one of the principal commanders of the barbarian troops who formed the military defense of Italy. The daughter of Wallia, king of the Visigoths, was the mother of Ricimer; but he was descended, on the father's side, from the nation of the Suevi: his pride or patriotism might be exasperated by the misfortunes of his countrymen; and he obeyed with reluctance an emperor in whose elevation he had not been consulted. His faithful and important services against the common enemy rendered him still more formidable; and, after destroying on the coast of Corsica a fleet of Vandals, which consisted of sixty galleys, Ricimer returned in triumph with the

Left: The Roman theater at Arles, where the annual assembly of seven provinces met to elect Avitus the Emperor of the West.
Top right: Geometrical floor mosaic among the ruins of Carthage. By 429 the Vandals had established themselves as a commanding power in North Africa with their headquarters in the northern granaries of the Empire at Carthage. Rome had relied on Africa for her supplies of grain and with the fall of her African colonies the economy of the Empire was effectively ruined.
Bottom right: The *loggia* and courtyard of the underground villa at Bulla Reggia, Tunisia.

appellation of the Deliverer of Italy. He chose that moment to signify to Avitus that his reign was at an end; and the feeble emperor, at a distance from his Gothic allies, was compelled, after a short and unavailing struggle, to abdicate the purple. By the clemency, however, or the contempt of Ricimer, he was permitted to descend from the throne to the more desirable station of bishop of Placentia: but the resentment of the senate was still unsatisfied; and their inflexible severity pronounced the sentence of his death. He fled towards the Alps, with the humble hope, not of arming the Visigoths in his cause, but of securing his person and treasures in the sanctuary of Julian, one of the tutelar saints of Auvergne. Disease, or the hand of the executioner, arrested him on the road, yet his remains were decently transported to Brivas, or Brioude, in his native province, and he reposed at the feet of his holy patron.

The successor of Avitus presents the welcome discovery of a great and heroic character, such as sometimes arises, in a degenerate age, to vindicate the honor of the human species. The emperor Marjorian has deserved the praises of his contemporaries and of posterity. His intimate connection with Count Ricimer was the immediate step by which he ascended the throne of the Western empire. During the vacancy that succeeded the abdication of Avitus, the ambitious barbarian, whose birth excluded him from the Imperial dignity, governed Italy, with the title of Patrician; resigned to his friend the conspicuous station of master-general of the cavalry and infantry, and, after an interval of some months, consented to the unanimous wish of the Romans, whose favor Marjorian had solicited by a recent victory over the Alemanni.

The private and public actions of Marjorian are very imperfectly known: but his laws, remarkable for an original cast of thought and expression, faithfully represent the character of a sovereign who loved his people, who sympathized in their distress, who had studied the causes of the decline of the empire, and who was capable of applying (as far as such reformation was practicable) judicious and effectual remedies to the public disorders.

Left: Richly worked Byzantine silk shroud. (Sixth century, British Museum)
Right: Statue from Ostia of a bearded man wearing a toga, a man of letters or philosopher, his book lying at his feet.
Below: The Vandals under their leader Genseric plunder the city of Rome AD 455.

While the emperor Marjorian assiduously labored to restore the happiness and virtue of the Romans, he encountered the arms of Genseric, from his character and situation their most formidable enemy. In the ensuing action the Roman fleet was destroyed at Carthegena and Marjorian was forced to accept Genseric's entreaties for a peaceful settlement.

The recent misfortune of Carthegena sullied the glory which had dazzled the eyes of the multitude: almost every description of civil and military officers were exasperated against the Reformer, since they all derived some advantage from the abuses which he endeavored to suppress; and the patrician Ricimer impelled the inconstant passions of the barbarians against a prince whom he esteemed and hated. The virtues of Marjorian could not protect him from the impetuous sedition which broke out in the camp near Tortona at the foot of the Alps. He was compelled to abdicate the Imperial purple; five days after his abdication it was reported that he died of a dysentery; and the humble tomb which covered his remains was consecrated by the respect and gratitude of succeeding generations.

It was not perhaps without some regret that Ricimer sacrificed his friend to the interest of his ambition: but he resolved in a second choice to avoid the imprudent preference of superior virtue and merit. At his command the obsequious senate of Rome bestowed the Imperial title on Libius Severus. History has scarcely deigned to notice his birth, his elevation, his character, or his death. Severus expired as soon as his life became inconvenient to his patron; and it would be useless to discriminate his nominal reign in the vacant interval of six years between the death of Marjorian and the elevation of Anthemius. During that period the government was in the hands of Ricimer alone; and although the modest barbarian disclaimed the name of king, he accumulated treasures, formed a separate army, negotiated private alliances, and ruled Italy with the same independent and despotic authority which was afterwards exercised by Odoacer and Theodoric.

The kingdom of Italy, a name to which the Western empire was gradually reduced, was afflicted, under the reign of Ricimer, by the incessant depredations of the Vandal pirates. In the spring of each year they equipped a formidable navy in the port of Carthage, and Genseric himself, though in a very advanced age, still commanded in person the most important expeditions.

The haughty Ricimer, who had long struggled with the difficulties of his situation, was at length reduced to address the throne of Constantinople in the humble language of a subject; and Italy submitted, as the price and security of the alliance, to accept a master from the choice of the emperor of the East.

Leo listened to the complaints of the Italians; resolved to extirpate the tyranny of the Vandals; and declared his alliance with his colleague Anthemius, whom he solemnly invested with the diadem and purple of the West.

In all his public declarations the emperor Leo assumes the authority, and professes the affection of a father for his son Anthemius, with whom he had divided the administration of the universe. The situation, and perhaps the character, of Leo dissuaded him from exposing his person to the toils and dangers of an African war. But the powers of the Eastern empire were strenuously exerted to deliver Italy and the Mediterranean from the Vandals; and Genseric, who had so long oppressed both the land and sea, was threatened from every side with a formidable invasion. The fleet that sailed from Constantinople to Carthage consisted of eleven hundred and thirteen ships, and the number of soldiers and mariners exceeded one hundred thousand men. Basiliscus, the brother of the empress Verina, was intrusted with this important command. His sister, the wife of Leo, had exaggerated the merit of his former exploits against the Scythians. But the discovery of his guilt, or incapacity, was reserved for the African war; and his friends could only save his military reputation by asserting that he had conspired with Aspar to spare Genseric, and to betray the last hope of the Western empire.

The formidable navy of Basiliscus pursued its prosperous navigation from the Thracian Bosphorus to the coast of Africa. He landed his troops at Cape Bona, or the promontory of Mercury, about forty miles from Carthage. The army of Heraclius, and the fleet of Marcellinus, either joined or seconded the Imperial lieutenant; and the Vandals who opposed his progress by sea or land were successively vanquished. If Basiliscus had seized the moment of consternation, and boldly advanced to the capital, Carthage must have surrendered, and the kingdom of the Vandals was extinguished. Genseric beheld the danger with firmness, and eluded it with his veteran dexterity. During this short interval the wind became favorable to the designs of Genseric. He manned his largest ships of war with the bravest of the Moors and Vandals; and they towed after them many large barks filled with combustible materials. In the obscurity of the night, these destructive vessels were impelled against the unguarded and unsuspecting fleet of the Romans. Their close and crowded order assisted the progress of the fire, which was communicated with rapid and irresistible violence. While they labored to extricate themselves from the fire-ships, and to save at least a part of the navy, the galleys of Genseric assaulted them with temperate and disciplined valor; and many of the Romans, who

escaped the fury of the flames, were destroyed or taken by the victorious Vandals. Basiliscus, whose station was the most remote from danger, disgracefully fled in the beginning of the engagement, returned to Constantinople with the loss of more than half of his fleet and army, and sheltered his guilty head in the sanctuary of St Sophia, till his sister, by her tears and entreaties, could obtain his pardon from the indignant emperor.

The peaceful and prosperous reign which Anthemius had promised to the West was soon clouded by misfortune and discord. Ricimer,

Left: The ruins of Thurburbo Majus, the ancient city of Tunisia, 34 miles south of Tunis, which had been made into a Roman colony in 27 BC.
Below: Theodoric the Ostrogoth's (AD 455–526) palace at Ravenna. (Mosaic from Saint Apollinaire Nuovo, sixth century)

apprehensive or impatient of a superior, retired from Rome and fixed his residence at Milan; an advantageous situation, either to invite or to repel the warlike tribes that were seated between the Alps and the Danube. Italy was gradually divided into two independent and hostile kingdoms. Ricimer suspended his ambitious designs till he had secretly prepared the engines with which he resolved to subvert the throne of Anthemius. The mask of peace and moderation was then thrown aside. The army of Ricimer was fortified by a numerous reinforcement of Burgundians and Oriental Suevi: he disclaimed all allegiance to the Greek emperor, marched from Milan to the gates of Rome, and, fixing his camp on the banks of the Anio, impatiently expected the arrival of Olybrius, his Imperial candidate.

The senator Olybrius, of the Anician family, might esteem himself the lawful heir of the Western empire. He had married Placidia, the younger daughter of Valentinian, after she was restored by Genseric, who still detained her sister Eudoxia, as the wife, or rather as the captive, of his son. The king of the Vandals supported, by threats and solicitations, the fair pretensions of his Roman ally; and assigned, as

one of the motives of the war, the refusal of the senate and people to acknowledge their lawful prince, and the unworthy preference which they had given to a stranger. The friendship of the public enemy might render Olybrius still more unpopular to the Italians; but when Ricimer meditated the ruin of the emperor Anthemius, he tempted, with the offer of a diadem, the candidate who could justify his rebellion by an illustrious name and a royal alliance. Olybrius yielded to the importunities of his friends, perhaps of his wife; rashly plunged into the dangers and calamities of a civil war; and, with the secret connivance of the emperor Leo, accepted the Italian purple, which was bestowed, and resumed, at the capricious will of a barbarian. He landed without obstacle (for Genseric was master of the sea) either at Ravenna or the port of Ostia, and immediately proceeded to the camp of Ricimer, where he was received as the sovereign of the Western world.

The patrician, who had extended his posts from the Anio to the Milvian bridge, already possessed two quarters of Rome, the Vatican and the Janiculum, which are separated by the Tiber from the rest of the city; and it may be conjectured that an assembly of seceding senators imitated, in the choice of Olybrius, the forms of a legal election. But the body of the senate and people firmly adhered to the cause of Anthemius; and the more effectual support of a Gothic army enabled him to prolong his reign, and the public distress, by a resistance of three months, which produced the concomitant evils of famine and pestilence. At length Ricimer made a furious assault on the bridge of Hadrian, or St Angelo; and the narrow pass was defended with equal valor by the Goths till the death of Gilimer, their leader. The victorious troops, breaking down every barrier, rushed with irresistible violence into the heart of the city, and Rome (if we may use the language of a contemporary pope) was subverted by the civil fury of Anthemius and Ricimer. The unfortunate Anthemius was dragged from his concealment and inhumanly massacred by the command of his son-in-law, who thus added a third, or perhaps a fourth, emperor to the number of his victims. Forty days after this calamitous event, the subject, not of glory, but of guilt, Italy was delivered, by a painful disease, from the tyrant Ricimer, who bequeathed the command of his army to his nephew Gundobald, one of the princes of the Burgundians. In the same year all the principal actors in this great revolution were removed from the stage; and the whole reign of Olybrius, whose death does not betray any symptoms of violence, is included within the term of seven months. He left one daughter, the offspring of his marriage with Placidia; and the family of the great Theodosius, transplanted from Spain to Constantinople, was propagated in the female line as far as the eighth generation.

While the vacant throne of Italy was abandoned to lawless barbarians, the election of a new colleague was seriously agitated in the council of Leo. The empress Verina, studious to promote the greatness of her own family, had married one of her nieces to Julius Nepos, who succeeded his uncle Marcellinus in the sovereignty of Dalmatia, a more solid possession than the title which he was persuaded to accept of Emperor of the West. But the measures of the Byzantine court were so languid and irresolute, that many months elapsed after the death of Anthemius, and even of Olybrius, before their destined successor could show himself, with a respectable force, to his Italian subjects. During that interval, Glycerius, an obscure soldier, was invested with the purple by his patron Gundobald; but the Burgundian prince was unable or unwilling to support his nomination by a civil war: the pursuits of domestic ambition recalled him beyond the Alps, and his client was permitted to exchange the Roman scepter for the bishopric of Salona. After extinguishing such a competitor, the emperor Nepos was acknowledged by the senate, by the Italians, and by the provincials of Gaul; his mortal virtues and military talents were loudly celebrated;

Theodoric's Mausoleum, at Ravenna. The tomb was built by his daughter Amulsuntha AD 520.

and those who derived any private benefit from his government announced in prophetic strains the restoration of the public felicity. Their hopes (if such hopes had been entertained) were confounded within the term of a single year; and the treaty of peace, which ceded Auvergne to the Visigoths, is the only event of his short and inglorious reign. The most faithful subjects of Gaul were sacrificed by the Italian emperor to the hope of domestic security; but his repose was soon invaded by a furious sedition of the barbarian confederates, who, under the command of Orestes, their general, were in full march from Rome to Ravenna. Nepos trembled at their approach; and, instead of placing a just confidence in the strength of Ravenna, he hastily escaped to his ships, and retired to his Dalmatian principality, on the opposite coast of the Hadriatic. By this shameful abdication he protracted his life about five years, in a very ambiguous state between an emperor and an exile, till he was assassinated at Salona by the ungrateful Glycerius, who was translated, perhaps as the reward of his crime, to the archbishopric of Milan.

The nations who had asserted their independence after the death of Attila were established, by the right of possession or conquest, in the boundless countries to the north of the Danube; or in the Roman provinces between the river and the Alps. But the bravest of their youth enlisted in the army of *confederates*, who formed the defense and the terror of Italy; and in this promiscuous multitude, the names of the Heruli, the Sciri, the Alani, the Turcilingi, and the Rugians, appear to have predominated. The example of these warriors was imitated by Orestes, the son of Tatullus, and the father of the last Roman emperor of the West. Orestes had never deserted his country. His birth and fortunes rendered him one of the most illustrious subjects of Pannonia. When that province was ceded to the Huns, he entered into the service of Attila, his lawful sovereign, obtained the office of his secretary, and was repeatedly sent ambassador to Constantinople, to represent the person and signify the commands of the imperious monarch. The death of that conqueror restored him to his freedom; and Orestes might honorably refuse either to follow the sons of Attila into the Scythian desert, or to obey the Ostrogoths, who had usurped the dominion of Pannonia. He preferred the service of the Italian princes, the successors of Valentinian; and, as he possessed the qualifications of courage, industry, and experience, he advanced with rapid steps in the military profession, till he was elevated, by the favor of Nepos himself, to the dignities of patrician and master-general of the troops. These troops had been long accustomed to reverence the character and authority of Orestes, who affected their manners, conversed with them in their own language, and was intimately connected with their national chieftains by long habits of familiarity and friendship. At his solicitation they rose in arms against the obscure Greek who presumed to claim their obedience; and when Orestes, from some secret motive, declined the purple, they consented, with the same facility, to acknowledge his son Agustulus as the emperor of the West. By the abdication of Nepos, Orestes had now attained the summit of his ambitious hopes; but he soon discovered, before the end of the first year, that the lessons of

The ruins of the theater at Carthage set into the hillside.

perjury and ingratitude which a rebel must inculcate will be retorted against himself, and that the precarious sovereign of Italy was only permitted to choose whether he would be the slave or the victim of his barbarian mercenaries. The dangerous alliance of these strangers had oppressed and insulted the last remains of Roman freedom and dignity. At each revolution their pay and privileges were augmented; but their insolence increased in a still more extravagant degree; they envied the fortune of their brethren in Gaul, Spain, and Africa, whose victorious arms had acquired an independent and perpetual inheritance; and they insisted on their peremptory demand that a *third* part of the lands of Italy should be immediately divided among them. Orestes, with a spirit which, in another situation, might be entitled to our esteem, chose rather to encounter the rage of an armed multitude than to subscribe the ruin of an innocent people. He rejected the audacious demand; and his refusal was favorable to the ambition of Odoacer, a bold barbarian. From all the camps and garrisons of Italy the confederates, actuated by the same resentment and the same hopes, impatiently flocked to the standard of this popular leader; and the unfortunate patrician, over-whelmed by the torrent, hastily retreated to the strong city of Pavia, the episcopal seat of the holy Epiphanites. Pavia was immediately besieged, the fortifications were stormed, the town was pillaged; and although the bishop might labor, with much zeal and some success, to save the property of the church and the chastity of female captives, the tumult could only be appeased by the execution of Orestes. His brother Paul was slain in an action near Ravenna; and the helpless Augustulus, was reduced to implore the clemency of Odoacer.

The barbarian, whose daring spirit accepted and ratified the pre-diction, was admitted into the service of the Western empire, and soon obtained an honorable rank in the guards. His manners were gradually polished, his military skill was improved, and the confederates of Italy would not have elected him for their general unless the exploits of Odoacer had established a high opinion of his courage and capacity. Their military acclamations saluted him with the title of king; but he abstained during his whole reign from the use of the purple and diadem, lest he should offend those princes whose subjects, by their accidental mixture, had formed the victorious army which time and policy might insensibly unite into a great nation.

The unfortunate Augustulus was made the instrument of his own disgrace; he signified his resignation to the senate; and that assembly, in their last act of obedience to a Roman prince, still affected the spirit of freedom and the forms of the constitution. An epistle was addressed, by their unanimous decree, to the emperor Zeno, the son-in-law and successor of Leo, who had lately been restored, after a short rebellion, to the Byzantine throne. They solemnly 'disclaim the necessity, or even the wish, of continuing any longer the Imperial succession in Italy; since, in their opinion, the majesty of a sole monarch is sufficient to pervade and protect, at the same time, both the East and the West. In their own name, and in the name of the people, they consent that the seat of universal empire shall be transferred from Rome to Con-stantinople; and they basely renounce the right of choosing their master, the only vestige that yet remained of the authority which had given laws to the world. The republic (they repeat that name without a blush) might safely confide in the civil and military virtues of Odoacer; and they humbly request that the emperor would invest him with the title of Patrician, and the administration of the *diocese* of Italy.' The deputies of the senate were received at Constantinople with some marks of displeasure and indignation: and when they were admitted to the audience of Zeno, he sternly reproached them with their treatment of the two emperors, Anthemius and Nepos, whom the East had successively granted to the prayers of Italy. 'The first (continued he) you have murdered; the second you have expelled: but the second is still alive, and whilst he lives he is your lawful sovereign.' But the prudent Zeno soon deserted the hopeless cause of his abdicated col-league. His vanity was gratified by the title of sole emperor, and by the statues erected to his honor in the several quarters of Rome; he entertained a friendly, though ambiguous, correspondence with the *patrician* Odoacer; and he accepted the Imperial ensigns which the barbarian was not unwilling to remove from the sight of the people.

The life of this inoffensive youth was spared by the generous clem-ency of Odoacer; who dismissed him, with his whole family, from the Imperial palace, fixed his annual allowance at six thousand pieces of gold, and assigned the castle of Lucullus, in Campania, for his exile.

Odoacer was the first barbarian who reigned in Italy, over a people who had once asserted their just superiority above the rest of mankind. The disgrace of the Romans still excites our respectful compassion, and we fondly sympathize with the imaginary grief and indignation of their degenerate posterity. But the calamities of Italy had gradually subdued the proud consciousness of freedom and glory. In the age of Roman virtue the provinces were subject to the arms, and the citizens to the laws, of the republic, till those laws were subverted by civil discord, and both the city and the provinces became the servile property of a tyrant. The forms of the constitution, which alleviated or disguised their abject slavery, were abolished by time and violence; the Italians alternately lamented the presence or the absence of the sovereigns whom they detested or despised; and the succession of five centuries inflicted the various evils of military license, capricious despotism, and elaborate oppression. During the same period, the barbarians had emerged from obscurity and contempt, and the warriors of Germany and Scythia were introduced into the provinces, as the servants, the allies, and at length the masters, of the Romans, whom they insulted or protected. The hatred of the people was suppressed by fear; they respected the spirit and splendor of the martial chiefs who were invested with the honors of the empire; and the fate of Rome had long depended on the sword of those formidable strangers. The stern Ricimer, who trampled on the ruins of Italy, had exercised the power, without assuming the title, of a king; and the patient Romans were insensibly prepared to acknowledge the royalty of Odoacer and his barbaric successors.

The king of Italy was not unworthy of the high station to which his valor and fortune had exalted him: his savage manners were polished by the habits of conversation; and he respected, though a conqueror and a barbarian, the institutions, and even the prejudices, of his subjects. After an interval of seven years, Odoacer restored the consulship of the West. For himself, he modestly, or proudly, declined an honor which was still accepted by the emperors of the East; but the curule chair was successively filled by eleven of the most illustrious senators; and the list is adorned by the respectable name of Basilius, whose virtues claimed the friendship and grateful applause of Sidonius, his client. The laws of the emperors were strictly enforced, and the civil administration of Italy was still exercised by the Prætorian præfect and his subordinate officers. Odoacer devolved on the Roman magistrates the odious and oppressive task of collecting the public revenue; but he reserved for himself the merit of seasonable and popular indulgence. Like the rest of the barbarians, he had been instructed in the Arian heresy; but he revered the monastic and episcopal characters; and the silence of the catholics attests the toleration which they enjoyed. The peace of the city required the interposition of his præfect Basilius in the choice of a Roman pontiff: the decree which restrained the clergy from alienating their lands was ultimately designed for the benefit of the people, whose devotion would have been taxed to repair the dilapidations of the church. Italy was protected by the arms of its conqueror; and its frontiers were respected by the barbarians of Gaul and Germany, who had so long insulted the feeble race of Theodosius. Odoacer passed the Hadriatic, to chastise the assassins of the emperor Nepos, and to acquire the maritime province of Dalmatia. He passed the Alps, to rescue the remains of Noricum from Fava, or Feletheus, king of the Rugians, who held his residence beyond the Danube. The king was vanquished in battle, and led away prisoner; a numerous colony of captives and subjects was transplanted into Italy; and Rome, after a long period of defeat and disgrace, might claim the triumph of her barbarian master.

Left: Vandal horseman leaving his villa. The Vandals soon adopted the Roman way of life. (Mosaic, fifth century AD, Carthage, Tunisia)
Right: The Attack on Rome by the Vandals.

Notwithstanding the prudence and success of Odoacer, his kingdom exhibited the sad prospect of misery and desolation. Since the age of Tiberius, the decay of agriculture had been felt in Italy; and it was a just subject of complaint that the life of the Roman people depended on the accidents of the winds and waves. In the division and the decline of the empire, the tributary harvests of Egypt and Africa were withdrawn; the numbers of the inhabitants continually diminished with the means of subsistence; and the country was exhausted by the irretrievable losses of war, famine, and pestilence. The decline of the arts reduced the industrious mechanic to idleness and want; and the senators, who might support with patience the ruin of their country, bewailed their private loss of wealth and luxury. One third of those ample estates, to which the ruin of Italy is originally imputed, was extorted for the use of the conquerors. Injuries were aggravated by insults; the sense of actual sufferings was embittered by the fear of more dreadful evils; and as new lands were allotted to new swarms of barbarians, each senator was apprehensive lest the arbitrary surveyors should approach his favorite villa, or his most profitable farm. The distress of Italy was mitigated by the prudence and humanity of Odoacer, who had bound himself, as the price of his elevation, to satisfy the demands of a licentious and turbulent multitude. The kings of the barbarians were frequently resisted, deposed, or murdered, by their *native* subjects; and the various bands of Italian mercenaries, who associated under the standard of an elective general, claimed a larger privilege of freedom and rapine. A monarchy destitute of national union and hereditary right hastened to its dissolution. After a reign of fourteen years Odoacer was oppressed by the superior genius of Theodoric, king of the Ostrogoths; a hero alike excellent in the arts of war and of government, who restored an age of peace and prosperity, and whose name still excites and deserves the attention of mankind.

I have now accomplished the laborious narrative of the decline and fall of the Roman empire, from the fortunate age of Trajan and the Antonines to its total extinction in the West, about five centuries after the Christian era. At that unhappy period the Saxons fiercely struggled with the natives for the possession of Britain: Gaul and Spain were divided between the powerful monarchies of the Franks and Visigoths and the dependent kingdoms of the Suevi and Burgundians: Africa was

Clovis, King of the Franks, established the Salian dynasty in France.
(*Ms Douce* 267, fol. 12ᵛ 57, The Bodleian Library, Oxford)

exposed to the cruel persecution of the Vandals and the savage insults of the Moors: Rome and Italy, as far as the banks of the Danube, were afflicted by an army of barbarian mercenaries, whose lawless tyranny was succeeded by the reign of Theodoric the Ostrogoth. All the subjects of the empire, who, by the use of the Latin language, more particularly deserved the name and privilege of Romans, were oppressed by the disgrace and calamities of foreign conquest; and the victorious nations of Germany established a new system of manners and government in the western countries of Europe. The majesty of Rome was faintly represented by the princes of Constantinople, the feeble and imaginary successors of Augustus. Yet they continued to reign over the East, from the Danube to the Nile and Tigris; the Gothic and Vandal kingdoms of Italy and Africa were subverted by the arms of Justinian; and the history of the *Greek* emperors may still afford a long series of instructive lessons and interesting revolutions.

The rise of a city, which swelled into an empire, may deserve, as a singular prodigy, the reflection of a philosophic mind. But the decline of Rome was the natural and inevitable effect of immoderate greatness. Prosperity ripened the principle of decay; the causes of destruction multiplied with the extent of conquest; and as soon as time or accident had removed the artificial supports, the stupendous fabric yielded to the pressure of its own weight. The story of its ruin is simple and obvious; and instead of inquiring *why* the Roman empire was destroyed, we should rather be surprised that it had subsisted so long. The victorious legions, who, in distant wars, acquired the vices of strangers and mercenaries, first oppressed the freedom of the republic, and afterwards violated the majesty of the purple. The emperors, anxious for their personal safety and the public peace, were reduced to the base expedient of corrupting the discipline which rendered them alike formidable to their sovereign and to the enemy; the vigor of the military government was relaxed and finally dissolved by the partial institutions of Constantine; and the Roman world was overwhelmed by a deluge of barbarians.

The decay of Rome has been frequently ascribed to the translation of the seat of empire; but this history has already shown that the powers of government were *divided* rather than *removed*. The throne of Constantinople was erected in the East; while the West was still possessed by a series of emperors who held their residence in Italy, and claimed their equal inheritance of the legions and provinces. This dangerous novelty impaired the strength and fomented the vices of a double reign: the instruments of an oppressive and arbitrary system were multiplied; and a vain emulation of luxury, not of merit, was introduced and supported between the degenerate successors of Theodosius. Extreme distress, which unites the virtue of a free people, embitters the factions of a declining monarchy. The hostile favorites of Arcadius and Honorius betrayed the republic to its common enemies; and the Byzantine court beheld with indifference, perhaps with pleasure, the disgrace of Rome, the misfortunes of Italy, and the loss of the West. Under the succeeding reigns the alliance of the two empires was restored; but the aid of the Oriental Romans was tardy, doubtful and ineffectual; and the national schism of the Greeks and Latins was enlarged by the perpetual difference of language and manners, of interests, and even of religion. Yet the salutary event approved in some measure the judgment of Constantine. During a long period of decay his impregnable city repelled the victorious armies of barbarians, protected the wealth of Asia, and commanded, both in peace and war, the important straits which connect the Euxine and Mediterranean seas. The foundation of Constantinople more essentially contributed to the preservation of the East than to the ruin of the West.

As the happiness of a *future* life is the great object of religion, we may hear without surprise or scandal that the introduction, or at least the abuse of Christianity, had some influence on the decline and fall of the Roman empire. The clergy successfully preached the doctrines of patience and pusillanimity; the active virtues of society were discouraged; and the last remains of military spirit were buried in the cloister: a large portion of public and private wealth was consecrated to the specious demands of charity and devotion; and the soldiers' pay was lavished on the useless multitudes of both sexes who could only plead the merits of abstinence and chastity. Faith, zeal, curiosity, and the more earthly passions of malice and ambition, kindled the flame of

The Coronation of Clovis who brought Christianity to the Northern barbarian tribes of Franks. (*Ms Douce* 267, fol. 12ᵛ, The Bodleian Library, Oxford)

and we may inquire, with anxious curiosity, whether Europe is still threatened with a repetition of those calamities which formerly oppressed the arms and institutions of Rome. Perhaps the same reflections will illustrate the fall of that mighty empire, and explain the probable causes of our actual security.

Yet the experience of four thousand years should enlarge our hopes and diminish our apprehensions: we cannot determine to what height the human species may aspire in their advances towards perfection; but it may safely be presumed that no people, unless the face of nature is changed, will relapse into their original barbarism. The improvements of society may be viewed under a threefold aspect. 1. The poet or philosopher illustrates his age and country by the efforts of a *single* mind; but these superior powers of reason or fancy are rare and spontaneous productions; and the genius of Homer, or Cicero, or Newton, would excite less admiration if they could be created by the will of a prince or the lessons of a preceptor. 2. The benefits of law and policy, of trade and manufactures, of arts and sciences, are more solid and permanent; and *many* individuals may be qualified, by education and discipline, to promote, in their respective stations, the interest of the community. But this general order is the effect of skill and labor; and the complex machinery may be decayed by time, or injured by violence. 3. Fortunately for mankind, the more useful, or, at least, more necessary arts, can be performed without superior talents or national subordination; without the powers of *one*, or the union of *many*. Each village, each family, each individual, must always possess both ability and inclination to perpetuate the use of fire and of metals; the propagation and service of domestic animals; the methods of hunting and fishing; the rudiments of navigation; the imperfect cultivation of corn or other nutritive grain; and the simple practice of the mechanic trades. Private genius and public industry may be extirpated; but these hardy plants survive the tempest, and strike an everlasting root into the most unfavorable soil. The splendid days of Augustus and Trajan were eclipsed by a cloud of ignorance; and the barbarians subverted the laws and palaces of Rome. But the scythe, the invention or emblem of Saturn, still continued annually to mow the harvests of Italy; and the human feasts of the Læstrigons have never been renewed on the coast of Campania.

Since the first discovery of the arts, war, commerce, and religious zeal have diffused among the savages of the Old and New World these inestimable gifts; they have been successively propagated; they can never be lost. We may therefore acquiesce in the pleasing conclusion that every age of the world has increased and still increases the real wealth, the happiness, the knowledge, and perhaps the virtue, of the human race.

theological discord; the church, and even the state, were distracted by religious factions, whose conflicts were sometimes bloody and always implacable; the attention of the emperors was diverted from camps to synods; the Roman world was oppressed by a new species of tyranny; and the persecuted sects became the secret enemies of their country. Yet party-spirit, however pernicious or absurd, is a principle of union as well as of dissension. The bishops, from eighteen hundred pulpits, inculcated the duty of passive obedience to a lawful and orthodox sovereign; their frequent assemblies and perpetual correspondence maintained the communion of distant churches; and the benevolent temper of the Gospel was strengthened, though confined, by the spiritual alliance of the catholics. The sacred indolence of the monks was devoutly embraced by a servile and effeminate age; but if superstition had not afforded a decent retreat, the same vices would have tempted the unworthy Romans to desert, from baser motives, the standard of the republic. Religious precepts are easily obeyed which indulge and sanctify the natural inclinations of their votaries; but the pure and genuine influence of Christianity may be traced in its beneficial, though imperfect, effects on the barbarian proselytes of the North. If the decline of the Roman empire was hastened by the conversion of Constantine, his victorious religion broke the violence of the fall, and mollified the ferocious temper of the conquerors.

This awful revolution may be usefully applied to the instruction of the present age. It is the duty of a patriot to prefer and promote the exclusive interest and glory of his native country: but a philosopher may be permitted to enlarge his views, and to consider Europe as one great republic, whose various inhabitants have attained almost the same level of politeness and cultivation. The balance of power will continue to fluctuate, and the prosperity of our own or the neighboring kingdoms may be alternately exalted or depressed; but these partial events can not essentially injure our general state of happiness, the system of arts, and laws, and manners, which so advantageously distinguish, above the rest of mankind, the Europeans and their colonies. The savage nations of the globe are the common enemies of civilized society;

St Augustine's Abbey, Canterbury, Kent, one of the earliest Roman cathedrals.

CHAPTER THIRTY

Byzantium – Theodora – the factions of the circus – the fall of Constantinople

THE emperor Justinian was born near the ruins of Sardica (the modern Sophia), of an obscure race of barbarians, the inhabitants of a wild and desolate country, to which the names of Dardania, of Dacia, and of Bulgaria have been successively applied.

In the exercise of supreme power, the first act of Justinian was to divide it with the woman whom he loved, the famous Theodora, whose strange elevation cannot be applauded as the triumph of female virtue. Under the reign of Anastasius, the care of the wild beasts maintained by the green faction at Constantinople was intrusted to Acacius, a native of the isle of Cyprus, who, from his employment, was surnamed the master of the bears. This honorable office was given after his death to another candidate, notwithstanding the diligence of his widow, who had already provided a husband and a successor. Acacius had left three daughters, Comito, THEODORA, and Anastasia, the eldest of whom did not then exceed the age of seven years. On a solemn festival, these helpless orphans were sent by their distressed and indignant mother, in the garb of suppliants, into the midst of the theater: the green faction received them with contempt, the blues with compassion; and this difference, which sunk deep into the mind of Theodora, was felt long afterwards in the administration of the empire. As they improved in age and beauty, the three sisters were successively devoted to the public and private pleasures of the Byzantine people; and Theodora, after following Comito on the stage, in the dress of a slave, with a stool on her head, was at length permitted to exercise her independent talents. She neither danced, nor sung, nor played on the flute; her skill was confined to the pantomime arts; she excelled in buffoon characters; and as often as the comedian swelled her cheeks, and complained with a ridiculous tone and gesture of the blows that were inflicted, the whole theater of Constantinople resounded with laughter and applause. The beauty of Theodora was the subject of more flattering praise, and the source of more exquisite delight. Her features were delicate and regular; her complexion, though somewhat pale, was tinged with a natural color;

every sensation was instantly expressed by the vivacity of her eyes; her easy motions displayed the graces of a small but elegant figure; and either love or adulation might proclaim that painting and poetry were incapable of delineating the matchless excellence of her form. But this form was degraded by the facility with which it was exposed to the public eye, and prostituted to licentious desire. Her venal charms were abandoned to a promiscuous crowd of citizens and strangers, of every rank and of every profession: the fortunate lover who had been promised a night of enjoyment was often driven from her bed by a stronger or more wealthy favorite; and when she passed through the streets, her presence was avoided by all who wished to escape either the scandal or the temptation. The satirical historian has not blushed to describe the naked scenes which Theodora was not ashamed to exhibit in the theater. After exhausting the arts of sensual pleasure, she most ungratefully murmured against the parsimony of Nature; but her murmurs, her pleasures, and her arts, must be veiled in the obscurity of a learned language. After reigning for some time the delight and contempt of the capital, she condescended to accompany Ecebolus, a native of Tyre, who had obtained the government of the African Pentapolis. But this union was frail and transient: Ecebolus soon rejected an expensive or faithless concubine; she was reduced at Alexandria to extreme distress; and in her laborious return to Constantinople, every city of the East admired and enjoyed the fair Cyprian, whose merit appeared to justify her descent from the peculiar island of Venus. The vague commerce of Theodora, and the most detestable precautions, preserved her from the danger which she feared; yet once, and once only, she became a mother. The infant was saved and educated in Arabia by his father, who imparted to him on his death-bed that he was the son of an empress. Filled with ambitious hopes, the unsuspecting youth immediately hastened to the palace of Constantinople, and was admitted to the presence of his mother. As he was never more seen, even after the decease of Theodora, she deserves the foul imputation of extinguishing with his life a secret so offensive to her imperial virtue.

Left: The Byzantine Empress Theodora (c AD 500–47), wife of Justinian I (Flavius Petrus) Sabbatus Justinianus AD 482–565; Roman Emperor AD 527–565). According to Procopius, Theodora was the daughter of Arcadius the Cypriot and before her marriage to Justinian had been actress and courtesan. She won the Emperor's heart and became his mistress, his wife and his close councilor, saving the throne by her courage during the Nika Riots. (Mosaic for the Basilica of San Vitale, sixth century, Ravenna)

Right: The extent of the Byzantine Empire during the reign of Justinian I. With the help of his general Belisarius (AD 505–565) he briefly restored the empire to its former glory by recapturing Gaul, Italy and the African provinces.

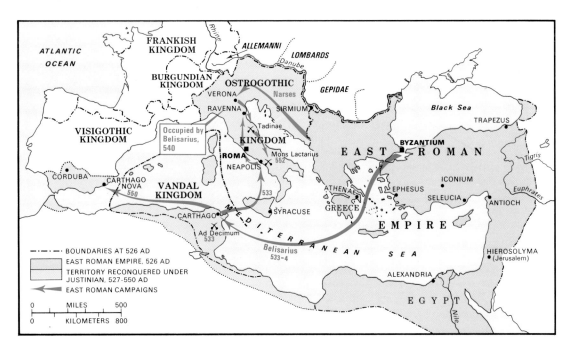

Left: The interior of the Great Dome of the Church of Santa Sophia looking to the East. Erected between AD 532–37 the Church was one of the most remarkable pieces of engineering of the period.
Right: Man feeding his donkey. (Mosaic from the floor of the Great Palace, Istanbul c 567–568)
Below right: View of the southwest of the great dome of the Church of Santa Sophia, Istanbul.

Above: The Emperor Justinian and his court. (Mosaic from the Basilica of San Vitale, Ravenna, Italy, sixth century)

In the most abject state of her fortune and reputation, some vision, either of sleep or of fancy, had whispered to Theodora the pleasing assurance that she was destined to become the spouse of a potent monarch. Conscious of her approaching greatness, she returned from Paphlagonia to Constantinople; assumed, like a skillful actress, a more decent character; relieved her poverty by the laudable industry of spinning wool; and affected a life of chastity and solitude in a small house, which she afterwards changed into a magnificent temple. Her beauty, assisted by art or accident, soon attracted, captivated, and fixed, the patrician Justinian, who already reigned with absolute sway under the name of his uncle. Perhaps she contrived to enhance the value of a gift which she had so often lavished on the meanest of mankind; perhaps she inflamed, at first by modest delays, and at last by sensual allurements, the desires of a lover who, from nature or devotion, was addicted to long vigils and abstemious diet. When his first transports had subsided, she still maintained the same ascendant over his mind by the more solid merit of temper and understanding. Justinian delighted to ennoble and enrich the object of his affection: the treasures of the East were poured at her feet, and the nephew of Justin was determined, perhaps by religious scruples, to bestow on his concubine the sacred and legal character of a wife. But the laws of Rome expressly prohibited the marriage of a senator with any female who had been dishonored by a servile origin or theatrical profession: the empress Lupicina or Euphemia, a barbarian of rustic manners, but of

irreproachable virtue, refused to accept a prostitute for her niece; and even Vigilantia, the superstitious mother of Justinian, though she acknowledged the wit and beauty of Theodora, was seriously apprehensive lest the levity and arrogance of that artful paramour might corrupt the piety and happiness of her son. These obstacles were removed by the inflexible constancy of Justinian. He patiently expected the death of the empress; he despised the tears of his mother, who soon sunk under the weight of her affliction; and a law was promulgated, in the name of the emperor Justin, which abolished the rigid jurisprudence of antiquity. A glorious repentance (the words of the edict) was left open for the unhappy females who had prostituted their persons on the theater, and they were permitted to contract a legal union with the most illustrious of the Romans. This indulgence was speedily followed by the solemn nuptials of Justinian and Theodora; her dignity was gradually exalted with that of her lover; and, as soon as Justin had invested his nephew with the purple, the patriarch of Constantinople placed the diadem on the heads of the emperor and empress of the East. But the usual honors which the severity of Roman manners had allowed to the wives of princes could not satisfy either the ambition of Theodora or the fondness of Justinian. He seated her on the throne as an equal and independent colleague in the sovereignty of the empire, and an oath of allegiance was imposed on the governors of the provinces in the joint names of Justinian and Theodora. The Eastern world fell prostrate before the genius and fortune of the daughter of Acacius. The pro-

stitute who, in the presence of innumerable spectators, had polluted the theater of Constantinople, was adored as a queen in the same city, by grave magistrates, orthodox bishops, victorious generals, and captive monarchs.

But the reproach of cruelty, so repugnant even to her softer vices, has left an indelible stain on the memory of Theodora. Her numerous spies observed and zealously reported every action, or word, or look, injurious to their royal mistress. Whomsoever they accused were cast into her peculiar prisons, inaccessible to the inquiries of justice; and it was rumored that the torture of the rack or scourge had been inflicted in the presence of a female tyrant, insensible to the voice of prayer or of pity. Some of these unhappy victims perished in deep unwholesome dungeons, while others were permitted, after the loss of their limbs, their reason, or their fortune, to appear in the world, the living monuments of her vengeance, which was commonly extended to the children of those whom she had suspected or injured. The senator or bishop whose death or exile Theodora had pronounced, was delivered to a trusty messenger, and his diligence was quickened by a menace from her own mouth. 'If you fail in the execution of my commands, I swear by him who liveth for ever that your skin shall be flayed from your body.'

If the creed of Theodora had not been tainted with heresy, her exemplary devotion might have atoned, in the opinion of her contemporaries, for pride, avarice, and cruelty; but if she employed her influence to assuage the intolerant fury of the emperor, the present age

Above: The triumphant entry of Belisarius into Rome, AD 547.
Left: The Archangel Michael. Angels were a recurring theme in Byzantine art. (Leaf of an early Christian ivory diptych probably made at Constantinople, early sixth century AD, British Museum, London)

will allow some merit to her religion, and much indulgence to her speculative errors. The name of Theodora was introduced, with equal honor, in all the pious and charitable foundations of Justinian; and the most benevolent institution of his reign may be ascribed to the sympathy of the empress for her less fortunate sisters, who had been seduced or compelled to embrace the trade of prostitution. A palace, on the Asiatic side of the Bosphorus, was converted into a stately and spacious monastery, and a liberal maintenance was assigned to five hundred women who had been collected from the streets and brothels of Constantinople. In this safe and holy retreat they were devoted to perpetual confinement; and the despair of some, who threw themselves headlong into the sea, was lost in the gratitude of the penitents who had been delivered from sin and misery by their generous benefactress. The prudence of Theodora is celebrated by Justinian himself; and his laws are attributed to the sage counsels of his most reverend wife, whom he had received as the gift of the Deity. Her courage was displayed amidst the tumult of the people and the terrors of the court. Her chastity, from the moment of her union with Justinian, is founded on the silence of her implacable enemies; and although the daughter of Acacius might be satiated with love, yet some applause is due to the firmness of a mind which could sacrifice pleasure and habit to the stronger sense either of duty or interest. The wishes and prayers of Theodora could never obtain the blessing of a lawful son, and she buried an infant daughter, the sole offspring of her marriage. Notwithstanding this disappointment, her dominion was permanent and absolute; she preserved, by art or merit, the affections of Justinian; and their seeming dissensions were always fatal to the courtiers who believed them to be sincere. Perhaps

two additional colors, a light *green* and a cærulean *blue*, were afterwards introduced; and, as the races were repeated twenty-five times, one hundred chariots contributed in the same day to the pomp of the circus. The four *factions* soon acquired a legal establishment and a mysterious origin, and their fanciful colors were derived from the various appearances of nature in the four seasons of the year; the red dog-star of summer, the snows of winter, the deep shade of autumn, and the cheerful verdure of the spring. Another interpretation preferred the elements to the seasons, and the struggle of the green and blue was supposed to represent the conflict of the earth and sea. Their respective victories announced either a plentiful harvest or a prosperous navigation, and the hostility of the husbandmen and mariners was somewhat less absurd than the blind ardor of the Roman people, who devoted their lives and fortunes to the color which they had espoused. Such folly was disdained and indulged by the wisest princes; but the names of Caligula, Nero, Vitellius, Verus, Commodus, Caracalla, and Elagabalus, were enrolled in the blue or green factions of the circus: they frequented their stables, applauded their favorites, chastised their antagonists, and deserved the esteem of the populace by the natural or effected imitation of their manners. The bloody and tumultuous contest continued to disturb the public festivity till the last age of the spectacles of Rome; and Theodoric, from a motive of justice or affection, interposed his authority to protect the greens against the violence of a consul and a patrician who were passionately addicted to the blue faction of the circus.

Constantinople adopted the follies, though not the virtues, of ancient Rome; and the same factions which had agitated the circus raged with redoubled fury in the hippodrome. Under the reign of Anastasius, this popular frenzy was inflamed by religious zeal; and the greens, who had treacherously concealed stones and daggers under baskets of fruit, massacred at a solemn festival three thousand of the blue adversaries. From the capital this pestilence was diffused into the provinces and cities of the East, and the sportive distinction of two colors produced two strong and irreconcilable factions, which shook the foundations of a feeble government. The popular dissensions, founded on the most serious interest or holy pretence, have scarcely equalled the obstinacy of this wanton discord, which invaded the peace of families, divided friends and brothers, and tempted the female sex, though seldom seen in the circus, to espouse the inclinations of their lovers, or to contradict the wishes of their husbands. Every law, either human or divine, was trampled under foot; and as long as the party was successful, its deluded followers appeared careless of private distress or public calamity. The license, without the freedom, of democracy, was revived at Antioch and Constantinople, and the support of a faction became necessary to every candidate for civil or ecclesiastical honors. A secret attachment to the family or sect of Anastasius was imputed to the greens; the blues were zealously devoted to the cause of orthodoxy and Justinian, and their grateful patron protected, about five years, the disorders of a faction whose seasonable tumults overawed the palace, the senate, and the capitals of the East. Insolent with royal favor, the blues affected to strike terror by a peculiar and barbaric dress – the long hair of the Huns, their close sleeves and ample garments, a lofty step, and a sonorous voice. In the day they concealed their two-edged poniards, but in the night they boldly assembled in arms and in numerous bands, prepared for every act of violence and rapine. Their adversaries of the green faction, or even inoffensive citizens, were stripped and often murdered by these nocturnal robbers, and it became dangerous to wear any gold buttons or girdles, or to appear at a late hour in the streets of a peaceful capital. A daring spirit, rising with impunity, proceeded to violate the safeguard of private houses; and fire was employed to facilitate the attack, or to conceal the crimes, of these factious rioters. No place was safe or sacred from their depredations; to gratify either avarice or revenge they profusely spilt the blood of the innocent; churches and altars were polluted by atrocious murders, and it was the boast of the assassins that their dexterity could always inflict a mortal wound with a single stroke of their dagger.

A sedition, which almost laid Constantinople in ashes, was excited by the mutual hatred and momentary reconciliation of the two factions. In the fifth year of his reign Justinian celebrated the festival of the ides of January: the games were incessantly disturbed by the clamorous

her health had been impaired by the licentiousness of her youth; but it was always delicate, and she was directed by her physicians to use the Pythian warm-baths. In this journey the empress was followed by the Prætorian præfect, the great treasurer, several counts and patricians, and a splendid train of four thousand attendants: the highways were repaired at her approach; a palace was erected for her reception; and as she passed through Bithynia she distributed liberal alms to the churches, the monasteries, and the hospitals, that they might implore Heaven for the restoration of her health. At length, in the twenty-fourth year of her marriage, and the twenty-second of her reign, she was consumed by a cancer; and the irreparable loss was deplored by her husband, who, in the room of a theatrical prostitute, might have selected the purest and most noble virgin of the East.

A material difference may be observed in the games of antiquity: the most eminent of the Greeks were actors, the Romans were merely spectators. The Olympic stadium was open to wealth, merit, and ambition; and if the candidates could depend on their personal skill and activity, they might pursue the footsteps of Diomede and Menelaus, and conduct their own horses in the rapid career. Ten, twenty, forty chariots, were allowed to start at the same instant; a crown of leaves was the reward of the victor, and his fame, with that of his family and country, was chanted in lyric strains more durable than monuments of brass and marble. But a senator, or even a citizen, conscious of his dignity, would have blushed to expose his person or his horses in the circus of Rome. The games were exhibited at the expense of the republic, the magistrates, or the emperors; but the reins were abandoned to servile hands; and if the profits of a favorite charioteer sometimes exceeded those of an advocate, they must be considered as the effects of popular extravagance, and the high wages of a disgraceful profession. The race, in its first institution, was a simple contest of two chariots, whose drivers were distinguished by *white* and *red* liveries:

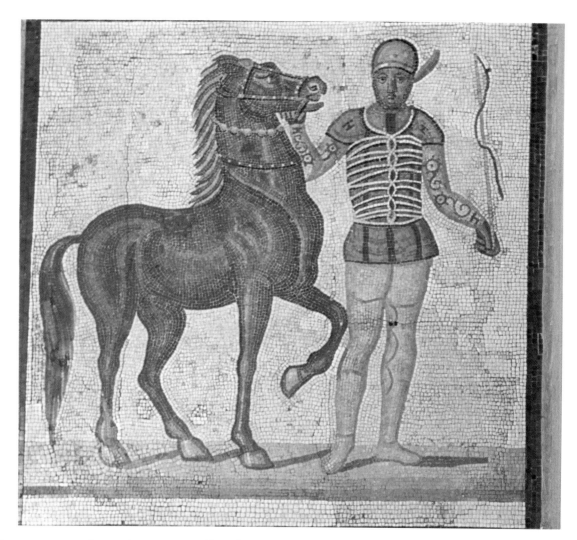

Right: A charioteer wears the racing colors of his club or faction. Known as the blues, greens, reds and yellows, charioteers and their supporters often caused severe civil discord. (First–second century AD, National Museum, Rome) *Below:* Charioteer of the Roman circus driving a two-horsed chariot. (Wall-painting from Ostia, Italy)

discontent of the greens; till the twenty-second race the emperor maintained his silent gravity; at length, yielding to his impatience, he condescended to hold, in abrupt sentences, and by the voice of a crier, the most singular dialogue that ever passed between a prince and his subjects. Their first complaints were respectful and modest; they accused the subordinate ministers of oppression, and proclaimed their wishes for the long life and victory of the emperor. 'Be patient and attentive, ye insolent railers!' exclaimed Justinian; 'be mute, ye Jews, Samaritans, and Manichæans!' The greens still attempted to awaken his compassion. 'We are poor, we are innocent, we are injured, we dare not pass through the streets; a general persecution is exercised against our name and color. Let us die, O emperor! but let us die by your command, and for your service!' But the repetition of partial and passionate invectives degraded, in their eyes, the majesty of the purple; they renouced allegiance to the prince who refused justice to his people, lamented that the father of Justinian had been born, and branded his son with the opprobrious names of a homicide, an ass, and a perjured tyrant. 'Do you despise your lives?' cried the indignant monarch. The blues rose with fury from their seats, their hostile clamors thundered in the hippodrome, and their adversaries, deserting the unequal contest, spread terror and despair through the streets of Constantinople. At this dangerous moment, seven notorious assassins of both factions, who had been condemned by the præfect, were carried round the city, and afterwards transported to the place of execution in the suburb of Pera. Four were immediately beheaded; a fifth was hanged; but, when the same punishment was inflicted on the remaining two, the rope broke, they fell alive to the ground, the populace applauded their escape, and the monks of St Conon, issuing from the neighboring convent, conveyed them in a boat to the sanctuary of the church. As one of these criminals was of the blue, and the other of the green, livery, the two factions were equally provoked by the cruelty of their oppressor or the ingratitude of their patron, and a short truce was concluded till they had delivered their prisoners and satisfied their revenge. The palace of the præfect, who withstood the seditious torrent, was instantly burned, his officers and guards were massacred, the prisons were forced open, and freedom was restored to those who could only use it for the public destruction. A military force which had been dispatched to the aid of the civil magistrate was fiercely encountered by an armed multitude, whose numbers and boldness continually increased: and the Heruli, the wildest barbarians in the service of the empire, overturned the priests and their relics, which, from a pious motive, had been rashly interposed to separate the bloody conflict. The tumult was exasperated by this sacrilege; the people fought with enthusiasm in the cause of God; the women, from the roofs and windows, showered stones on the heads of the soldiers, who darted firebrands against the houses; and the various flames, which had been kindled by the hands of citizens and strangers, spread without control over the face of the city. The conflagration involved the cathedral of St Sophia, the baths of Zeuxippus, a part of the palace from the first entrance to the altar of Mars, and the long portico from the palace to the forum of Constantine: a large hospital, with the sick patients, was consumed; many churches and stately edifices were destroyed; and in immense treasure of gold and silver was either melted or lost. From such scenes of horror and distress the wise and wealthy citizens escaped over the Bosphorus to the Asiatic side, and during five days Constantinople was abandoned to the factions, whose watchword, NIKA, *vanquish!* has given a name to this memorable sedition.

As long as the factions were divided, the triumphant blues and desponding greens appeared to behold with the same indifference the disorders of the state, and the emperor, alarmed by their distrust,

Right: Men fighting lions at the 'games.' (Ivory diptych from Istanbul, c AD 500, Hermitage Museum, Leningrad)

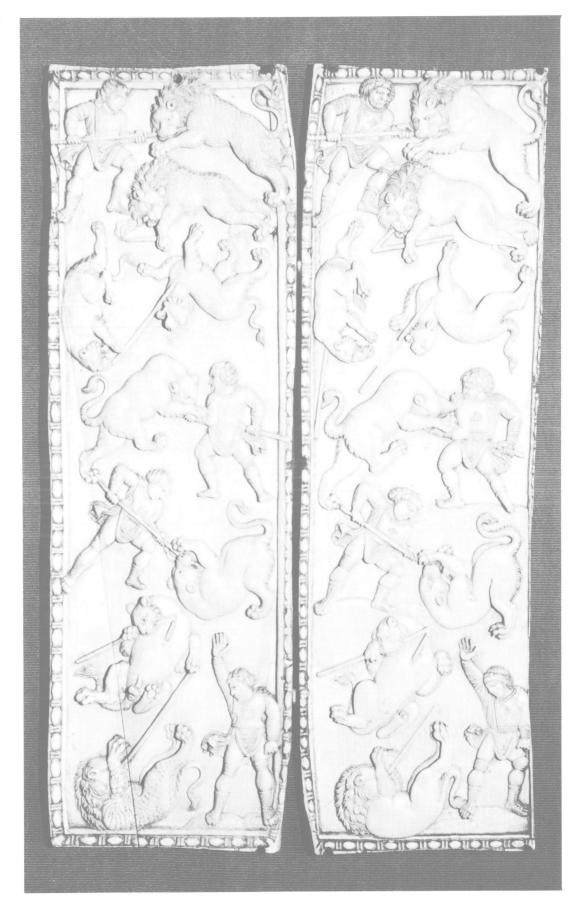

retreated with precipitation to the strong fortress of the palace. The obstinacy of the tumult was now imputed to a secret and ambitious conspiracy, and a suspicion was entertained that the insurgents, more especially the green faction, had been supplied with arms and money by HYPATIUS and POMPEY, two patricians who could neither forget with honor, nor remember with safety that they were the nephews of the emperor Anastasius. Capriciously trusted, disgraced, and pardoned by the jealous levity of the monarch, they had appeared as loyal servants before the throne, and, during five days of the tumult, they were detained as important hostages; till at length, the fears of Justinian prevailing over his prudence, he viewed the two brothers in the light of spies, perhaps of assassins, and sternly commanded them to depart from the palace. After a fruitless representation that obedience might lead to involuntary treason, they retired to their houses, and in the morning of the sixth day Hypatius was surrounded and seized by the people, who, regardless of his virtuous resistance and the tears of his wife, transported their favorite to the forum of Constantine, and, instead of a diadem, placed a rich collar on his head. If the usurper, who afterwards pleaded the merit of his delay, had complied with the advice of his senate, and urged the fury of the multitude, their first irresistible effort might have oppressed or expelled his trembling competitor. The Byzantine palace enjoyed a free communication with the sea, vessels lay ready at the garden-stairs, and a secret resolution was already formed to convey the emperor with his family and treasures to a safe retreat at some distance from the capital.

Justinian was lost, if the prostitute whom he raised from the theater had not renounced the timidity as well as the virtues of her sex. In the midst of a council where Belisarius was present, Theodora alone displayed the spirit of a hero, and she alone, without apprehending his future hatred, could save the emperor from the imminent danger and his unworthy fears. 'If flight,' said the consort of Justinian, 'were the only means of safety, yet I should disdain to fly. Death is the condition of our birth, but they who have reigned should never survive the loss of dignity and dominion. I implore Heaven that I may never be seen, not a day, without my diadem and purple; that I may no longer behold the light when I cease to be saluted with the name of queen. If you resolve, O Cæsar! to fly, you have treasures; behold the sea, you have ships; but tremble lest the desire of life should expose you to wretched exile and ignominious death. For my own part, I adhere to the maxim of antiquity, that the throne is a glorious sepulcher.' The firmness of a woman restored the courage to deliberate and act, and courage soon discovers the resources of the most desperate situation. It was an easy and a decisive measure to revive the animosity of the factions; the blues were astonished at their own guilt and folly, that a trifling injury should provoke them to conspire with their implacable enemies against a gracious and liberal benefactor; they again proclaimed the majesty of Justinian; and the greens, with their upstart emperor, were left alone in the hippodrome. The fidelity of the guards was doubtful; but the military force of Justinian consisted in three thousand veterans, who had been trained to valor and discipline in the Persian and Illyrian wars. Under the command of Belisarius and Mundus, they silently marched in two divisions from the palace, forced their obscure way through narrow passages, expiring flames, and falling edifices, and burst open at the same moment the two opposite gates of the hippodrome. In this narrow space the disorderly and affrighted crowd was incapable of resisting on either side a firm and regular attack; the blues signalized the fury of their repentance, and it is computed that above thirty thousand persons were slain in the merciless and promiscuous carnage of the day. Hypatius was dragged from his throne, and conducted with his brother Pompey to the feet of the emperor; they implored his clemency, but their crime was manifest, their innocence uncertain, and Justinian had been too much terrified to forgive. The next morning the two nephews of Anastasius, with eighteen *illustrious* accomplices, of patrician or consular rank, were privately executed by the soldiers, their bodies were thrown into the sea, their palaces razed, and their fortunes confiscated. The hippodrome itself was condemned, during several years, to a mournful silence; with the restoration of the games the same disorders revived, and the blue and green factions continued to afflict the reign of Justinian, and to disturb the tranquility of the Eastern empire.

EVENTS TO THE FALL OF CONSTANTINOPLE

Justinian's (Flavius Anicius Justinian c 482–565) reign was marked by a splendid display of magnificence and a series of conquests that returned to the Roman Empire much of its ancient glory. He imported silkworms from the East and established a flourishing silk trade, founded various schools to replace the School of Athens, and crowned his exploits by the building of the magnificent cathedral of Santa Sophia. His reign represents the late flowering of Graeco-Romano antiquity. Under his generals, he routed the African vandals in a three-month campaign and succeeded with an astonishingly

small force of 5000 cavalry in retaking the ancient colonies of Carthage and Hippo Regius. The African war was shortly followed by the submission of Italy. Justinian had no doubt noticed that the barbarian tribes had little organization and intertribe fighting left them open to attack.

The extravagance of Justinian's campaigns in the West has often been criticized in that by so doing he sacrificed his interest in the East; in particular the fortification of the Danube soon after his death was left to the incursions of the Huns and Bulgars. But if Justinian underestimated his resources it was in the main due to the two Persian wars he was forced to undertake in 532 and 540 – neither brought conclusive

victories to the Byzantine forces.

However Justinian's conquests were fleeting and in the years succeeding his reign Byzantium was never at peace. By the ninth century the Moslems had overrun much of the territory and had established extensive domains in the Holy Land, an event which led directly to the sack of Constantinople by the Latins during the First Crusade.

Eventually, an overwhelming desire to conquer Constantinople filled the Moslems and the city finally fell to them in 1453 after a forty-day siege – one of the most extensive sieges ever raised in Medieval times.

While Rome had declined in majesty, Constantinople represented the rise of a Christian world, its riches and

magnificent buildings far surpassing even those found in cities such as Baghdad. When it fell its fugitives took with them their classical learning and in so doing sowed the seeds for the Renaissance and the basis for our present culture.

The concept of the Roman Emperor embodied in the title of Holy Roman Emperor was a tradition that continued through the ages. It was the dream of Charlemagne and the Hohenstaufen emperors; it was one that inspired the passions of Napoleon and Kaiser Wilhelm – and remains the ideal for all those who aspire to power on a similar scale.

Above: The Bulgars attacking Constantinople during the century.

Left: The Siege of Constantinople by the Turks, 1453. (Ms Fr 9087, fol 207v, fifteenth century, Bibliothèque Nationale, Paris)

Extreme left: Church of Justinian at Leptis Magna, Tripolitania, Libya.

Below: The Sultan's Guard sounding their trumpets. (Arab Ms *Les Séances d'Harari*, fourteenth century, Bibliothèque Nationale, Paris)

EPILOGUE

Prospect of the ruins of Rome – four causes of decay and destruction – example of the Colosseum – the conclusion of the whole work

I N proportion to her former greatness, the fall of Rome was the more awful and deplorable.

After a diligent inquiry I can discern four principal causes of the ruin of Rome, which continued to operate in a period of more than a thousand years. I. The injuries of time and nature. II. The hostile attacks of the barbarians and Christians. III. The use and abuse of the materials. And, IV. The domestic quarrels of the Romans.

I. The art of man is able to construct monuments far more permanent than the narrow span of his own existence: yet these monuments, like himself, are perishable and frail; and in the boundless annals of time his life and his labors must equally be measured as a fleeting moment. Of a simple and solid edifice it is not easy however to circumscribe the duration. As the wonders of ancient days, the pyramids attracted the curiosity of the ancients: a hundred generations, the leaves of autumn, have dropped into the grave; and after the fall of the Pharaohs and Ptolemies, the Cæsars and caliphs, the same pyramids stand erect and unshaken above the floods of the Nile. A complex figure of various and minute parts is more accessible to injury and decay; and the silent lapse of time is often accelerated by hurricanes and earthquakes, by fires and inundations. The air and earth have doubtless been shaken; and the lofty turrets of Rome have tottered from their foundations; but the seven hills do not appear to be placed on the great cavities of the globe; nor has the city, in any age, been exposed to the convulsions of nature, which, in the climate of Antioch, Lisbon, or Lima, have crumbled in a few moments the works of ages into dust. Fire is the most powerful agent of life and death: the rapid mischief may be kindled and propagated by the industry or negligence of mankind; and every period of the Roman annals is marked by the repetition of similar calamities. A memorable conflagration, the guilt or misfortune of Nero's reign, continued, though with unequal fury, either six or nine days. Innumerable buildings, crowded in close and crooked streets, supplied perpetual fuel for the flames; and when they ceased, four only of the fourteen regions were left entire; three were totally destroyed, and seven were deformed by the relics of smoking and lacerated edifices. In the full meridian of empire the metropolis arose with fresh beauty from her ashes; yet the memory of the old deplored their irreparable losses, the arts of Greece, the trophies of victory, the monuments of primitive or fabulous antiquity. In the days of distress and anarchy every wound is mortal, every fall irretrievable; nor can the damage be restored either by the public care of government, or the activity of private interest. Yet two causes may be alleged which render the calamity of fire more destructive to a flourishing than a decayed city. 1. The more combustible materials of brick, timber, and metals, are first melted or consumed; but the flames may play without injury or effect on the naked walls and massy arches that have been despoiled of their ornaments. 2. It is among the common and plebeian habitations that a mischievous spark is most easily blown to a conflagration; but as soon as they are devoured, the greater edifices which have resisted or escaped are left as so many islands in a state of solitude and safety. From her situation, Rome is exposed to the danger of frequent inundations. Without excepting the Tiber, the rivers that descend from either side of the Apennine have a short and irregular course; a shallow stream in the summer heats; an impetuous torrent when it is swelled in the spring or winter, by the fall of rain and the melting of the snows. When the

The Roman Forum, seen from Palatine Hill.

current is repelled from the sea by adverse winds, when the ordinary bed is inadequate to the weight of waters, they rise above the banks, and overspread, without limits or control, the plains and cities of the adjacent country. Soon after the triumph of the first Punic war the Tiber was increased by unusual rains; and the inundation, surpassing all former measure of time and place, destroyed all the buildings that were situate below the hills of Rome. According to the variety of ground, the same mischief was produced by different means; and the edifices were either swept away by the sudden impulse, or dissolved and undermined by the long continuance, of the flood. Under the reign of Augustus the same calamity was renewed: the lawless river overturned the palaces and temples on its banks; and, after the labors of the emperor in cleansing and widening the bed that was encumbered with ruins, the vigilance of his successors was exercised by similar dangers and designs. The project of diverting into new channels the Tiber itself, or some of the dependent streams, was long opposed by superstition and local interests; nor did the use compensate the toil and cost of the tardy and imperfect execution. The servitude of rivers is the noblest and most important victory which man has obtained over the licentiousness of nature; and if such were the ravages of the Tiber under a firm and active government, what could oppose, or who can enumerate, the injuries of the city after the fall of the Western empire? A remedy was at length produced by the evil itself: the accumulation of rubbish and the earth that has been washed down from the hills is supposed to have elevated the plain of Rome fourteen or fifteen feet, perhaps, above the ancient level; and the modern city is less accessible to the attacks of the river.

II. The crowd of writers of every nation, who impute the destruction of the Roman monuments to the Goths and the Christians, have neglected to inquire how far they were animated by a hostile principle, and how far they possessed the means and the leisure to satiate their enmity. In the preceding volumes of this History I have described the triumph of barbarism and religion; and I can only resume, in a few words, their real or imaginary connection with the ruin of ancient Rome. Our fancy may create, or adopt, a pleasing romance, that the Goths and Vandals sallied from Scandinavia, ardent to avenge the flight of Odin; to break the chains, and to chastise the oppressors, of mankind; that they wished to burn the records of classic literature, and to found their national architecture on the broken members of the Tuscan and Corinthian orders. But in simple truth, the northern conquerors were neither sufficiently savage, nor sufficiently refined, to entertain such aspiring ideas of destruction and revenge. The shepherds of Scythia and Germany had been educated in the armies of the empire, whose discipline they acquired, and whose weakness they invaded: with the familiar use of the Latin tongue they had learned to reverence the name and titles of Rome; and, though incapable of emulating, they were more inclined to admire than to abolish the arts and studies of a brighter period. In the transient possession of a rich and unresisting capital, the soldiers of Alaric and Genseric were stimulated by the passions of a victorious army; amidst the wanton indulgence of lust or cruelty, portable wealth was the object of their search: nor could they derive either pride or pleasure from the unprofitable reflection that they had battered to the ground the works of the consuls and Cæsars. Their moments were indeed precious: the Goths evacuated Rome on the sixth, the Vandals on the fifteenth day; and, though it be far more difficult to build than to destroy, their hasty assault would have made a slight impression on the solid piles of antiquity. We may remember that both Alaric and Genseric affected to spare the buildings of the city; that they subsisted in strength and beauty under the auspicious government of Theodoric; and that the momentary resentment of Totila was disarmed by his own temper and the advice of his friends and enemies. From these innocent barbarians the reproach may be transferred to the Catholics of Rome. The statues, altars, and houses of the demons were an abomination in their eyes; and in the absolute command of the city, they might labor with zeal and perseverance to erase the idolatry of their ancestors. The demolition of the temples in the East affords to *them* an example of conduct, and to *us* an argument of belief; and it is probable that a portion of guilt or merit may be imputed with justice to the Roman proselytes. Yet their abhorrence was confined to the monuments of heathen superstition; and the civil structures that were dedicated to the business or pleasure of society might be preserved without injury or scandal. The change of religion was accomplished, not by a popular tumult, but by the decrees of the emperors, of the senate, and of time. Of the Christian hierarchy, the bishops of Rome were commonly the most prudent and least fanatic; nor can any positive charge be opposed to the meritorious act of saving and converting the majestic structure of the Pantheon.

III. The value of any object that supplies the wants or pleasures of mankind is compounded of its substance and its form, of the materials and the manufacture. Its price must depend on the number of persons by whom it may be acquired and used; on the extent of the market; and consequently on the ease or difficulty of remote exportation, according to the nature of the commodity, its local situation, and the temporary circumstances of the world. The barbarian conquerors of Rome usurped in a moment the toil and treasure of successive ages; but, except the luxuries of immediate consumption, they must view without desire all that could not be removed from the city in the Gothic wagons or the fleet of the Vandals. Gold and silver were the first objects of their avarice; as in every country, and in the smallest compass, they represent the most ample command of the industry and possessions of mankind. A vase or a statue of those precious metals might tempt the vanity of some barbarian chief; but the grosser multitude, regardless of the form, was tenacious only of the substance; and the melted ingots might be readily divided and stamped into the current coin of the empire. The less active or less fortunate robbers were reduced to the baser plunder of brass, lead, iron, and copper: whatever had escaped the Goth and Vandals was pillaged by the Greek tyrants; and the emperor Constans, in his rapacious visit, stripped the bronze tiles from the roof of the Pantheon. The edifices of Rome might be considered as a vast and various mine; the first labor of extracting the materials was already performed; the metals were purified and cast; the marbles were hewn and polished; and after foreign and domestic rapine had been satiated, the remains of the city, could a purchaser have been found, were still venal. The monuments of antiquity had been left naked of their precious ornaments; but the Romans would demolish with their own hands the arches and walls, if the hope of profit could surpass the cost of the labor and exportation. If Charlemagne had fixed in Italy the seat of the Western empire, his genius would have aspired to restore, rather than to violate, the works of the Cæsars; but policy confined the French monarch to the forests of Germany; his taste could be gratified only by destruction; and the new palace of Aix-la-Chapelle was decorated with the marbles of Ravenna and Rome. Five hundred years after Charlemagne, a king of Sicily, Robert, the wisest and most liberal sovereign of the age, was supplied with the same materials by the easy navigation of the Tiber and the sea; and Petrarch sighs an indignant complaint, that the ancient capital of the world should adorn from her own bowels the slothful luxury of Naples. But these examples of plunder or purchase were rare in the darker ages; and the Romans, alone and unenvied, might have applied to their private or public use the remaining structures of antiquity, if in their present form and situation they had not been useless in a great measure to the city and its inhabitants. The walls still described the old circumference, but the city had descended from the seven hills into the Campus Martius; and some of the noblest monuments which had braved the injuries of time were left in a desert far remote from the habitations of mankind. The palaces of the senators were no longer adapted to the manners or fortunes of their indigent

successors: the use of baths and porticoes was forgotten: in the sixth century the games of the theater, amphitheater, and circus had been interrupted: some temples were devoted to the prevailing worship; but the Christian churches preferred the holy figure of the cross; and fashion, or reason, had distributed after a peculiar model the cells and offices of the cloister. Under the ecclesiastical reign the number of these pious foundations was enormously multiplied; and the city was crowded with forty monasteries of men, twenty of women, and sixty chapters and colleges of canons and priests, who aggravated instead of relieving, the depopulation of the tenth century. But if the forms of ancient architecture were disregarded by a people insensible of their use and beauty, the plentiful materials were applied to every call of necessity or superstition; till the fairest columns of the Ionic and Corinthian orders, the richest marbles of Paros and Numidia, were degraded, perhaps to the support of a convent or a stable. The daily havoc which is perpetrated by the Turks in the cities of Greece and Asia may afford a melancholy example; and in the gradual destruction of the monuments of Rome, Sixtus the Fifth may alone be excused for employing the stones of the Septizonium in the glorious edifice of St Peter's. A fragment, a ruin, howsoever mangled or profaned, may be viewed with pleasure and regret; but the greater part of the marble was deprived of substance, as well as of place and proportion; it was burnt to lime for the purpose of cement. Since the arrival of Poggius the temple of Concord and many capital structures had vanished from his eyes; and an epigram of the same age expresses a just and pious fear that the continuance of this practice would finally annihilate all the monuments of antiquity. The smallness of their numbers was the sole check on the demands and depredations of the Romans. The imagination of Petrarch might create the presence of a mighty people; and I hesitate to believe that, even in the fourteenth century, they could be reduced to a contemptible list of thirty-three thousand inhabitants. From that period to the reign of Leo the Tenth, if they multiplied to the amount of eighty-five thousand, the increase of citizens was in some degree pernicious to the ancient city.

IV. I have reserved for the last the most potent and forcible cause of destruction, the domestic hostilities of the Romans themselves. Under the dominion of the Greek and French emperors the peace of the city was disturbed by accidental, though frequent, seditions: it is from the decline of the latter, from the beginning of the tenth century, that we may date the licentiousness of private war, which violated with impunity the laws of the Code and the Gospel, without respecting the majesty of the absent sovereign, or the presence and person of the vicar of Christ. In a dark period of five hundred years Rome was perpetually afflicted by the sanguinary quarrels of the nobles and the people, the Guelphs and Ghibelines, the Colonna and Ursini; and if much has escaped the knowledge, and much is unworthy of the notice, of history, I have exposed in the two preceding chapters the causes and effects of the public disorders. At such a time, when every quarrel was decided by the sword, and none could trust their lives or properties to the impotence of law, the powerful citizens were armed for safety, or offense, against the domestic enemies whom they feared or hated. Except Venice alone, the same dangers and designs were common to all the free republics of Italy; and the nobles usurped the prerogative of fortifying their houses, and erecting strong towers that were capable or resisting a sudden attack. The cities were filled with these hostile edifices; and the example of Lucca, which contained three hundred towers; her law, which confined their height to the measure of fourscore feet, may be extended with suitable latitude to the more opulent and populous states. The fist step of the senator Brancaleone in the establishment of peace and justice was to demolish (as we have already seen) one hundred and forty of the towers of Rome; and, in the last days of anarchy and discord, as late as the reign of Martin the Fifth, forty-four still stood in one of the thirteen or fourteen regions of the city. To this mischievous purpose the remains of antiquity were most readily adapted: the temples and arches afforded a broad and solid basis for the new structures of brick and stone; and we can name the modern turrets that were raised on the triumphal monuments of Julius Cæsar, Titus, and the Antonines. With some slight alterations, a theater, an amphitheater, a mausoleum, was transformed into a strong and spacious citadel. I need not repeat that the mole of Hadrian has assumed the title and form

Sunset over the theater at Leptis Magna, Tripolitania.

of the castle of St Angelo; the Septizonium of Severus was capable of standing against a royal army; the sepulcher of Metella has sunk under its outworks; the theaters of Pompey and Marcellus were occupied by the Savelli and Ursini families; and the rough fortress has been gradually softened to the splendor and elegance of an Italian palace. Even the churches were encompassed with arms and bulwarks, and the military engines on the roof of St Peter's were the terror of the Vatican and the scandal of the Christian world. Whatever is fortified will be attacked; and whatever is attacked may be destroyed. Could the Romans have wrested from the popes the castle of St Angelo, they had resolved by a public decree to annihilate that monument of servitude. Every building of defense was exposed to a siege; and in every siege the arts and engines of destruction were laboriously employed. After the death of Nicholas the Fourth, Rome, without a sovereign or senate, was abandoned six months to the fury of civil war. 'The houses,' says a cardinal and poet of the times, 'were crushed by the weight and velocity of enormous stones; the walls were perforated by the stokes of the battering-ram; the towers were involved in fire and smoke; and the assailants were stimulated by rapine and revenge.' The work was consummated by the tyranny of the laws; and the factions of Italy alternately exercised a blind and thoughtless vengeance on their adversaries, whose houses and castles they razed to the ground. In comparing the *days* of foreign with the *ages* of domestic hostility, we must pronounce that the latter have been far more ruinous to the city; and our opinion is confirmed by the evidence of Petrarch. 'Behold,' says the laureate, 'the relics of Rome, the image of her pristine greatness! neither time nor the barbarian can boast the merit of this stupendous destruction: it was perpetrated by her own citizens, by the most illustrious of her sons; and your ancestors (he writes to a noble Annibaldi) have done with the battering-ram what the Punic hero could not accomplish with the sword.' The influence of the two last principles of decay must in some degree be multiplied by each other; since the houses and towers which were subverted by civil war required a new and perpetual supply from the monuments of antiquity.

These general observations may be separately applied to the amphitheater of Titus, which has obtained the name of the COLISEUM, either from its magnitude, or from Nero's colossal statue: an edifice, had it been left to time and nature, which might perhaps have claimed an eternal duration. The curious antiquaries, who have computed the numbers and seats, are disposed to believe that above the upper row of stone steps the amphitheater was encircled and elevated with several stages of wooden galleries, which were repeatedly consumed by fire, and restored by the emperors. Whatever was precious, or portable, or profane, the statues of gods and heroes, and the costly ornaments of sculpture, which were cast in brass, or overspread with leaves of silver and gold, became the first prey of conquest or fanaticism, of the avarice of the barbarians or the Christians. In the massy stones of the Coliseum many holes are discerned; and the two most probable conjectures represent the various accidents of its decay. These stones were connected by solid links of brass or iron, nor had the eye of rapine overlooked the value of the baser metals; the vacant space was converted into a fair or market; the artisans of the Coliseum are mentioned

in an ancient survey; and the chasms were perforated or enlarged to receive the poles that supported the shops or tents of the mechanic trades. Reduced to its naked majesty, the Flavian amphitheater was contemplated with awe and admiration by the pilgrims of the North; and their rude enthusiasm broke forth in a sublime proverbial expression, which is recorded in the eighth century, in the fragments of the venerable Bede: 'As long as the Coliseum stands, Rome shall stand; when the Coliseum falls, Rome will fall; when Rome falls, the world will fall.' In the modern system of war, a situation commanded by three hills would not be chosen for a fortress; but the strength of the walls and arches could resist the engines of assault; a numerous garrison might be lodged in the enclosure; and while one faction occupied the Vatican and the Capitol, the other was intrenched in the Lateran and the Coliseum.

The abolition at Rome of the ancient games must be understood with some latitude; and the carnival sports, of the Testacean mount and the Circus Agonalis, were regulated by the law or custom of the city. The senator presided with dignity and pomp to adjudge and distribute the prizes, the gold ring, or the *pallium*, as it was styled, of cloth or silk. A tribute on the Jews supplied the annual expense; and the races, on foot, on horseback, or in chariots, were ennobled by a tilt and tournament of seventy-two of the Roman youth.

This use of the amphitheater was a rare, perhaps a singular festival: the demand for the materials was a daily and continual want, which the citizens could gratify without restraint or remorse. In the fourteenth century a scandalous act of concord secured to both factions the privilege of extracting stones from the free and common quarry of the Coliseum; and Poggius laments that the greater part of these stones had been burnt to lime by the folly of the Romans. To check this abuse, and to prevent the nocturnal crimes that might be perpetrated in the vast and gloomy recess, Eugenius the Fourth surrounded it with a wall; and, by a charter, long extant, granted both the ground and edifice to the monks of an adjacent convent. After his death the wall was overthrown in a tumult of the people; and had they themselves respected the noblest monument of their fathers, they might have justified to resolve that it should never be degraded to private property. The inside was damaged; but in the middle of the sixteenth century, an era of taste and learning, the exterior circumference of one thousand six hundred and twelve feet was still entire and inviolate; a triple elevation of fourscore arches, which rose to the height of one hundred and eight feet. Of the present ruin the nephews of Paul the Third are the guilty agents; and every traveller who views the Farnese palace may curse the sacrilege and luxury of these upstart princes. A similar reproach is applied to the Barberini; and the repetition of injury might be dreaded from every reign, till the Coliseum was placed under the safeguard of religion by the most liberal of the pontiffs, Benedict the Fourteenth, who consecrated a spot which persecution and fable had stained with the blood of so many Christian martyrs.

Of these pilgrims, and of every reader, the attention will be excited by a History of the Decline and Fall of the Roman Empire; the greatest, perhaps, and most awful scene in the history of mankind. The various causes and progressive effects are connected with many of the events most interesting in human annals: the artful policy of the Cæsars, who long maintained the name and image of a free republic; the disorders of military despotism; the rise, establishment, and sects of Christianity; the foundation of Constantinople; the division of the monarchy; the invasion and settlements of the barbarians of Germany and Scythia; the institutions of the civil law; the character and religion of Mohammed; the temporal sovereignty of the popes; the restoration and decay of the Western empire of Charlemagne; the crusades of the Latins in the East; the conquests of the saracens and Turks; the ruin of the Greek empire; the state and revolutions of Rome in the middle ages. The historian may applaud the importance and variety of his subject; but, while he is conscious of his own imperfections, he must often accuse the deficiency of his materials. It was among the ruins of the Capitol that I first conceived the idea of a work which has amused and exercised near twenty years of my life, and which, however inadequate to my own wishes, I finally deliver to the curiosity and candor of the public.

LAUSANNE,
27 June, 1787.

Emperors of Rome

AUGUSTUS
23 BC–AD 14

TIBERIUS
14–37

CALIGULA
37–41

CLAUDIUS I
41–54

NERO
54–68

GALBA
68–69

OTHO
69

VITELLIUS
69

VESPASIAN
69–79

TITUS
79–81

DOMITIAN
81–96

NERVA
96–98

TRAJAN
98–117

HADRIAN
117–138

ANTONIUS PIUS
138–161

MARCUS AURELIUS
161–180

Lucius Verus 161–169
Commodus 176–180

COMMODUS
180–192

PERTINAX
193

DIDIUS JULIANUS
193

SEPTIMIUS SEVERUS
193–211

Caracalla 198–211
Geta 209–211

CARACALLA
211–217

Geta 211–212

MACRINUS
217–218

ELAGABALUS
218–222

SEVERUS ALEXANDER
222–235

MAXIMINUS
235–238

GORDIAN I
238

GORDIAN II
238

BALBINUS
238

PUPIENUS
238

GORDIAN III
238–244

PHILIP
244–249

DECIUS
249–251

TREBONIANUS GALLUS
251–253

AEMILIANUS
253

VALERIANUS
253–259

Gallienus 253–259

GALLIENUS
259–268

Postumus (in Gaul) 258–267

CLAUDIUS II
268–270

Tetricus (in Gaul) 268–273

QUINTILLUS
270

AURELIAN
270–275

TACITUS
275–276

FLORIANUS
276

PROBUS
276–282

CARUS
282–283

CARINUS
283–285

Numerianus 283–284

DIOCLETIAN
284–305

Maximian 286–305

GALERIUS and CONSTANTIUS 305	Emperors Following the Division of the Empire	

GALERIUS and SEVERUS
306

	EMPERORS OF THE WESTERN EMPIRE AFTER THEODOSIUS I	EMPERORS OF THE EASTERN EMPIRE AFTER THEODOSIUS I

GALERIUS, LICINIUS, CONSTANTINE, DAIA, and MAXENTIUS
307–
(Galerius d.311, Maxentius d. 312, Daia d. 313, Licinius defeated 324)

HONORIUS
394–423

ARCADIUS
395–408

CONSTANTINE I
324–337

VALENTINIAN III
423–455

THEODOSIUS II
408–450

CONSTANTINE II
337–340

Constans 337–340
Constantius 337–340

MAXIMUS
455

MARCIAN
450–457

CONSTANS
340–350

AVITUS
455–456

LEO I
457–474

CONSTANTIUS
340–361

MAJORIAN
457–461

LEO II
474

JULIAN
361–363

SEVERUS
461–465

ZENO
474–491

JOVIAN
363–364

No Emperor
465–467

ANASTASIUS I
491–518

VALENTIAN I
364–375

Valens 364–375
Gratian 367–375

ANTHEMIUS
467–472

JUSTIN I
518–527

OLYBRIUS
472

JUSTINIAN I
527–565

VALENS
375–378

GLYCERIUS
473–474

The Emperors of the Eastern Empire continued to reign until the Fall of Constantinople, 1453.

GRATIAN
378–383

NEPOS
474–475

VALENTINIAN II
375–392

Theodosius I 379–392

ROMULUS AUGUSTULUS
475–476

THEODOSIUS I
392–395

Arcadius 383–395
Honorius 394–395

*End of Western Empire:
Odoacer, King of Italy*

Index

Acknowledgments

ARCHEOLOGICAL MUSEUM, LENINGRAD: 191

ARMS AND ARMOUR PRESS: 16, 17, 20, 21 (right and bottom two)

BASILICA OF ST AMBROGIO, MILAN: 201 (top)

BIBLIOTHEQUE NATIONALE, PARIS: 146–47, 243 (bottom left and right)

BODLEIAN LIBRARY: 232, 233 (top)

BRITISH MUSEUM: 10, 11, 19 (all three), 24 (bottom), 66, 67, 70, 74, 75 (both), 79, 88, 93 (top), 102 (top), 119 (bottom), 135, 137, 139, 141, 142, 144, 158, 161 (bottom left and right), 165, 166, 172 (both), 173 (both), 200 (top), 201 (top right and bottom left), 203, 220 (left), 226 (top left and top right), 230 (all three), 231 (top right), 236 (top left and top right), 238 (left)

BRITISH MUSEUM LIBRARY BOARD: 11

BRITISH TOURIST BOARD: 1, 100 (top and bottom two), 101, 166, 210 (all three), 233 (bottom)

BYZANTINE MUSEUM, ATHENS: 119 (top)

DEUTSCHES ARCHAEOLOGISCHES INSTITUT, ROME: 71 (top)

EDIZIONE SALVUCCI, URBISAGLIA: 207 (top)

EGYPTIAN TOURIST OFFICE: 85, 89

FONDAZIONE TRECCANI, DESENZANO: 204 (both)

HANS KOCH: 177 (both), 184–85 (all four)

HERMITAGE MUSEUM, LENINGRAD: 241

LONDON MUSEUM: 12 (bottom right), 13 (center), 24 (top three), 42 (top left) 43 (top right), 116, 137 (top), 138, 166–67, 230

LOUVRE, PARIS: 55 (left), 148

MANSELL COLLECTION, LONDON: 24 (bottom), 25 (top), 26, 28, 42 (bottom), 43 (bottom), 46, 49, 56 (bottom), 78 (top), 84, 88, 92, 99 (bottom), 106–107 (top and bottom), 121, 124, 125, 143, 145, 152 (left), 192, 194, 200 (bottom), 201 (top), 207 (bottom), 216, 231, 234

MANSELL/ALINARI: 46, 56 (bottom), 78 (top), 92, 96, 106–107 (top), 121, 124, 125, 145, 170

MANSELL/ANDERSON: 26, 29, 49, 84, 99, 152 (left), 192, 194, 200 (bottom), 201 (top), 206 (bottom), 234

MANSELL/EDIZIONI BROGI: 216

MARY EVANS: 7, 47, 52, 53, 71 (bottom), 98, 102, 107 (bottom), 150 (bottom), 160, 202, 207 (bottom), 209 (bottom), 227, 238–39 (center)

MITTELRHEINISCHES LANDESMUSEUM, MAINZ: 16

MOSTRA AUGUSTEA: 56 (bottom), 78 (top), 92, 106, 121, 135, 152 (left), 206 (bottom)

MUNICH MUSEUM, MUNICH: 25

MUSEO CAPITOLINO, ROME: 29 (bottom), 36, 41, 96

MUSEO CRISTIANO, BRESCIA: 201 (right)

MUSEO DELLA CIVILTA, ROME: 24 (bottom)

MUSEO LATERANO, ROME: 49

MUSEO NAZIONALE, ROME: 39 (bottom), 46, 86 (top), 125, 192, 194, 240 (top)

MUSEO PIO CLEMENTINO, VATICAN, ROME: 105

MUSEUM DER STATS WORMS: 21 (bottom right)

MUSEUM OF ANTIQUES, NEWCASTLE: 21 (left)

NATIONAL ARCHEOLOGICAL MUSEUM, NAPLES: 33 (top two), 86 (bottom)

NATIONAL MUSEUM OF BELGRADE: 120

NATIONAL MUSEUM OF RAVENNA: 13

NATIONAL MUSEUM, ROME: 58 (bottom), 240 (top)

PALAZZO VECCHIO, FLORENCE: 122

PAUL ARTHUR: 103, 214, 215, 219 (top and bottom), 242

PETER CLAYTON: 162 (top)

PHOTO GIRAUDON: 43 (bottom), 174

PHOTO MAS, BARCELONA: 109 (top)

PHOTO OSCA SAVIO: 109 (top)

PHOTORESOURCES: 2, 8, 10, 13 (top), 14 (all three), 15 (all four), 18 (both), 22, 23, 25 (bottom), 30 (both), 31 (bottom), 33 (top two), 34 (right), 35, 36, 38 (bottom), 39 (bottom), 40, 41, 55 (both), 58 (both), 59 (both), 69, 82, 83, 86 (both), 87 (bottom right), 94 (both), 97, 100 (cen-ter), 104, 108 (top), 109 (both), 112 (both), 115 (bottom), 118, 119 (both), 123 (bottom), 151 (top), 157, 165, 172–73, 174, 182–83, 186, 187 (two), 190, 191 (top), 192 (right), 203, 208 (both), 228 (bottom), 229 (top), 236 (both), 237 (both), 240 (both), 241, 242 (right)

RADIO TIMES HULTON PICTURE LIBRARY: 13 (bottom right), 29 (top), 32 (both), 33 (bottom), 34, 35, 38 (top), 39 (top), 42 (top), 43 (top), 50, 56 (top), 57, 78 (bottom), 81, 113, 117, 118, 151 (bottom), 153 (both), 212, 217, 221, 224

RAPUZZI: 136

RAY GARDNER: 66, 67, 70, 99 (top), 102 (top), 186, 203, 206 (top), 230 (top), 231 (top and bottom right), 220 (left)

ROGER WOOD STUDIOS: 3, 37, 50 (left), 51, 161 (top), 213, 214 (right), 247

RONALD SHERIDAN: 6, 48 (both), 68, 87 (top), 108 (bottom), 114 (bottom), 134, 140, 154, 155, 159, 195 (right), 211 (top)

SCALA: 31 (top), 87 (center), 91, 105, 114 (top), 120, 122, 156, 191 (bottom), 214 (left), 215, 218 (top), 219 (top and bottom), 218–19 (center)

SOUSSE MUSEUM, TUNISIA: 58 (top)

STRAUBING MUSEUM: 16, 21

TUNISIAN TOURIST BOARD: 22, 223, 228 (top), 229 (bottom)

TURKISH MINISTRY OF TOURISM AND INFORMATION: 90, 150 (top), 188

UFFIZI GALLERY, FLORENCE: 124

VATICAN, ROME: 28, 99, 106–107, 114 (top), 149, 156, 243 (top)

WERNER FORMAN ARCHIVE: 54, 76, 77, 80 (both), 196, 199 (bottom), 225 (both)

The editor and publishers extend their grateful thanks to Richard Natkiel for the provision of maps and to Arms and Armour Press for the use of illustrations from their publication THE ARMS OF IMPERIAL ROME.